DICKENS STUDIES ANNUAL
Essays on Victorian Fiction

DICKENS STUDIES ANNUAL
Essays on Victorian Fiction

EDITORS

Michael Timko
Fred Kaplan
Edward Guiliano

DICKENS STUDIES ANNUAL

Essays on Victorian Fiction

VOLUME
12

Edited by
Michael Timko, Fred Kaplan,
and Edward Guiliano

AMS PRESS, INC.
NEW YORK, N.Y.

DICKENS STUDIES ANNUAL
ISSN 0084-9812

International Standard Book Number
Series: 0-404-18520-7
Vol. 12: 0-404-18532-0

Dickens Studies Annual: Essays on Victorian Fiction welcomes essay and mono-graph-length contributions on Dickens as well as on other Victorian novelists and on the history or aesthetics of Victorian fiction. All manuscripts should be double-spaced, including footnotes, which should be grouped at the end of the submis-sion, and should be prepared according to current MLA style. An editorial deci-sion can usually be reached more quickly if two copies are submitted. The pre-ferred editions for citations from Dickens' works are the Clarendon and the Norton Critical when available, otherwise the Oxford Illustrated Dickens or the Penguin.

Please send submissions to the Editors, *Dickens Studies Annual,* Room 1522, Graduate School and University Center, City University of New York, 33 West 42nd Street, New York, N.Y. 10036; please send subscription inquiries to AMS Press, Inc., 56 East 13th Street, New York, N. Y. 10003.

Contents

List of Illustrations

Overleaf: Wrapper of the first monthly installment of *A Tale of Two Cities*.

Courtesy of The Henry W. and Albert A. Berg Collection, The New York Public
Library, Astor, Lenox, and Tilden Collections.

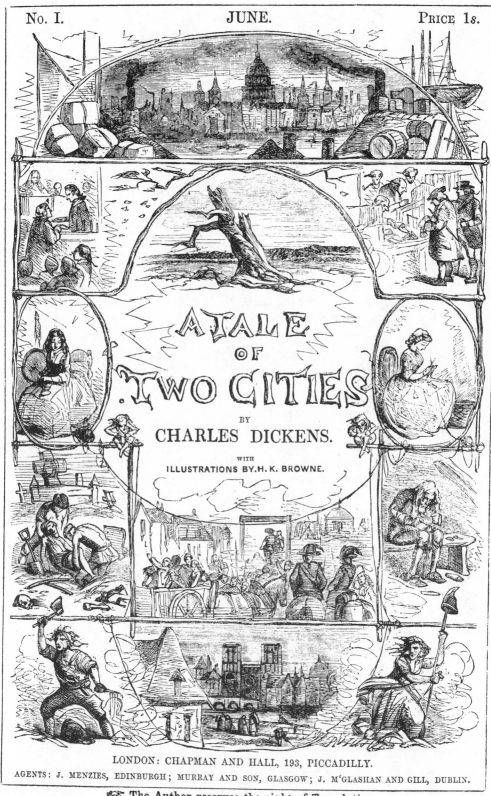

A TALE
OF
TWO CITIES

BY
CHARLES DICKENS.

WITH
ILLUSTRATIONS BY H. K. BROWNE.

LONDON: CHAPMAN AND HALL, 193, PICCADILLY.

AGENTS: J. MENZIES, EDINBURGH; MURRAY AND SON, GLASGOW; J. M'GLASHAN AND GILL, DUBLIN.

Preface

The essays in Volume 12 of *DSA* demonstrate vividly a number of vital points that can and should be made about Dickens and his age. The first, perhaps the most obvious, but one that has to be made from time to time, is that interest in Dickens and his work continues to be high among scholars, critics, and readers. One also notes that there is still more to Dickens than *Nicholas Nickleby*, even though the popularity of the recent British production and the deluge of paperback editions of that novel seemed determined to turn him into a one-novel author. The essays on *Bleak House*, *Oliver Twist*, *Our Mutual Friend*, and *A Tale of Two Cities* reveal the range of his concern and the depth of his art and thought.

That range and depth are further shown by the other analytic essays on the relationship of Dickens and Carlyle, the subject of the annual conference of the California Dickens Institute at the University of California at Santa Cruz this past year. That Carlyle's *The French Revolution* had a profound influence on Dickens, and particularly on *A Tale of Two Cities*, has always been known; however, these recent studies indicate the true extent of that influence and the huge debt that Dickens owed to the Sage of Chelsea. These studies also serve to document the fierce independence of the novelist and the artistic skill by which he transformed Carlylian rhetoric and "doctrine" into Dickensian narrative and vision. Finally, in keeping with the wider scope of *DSA*, the essays on Dickens' contemporaries, Collins, Eliot, and Thackeray, provide more evidence for the complexity of the Victorian Age itself and the reasons for which the novel in that Age continues to be held in such high esteem in our own.

Once more we wish to thank those who provided encouragement and support: Presidents Saul Cohen and Harold Proshansky, Queens College and the Graduate Center of The City University of New York respectively; Provost William Hamovitch and Dean John H. Reilly, Queens College, CUNY; Provost Stanley Waren, Dean Steven Cahn, and Associate Dean Richard A. Styskal, Graduate Center, CUNY; Professor Lillian Feder, Executive Officer of the Ph.D. Program in English, CUNY; Professor Lois Hughson, Chair of the Department of English, Queens College, CUNY; Gabriel Hornstein, President, AMS Press, and William Long, Editor.

We also express thanks to all our colleagues who have given generously of their time to read manuscripts. Omar Addi deserves our appreciation for serving efficiently as our editorial assistant for this volume.

Notes on Contributors

MURRAY BAUMGARTEN, Director of the Dickens Project, teaches English and Comparative Literature at the University of California, Santa Cruz. He has written on the novel, Victorian literature, and the Bible. His book, *City Scriptures: Modern Jewish Writing*, was published in 1982.

H. PHILIP BOLTON, Associate Professor of English and Chair, Arts and Humanities Department of Mount Vernon College, Washington, D. C., has for fifteen years been preparing a book about stage versions of novels in England from 1800 to 1900. The novels are long; the plays are legion: finding and reading them has slowed the process of Professor Bolton's whole life.

ROBERT A. COLBY, Professor, Graduate School of Library and Information Studies, Queens College, City University of New York, has a special interest in the Victorian novelist as public educator. Thackeray, the center of one of his previous books, will figure peripherally in his work in progress "The Uses of Fiction."

PATRICK J. CREEVY is currently Associate Professor of English at Mississippi State University. He has published articles on the poetry of Matthew Arnold as well as on the relations between Victorian science and theology. He is working now on the poetics of J. S. Mill.

RICHARD J. DUNN is Professor and Chairman of the English Department at the University of Washington. He has published widely on Victorian novelists and recently has compiled *David Copperfield: An Annotated Bibiography*. His *Approaches to Teaching Dickens's David Copperfield* is scheduled for publication in 1984. Formerly Secretary-treasurer and

President of the Dickens Society, Professor Dunn now serves on its board of trustees.

EDWIN M. EIGNER is Professor of English and Creative Writing at the University of California, Riverside, and author of *Robert Louis Stevenson and Romantic Tradition* (1966) and *The Metaphysical Novel in England and America: Dickens, Bulwer, Hawthorne, Melville* (1978). He and George J. Worth are currently editing a collection of Victorian Criticism of Fiction.

CATHERINE GALLAGHER is an Assistant Professor of English at the University of California, Berkeley. She has published articles on both Victorian fiction and critical theory in such periodicals as *Nineteenth-Century Fiction*, *Theory and Society*, and *Diacritics*, and she has just finished a book explaining the connection between the industrial revolution and the formal development of the English novel.

BARBARA GATES is Associate Professor of English at the University of Delaware. Her published work includes articles on a wide range of Romantic and Victorian writers and has appeared in journals such as *Criticism*, *Victorian Poetry* and *The Victorian Newsletter*. Currently she is completing a book-length study of suicide and the Victorians.

ELLIOT L. GILBERT is Professor of English at the University of California, Davis, where he edits the *California Quarterly*. He has written on such nineteenth-century literary figures as Dickens, Poe, Tennyson, Carlyle, George Moore, and Oscar Wilde, and for his most recent project has compiled and edited *"O Beloved Kids": Rudyard Kipling's Letters to His Children*, just issued in England and scheduled for American publication next spring.

MICHAEL GOLDBERG is Professor of English at the University of British Columbia. The author of *Carlyle and Dickens* (1972) and a section on the reception of Carlyle's Pamphlets in *Carlyle and His Contemporaries* (1976), his most recent involvement with Carlyle has been an edition of Carlyle's *Latter-Day Pamphlets* (with Jules Seigel) and an edition of *Heroes and Hero-Worship* (in progress). A frequent contributor to CBC Radio programs on literature and the arts he has published in a wide variety of scholarly journals on such authors as Shaw, Byron, Bentham, D. H. Lawrence, Carlyle, Dickens, and Roy Fuller.

ALBERT D. HUTTER is currently an Associate Professor of English and Comparative Literature at UCLA and a research psychoanalyst with the Southern California Psychoanalytic Institute. He has published articles on critical theory, Shakespeare, detective fiction, and psychoanalysis, as well as numerous articles on Dickens; his *Dickens and Detective Fiction* will be published next year. He also writes fiction and crime fiction; his novel, *The Death Mechanic*, was published in 1980.

ROBERT KIELY is Professor of English at Harvard University. He is the author of *Beyond Egotism: the Fiction of James Joyce, Virginia Woolf, and D. H. Lawrence*; *The Romantic Novel in England*; and *Robert Louis Stevenson and the Fiction of Adventure*. Last year he taught *Oliver Twist* in the People's Republic of China where Dickens is revered, along with Shakespeare and Jack London, as one of the great pre-Revolutionary writers in the Western Tradition. Professor Kiely taught his Chinese students that, in the Pickwickian sense, their passion for Dickens was laudable, commendable, and, in short, fully deserving of praise.

JOHN KUCICH is Wilhartz Assistant Professor of English at the University of Michigan, Ann Arbor. He has published *Excess and Restraint in the Novels of Charles Dickens* (1981), as well as several assays on Dickens and a number of reviews. Having received fellowships from both NEH and the University of Michigan, he is currently writing a book on repression in Victorian fiction.

MICHAEL LUND, Associate Professor of English at Longwood College in Virginia, has published articles on readers' responses to the serialization of major novels (many by Thackeray) in a variety of journals. With the appearance of this essay, and several more due out in the next year, he may soon make the claim of having published a critical book in installments.

CAROL HANBERY MACKAY is an Assistant Professor of English at the University of Texas, Austin. A participating member of the University of California Dickens Project, she has written articles on Dickens, Thackeray, and Anne Thackeray Ritchie. She is currently completing a book-length study of soliloquy in nineteenth-century fiction.

SYLVÈRE MONOD has edited many Dickens novels in France and in the United States, and he is the author of several books and articles on Dickens. He retired from the Sorbonne in 1982. His essay for this volume is thus one of the first fruits of his early retirement. The characteristic acid flavor shows that the autumn of his life is not entirely the season of "mellow fruitfulness."

The late BRANWEN BAILEY PRATT was Associate Professor of English Literature at San Francisco State University. The recipient of several research fellowships, she had written a number of articles on Dickens, Victorian literature, and psychology and literature.

MICHAEL TIMKO, Professor of English at Queens College and the Graduate Center, City University of New York, has written extensively on Victorian literature, including *Innocent Victorian: The Satiric Poetry of A. H. Clough*. Most recently, he has been a Fellow of the Institute for Advanced Studies in the Humanities at the University of Edinburgh and an NEH-Huntington Library Fellow.

BURTON M. WHEELER is Professor of English and Religious Studies at Washington University, St. Louis. Confined to Administration for eighteen years (including twelve as Dean of the College of Arts and Sciences), he was "Recalled to Life" in 1979. Like Dr. Manette, he returns at moments of stress to his cobbler's bench, but his efforts to regain sanity through teaching and writing on nineteenth- and twentieth-century fiction are thus far encouraging. The first evidence of recovery appeared in *Contemporary Literature*, 23, No. 3 (1982).

CHRIS R. VANDEN BOSSCHE is Visiting Lecturer at the University of California, Santa Cruz, and is Associate Director of the University of California Dickens Project. He has written extensively on Carlyle as well as on the problem of history in Tennyson's *Maud*, and the relationship of Queen Victoria's widowhood to the iconography of widowhood in Victorian art and literature.

The Novelist as Resurrectionist: Dickens and the Dilemma of Death

Albert D. Hutter

"By what means were these fearful atrocities perpetrated?"—"By suffocation. We made the persons drunk, and then suffocated them by holding the nostrils and mouth, and getting on the body; sometimes I held the mouth and nose, while Hare knelt upon the body; and sometimes Hare held the mouth and nose, while I placed myself upon the body. . . . he was on the body assisting me with all his might, while I held the nostrils and mouth with one hand, and choked her under the throat with the other; we sometimes used a pillow, but did not in this case."

* * *

"To whom were the bodies so murdered sold?"—"To Dr.— —. We took the bodies to his rooms . . . , and then went to his house to receive the money for them . . . . No questions were ever asked as to the mode in which we had come by the bodies. . . ."

"You have been a resurrectionist (as it is called), I understand?" "No, neither Hare nor myself ever got a body from a churchyard. All we sold were murdered, save the first one, which was that of the woman who died a natural death in Hare's house. We began with that: our crimes then commenced. The victims we selected were generally elderly persons. They could be more easily disposed of than persons in the vigour of youth."

New Newgate Calendar

This is William Burke, coolly describing the series of murders he and his accomplice, William Hare, committed between 1827 and 1829 in order to sell their victims for medical dissection. His trial was probably the most sensational in a century known for sensational trials—and much given to publicizing them. Indeed, Burke's name was more than a household word: it entered the language, and "burking" is still used to describe a kind of strangulation. The financial incentive for selling cadavers was also notorious in the period, and the grisly occupation of stealing bodies from graves had its own slang label, the ironic "resurrectionist," which came into existence sometime in the eighteenth century.[1] "Resurrecting" was quite specialized, as Burke's testimony makes clear: he denies being a resurrectionist because "neither Hare nor myself ever got a body from a churchyard." Those who took their "goods" fresh off the streets formed a separate branch of the body-snatching business. But the aim of this trade was always the same: to sell corpses for dissection to the doctors, the anatomists, and the medical students. The trade was to build throughout the eighteenth century; by the beginning of the nineteenth century, the body business was booming.

During the course of the eighteenth century, medical schools had begun to place more value on a knowledge of practical anatomy, on dissection. In keeping with the spirit of the Enlightenment, anatomy was already prized on the Continent "as a path toward the knowledge of God, at any rate the God of the eighteenth century." Dissection was, at times, even turned into a strange form of public ritual and celebration: "The anatomy lesson that was so often depicted in the engravings and paintings of the seventeenth century was, like the defense of a thesis or a college play, a great social event that the whole town attended, with masks, refreshments, and diversions." Collections of anatomical plates were much sought after as rare and beautiful books. And for the very wealthy a special dissecting room was sometimes set aside: "A rich man who was interested in nature might have his own private dissecting room, just as he might have his own chemical laboratory. But this room had to be supplied with bodies."[2]

On the Continent the supply of bodies was generally more adequate than in the British Isles because British governmental and public attitudes combined to make it difficult or impossible for corpses to be turned over legally to surgeons or bought by private anatomists from various public sources—prison, workhouse, hospital, morgue. Since the corpses traditionally delivered to the Company of Barber-Surgeons for dissection were the bodies of notorious criminals, from the Renaissance on dissection came to be viewed as a postmortem continuation of punishment. When, in 1540, the Guild of Surgeons and the Company of Barber-Surgeons were consolidated and incorporated by Parliament (32 Hen. VIII, Cap. 42), they were awarded four bodies of executed felons a year, to be given without charge: "to make incision of the same dead bodies or otherwyse to order the same after their saide discrecions at their pleasures for their further and better knowledge instruction, insight, learnyng and experience in the sayde scyence or faculty of surgery." Four bodies was a meager requisition, although Scotland in the same period was worse off: until 1694, Scottish surgeons were legally restricted to the dissection of a single body.[3]

The difficulties imposed by these regulations were compounded by an often quite literal belief in resurrection and the judgment day: mutilation of the corpse might prevent the soul from being "raised," since the resurrectionist had already raised it once before and, in the process, helped to destroy the body, the soul's container. Citing St. Paul, Thomas Greenhill claimed "that Bodies are piously to be laid up in the Earth, like to Corn sowed, to confirm the assured Hope of the *Resurrection*."[4] Greenhill's *The Art of Embalming* (1705) repeatedly testifies to the importance of preserving the body to prepare for resurrection, while it also offers a series of citations and anecdotes demonstrating that the violation of the body is a punishment for earthly sin, a violation which in turn threatens the eternal life of the soul. Greenhill argues, for example, that although

> the Body be not sensible, yet the Soul which cannot die, mourns sadly when its Companion is either ill treated or neglected; but on the contrary rejoyces when it is Honour'd and taken Care of. . . . The Soul is the most precious Thing in this World, and accordingly GOD has enclos'd it with a Cover, the Body, the most beautifully compos'd next to it that can be; Shall we despise therefore this Cover, because Death has separated it from the Soul? No, let us rather esteem it the more, and take the more Care to preserve it, inasmuch as it has once been the Casket of that noble Jewel, and is the only Way of representing that Divine Form which GOD Almighty was pleas'd to impress on it.[5]

First citing the Egyptian belief that the soul would only desert a corrupted or putrified habitation, Greenhill goes on to quote (and broadly reinterpret) *Proverbs* 7: "by its [the body] being dress'd in fine Linnen, [it] might court and incline its best Companion, the Soul, to cohabit with it."[6] He later adds that "Bodies Embalm'd . . . seem not to be dead, but only asleep, waiting for the Resurrection,"[7] and he concludes this line of argument by describing the process of embalming as a kind of "Looking-Glass, a Praeludium and Argument of the Resurrection."[8]

Whatever position theologians might take on the separation of body and soul (and hence on the importance or irrelevance of the physical condition of the body after death), superstition and custom combined to make the body after death inviolate.[9] It was thus virtually impossible for a corpse to be obtained for British medical schools without recourse to body snatching. As more and more students attended medical schools and the private schools of anatomy which grew up around them, and as the need to learn how to operate on a living body was inevitably tied to practical anatomy, the laws of supply and demand took over. The important work of first John Hunter and then Astley Cooper helped to reverse the deplorable ignorance of many, indeed most, surgeons in Britain, who often operated without knowledge of the body as a whole and invariably operated on new cases without prior experience of the same operation on a cadaver. Experience had to be obtained (certainly from the patient's point of view) the hard way. As Sir Astley Cooper put it, a surgeon "must mangle the living, if he has not operated on the dead." This comment was made in 1828, when Sir Astley could confidently reply to a question on the necessity for dissection in medical education "that without dissection there can be no anatomy, and that anatomy is our polar star, for, without anatomy a surgeon can do nothing, certainly nothing well."[10]

Cooper was the first witness to appear before the Select Committee on Anatomy, appointed by the House of Commons to investigate a problem which, in 1828, had assumed epidemic proportions. Yet public resistance to change was massive. In spite of the overwhelming evidence presented to the committee and the committee's own clear endorsement, the Anatomy Act itself, which provided that the necessary bodies for dissection be made available to medical schools, was not passed until 1832—until the publicity occasioned by the horrible murders of Burke and Hare had been supplemented by a similar series of London killings.[11] Finally, the public's outrage overwhelmed their long-standing hatred and fear of dissection itself and their consequent repugnance toward the new legislation.

Whether bodies were to be obtained legally from hospitals and workhouses, or illegally from cemeteries, or even murderously on the public streets, the poor were almost always to be the victims.[12] As one grave-robber testified before the Select Committee: "When I go to work, I like to get those [bodies] of poor people buried from the workhouses, because, instead of working for one subject, you may get three of four; I do not think during the time I have been in the habit of working for the schools, I got half a dozen of wealthier people."[13] Another anonymous grave-robber, when asked whether the bodies he raised were "principally . . . bodies of rich or poor?" replied, quite succinctly: "Both classes; but we could not obtain the rich so easily, because they were buried so deep."[14] Not only were the rich buried deeper and alone; they could also afford to be buried in more secure places, or even to hire people to protect them until the body decomposed far enough to escape dissection. They might even have bought one of the newly patented devices which ingeniously shielded the dead: these were "mortsafes," iron cages built over the grave to keep the living out and the dead in; or specially patented iron coffins, sealed in such a way that they could not be reopened; or spring guns and other traps set up during the day to keep the body snatchers away at night. Robert Southey's "The Surgeon's Warning" is a satiric poem depicting a surgeon who is desperate not to fall victim to the dissecting knife he himself has wielded and who has means enough, he hopes, to save his corpse: "Bury me in lead when I am dead," he begs his fellows,

> And see the coffin weigh'd
>
> . . . .
>
> And let it be solder'd closely down
> Strong as strong can be . . .
> And put it in a patent coffin,
> That I may rise no more.

He also asks for a three-man watch, with a five guinea reward if any of them "shoot / A Resurrection Man." He is, of course, doomed in spite of all his precautions, and presumably doomed precisely because of what creates those fears—his own much despised professional acquaintance with corpses and their dissection.[15]

The body snatchers responded with remarkable ingenuity to each new obstacle: they often sent their women, dressed as mourners, to attend burial services to mark the site of the new grave and the depth of the coffin, and also to observe the location and nature of the traps. Sometimes posing as near-relations who had heard of the death of someone otherwise likely to be unclaimed, they quickly bore off the friendless corpse. For parish workhouses such seemingly miraculous appearances would be especially welcome, since it would save them the cost of the burial.[16]

As a group, body snatchers were universally despised; even other criminals considered them of a lower order. Their work, however, required daring, immense physical strength, and great energy. Some of them, like the notorious Ben Crouch, who worked closely with Robert Liston for a long period of time and headed the "Borough Gang" that supplied most of the cadavers for the London hospitals and anatomy schools in the early 1800s, were usually portrayed romantically. Certainly Crouch's exploits in securing particularly valuable and well-protected corpses were often chronicled, and very likely exaggerated. Crouch himself seems to have been something of a dandy and "a powerful, overbearing man with a pock-marked face and a filthy temper; . . . of superior intelligence." He could also control his drinking in a trade where drunkenness was an occupational disease: drink offered a way to keep warm and instill courage in lonely graveyards at night. The "trade" was deliberately made mysterious by the resurrectionists themselves, who often described quite elaborate, and seemingly impossible, techniques for angling at a coffin, rather than disturbing the site itself and betraying their presence the next day. They would then, they claimed, extract the corpse by means of various tools, pulling it out of the long tunnel which they had dug to the top of the coffin.[17]

Everything about the resurrectionists—their connection with crime, their arcane, grisly occupation, the public uproar they caused, their exploitation of the poor, and the hypocrisy involved in their complex relations with the doctors who employed them—touch on issues that were bound to interest Dickens. In addition, the sensational crimes blamed on the resurrectionists occurred as Dickens was growing up, while the Special Parliamentary Committee on Anatomy was called in the same year that Dickens' uncle, Charles Barrow, began his *Mirror of Parliament*. Dickens would soon work for this journal, which recorded Parliamentary debate, and his occupation, in turn, must have made him still more aware of the issues discussed before Parliamentary committees.[18] If anything, it seems surprising that Dickens waited until 1859 to introduce a resurrectionist as a significant character in his fiction. Jerry Cruncher of *A Tale of Two Cities* has, of course, some Dickensian antecedents. Even Bill Sikes, who resembles Ben Crouch in a number of ways (appearance, strength, brutality, "filthy temper"), is apparently not above turning a body to profit. He tells Fagin that if he were one of Fagin's boys he would have murdered him " 'long ago; and—no, I couldn't have sold you arterwards, though; for you're fit for nothing but keeping as a curiosity of ugliness in a glass bottle, and I suppose they don't blow glass bottles large enough' " (xiii, 77).

Jerry has a number of successors in Dickens' fiction. The central theme of dragging bodies from the Thames in *Our Mutual Friend* bears a close resemblance to Jerry's trade—the difference being that Gaffer Hexam or Rogue Riderhood found rifling the bodies more profitable than selling them, thanks to the passage of the Anatomy Act. Durdles, of *The Mystery of Edwin Drood*, is in many ways the most obvious successor to Jerry: they both like to drink; they are both somewhat bad-tempered and considered "characters"; and they both bear the physical markings of their profession: Cruncher cannot scour away his perpetual rust, while Durdles, from working constantly "in the gravestone, tomb, and monument way," is "wholly of their color from head to foot" (ix, 28). Durdles is always promising to clean himself, but, like Jerry, he always shows an inevitable outward manifestation of his work (xii, 102). He even names the physical aches and pains occasioned by nocturnal activity in the cold of graves and sepulchers: "'I've got a touch of the Tombatism,'" he tells Jasper. And when Sapsea corrects him ("'You mean the Rheumatism'") he emphatically denies it: "'I mean, Mr. Sapsea, the Tombatism. It's another sort from Rheumatism. . . . You get among them Tombs afore it's well light on a winter morning, and keep on, as the Catechism says, a walking in the same all the days of your life, and *you*'ll know what Durdles means'" (iv, 30).

To see Durdles as Jerry's successor, the ultimate Cruncher of Dickensian fiction, we must recognize that he simultaneously enacts both of Jerry's grave-related occupations: digging up bodies, as Jerry does in the novel, and returning them to the grave, as he promises to do in the future should he escape Paris with his life.[19] Durdles combines these functions. Durdles also develops an aspect of Cruncher's work, important and implicit in all that Jerry does, which, as I shall show later, tends to transform Jerry into a kind of novelist or narrator. About Durdles, however, there can be no question, for Durdles "often speaks of himself in the third person; perhaps being a little misty as to his own identity when he narrates" (iv, 29). And what he narrates about himself confirms Dickens' judgment that "with the Cathedral crypt he is better acquainted than any living authority; it may even be than any dead one" (iv, 28). His own authority has a peculiarly ambiguous aspect: he locates and identifies corpses long-forgotten and lost and then turns them to dust.

> Thus he will say, touching his strange sights: "Durdles come upon the old chap," in reference to a buried magnate of ancient time and high degree, "by striking right into the coffin with his pick. The old chap gave Durdles a look with his open eyes, as much as to say 'Is your name Durdles? Why, my man, I've been waiting for you a Devil of a time!' And then he turned to powder" (iv, 29).

* * *

> Let's talk of graves, of worms, and epitaphs,
> Make dust our paper, and with rainy eyes
> Write sorrow on the bosom of the earth.
> *(Richard II)*

Dickens' concern with graves and burial and disinterment reflects the concerns of his age, including the sensational crimes that firmly fixed the business of "resurrecting" in the public mind. But Dickens also characteristically reflects the unstated and largely unconscious concerns of the Victorians in his repeated use and development of figures like Cruncher or Durdles. To the extent that this concern involves a denial of the emptiness of death, it is much older than the Victorian age. Shakespeare's Richard II, for example, seems to be resigning himself to death, but in effect he denies the horror of death as change by immediately surrounding "worms" with "graves" on one side and "epitaphs" on the other. He has symbolically erected his own monument in the very act of imagining himself dead, just as in response to the more annihilating image of "make dust our paper" he proceeds to "write" again almost instantly, transforming self-pity into theatrical statement. In this complex speech every movement toward the naked and appalling emptiness of death ("barren earth / Which serves as paste and cover to our bones") is countered by language and narrative as a fixing and identifying act, an act which covers over the bare ground itself ("let us sit upon the ground / And tell sad stories of the death of kings"). Richard seems to face what Shakespeare calls, in Sonnet 64, "Time's fell hand," that which makes "brass eternal slave to mortal rage." Thus, Richard speaks of the "vain conceit" which allows us to believe that "this flesh which walls about our life / Were brass impregnable." Richard seems to know better, but his strategy throughout the play is to substitute the drama of the self, the narrative of a life, for emptiness and decay. If flesh is impermanent, then the name on the grave, the inscription, or the stories told about the dead will effectively "wall[s] about our life" like "brass impregnable." When Richard urges Isabel in V, i to go to France and tell his "lamentable tale" to the court, to "send the hearers weeping to their beds," he is creating his own epitaph—and his own permanence. His story frames him, fixes him, immortalizes him. He has substituted—as we all do in using a crypt, or marker, or epitaph—the container for the thing contained.[20]

It has, however, grown more and more difficult to sustain this substitution, particularly in Western culture, because of a steady loss of faith in Christian doctrine since the Renaissance; the accepted rituals of burial and of mourning have consequently lost some of their power to assuage or to make us believe in a permanence which now seems quite illusory. According to writers like Philippe Ariès, the result of such a loss of faith is the gradual emergence of a peculiarly modern fear of death. Ariès chronicles the various ways in which we have attempted to acknowledge that fear while also denying it or disposing of it:

> For until now, incredible as it may seem, human beings as we are able to perceive them in the pages of history have never really known the fear of death. Of course, they were afraid to die; they felt sad about it, and they said so calmly. But this is precisely the point: Their anxiety never crossed the threshold into the unspeakable, the inexpressible. It was translated into soothing words and channeled into familiar rites. People paid attention to death. Death was a serious matter, . . . a dramatic moment in life, . . . but not so formidable that they were tempted to push it out of sight, run away from it, act as if it did not exist, or falsify its appearances.[21]

Nineteenth-century literature offers repeated evidence of a cultural fascination with death and its simultaneous denial, an attempt to work out what was felt at the time to be the increasing dilemma of death. Poe, for example, progresses quite logically from stories of cryptography to stories of mystery and detection because he is in fact creating surfaces of mystery and clue which effectively conceal the larger and more frightening issues of death and mutability. In the classic detective story, which he helped to invent, time is reduced to the special time and circumstances of the specific crime, so that a resolution of that crime always implies control over temporality. In other ways the deliberate imposition of an unresolvable conflict of competing stories or even chaotic visions, as we find them in modern art and modern fiction, function as elaborate screens: if we cannot know what we really see or the meaning of what we read, we cannot, under any circumstances, look at or know the naked, unrelenting facts of death, decay, of "barren earth."[22]

Ariès asserts that "when people started fearing death in earnest, they stopped talking about it."[23] This assertion is only partially true. Our popular culture and our rituals may indeed seek to deny death by relegating our dying to hospitals and to what Ariès calls the "invisible death" of this century; but in virtually all major contemporary writers there is a clear attempt to confront death in its most annhilating form. Serious twentieth-century literature continues the Victorians' exploration of the fearful facelessness of death. This passage, from Beckett, is characteristic:

> White planes no trace shining white one only shining white infinite but that known not. Light heat all known all white heart breath no sound. Head haught eyes white fixed front old ping last murmur one second perhaps not alone eye unlustrous black and white half closed long lashes imploring ping silence ping over.

These lines close the short sketch "Ping," an odd and difficult piece which, as far as most critics decipher it, seems to be about Christ and about the state of death itself.[24] It opens with a corpse very likely in a tomb or coffin: "All known all white bare white body fixed one yard legs joined like sewn. . . . White walls one yard by two white ceiling one square yard never seen."[25] Its effect, like that of the closely related "Imagination Dead Imagine," is to provide the reader with an image of imagelessness, of what would happen if, to paraphrase, our imagination were to die: might we then imagine such a state of death, death without body and death without mind? The task is of course impossible, since we cannot imagine death without imagining, without an act of mind. John Irwin points to this problem as it affected Poe more than a century earlier:

> This substitution involves a subtle shift between two different aspects of death in that the split and doubled self images its own death *as if* it were the death of another person. Yet the very act of *witnessing* a death always implies the persistence of the observer's consciousness beyond that death. By its very nature, then, any *image* of death (even the image of oneself as a corpse) bears within it the notion of the survival of consciousness, the survival of oneself as *observer of the image*. But one's own death is the destruction of observing.[26]

Beckett's technical virtuosity considerably extends the range of what Poe could do with this problem because Beckett recreates the sense of death and loss through language and syntax, through the very absences and spaces of words themselves, while Poe was operating primarily at the level of plot (the use of the double which Irwin describes). Thus Beckett helps us to imagine the blindness of whiteness, white light everywhere, illuminating the coffin itself into an eternal white emptiness. The trick of "Ping" is that he must lead us to imagine the state of being dead by seeming to start in the crypt but in fact switching us from inside to outside and back inside the coffined figure until, at the close, we witness its death and our own, at the very moment of the death (ending) of the story: "ping silence ping over."

Irwin rightly asserts that any image of death, "even the image of oneself as corpse," must imply a conscious act of observation, of reading the words of the text and imagining the body described. But what if the reader is led to expect precisely this awful image of the dead, with its implicit consolation of a life-asserting reflection back to the reader, whose life is thus ironically affirmed in the mirroring presence of death, of the corpse—and then the image is suddenly emptied? What if we go to the grave, dig up the coffin, open it up, and, like Jerry Cruncher, discover—nothing?

Jacques Derrida has written at length about the double image of the crypt as container and as false container, about its attempt to confine or surround what is in fact uncontainable: the decomposing body, or the life and even the soul within that body, all of which the crypt is designed to "contain" and bear witness to. Derrida describes the crypt as at once suggesting "the hermeticism of a stronghold or strongbox—safe—and a certain ceaselessly threatening instability. . . . it is erected by its very ruin, held up by what never stops eating away at its foundation."[27] He sees in the image of the crypt a prime image of language itself; we use language to define and to hold meaning but it always fails to some degree because it cannot define absolutely. Grave robbing or disinterment seem apt images for the act of writing: society inscribes the grave and helps us to "write sorrow on the bosom of the earth"; we all hope to fix that which cannot be held unchanged. Derrida's topic in this essay is Freud's "Wolf-Man" case, and more generally the subject of psychoanalysis. But his comments are readily extended to any act of writing that analyzes, whether it is in the novelist's implicit analysis of character or culture or criticism's formal analysis of text: "To track down the path to the tomb, then to violate a sepulcher: that is what the analysis of a cryptic incorporation is like."[28] Ultimately the crypts within the "cemetery-guard" of the Self are in the realm of the unconscious, the repressed; they symbolize the innermost, secret, personal history of each individual.[29] And novelists (or literary critics) are inevitably engaged in violating such memorials, probing and exploring them. Like the historian and the archaeologist, they disinter, unlock, and decode what has deliberately been buried and enclosed, renamed or disguised. Novelists and critics resemble, in this unearthing of the soul, literary resurrectionists. They help to disinter, exhibit, and dissect the body; they help their readers to see, or view, the corpse on display in the morgue of literary history.

The comparison of a *corpus* of literature with the display of bodies in a real morgue is not as outrageous as it may first sound, given the history of the morgue itself and of the public's relationship to the morgue as theater, where the bodies were displayed as they might have been at a waxwork. In the nineteenth century, the morgue evoked two very different feelings in the ever-increasing number of spectators who came there not just to identify bodies but to *view* them as spectacle. It was, in one way, the most concrete and unflinching proof of the corpse as lifeless and soulless; it was a kind of medical temple which replaced the Christian temple with a terrible vengeance, because we could now see ourselves reflected in the corpses and see our futures in the cold and empty death before us. But in another way the very presence and accessibility of the morgue allowed us to make what has become a cliché of the crime story: "positive identification." What we are asserting as positive and identifying when we go to the morgue to view a body is not so much the existence of someone else but of ourselves.

The scientific morgue became what Allan Mitchell, in an article on "The Paris Morgue as a Social Institution in the Nineteenth Century," calls "a sort of lost-and-found department of the dead." The morgue became "an essential agency for law enforcement and the detection of criminals," and it became as well a tourist attraction, "invariably listed in the guidebooks of the nineteenth century." It drew millions of spectators, and it was, as Mitchell demonstrates clearly, "more than a temple of suicide," but rather "the shrine of positivism. . . . inseparable from the growing prestige of nineteenth-century science."[30]

Dickens' lifelong fascination with morgues, and tombs, and burial sites is in one sense characteristic of his age; but Dickens' reflections on what he saw offer us a profound vision into the meaning of such morbid tourism. Certainly he acknowledged his curiosity about death quite openly: "Whenever I am at Paris," he writes, in 1860, as the "Uncommercial Traveller," "I am dragged by invisible force into the Morgue."[31] He and Collins often went to morgues and prisons. Referring to the Paris trip of 1846–47, Forster remarks that Dickens "went at first rather frequently to the Morgue, until shocked by something so repulsive that he had not courage for a long time to go back" (F, II, 294). But he did indeed go back, and over the next twenty years Dickens would visit morgues, catacombs, and tombs with an almost morbid regularity, indeed, as the Uncommercial Traveller suggests, obsessively:

> Whenever I am at Paris, I am dragged by invisible force into the Morgue. I never want to go there, but am always pulled there. One Christmas Day, when I would rather have been anywhere else, I was attracted in, to see an old grey man lying all alone on his cold bed, with a tap of water turned on over his grey hair, and running, drip, drip, drip, down his wretched face until it got to the corner of his mouth, where it took a turn, and made him look sly. One New Year's Morning (by the same token, the sun was shining outside, and there was a mountebank balancing a feather on his nose, within a yard of the gate), I was pulled in again to look at a flaxen-haired boy of eighteen, with a heart hanging on his breast—"from his mother," was engraven on it—who had come into the net across the river, with a bullet wound in his fair forehead and his hands cut with a knife, but whence or how was a blank mystery. This time, I was forced into the same dread place, to see a large dark man whose disfigurement by water was in a frightful manner comic, and whose expression was that of a prize-fighter who had closed his eyelids under a heavy blow, but was going immediately to open them, shake his head, and "come up smiling." Oh what this large dark man cost me in that bright city!   (UT, pp. 64–65)

Although Dickens emerges from the morgue to the bright Paris streets and to a characteristic round of activity, he cannot get the images, the figures and faces he has seen and the fancies he has created from them, out of his mind; and he makes another visit to the morgue "to look at [the] clothes" of "the large dark creature," and is still thinking about him when he leaves Paris for Switzerland (*UT*, p. 67). This pattern—obsessive and concentrated observation, leading to elaborate fantasies on the lives of figures he has seen and then dwelt upon imaginatively, alleviated but not eliminated by brisk activity in the bright world outside—resembles nothing so much as Dickens' own relationship to his work.[32] Visits to the morgue came to represent for Dickens an experience which led from the observation of cold dead fact and detail to the process of imagination and the transformations of writing. Thus when he writes to Forster (in 1847) of having visited the Paris Morgue and develops his first glimpse of the *"old man with a grey head lying there"* (*P*, V, 3), Dickens muses on the thing observed and his own perception of it: "It seemed the strangest thing in the world that it should have been necessary to take any trouble to stop such a feeble, spent, exhausted morsel of life." He then passes on to a sense of place and his own relationship to it before he quickly and imaginatively generalizes from the individual observed to the year itself. Such generalizing inevitably makes him aware of his own gift, his vocation and his style, so that he closes the quick movement—from corpse to self to context to symbolic statement of a period—by an ironic reference to his writerly self. And in this sudden self-consciousness, he ends abruptly:

> It was just dusk when I went in; the place was empty; and he lay there, all alone, like an impersonation of the wintry eighteen hundred and forty-six . . . . I find I am getting inimitable, so I'll stop.[33]

In the later version of this incident, the Uncommercial Traveller piece entitled "Some Recollections of Mortality," Dickens at first describes a Parisian crowd eager to view a recently delivered corpse, while the Uncommercial's interest passes very quickly from the corpse to the observers, and especially to their attempts to transform the experience of viewing the dead into a story or history, or at least into something which could be pegged and catalogued: "And there was a much more general, purposeless, vacant staring at it—like looking at waxwork, without a catalogue, and not knowing what to make of it. But all these expressions concurred in possessing the one underlying expression of *looking at something that could not return a look*" (*UT*, p. 192). In effect Dickens senses the doubleness and the tension inherent in this Victorian viewing of the morgue's "great exhibition": the simultaneous need to identify the corpse and thereby affirm one's own existence at what Mitchell calls "the shrine of posivitism" along with a dread in the face of emptiness, of vacuum.[34] One challenge in looking at a body with the life gone out of it—a challenge of the most disturbing kind—is to allow into consciousness the opposing sense of life in us and death in the mirror we face. We look, but the gaze cannot be returned. Perhaps the novelist may confront this more readily than others because he has at least the illusion of breathing life back into the lifeless object, of a kind of fictive resurrection. And such novelistic power is inevitably linked, in the nineteenth century, with the power of observation.

As Dickens repeatedly demonstrates in his visits to the morgue, or indeed to prisons or post offices or anywhere he goes with an eye toward writing fiction or journalism, the static or inanimate world he sees is brought to life by the close and original observation of detail, the detail, for example, with which Dickens describes the morgue in "Some Recollections . . .": the people there, the insignificant body which is the peculiarly absent center of their concentrated gaze. And from this scene Dickens thinks back to "one day in the hard winter of 1861," when he was walking near the Regent's Canal and he noticed a policeman and a cabman hurrying to the river, carrying a long pole. Dickens races after them in time to see the figure they have pulled out of the water:

> I saw, lying on the towing-path with her face turned up towards us, a woman, dead a day or two, and under thirty, as I guessed, poorly dressed in black. The feet were lightly crossed at the ankles, and the dark hair, all pushed back from the face, as though that had been the last action of her desperate hands, streamed over the ground. Dabbled all about her, was the water and the broken ice that had dropped from her dress, and had splashed as she was got out.   (*UT*, p. 193)

Detail leads rapidly to mystery and the woman becomes, like the dead man who came to represent the year 1846, an emblem—at least for the narrator and his readers. Dickens seems to suggest in her a type of Christ ("feet . . . lightly crossed at the ankles"), and he makes us powerfully aware of her final moments by the imagined "action of her desperate hands." This condensed but masterful sketch finishes with a strangely mixed frieze, the water and the broken ice, both held in space as in a picture, as in a "tableau vivant" of the dead. All this Dickens sees and communicates in a few sentences to his readers. But among the observers Dickens sees repeated "that stare at it [the corpse] which I have likened to being at a waxwork exhibition without a catalogue." The policeman, like Mr. Inspector of *Our Mutual Friend*, meanwhile takes stock "with professional stiffness and coolness." Indeed the whole scene, lodging itself in

Dickens' memory some three years before beginning *Our Mutual Friend*, may well have contributed to the images and concerns of that book, and particularly to the idea of recovering the dead, the lifeless, from the river and, more profoundly, from the inhumane indifference which represents the true and deadly threat of that novel. Dickens closes his description of the woman's body on just such a note:

A barge came up, breaking the floating ice and the silence, and a woman steered it. The man with the horse that towed it, cared so little for the body, that the stumbling hoofs had been among the hair, and the tow-rope had caught and turned the head, before our cry of horror took him to the bridle. At which sound the steering woman looked up at us on the bridge, with contempt unutterable, and then looking down at the body with a similar expression—as if it were made in another likeness from herself, had been informed with other passions, had been lost by other chances, had had another nature dragged down to perdition—steered a spurning streak of mud at it, and passed on.   (*UT*, p. 194)

Finally, Dickens moves from the present viewing of the corpse in the Paris morgue, through this recollection of a drowned woman, to a much earlier memory, "say five-and-twenty years ago" (*UT*, p. 194), when he was put on his first jury and asked to decide whether a mother had murdered her newborn infant or merely concealed the body once it was dead. Dickens was moved by the mother, whom he felt to be innocent of the greater crime, as he felt moved against the beadle who summoned him and those jury members whom he found narrow and hard-hearted. Indeed, in a variety of ways, this event, which Dickens himself dates to the period around 1836–37, reflects many of the concerns of *Oliver Twist*.[35] And what captures his imagination in the telling of this last recollection of mortality is the image of the dead child, which may well have had for Dickens associations with Oliver, whom we first see very reluctant "to take upon himself the office of respiration," lying instead "gasping on a little flock mattress, rather unequally poised between this world and the next: the balance being decidedly in favour of the latter" (I, 1). Both children may also suggest to Dickens his own sense of himself as a child, a "poor little lad," turned into a crushed castaway and sent down to the vaults of Warren's Blacking Warehouse, "thrown away" at such an age (*F*, I, 28). But the child whom we now see as the final image of death in "Some Recollections . . ." is a most disturbing reminder of the death we all feel in relationship to our own pasts and, perhaps, as well, to our sense of a future beyond our lives.

> In a kind of crypt devoted to the warehousing of the parochial coffins, and
> in the midst of a perfect Panorama of coffins of all sizes, it was stretched on
> a box; the mother had put it in her box—this box—almost as soon as it was
> born, and it had been presently found there. It had been opened, and neatly
> sewn up, and regarded from that point of view, it looked like a stuffed crea-
> ture. It rested on a clean white cloth, with a surgical instrument or so at
> hand, and regarded from that point of view, it looked as if the cloth were
> "laid," and the Giant were coming to dinner. There was nothing repellant
> about the poor piece of innocence, and it demanded a mere form of looking
> at. So, we looked at an old pauper who was going about among the coffins
> with a foot rule, as if he were a case of Self-Measurement; and we looked at
> one another.   (*UT*, p. 196)

In the image of an infant as "a stuffed creature," Dickens anticipates
the peculiar but powerful unreality of Mr. Venus's shop in *Our Mutual
Friend*, with its bottled hindoo babies and skeletons and body parts nearly
restored to life, "paralytically animated" in the moment that Wegg peers
back at them from the darkness just outside Venus's shop (I, vii, 85). Yet
as the Uncommercial Traveller said earlier about the viewers rushing to
see the newly arrived corpse, the gaze directed at that which cannot return
our gaze has the most disturbing consequences. The effect in Dickens'
mind—and therefore in ours as we read—is to move from the dead child
to the dead future ("an old pauper . . . going about among the coffins
with a foot rule, as if he were a case of Self-Measurement"), to a disturbing connection between the dead child and the pauper nearly dead, to the
present and living—and then to us ("and we looked at one another").

In this short but quite remarkable piece, Dickens uses the morgue as a
kind of *theatrum mundi*, and he offers us a quick reverse look at the ages
of man: old man, young woman, infant. As he does so, Dickens also seems
to touch on the sources of some of his own fiction and, more interestingly,
on the process of writing that fiction—the movement from observed detail to the art that breathes life into the corpses observed as into the observers themselves. But while doing all this, Dickens returns us again and
again to an uncanny, riveting prospect: "*looking at something that could
not return a look*," "looking at waxwork," "that stare . . . [like] being at a waxwork exhibition without a catalogue," all leading to an un-
nerving self-reflexive gaze ("and we looked at one another"). In cata-
loguing his own memories and obsessions around the theme of death and
in the locale of the morgue, Dickens vividly renders the uncomfortable
duality experienced by the Victorians, who both fixed an unflinching gaze
of positivism on the corpse and glimpsed, through it, the abyss of
nihilism.[36]

* * *

A wonderful fact to reflect upon, that every human creature is constituted to be that profound secret and mystery to every other. A solemn consideration, when I enter a great city by night, that every one of those darkly clustered houses encloses its own secret; that every room in every one of them encloses its own secret; that every beating heart in the hundreds of thousands of breasts there, is, in some of its imaginings, a secret to the heart nearest it! Something of the awfulness, even of Death itself, is referable to this. No more can I turn the leaves of this dear book that I loved, and vainly hope in time to read it all. No more can I look into the depths of this unfathomable water, wherein, as momentary lights glanced into it, I have had glimpses of buried treasure and other things submerged. It was appointed that the book should shut with a spring, for ever and for ever, when I had read but a page. It was appointed that the water should be locked in an eternal frost, when the light was playing on its surface, and I stood in ignorance on the shore. My friend is dead, my neighbour is dead, my love, the darling of my soul, is dead; it is the inexorable consolidation and perpetuation of the secret that was always in that individuality, and which I shall carry in mine to my life's end. In any of the burial-places of this city through which I pass, is there a sleeper more inscrutable than its busy inhabitants are, in their innermost personality, to me, or than I am to them?   (I, iii, 10)

This well-known opening of Chapter Three of *A Tale of Two Cities* interrupts the suspenseful account of Mr. Lorry, on the night-mail to Dover, who had received the strange message from Jerry Cruncher: "Recalled to Life." The intimate, slightly mournful tone of this opening is as different from the preceding chapters as the quickly paced narrative and dialogue of Chapter Two, "The Mail," was different from the famously balanced oratory of the novel's very first paragraphs. Indeed the chapter headings themselves suggest a progress from public view and public oratory ("The Period"), to adventure ("The Mail"), to the kind of philosophical, melancholic, and personal musing we find here at the beginning of Chapter Three, "The Night Shadows." As Dickens makes clear in this first paragraph, "shadows" refer with deliberate ambiguity to the living—the inscrutable and busy inhabitants of this city as dead to the speaker as are those buried nearby—and to the dead themselves, whose souls, having shed the body, will rise like shadows and whose long historical shadows are projected through past letters, past deeds, past actions, across the landscape of the narrative which is to come. The final sentence of this paragraph will gain in complexity and significance through the course of the book. At first, it seems the most pessimistic of visions: those who live, even those who are closest to me, are as effectively dead to my understanding as the inhabitants of cemeteries; I shall never know how they truly feel or what they truly think, any more than they will ever know me. Such a vision of secrecy, repression, distrust, or the simple absence of knowledge provides the psychological background—and the psychological power—which Dickens draws on to create the mood of political repression and secrecy in pre-Revolutionary France; such a vision has in it, as Dickens says, "something of the awfulness, even of Death itself." But another reading—backward from the close of the novel, from Carton's sacrifice, from information gleaned in the cemeteries of London, from the recurrent theme of resurrection—is that, if in one light the living appear dead to us, the dead may appear to be alive and to give life.

We might, from the knowledge of the whole story that Dickens is about to tell, answer his last question ("is there a sleeper more inscrutable . . . ?") with a paradoxically negative affirmation: There is no sleeper more inscrutable in the graveyards than my living contemporaries or my closest friends, but those very sleepers in the graveyard will soon yield up a knowledge that will transform the most secretive and unlikely of men, men like Carton. Those secrets will not only save the living but give new meaning to their lives. Here "cemetery" may be used with etymological accuracy, to designate a place where the living merely "sleep," in transition from one world to the next.[37] Such a transition, at least in Christian tradition, is a passage from a vale of tears to a world of clarity, of total and transparent meaning. Finally, Dickens' fame, in his own time as well as a century later, adds yet another meaning to his musing on that which is buried and inscrutable as opposed to that which is living. As we now read him we are aware of Dickens, the man, alive and sharing his thoughts, as we are also aware of the Dickens who is at once dead and immortally present before us, on the page. It is hard not to imagine that Dickens, at the height of his fame and in such a pensive mood about his own life and his relationship to others[38]—in the present and in the future—is not himself thinking about the irony of his own position and the reception of his words. He may well be imagining his own paradoxical future: as a corpse, and as a textual presence more powerful than any living personality. The dead always teach us about the living, and what we learn from a Shakespeare or a Dickens may perhaps prove more revelatory—even more intimate—than any observations we make about ourselves or our friends.

The opening paragraph of "The Night Shadows" suggests in effect the impossibility of what we, as readers, are inevitably attempting with Dickens at the outset of this novel: to explore that profound mystery which is the impenetrable, monumental grave, that crypt which is the secret self of every other being. The passage is characterized by a tension between the closed world of death—"the awfulness, even of Death itself," "the burial places of this city"—and an attempt to open it by language, by description, and by repeated references within the paragraph to the act of reading: "No more can I turn the leaves of this dear book . . . in time to read it all," "It was appointed that the book should shut . . . when I had read but a page." Dickens follows, in this respect, the strategy of Shakespeare's Richard II. The apparent impossibility of seeing into the cryptically guarded secret of others is implicity broken, within the passage itself, by self-consciousness about narration and the act of reading, and it is still further broken by the surprisingly intimate tone, so different from everything preceding it. And as soon as we respond to the intimacy and nod agreement with the narrator, we have been allied most directly with the secret soul of another.

The act that makes us allies is a common act of narrational curiosity, looking into others as we would look into a crypt, baffled by the seeming impossibility of knowing the secrets of our neighbors any more than we can know the secrets of the dead. Author and reader have both become, for the moment, resurrectionists. As we have seen, Dickens' own fascination with morgues and corpses suggests how much can be learned, even from a dead body. Certainly it suggests the author's need to know, to resurrect the corpse into a living narrative, a history, while it suggests at the same time the unspeakable fear aroused by such an act, by any direct confrontation with the dead, with the encrypted past.

The dilemma that this passage poses—at once announcing the isolation of one person from another and also affirming a connection through the narrational act itself—will be resolved in two ways in this novel. The positive solution, the affirmative sacrifice, will be Carton's. But another kind of doubling, comic yet more deeply subversive, even nihilistic—will be that of Jerry Cruncher, whose literal resurrections do more than lampoon or satirize the Christian meaning of the myth, the serious significance of Carton's sacrifice. Cruncher shows us what Carton cannot see: the emptiness of death, the nothingness of dust.

Carton's life follows the typical pattern of the fictive criminal of the eighteenth and nineteenth centuries, the "hero" of the purportedly true accounts of the *Newgate Calendar* and the more sensational reports which accompanied every major public execution: born with the capacity for better things but also fatally flawed, the criminal-hero marches steadily toward his own destruction. Women and drink and gambling were the most obvious temptations, and Carton is clearly susceptible to all three. He even calls himself a profligate, refers to his own "sloth and sensuality," and Dickens follows these comments by Lucie's presumed thoughts (certainly Dickens' own moral position): "It was so sad to think, how much he had thrown away, and how much he every day kept down and perverted" (II, xiii, 143–145).

Given the dramatic stage, the "platform" of a Newgate or a Tyburn hanging, the criminal sees what might have been; and we, his audience, feel both identified with him and, presumably, warned in time. One of the extraordinary effects of reading through the two-volume *Newgate Calendar* is to become aware of the powerful impact of the moment of death and the astonishing drama—surely nothing can rival it—of imagining what it would be like to know we were about to die. There are of course many variations on the model I have ascribed to Carton—we read of "born" villains or the unrepentant, defiant condemned—but the image of the young man of promise betrayed by loss of control or of will and led to his own death runs from Defoe's criminal protagonists through the period immediately preceding *A Tale of Two Cities*.[39] Carton is very much within this tradition until the closing section of the novel, where he is deliberately elevated into a type of Christ. And as he ascends, both literally and figuratively, toward the final, climactic, and transcendent death of the book, Jerry Cruncher descends. Carton comes to stand for the idealized and religious concept of "Resurrection"; Jerry for the ironic slang meaning of the same term. Carton is the Saviour, whereas Cruncher's very presence leads toward Apocalypse: " 'What a night it has been! Almost a night, Jerry,' said Mr. Lorry, 'to bring the dead out of their graves' " (I, vi, 97). Carton reassures us; Cruncher disturbs us.

Certainly, what he sees disturbs us—when we are finally allowed to see it. Both within the text and extratextually, in the illustrations, everything is done to delay or deny the very emptiness of Jerry's own vision. That vision occurs in Chapter xiv of Book II, "The Honest Tradesman." The chapter itself begins as Dickens identifies Cruncher with the artist and philosopher and simultaneously denies that connection by a series of mock-heroic comparisons. Like Dickens himself, Cruncher observes all the bustle and excitement in the London streets: "To the eyes of Mr. Jeremiah Cruncher . . . a vast number and variety of objects in movement were every day presented." Jerry sees two streams of humanity, and his vision is at first a grand one: "two immense processions, one ever tending westward with the sun, the other tending eastward from the sun, both ever tending to the plains beyond the range of red and purple where the sun goes down!'' Jerry is then compared to "the heathen rustic who has for several centuries been on duty watching one stream," but such quasi-mythological comparisons only reaffirm Jerry's own banality: first we have an extended comparison of Jerry to a kind of cockney Charon, "deriving a small part of his income . . . from the pilotage of timid women . . . from Tellson's side of the tides to the opposite shore"; then this image, which informs the subsequent paragraph:

> Time was, when a poet sat upon a stool in a public place, and mused in the sight of men. Mr. Cruncher, sitting on a stool in a public place, but not being a poet, mused as little as possible, and looked about him.[40]

Repeatedly, as this chapter begins, Jerry is made to seem a type of the poet or author or philosophical viewer of humanity—and then denied that association. We might say that the comedy of his presentation is a stylistic attempt to deny, at every point, what he does or what we come to see through him. And even that slender humor is almost overwhelmed by a barely disguised aggression in this chapter, particularly in Jerry's treatment of his wife, which threatens to ruin the comedy altogether.[41]

The climax of the chapter is the "fishing expedition" of Cruncher, Sr., witnessed, at least for a time, by Jerry, Jr.:

> But, his long-cherished desire to know more about these matters, not only stopped him in his running away, but lured him back again. They were still fishing perseveringly, when he peeped in at the gate for the second time; but, now they seemed to have got a bite. There was a screwing and complaining sound down below, and their bent figures were strained, as if by a weight. By slow degrees the weight broke away the earth upon it, and came to the surface. Young Jerry very well knew what it would be; but, when he saw it, and saw his honoured parent about to wrench it open, he was so frightened, being new to the sight, that he made off again, and never stopped until he had run a mile or more.   (II, xiv, 154)

By switching to young Jerry's point of view in this chapter, Dickens promotes a comic perspective not unlike Pip's vision of Magwitch and his terrible imaginary companion at the beginning of *Great Expectations*; yet in *A Tale of Two Cities* the narrative perspective of the frightened child also succeeds in preventing us from viewing a coffin which is to prove empty. Instead the novelist's camera-eye follows Jerry, Jr., and plays up the superficial terror associated with horror and ghost stories:

> He had a strong idea that the coffin he had seen was running after him; and, pictured as hopping on behind him, bolt upright, upon its narrow end, always on the point of overtaking him and hopping on at his side—perhaps taking his arm—it was a pursuer to shun. It was an inconsistent and ubiqui-

tous fiend too, for, while it was making the whole night behind him dreadful, he darted out into the roadway to avoid dark alleys, fearful of its coming hopping out of them like a dropsical boy's-Kite without tail and wings. It
hid in doorways too, rubbing its horrible shoulders against doors, and drawing them up to its ears, as if it were laughing. It got into shadows on the
road, and lay cunningly on its back to trip him up. All this time it was inces-
santly hopping on behind and gaining on him, so that when the boy got to
his own door he had reason for being half dead. And even then it would not
leave him, but followed him up-stairs with a bump on every stair, scrambled
into bed with him, and bumped down, dead and heavy, on his breast when
he fell asleep.   (II, xiv, 154–155)

All these fantasies imply that the coffin, or its occupant, is alive. The underlying terror of that cliché of horror stories is not the resurrection of the
body but a blurring of the boundaries between the living and the dead.
The blank gaze of the dead object, the dead mirror into which we stare
when we look at the body in the coffin, create the fear Dickens repeatedly
describes in his accounts of the morgue. Bringing the body back to life
and action is far less horrifying than the vision that we have been denied at
this moment in the story, that we get only by indirection and that forms
one of the trump cards Carton will be able to play, in the closing chapters
of the novel, to oblige Barsad to cooperate with him. Here Jerry himself
speaks as if for the dead, touching Barsad

> on the shoulder like a ghostly bailiff.
> "That there Roger Cly, master," said Mr. Cruncher, with a taciturn and
> iron-bound visage. "So *you* put him in his coffin?"
> "I did."
> "Who took him out of it?"
> Barsad leaned back in his chair, and stammered, "What do you mean?"
> "I mean," said Mr. Cruncher, "that he warn't never in it. No! Not he! I'll
> have my head took off, if he was ever in it."
> The spy looked round at the two gentlemen; they both looked in unspeak-
> able astonishment at Jerry.
> "I tell you," said Jerry, "that you buried paving-stones and earth in that
> there coffin."   (III, viii, 288–289)

The paving stones may carry the suggestion of revolutionary weapons,
but the force of the image is on the absence of the body and the presence
of that to which the body must return—to earth, to ashes, to dust, or to
the absolute inanimate life of stones. The utter deadness of the paving
stones echoes Wordsworth's famous image of Lucy, who "neither sees
nor hears / Rolled round in earth's diurnal course, / With rocks, and
stones, and trees."

Later Jerry will try to deny his mortifying revelation, and, in answer to Lorry asking him " 'What have you been, besides a messenger?' " he replies " 'Agricultooral character.' " Lorry is having none of that and refers obliquely to " 'an unlawful occupation of an infamous description.' " Although he is speaking sternly, Lorry's refusal to name the trade, combined with Jerry's comical circumlocutions and evasions, all further our sense that what Jerry does and what he has seen must be refuted. Jerry himself will attempt this refutation by a kind of vocational act of undoing. He offers to " 'make amends for what he would have un-dug—if it wos so—by diggin' of 'em in with a will, and with conwictions respectin' the futur' keepin' of 'em safe' "   (III, ix, 291–292).

But Jerry need not have worried: Dickens and his illustrator had already seen to that. To the best of my knowledge, no one has commented on the inaccuracy of Phiz's front wrapper illustration, which shows Jerry digging up what is unmistakably a corpse. Indeed, Jane R. Cohen, in her recent comprehensive study of *Charles Dickens and his Original Illustrators*, comments that Browne's "wrapper design clearly depicts its [the novel's] main characters and incidents," although in general, according to Cohen, Browne "failed to respond to the author's new interests as they were suggested on the wrapper and developed in the text."[42] In the middle of the left side of the wrapper, mirroring a picture of the imprisonment or living burial of Manette in the tomb of the Bastille on the right, Cruncher removes a body.

If we were to argue that Phiz was merely illustrating Jerry's vocation in general rather than the specific instance of it found in the novel, we would only be rationalizing the mistake, not explaining it. Such a generic illustration (rather than the specific textual one) would be extraordinary for any of Dickens' illustrators, whether on the wrappers or in individual illustrations. Further, we know that Dickens scrutinized these illustrations with great care and that although he was critical of Phiz he apparently offered no correction of the mistake. Indeed, had he perceived it or perceived it as an error, we know that he would certainly have seen it remedied; Dickens was almost fanatical about such details.[43] Rather, Dickens—like young Jerry, like "Phiz," like most of his readers—must have ultimately found it less frightening to visualize a corpse where there had been in the reality of the text nothing but dirt and stones: In the first (wrapper) illustration, Dickens and Browne offer us presence where Cruncher had in fact discovered absence.

The novel's repeated motif of being "buried alive"—the theme of recovering the Bastille prisoner from a living grave—is similarly predicated on a notion that we are witnessing the worst possible dilemma of the human condition. But in fact the worst dilemma would be that which is initially threatened to young Manette: total emptiness, a life dissolved and forgotten, as our bodies must some day dissolve and become indistinguishable from the earth in which they are buried. Everything in the novel seems to work against this fate, since not only is Manette "dug out" and "resurrected," but the thoughts and writings of his greatest period of despair and oblivion are recovered and made powerful: everything about his presumed "burial" is finally given substance and power. At the start of the novel, Lorry has a nightmare about digging out Manette only to have him turn to dust—a nightmare which anticipates Durdles's "old chap" who "turns to powder" on touch. More important, Lorry's nightmare anticipates Jerry's discovery of nothingness, and the old banker will do everything in his power to prevent such a vision from becoming fact. He is riding along thinking repeatedly that "he was on his way to dig some one out of a grave":

> After such imaginary discourse, the passenger in his fancy would dig, and dig, dig—now, with a spade, now with a great key, now with his hands—to dig this wretched creature out. Got out at last, with earth hanging about his face and hair, he would suddenly fall away to dust. The passenger would then start to himself, and lower the window, to get the reality of mist and rain on his cheek.   (I, iii, 13)

The action of the novel is designed to deny this vision, to reaffirm continually not only the possibility of digging up a corpse but also of reviving it, of always making sense of the inchoate mumblings of the doctor—or, for that matter, even of the young peasant brother and sister who first lead the doctor into danger.[44] Sense is made of every fact, of every action; and when characters attempt to subvert the clarity, the "life" of such a world, they are made to pay a heavy price. Barsad will be obliged to risk his life, indeed he is virtually certain he will lose it, when his attempt to make his associate Cly "disappear" (by seeming to be dead) is discovered. Old Foulon is less fortunate:

> Defarge stood, panting, against a background of eager eyes and open mouths, formed outside the door; all those within the wine-shop had sprung to their feet.
>   "Say then, my husband. What is it?"
>   "News from the other world!"
>   "How, then?" cried madame, contemptuously. "The other world?"
>   "Does everybody here recall old Foulon, who told the famished people that they might eat grass, and who died, and went to Hell?"

"Everybody!" from all throats.

"The news is of him. He is among us!"

"Among us!" from the universal throat again. "And dead?"

"Not dead! He feared us so much—and with reason—that he caused him-self to be represented as dead, and had a grand mock-funeral. But they have found him alive, hiding in the country, and have brought him in. I have seen him but now, on his way to the Hôtel de Ville, a prisoner. I have said that he had reason to fear us. Say all! *Had* he reason?"   (II, xxii, 212)

One way Dickens makes the madness of the revolutionaries so chilling is in the simple question uttered by "the universal throat": is he "among us . . . and dead?" Far more than Mme. Defarge's contemptuous refer-ence to the notion of "the other world" or her husband's equally glib and ironic formula of the man who "died, and went to hell," that universal question points to the depravity of a world so fallen that the living and the dead are mixed, that the reassuring boundaries of Christianity are dis-solved. In such a world, Dickens implies, nothing that *we* know is clear. The revolutionaries have created their own Terror and their own night-mare vision of a world in which the dead might well come alive, not as Christ had done but through a confusion of living and dead, a mistaken resurrection. But even for the revolutionaries, there must be a sense of order and clarity. They have many reasons for wishing to torment and then kill Foulon, but his attempt to fool them over death is perhaps the most provoking act in a life of provocation and insult. For a people now committed to watching and counting with satisfaction the regular severing of heads from bodies, the precise and deadly moment when La Guillotine carefully translates a person from one world to the next, Foulon's decep-tion is the most inexcusable act of all.

The overt and seemingly relentless subtext of this novel is to give mean-ing to death or to the past, to disinter the historical moment and make it come alive, to recover bodies and letters and everything that may presum-ably have disappeared and to resurrect them, to give them meaning. Most often, death is made to enhance life, as Darnay's near execution enhances his value for Lucie:

He had loved Lucie Manette from the hour of his danger. He had never heard a sound so sweet and dear as the sound of her compassionate voice; he had never seen a face so tenderly beautiful, as hers when it was confronted with his own on the edge of the grave that had been dug for him.

(II, x, 123–124)

Here we are in the world of Dickens' earliest—and most sentimental—fiction, a world in which the memory of the dead always enriches the life of the living, in which the boundaries between the living and the dead are as firm and secure as the plot in which they are stated. Death and closure are inevitably connected in these works, as in the final paragraph of *Nicholas Nickleby*, where Smike's otherworldly presence completes the positive resolution of all the lives of the surviving characters:

> The grass was green above the dead boy's grave, and trodden by feet so small and light, that not a daisy drooped its head beneath their pressure. Through all the spring and summer-time, garlands of fresh flowers, wreathed by infant hands, rested on the stone; and, when the children came there to change them lest they should wither and be pleasant to him no longer, their eyes filled with tears, and they spoke low and softly of their poor dead cousin.   (lxv, 831)

At its close *Oliver Twist* offers us the most reactionary image of death, because here Oliver's mother—who bore him illegitimately, whose tomb holds neither coffin nor corpse, whose first name only is inscribed, whose absence throughout the text has served to affirm Oliver's sentimental presence—is positively identified and located even though her body remains missing, so that she completes the happiness of all those who have survived her. Again, this vision is affirmed in the last paragraph of the novel. In both *Nicholas Nickleby* and *Oliver Twist* these paragraphs, describing a death that offers closure, provide as well the basis for the final illustration, the closing image, quite literally, of the text:

> Within the altar of the old village church, there stands a white marble tablet, which bears as yet but one word,—"Agnes!" There is no coffin in that tomb; and may it be many, many years, before another name is placed above it! But, if the spirits of the Dead ever come back to earth, to visit spots hallowed by the love—the love beyond the grave—of those whom they knew in life, I believe that the shade of Agnes sometimes hovers round that solemn nook. I believe it none the less, because that nook is in a Church, and she was weak and erring.   (liii, 368)

The affirmation of Agnes even in her bodily absence and in her death parallels the affirmation of Carton and Darnay at the close of *A Tale of Two Cities*: At his sublime death Carton is, in effect, Darnay, and we see him, in the familiar words which end that novel, living on through generations of children who bear his name. Even when Darnay is in prison and looking into what seems to him to be his own grave, his vision of the decay of the body only elevates his, and our, sense of the sublimity of the soul; at first,

> when the gaoler was gone, he thought in the same wandering way, "Now am I left, as if I were dead." Stopping then, to look down at the mattress, he

turned from it with a sick feeling, and thought, "And here in these crawling creatures is the first condition of the body after death."   (III, i, 244)

But Darnay will triumph over his fear and revulsion not simply by strength of character but, from the reader's point of view, by the presence of Carton, just as Carton's true life is ensured by his death and his rebirth as Darnay at the close of the text. Thus Darnay's use of his prison thoughts as stepping stones to a "higher" frame of mind effectively denies them, and with them the negating power of death. Like Carton, and like many of the central figures of Dickens' earlier fiction, he will attempt to "solve" the dilemma of death by a separation of soul from body that encourages us then to evade, and finally to deny altogether, the decaying corpse and the absence after life has left the body. What Jerry sees, however—indeed what Jerry does, the very literalness of his "resurrecting"—brings us to a much more disturbing vision.

And this deeply disturbing aspect of Jerry's work and the visions to which it leads us account to some extent for the peculiar lack of comedy most critics have decried in this novel. Mark Twain mentioned "the body-snatcher in *A Tale of Two Cities*" (along with all of *Pickwick*!) as rare instances of failed comedy in Dickens.[45] And John Gross writes:

> But it must be admitted that the *Tale* is in many ways a thin and uncharacteristic work, bringing the mounting despair of the eighteen-fifties to a dead end rather than ushering in the triumphs of the 'sixties. In no other novel, not even *Hard Times*, has Dickens's natural profusion been so drastically pruned. Above all, the book is notoriously deficient in humour. One falls— or flops—back hopefully on the Crunchers, but to small avail. True, the comic element parodies the serious action: Jerry, like his master, is a "Resurrection-Man," but on the only occasion that we see him rifling a grave it turns out to be empty, while his son's panic-stricken flight with an imaginary coffin in full pursuit is nightmarish rather than funny. As comic characters the Crunchers are forced and mechanical; . . . Obviously Dickens's humour is many things, but it is usually bound up with a sense of almost magical power over nature: to distort, exaggerate, yoke together or dissolve is to manipulate and control external reality.[46]

I agree that Cruncher, by implication, fails to give us this sense of a "magical power over nature," although I'm not sure this lack deserves criticism. It may make Jerry and resurrectionism less funny and more serious, but it allows Dickens, through this comic subplot, to develop a dark vision which he had intimated in the novels of the 1850s and would expand powerfully in his final works. The Crunchers themselves may be too slight in conception to bear the burden that they actually do assume through the course of the novel;[47] they are not successfully comic in the manner of

Pickwick or Sam Weller or Quilp. But Gross should not dismiss the resurrection theme so quickly, just as he is surely wrong to offer the image of the "grave [which] turns out to be empty" as some sort of proof for the anticlimactic or inadequate nature of this scene. The grave's emptiness makes Jerry's function within the novel particularly unsettling.[48] The Cruncher subplot is more than a slick and vaguely comic echo of the serious theme of Christ's resurrection; it is a revolutionary image of death, a subversive version of a myth, which the novel follows out in the story of Carton's Christlike sacrifice. In effect the Cruncher subplot brings to the surface of the text the contradiction implicit but hidden in our culture's concept of the tomb and burial, a contradiction implicit in the story of Christ's own resurrection:

> what the New Testament accounts of the ascension *do* is to effect a massive reversal of their own sense of the resurrection as visible proof. For the disciples, within the text, the proof of a nonbodily life after death is the presence of Christ's resurrected body, but for the readers of the text, the proof of that life will be, through the device of the ascension, the absence of Christ's resurrected body. The visible sign of an imageless, nonbodily life will be, henceforth, that Christ's body is no longer visible. . . . What the New Testament stories do is to rename an absence as a presence, to call physical death "eternal life" by making a subtle shift in the absence they rename; for what the New Testament explains as the absence of a resurrected body is literally the absence of a corpse. And that absence can be renamed as visible proof that Christ has returned to life and ascended into heaven precisely because it preempts the major proof to the contrary—the presence of a dead body.[49]

Carton will transform his own "wasted life" into a sacrifice that allows not just Darnay to be reborn but also Carton himself to be reborn through generations of children named after him. The image that counters such symbolic fertility is not so much the murderous destruction of the Revolution as the absence of presence, the emptiness of the coffin, discovered by Cruncher. The irony of the term "resurrectionists" for body snatchers underscores the sacrilegious nature of the act: it vulgarizes the Christian belief in the ascent to heaven (the commonplace irony of referring to resurrectionists "raising" bodies); and it dramatizes primitive superstition and custom, which affirm the sanctity of the intact corpse, the corpse that will "rise" on the Day of Judgment.

Dickens thus dramatizes an unconscious conflict of his culture: a struggle between two competing images of death and the dead body. The first image, as epitomized by Carton, is conservative and religious; the second image, established through Cruncher, is subversive, even nihilistic, and it leads us in turn toward a modern perspective on the dilemma of death.

Acknowledgments

I wish particularly to thank Susan Crow, and Professors A. R. Braunmuller and Susan Brienza for their comments on this paper. Professor Joseph N. Riddel did his best to explain Derrida and should not be held responsible for any of my subsequent deconstructions of Derrida's work. I also feel a considerable debt to all of the participating faculty at the Santa Cruz Dickens Conference for their provocative comments on Dickens and their specific suggestions for this paper; I am especially grateful to the organizers of this splendid scholarly event, Professors Murray Baumgarten and John Jordan of the University of California at Santa Cruz, and Professor Edwin Eigner of the University of California, Riverside.

NOTES

All quotations of Dickens' works are from the *New Oxford Illustrated Dickens* (London: Oxford University Press, 1947-59), except for *Oliver Twist*, ed. Kathleen Tillotson, and *The Mystery of Edwin Drood*, ed. Margaret Cardwell, which are from the more recent *Clarendon Dickens* (London: Oxford University Press, 1966-). All citations to Dickens' works will be given parenthetically; citations to Dickens' novels will include book and/or chapter number as well as page references. All references to Dickens' letters through 1849 are to *The Pilgrim Edition* of *The Letters of Charles Dickens*, Madeline House and Graham Storey, eds. (Oxford: The Clarendon Press, 1965-), and will be shown by the abbreviation *P* followed by volume and page number; letters appearing after 1849 will be quoted from *The Nonesuch Dickens: The Letters of Charles Dickens*, ed. Walter Dexter, 3 vols. (London: The Nonesuch Press, 1938), and will be shown by the abbreviation *N* followed by volume and page number. Similarly, all references to John Forster's *The Life of Charles Dickens*, 3 vols. (London: Chapman and Hall, 1872-74) will by shown parenthetically with the abbreviation *F* followed by volume and page.

1. The first *Oxford English Dictionary* listing under "resurectionist" is: "An exhumer and stealer of corpses; a resurrection man"; the first example is taken from *The Annual Register* of 1776.

2. Philippe Ariès, *The Hour of Our Death* (New York: Random House, 1982), pp. 365, 366.

3. Cecil Howard Turner, *The Inhumanists* (London: Alexander Ouseley, 1932), p. 32.

4. Thomas Greenhill, *NekpokhΔeia: or, the Art of Embalming; wherein is shewn The Right of Burial, The Funeral Ceremonies and the several Ways of Preserving Dead Bodies in Most Nations of the World* (London: privately printed, 1705), p. 17. Here and throughout I have modernized the "long *s*."

5. *Ibid.*, pp. 104-106.

6. *Ibid.*, p. 106.

7. *Ibid.*, p. 110.

8. *Ibid.*, p. 112.

9. In *The Encyclopaedia of Religion and Ethics*, ed. James Hastings, 13 vols. (New York: Charles Scribner's Sons, 1908-26), under the heading "Death and Disposal of the Dead (Early Christian)," we are offered repeated evidence of the care and respect for corpses themselves as "temples of the Holy Ghost." Referring to medieval Europe, Ariès writes that "there was an unstated relationship between the preservation of the body and that of the soul" (p. 261); and by the eighteenth century, he notes, "the increasing importance of the burial vault corresponded to a growing concern on the part of the survivors for the physical preservation of the body." Ariès then adds:

> Thus, the dead have also obtained a space of their own, a vaulted cavern where they will remain—this is promised—forever, exempt from the traditional disruption of having their dried-out bones transported to the charnels. This space for the dead is the subterranean counterpart of the space for the living, the chapel in which the latter gather to attend services. We are now in the presence of a new type of burial and a new attitude toward the dead, which in the nineteenth century will overtake all of society.   (p. 292)

See also Ariès, pp. 32 and 355-356.

Greenhill, *Art of Embalming*, lists five reasons for burying—while also preserving—bodies. He begins by noting that such a practice prevents disease (plague) from being passed back to the living; that it removes a painful image from our sight; and that it frees us from the terror of death (because it removes the sight of the dead body while we also know that the body will remain preserved). He then concludes: "So that we will account the *Fourth Reason for Burial*, to be the *Excellency of Man's Body*, to which we ought to show the greater Honour and Respect, in that it is the Receptacle of the *Immortal Soul.* . . . But the *Fifth Cause* and *ultimate End of Burial* is in order to [sic] a future *Resurrection*" (p. 17).

Official Christian doctrine did not always insist on the preservation of the body. The church has altered its attitude toward practices like cremation, in part influenced by pressures for public health and safety (for example, the need to cremate the bodies of plague victims to protect the living). But modern western practices derive from assumptions that come from pagan rituals, Egyptian mummification, and Hebrew custom. "Like other Semites," write Habenstein and Lamers in their *History of American Funeral Directing* (Milwaukee: Bulfin, 1955), "the Hebrews believed that the soul kept a close connection with the dead body, so that when the corpse was hurt the soul suffered" (p. 52). And for the Egyptians they write that "the body, itself, was therefore to be preserved in natural form so that the restoration of *the person* in its complex parts, the bringing together of the elements which at death had been separated, might take place" (p. 9).

10. "Dissection in Schools of Anatomy," *British Parliamentary Papers: Health: Medical Profession*, 5 vols., *Reports from Select Committees on the Schools*

and Science of Anatomy and on the Education and Practice of the Medical Profession in the United Kingdom (Shannon, Ireland: Irish University Press, 1968), I, 15, 14.

11. These were the killings by John Bishop and Thomas Williams in London. Bishop and Williams were finally apprehended in November, 1831, for the murder of an Italian boy whose body they then attempted to sell for dissection. They were executed the following month, in December, 1831; in 1832, the Anatomy Act was passed.

    The bodies of Bishop and Williams were dissected at two major schools of anatomy in London, with a large crowd in attendance, and their skeletons subsequently went on permanent exhibit at the schools: see Camden Pelham, *The Chronicles of Crime, or, The New Newgate Calendar* (London: T. Miles, 1887), II, 302. Death masks were made of both men, and Dickens describes seeing the masks on exhibit at Newgate Prison ("Visit to Newgate," *Sketches by Boz*). According to Dickens, Bishop, "in particular, exhibit[ed] a style of head and set of features, which might have afforded sufficient moral grounds for his instant execution at any time, even had there been no other evidence against him" (202–203).

    Stanley Tick suggests that the two death masks in Jaggers's office in *Great Expectations* are of Bishop and Williams; see "Cruncher on Resurrection: A Tale of Charles Dickens," *Renascence*, 33 (1981), 98.

12. Professor Catherine Gallagher and I both came to the Santa Cruz conference with papers on the subject of resurrectionists and *A Tale of Two Cities*. Her numerous comments in various discussions and the splendid talk she gave have influenced what I now see in the novel; her approach has certainly affected my revisions of my own talk. Two of her central concerns that I had not sufficiently considered before hearing her paper are the economic and social implications of the resurrectionists' activities, as I outline them in this paragraph.

13. "Dissection in Schools of Anatomy," *British Parliamentary Papers*, I, 72.

14. *Ibid.*, I, 119.

15. Robert Southey, "The Surgeon's Warning," *The Poetical Works of Robert Southey, Collected by Himself*, 10 vols. (London: Longman, Orme, Brown, Green, and Longmans, 1838), VI, 184–191.

    For general background on the resurrectionists and the body-snatching trade I have principally relied upon four works. The most complete and modern summary I know of is Hubert Cole's *Things for the Surgeon: A History of the Resurrection Men* (London: Heinemann, 1964). A useful, if largely anecdotal and earlier work, which I have cited above, is Cecil Howard Turner, *The Inhumanists* (London: Alexander Ouseley, 1932). A good short history of the resurrectionists is offered along with a detailed account of Burke and Hare and their trial in a volume from "The Notable British Trials" series: *Burke and Hare*, ed. William Roughead (Edinburgh and London: William Hodge, 1921). Finally, the anonymous *Diary of a Resurrectionist, 1811-1812*, ed. James Blake Bailey (London: Swan Sonnenschein, 1896) also offers a helpful "Account of the Resurrection Men in London," and "A Short History of the Passing of the Anatomy Act" by the editor.

16. Cole, *Things*, observes that resurrection men had to remove bodies without leaving visible

> signs that the grave had been disturbed; otherwise the whole grave-yard might be "spoiled" for months to come. As thefts became more common, relations became more suspicious and would scatter grave flowers, shells, pebbles, and other markers. . . . Immediately after a funeral, if the graveyard staff were not in the resurrectionists' pay, a member of the gang or his wife would stroll through the cemetery and note the position of the new grave, the existence of any particular safeguards and obstacles (such as trip-wires leading to spring-guns. . . .), and the exact distribution of any articles that had been placed on the surface of the grave.   (p. 17)

And Bailey, introducing *The Diary of a Resurrectionist*, writes that

> a favourite trick . . . was that of claiming the bodies of friendless persons who died in workhouses, or similar institutions. . . . a man and woman, decently clad in mourning, in great grief, and often in tears, called at the workhouse to take away the body of their dear departed relative.   (p. 55)

He adds that

> subjects, too, were obtained from cheap undertakers, who kept the bodies of the poor until the time for burial. The coffin was weighted so as to conceal the fraud, and the mockery of reading the Burial Service over it was gone through in the presence of unsuspecting relatives.   (p. 55)

See also Turner, *Inhumanists*, "Body Snatching Without Labour," pp. 143–164.

17. Crouch is described by Cole, *Things*, p. 15; the more general practices of the body snatchers described here are outlined in Turner, *Inhumanists*, pp. 113–123.

18. See Edgar Johnson, *Charles Dickens: His Tragedy and Triumph*, 2 vols. (New York: Simon and Schuster, 1952), I, 61–65.

Andrew Sanders's recent study of *Charles Dickens: Resurrectionist* (New York: St. Martin's Press, 1982), begins by quoting an anecdote from J. C. Hotten's nineteenth-century biography of Dickens. The young Dickens, when asked to provide a calling card, wrote out: "CHARLES DICKENS, / Resurrectionist, / In search of a subject." Hotten commented that " 'Some recent cases of body-snatching had then made the matter a general topic for public discussion,' " and noted that " 'the strange address card' " was posted " 'for the amusement of medical students who patronised' " the oyster bar where Dickens wrote it. It was still up when *Pickwick Papers* first made Dickens a public figure (quoted from Sanders, *Dickens*, p. ix).

Sanders's book appeared after the Santa Cruz conference, but it offers additional and excellent documentation for an issue addressed by several of the

Santa Cruz participants: the connection between Dickens and the concept of resurrection, particularly the Christian view of Resurrection as it appears throughout Dickens' works. Insofar as my reading of Dickens emphasizes what I call the subversive or revolutionary meanings of resurrection, I disagree with Sanders; yet I find his study both valuable and persuasive. Sanders effectively argues a traditional positive reading—which Sydney Carton illustrates perfectly—whereas I am arguing for a central tension in Dickens' later novels between the traditional and the subversive, the positive and the nihilsitic, between Carton and Cruncher.

19. Jerry promises Lorry that he will " 'make amends for what he would have un-dug—if it wos so—by diggin' of 'em in with a will, and with conwictions respectin' the futur' keepin' of 'em safe' " (III, ix, 292).

20. I am necessarily reducing Shakespeare's subtle sense of the relationship between the death and decay of the body and the transmigration of the soul. Stephen Booth's rich reading of Sonnet 146 deals, in large part, with this complex and shifting relationship between "soul" and "earth," and the sonnet itself illustrates the Renaissance habit of reminding us of the decay of the flesh and of the worms who are "inheritors of this excess." On the opening line—"Poor soul, the center of my sinful earth"—Booth writes:

> Line 1 prepares the way for all the ideas from which and toward which the poem develops: it reaches toward the intermeshed paradoxes by which man is made of earth and has dominion over earth. . . . This opening line suggests the beginning of human history, implies its course, and implies its end, which is also the focus of the poem's end, the Last Judgment, doomsday—when the bodies and souls of the righteous shall be reunited in eternal life and death shall have "no more dominion" over them.

See Stephen Booth, *Shakespeare's Sonnets* (New Haven and London: Yale University Press, 1977), p. 503.

More broadly, J. V. Cunningham traces the development in Shakespeare of an acceptance of death, culminating in Edgar's "Ripeness is all" in *King Lear*, which Cunningham defines as an Elizabethan commonplace. After discussing *Hamlet*'s "the readiness is all," with a backward look at *Richard II*, Cunningham points toward the powerfully condensed line from *Lear*: "the metaphor shifts our point of view from a man's attitude toward death, from the 'readiness' of Hamlet and the 'men must endure' of the first part of Edgar's speech, to the absoluteness of the external process of Providence on which the attitude depends." On the difference between modern and Shakespearean views of death, Cunningham adds: "ours looks toward life and his toward death; ours finds its locus in modern psychology and his in Christian theology." See J. V. Cunningham, "Introduction: Ripeness is all," *Woe or Wonder: The Emotional Effect of Shakespearean Tragedy* (Chicago: Swallow Press, 1969), pp. 7–13.

It seems to me that Shakespeare, characteristically, anticipates a modern preoccupation with the emptiness of death but also that this view is not necessarily his own: certainly Shakespeare does not present it in isolation or in triumph over Renaissance views. In effect, he offers us a dramatic version of the denial of death in the very acceptance of it, as with *Richard II*, while he also provides a much broader and complicated vision—at once stoical, Biblical, Renaissance, and modern. His work helps us see Dickens in a fuller historical context.

21. Ariès, *Hour*, p. 405.

22. Certain characteristic techniques of modern literature or modern art make aesthetically attractive—while to some degree they minimize or obscure—the subject matter of death. A good (and very early) example is Monet's painting of his wife on her deathbed, "Camille sur son lit de Mort" (1879), in which the technical beauty of the painting is itself alluring while it also tends to blend Camille with the bedclothes and gauze coverings that surround her. Impressionist technique here calls attention to itself, and it has immense beauty and power; at the same time, it seems to be suggesting (in the most "aesthetic" and painless way) the fate of any corpse, of the body transforming itself into its surroundings, merging with them, before our eyes. We see Camille's face, the teeth especially pronounced (as in a skull), while her body has disappeared into—or become part of—the shroud and coverings.

Sylvie Gache, describing the picture in *Hommage à Claude Monet* (Paris: Editions de la Reunion des musées nationaux, 1980), p. 201, writes: "Monet was always interested in the ephemeral character of beings and objects: it is not surprising that viewing a corpse would have elicited the need to transform it into a work of art" (my translation). But Gache is responding to Monet's own remarkable statement about this experience of seeing someone so beloved dead before his eyes and finding himself searching for the " 'gradations of color which death had just imposed on the immobile face. Tones of blue, yellow, gray...' " (p. 201, my translation). He wishes to record the last viewing of a beloved face. He is also accurately trying to record her suffering (Joel Isaacson calls it "a painful and haunting portrait, her face gray and frozen in a grimace that reveals the agony of her last months"—see *University of Michigan Museums of Art and Archaeology Bulletin*, 1 [1978], 2). But finally, Monet is using art—particularly the potential for merging, fragmentation, and a certain kind of aesthetic obscurity—to disguise the effect of death at the same time that it transmits death's most disturbing qualities: the loss of separateness, of identity, and the merger with things, ultimately with dust itself.

23. Ariès, *Hour*, p. 406.

24. Samuel Beckett, "Ping," *First Love and Other Shorts* (New York: Grove Press, 1974), pp. 67–72. David Lodge, "Some *Ping* Understood," *Encounter*, 30 (1968), 85–89, is the first critic to talk about Beckett's attempt in "Ping" to recreate the consciousness of impending death. Eric Levy, *Beckett and the Voice of Species* (Totowa, N. J.: Barnes and Noble, 1980), p. 101, describes the later Beckett fiction (including "Ping") as expressing "Nothing... from the outside by means of images which communicate an experience with less and less content until reaching a state of complete absence. This is the only goal left to imagination and one whose utter impoverishment renders even more vivid the

experience of Nothing it tries to escape." Elizabeth Bregman Segrè, "Style and Structure in Beckett's 'Ping,'" *Journal of Modern Literature*, 6 (1977), 127-147, argues that in this story Beckett is "'destructuring' both the conventional narrative and the language which composes it" (146). Susan D. Brienza offers the most helpful, detailed reading of the story in her chapter on "Ping" from a book in preparation on *Samuel Beckett's New Styles*. In an earlier article on "Imagination Lost and Found: Beckett's Fiction and Frye's *Anatomy*," *Modern Language Notes*, 95 (1980), 980-994, Brienza and Peggy A. Knapp suggest that the subject is enclosed in a coffin ("perhaps with the nails—ping—being pounded in") while the character/creature itself "conjures up the image of a mummy. As everything, all colors, wash to white, and as the creature clings to one last memory, the reader experiences the ebbing of consciousness and the flashes from the past which supposedly constitute death" (988-989).

25. Beckett, "Ping," p. 69.

26. John T. Irwin, *American Hieroglyphics* (New Haven: Yale University Press, 1980), p. 190.

27. "Fors," *Georgia Review*, 31 (1977), 80.

28. *Ibid.*, p. 97.

29. Derrida presses this issue much further than I am prepared to do here: for Derrida, the movement inside the crypt or sepulcher, the tearing away of a false front (monumental exterior) and the tearing down of a false dichotomy (outside/inside) would be endlessly repeated. When we move from the outside (crypt) to the inside (corpse), we are merely faced with another outside symbolizing something we cannot see directly—death itself—in the external shape of the dead body. I am suggesting that the closest we can come to "seeing" death is one move closer to the "inside"—namely the substitution of dust or bones or simply nothing, emptiness, for the corpse itself; but my own continued insistence on getting "inside" (or even closer to what is inside), to the direct experience of death itself, is precisely what Derrida argues against. See also Derrida's *Marges de la Philosophie* (Paris: Editions de Minuit, 1972), especially the section on "*le puits et la pyramide*."

30. *Francia*, 4 (1976), 588, 582, 596.

31. "Travelling Abroad," from *The Uncommercial Traveller & Reprinted Pieces* (hereafter abbreviated *UT*), p. 64.

32. Dickens was an inveterate and seemingly indefatigable walker. Walking allowed him to observe—and record—the life around him, even as it also served as a necessary release and change from the intensity of his work. Forster describes the regularity of his working life and the methodical nature of his relationship to work and to home, suggesting that perhaps Dickens exaggerated order and regularity: he tried to work every morning, and his afternoon walks seemed a "necessity," even "indispensable" (*F*, III, 475-476). Dickens repeatedly described his work with phrases like "I have hammered at it more or less" (To W. H. Wills, 31 July 1868: *N*, III, 661), and he would refer

to the writing of "long and heavy pages . . . as I have heretofore proved and demonstrated with the sweat of my brow" (to Wilkie Collins, 2 July 1867: *N*, III, 535).

The correspondence with Collins in particular suggests a shared bond of something like a prison sentence to work, along with the joys of inspiration and creativity. "I am so undoubtedly one of the sons of toil," he remarks, in the letter just quoted; and, typically, Dickens tells Collins that he knew Collins would "come ahead of all the Field . . . with that invincible determination to work, and that profound conviction that nothing of worth is to be done without work, of which triflers and feigners have no conception" (20 September 1862: *N*, III, 304). Surely Dickens is describing not only Collins but himself. Sue Lonoff, in *Wilkie Collins and his Readers* (New York: AMS Press, 1982), p. 20, remarks that "one of the strongest bonds that united [Dickens and Collins] was their common belief in the craft of fiction, their mutual conviction of the need for taking pains." When he was hard at work (writing or on tour), Dickens made a point of turning down all engagements and would describe himself in terms that suggest obsession, even monomania. Typical is this remark to Percy Fitzgerald: "I have. . . forsworn all pleasure engagements whatsoever during its [the reading tour's] progress, I accept no invitations, see no one, and am perfectly heroic against my nature and my will" (9 August 1858: *N*, III, 37).

33. *P*, V, 3. In note 2 (same page), the Pilgrim editors call "the description . . . extremely characteristic of CD," and they go on to list the various appearances of the old man described as well as other related references to the Morgue.

34. In reference to this passage, Sanders writes that "Dickens appears to be fascinated by a *horror vacui*, an emptiness shared by the living and the dead. He is disturbed too by the vacancy and loneliness of death in a public place." Sanders goes on to contrast this scene with Scrooge seeing his own corpse, and he compares Dickens' view of those who died friendless as opposed to those who died beloved by family and friends. "The deaths of the unloved, the unmissed and the unhoused seem to have troubled him and to have stimulated a different kind of meditation than those of friends, or characters, to whom he felt close" (*Charles Dickens: Resurrectionist*, p. 48). The point is well taken, although Dickens, as he grew older, seems to have identified increasingly with those very figures, like John Harmon and John Jasper, who were outcast or never fully understood—even by those closest to them. I believe that the graphic isolation and neglect implied by the appearance of a corpse waiting to be identified in the morgue fascinated Dickens not so much because he was then so far outside his normal experience but rather because it exaggerated and dramatized Dickens' growing internal sense of separation and profound isolation.

35. The Beadle has clear traces of Bumble upon him, while the general hard-heartedness of some jury members sounds remarkably like the meetings of the parochial board in *Oliver Twist*. But most central are the parallel concerns of the abandoned or illegitimate child and of the victimized young mother—a set of concerns that would continue throughout Dickens' adult life and throughout his writings.

36. In contrast, Greenhill's eighteenth-century treatise asserts the reassuring power of the very presence of the dead body (as long as it was preserved): mere statues or monuments, Greenhill argues, "but very faintly and imperfectly represent that Body, to which *Embalming* gives a real Presence, and which may at any Time be essay'd by our Senses" (*Art of Embalming*, p. 106). As cited above, Greenhill describes the preserved corpse most positively as "*a Looking-Glass, a Praeludium and Argument of the Resurrection, a Symbol of our Future Integrity. . . and Everlasting Eternity*" (p. 112). As opposed to Dickens' decidedly more modern reaction when faced with death itself, Greenhill shows no indication of being disturbed by that gaze which cannot return our gaze; it is for him quite explicitly a reassuring presence, a denial of death as absence.

37. The English word is derived from the Greek *Koimētērion* (sleeping chamber, burial place) and is akin to the Latin *cunae* (cradle). Habenstein and Lamers (*History*, pp. 60–61), begin a section on "*Death as Sleep*" by noting:

> The tone and direction of Christian funeral practices were set by the Christian belief in the resurrection. To non-Christians and the very early Hebrews, death was an uninviting reality in which the promise of an agreeable or intolerable afterlife was at best given only to a select few. The changed outlook produced by Christianity is to be clearly seen in the new metaphor in which death is represented as sleep. The "Cemetery" by its etymology designates a sleeping place, where those rest for a while in Christ until they rise with Him in the general resurrection. The concept and terminology of death as sleep have carried through almost two thousand years into modern funerary usage.

38. Johnson writes that the idea for *A Tale of Two Cities* "had come to Dickens more than a year before, in the midst of the turmoil and anguish of his disintegrating marriage" (II, 947). The new novel itself was a great success, as was Dickens' reading tour, begun in 1858 and continuing into 1859. Forster (III, 208) reminds us that in 1858 "the first collection of his writings into a succinct library form" was brought out, an event that must have surely marked his sense of his future fame. During this same period he also broke with his publishers of sixteen years and began a new journal of his own. He was, of course, now involved with Ellen Ternan, and the range and power of his writing—although he received immense praise for *A Tale of Two Cities* from those he most admired, like Forster and Carlyle—would continue to grow with the two novels after *A Tale of Two Cities* (*Great Expectations* and *Our Mutual Friend*). Because of the combined successes of his writing and his readings, in combination with his sense of ending a miserable portion of his life and beginning fresh, Dickens' pervasive mood during this period was triumphant and forward looking. See, generally, Johnson's first two chapters of Part Nine, "The Track of a Storm," II, 929–952, and 'Surface Serene," 953–971.

39. The most helpful and comprehensive account of this fictional genre is Keith Hollingsworth, *The Newgate Novel* (Detroit: Wayne State University Press, 1963).

40. Dickens may have been thinking of a general type, a kind of poetic *topos*, or he may have had Dante specifically in mind: In *Little Dorrit*, Mr. Sparkler knows Dante "as an eccentric man in the nature of an Old File, who used to put leaves round his head, and sit upon a stool for some unaccountable purpose, outside the cathedral at Florence" (II, vi, 499).

41. See my article, "Nation and Generation in *A Tale of Two Cities*," *PMLA*, 93 (1978), 454–455.

42. Jane R. Cohen, *Charles Dickens and his Original Illustrators* (Columbus: Ohio State University Press, 1980), p. 118.

43. Cohen's excellent study builds from the axiom that

> Dickens exerted unprecedented authority over everything but the actual execution of the illustrations to his works. With few exceptions, he selected and entitled (often ironically) the subjects, provided the proofs or précis, and suggested conceptions, models, and details. He usually inspected not only the final drawings, but the preliminary sketches as well. (p. 5)

44. The conscious plot of the novel thus always pushes us toward the reaffirmation of memory and logic. The discovery of Manette's letter and its introduction into the text itself is used by the Defarges in the most destructive way—to annihilate the Evremondes. But for Dickens' audience, indeed for any reader of the novel, the letter reaches us through all time, as if we were beyond time, hearing it on the Day of Judgment, the day of universal resurrection: "'I solemnly declare,'" writes Manette, "'that my memory is exact and circumstantial—and that I write the truth as I shall answer for these my last recorded words, whether they be ever read by men or not, at the Eternal Judgment-seat'" (III, x, 303).

45. Twain recorded the remark in a notebook for 1885; see *Mark Twain's Notebooks & Journals*, vol. 3, R. P. Browning, M. B. Frank and L. Salamo, eds. (Berkeley and Los Angeles: University of California Press, 1979), 172 and Walter Blair, *Mark Twain and Huck Finn* (Berkeley and Los Angeles: University of California Press, 1960), p. 61.

46. "*A Tale of Two Cities*," in *Twentieth-Century Interpretations of A Tale of Two Cities*," ed. Charles E. Beckwith (Englewood Cliffs, New Jersey: Prentice-Hall, 1972), p. 26.

47. In "Nation and Generation," I try to substantiate the view that "the comedy [of *A Tale of Two Cities*] revises the novel's central conflicts and offers its own resolution. But that resolution cannot be sustained, and both the language and the setting of the comedy too strongly reveal the nightmare that informs it" (455). Sanders argues that "the idea of a 'recall to life' is so firmly established that Dickens even allows himself a comic Shakespearian play on his central theme. The nefarious activity of the 'resurrection man,' Jerry Cruncher, in fact complements rather than undermines a dominant idea" (*Charles Dickens: Resurrectionist*, p. 169).

48. Jerry himself is, of course, neither a political radical or a radical thinker. His function is, in effect, to be able to view the empty tomb (perhaps something he alone can do precisely because he thinks so little about it) and to report that vision, to transmit it through the text to us.

49. Irwin, *Hieroglyphics*, p. 144.

The Text and Plan of *Oliver Twist*

Burton M. Wheeler

Oliver Twist poses unique problems for Dickensian scholars. While there is general agreement that it is a work of remarkably evocative power, there is substantial disagreement about its coherence. This study maintains that the disagreements stem in large part from mistaken assumptions about the genesis and development of the novel. It advances the hypothesis, based on the text as it first appeared in *Bentley's Miscellany*, that "The Adventures of Oliver Twist, or, The Parish Boy's Progress" was begun as a short serial, that Dickens had already published four installments before deciding to convert it into a novel, and that its plot did not take shape even in general form until he had published yet another three installments.

Determining to meet one of his commitments to Richard Bentley by extending the serial into a novel, Dickens decided to rescue Oliver from a representative "Parish Boy's Progress," that is, from workhouse to criminal associates to deportation or the gallows. He then settled upon Nancy as the character who, replacing Oliver as the central focus of the work, could sustain the theme that private benevolence must rescue children from the corruptive forces of society. Only later, to achieve a semblance of unity, did he graft on the melodramatic plot replete with lockets, wills, villains, and bucolic conclusion. Efforts to represent *Oliver Twist* as a unified, planned work are, I think, misbegotten, a misrepresentation of the nature of Dickens' early genius.

Sylvère Monod, who worked with the extant manuscript of *Oliver Twist* in the Forster collection before the publication of Kathleen Tillotson's Clarendon edition, seems perplexed by the problems of the novel. "Thus does *Oliver Twist* in the first place strike us as a novel composed and published in small fragments over many months and subjected to many vicissitudes and accidents." He declares that "the story has not been completely thought out in advance," but nevertheless argues that the work has

41

"real unity . . . its parts are firmly held together, with excess, indeed, rather than lack of firmness."[1] Arnold Kettle, surely the most explicit critic of the flaws of *Oliver Twist*, complains:

> The struggle throughout *Oliver Twist* between the plot and the pattern is indeed a life and death struggle, a struggle as to whether the novel shall live or not. And in so far as the plot succeeds in twisting and negating the pattern the value of the novel is in fact weakened. To a considerable degree, the novel *is* thus ruined; the loss of tension in the third quarter and the dubious close are the testimony. But the total effect is not one of disaster. The truth and depth of the central vision are such that a vitality is generated which struggles against and survives the plot.[2]

Such criticism stresses the disparity between design and execution. A close examination of the passages deleted from the *Miscellany* text for the 1838 three-volume edition, however, suggests that the problem does not lie in Dickens' failure to execute his original design. Rather, his failure, if it can be called that, lay in his brash confidence that he could radically alter his plan after a portion of the work was already in the hands of his readers.

Because the generally accepted view that Dickens conceived *Oliver Twist* as a novel from the outset rests upon external evidence, it is first necessary to examine the grounds for that contention. Kathleen Tillotson, whose prodigious labor in preparing the Clarendon edition commands respect, believes that Dickens may have conceived *Oliver Twist* as early as 1833. She cites a letter from Dickens to Henry Kolle which refers to a series of papers to be called *The Parish*. Dickens wrote: "Should they be successful . . . I shall cut my proposed Novel up into little Magazine Sketches." Mrs. Tillotson also offers the preface to the 1841 edition, to which I shall return later, as evidence.[3] The assumption that the letter to Kolle refers to *Oliver Twist* has not been supported, however. Even with the use of the word "Novel," a most imprecise term, it is surely possible that Dickens was speaking of *Sketches by Boz*, some of which he was writing at the time. John Forster has been cited by Steven Marcus as implying that Dickens was writing *Oliver Twist* during the summer of 1836,[4] but in the passage cited, Forster first confuses an agreement of August 22 with Richard Bentley for "two novels" with an agreement of November 4 to edit the *Miscellany*. He then adds, "Under these Bentley agreements he was now writing, month by month, the first half of *Oliver Twist*." In his next sentence, Forster cites a letter from Dickens, but gives no date.[5] The editors of the Pilgrim *Letters* propose June 9, 1837 for the letter, not 1836. Indeed the November 4 agreement with Bentley calls for Dickens to provide the new periodical "an original *article* (italics mine) of his own writing, every monthly Number, to consist of about a sheet of 16 pages.''[6] As subsequent angry negotiations between Dickens and Bentley prove, the publisher did not intend the November 4 agreement to modify the earlier contract for two novels.

The best available evidence indicates that the first chapters were not completed before January, 1837. Richard Bentley's aide and accountant, E. S. Morgan, prepared a "brief retrospect" of his associations with Henry Colburn and Bentley in July, 1873. Although Morgan ends his recollections with an apology for his "enfeebled powers of brain" and "this imperfect sketch" after a thirty-six year lapse,[7] his evidence is, unlike Forster's, first-hand. Morgan recalls:

> It had been at first intended that the Miscellany should open with the Story of 'Oliver Twist', but this was frustrated by the illness of Mr. Dickens. He had been attacked by influenza, then raging as an epidemic, and I remember calling upon him at his then lodgings at Furnivals Inn for Copy, when he explained to me the cause of the delay, promising that the opening chapter should be delivered in time for the 2nd Number, to appear on the 1st of February, 1837.[8]

Morgan's evidence does not provide assistance in determining the scope and proposed length of "Oliver Twist," but it appears to preclude earlier composition than 1837. Further, the prospectus for *Bentley's Miscellany* gives no indication that a lengthy serial or novel would be a feature. Morgan, who claims to have prepared the prospectus, recalls that the *Miscellany* was "to be devoted to humorous papers by popular writers."[9] The proposed title, "The Wit's Miscellany," emphasized that expectation. A copy of the prospectus in Dickens' own hand contains the statement: "These papers will be the exclusive copyright of Mr. Bentley. They will be found nowhere else, and will never be collected in any other form."[10] Within a matter of months, Dickens would accept neither of these conditions.

Dickens' own comments in the correspondence available to us about the writing of *Oliver Twist* are also instructive. The first reference to *Oliver Twist* by name appears in a letter to Bentley dated January 20, 1837 by the Pilgrim editors.[11] Two days earlier he had written Bentley, "I am very happy to say that I think the next No. will be an exceedingly good one. I have bestowed great pains and time upon it, and shall consider the arrangement, well. Moreover, I think I have hit on a capital notion for myself, and one which will bring Cruikshank out."[12] On January 24 he informed Bentley. "I have thrown my whole heart and soul into Oliver Twist, and most confidently believe he will make a feature in the work, and be very popular.''[13] On June 26 he advised Bentley, ''Read Oliver. I think he flourisheth this month.''[14] Dickens' first explicit reference to *Oliver Twist* as a novel does not appear until July 14 when he first proposed that it be accepted as the second novel of the August, 1836 contract.[15] Bentley's understandable anger that Dickens wished to incorporate into the first agreement work for which he was being paid under the second agreement was to no avail. Faced with Dickens' threat in September, 1837 to resign the editorship after the October number and to discontinue ''contributing to it in anyway,''[16] Bentley capitulated and signed a new agreement on September 28, 1837.

Throughout the correspondence of 1837–1838 Dickens refers to having just completed copy or to his need to finish an installment. Although most of these comments are of limited significance, several are particularly relevant to the question of when Dickens' plans for *Oliver Twist* took shape. In a letter dated October 13, 1837 by the editors of the Pilgrim *Letters*, Dickens wrote to Morgan requesting a copy of Volume I of the *Miscellany* (containing the issues of January through June, 1837), indicating ''I have distributed all I had of that part, and have nothing to refer to for that portion of Oliver's history.''[18] Dickens was then in the process of writing Chapters XVI and XVII in which he takes the reader back to Oliver's birthplace. Dickens' failure to retain a copy of the early portions, even in manuscript, may have been sheer carelessness, of course, but raises the possibility that he had not anticipated any need to refer to the details of the first chapters. My hypothesis is that only as he was writing the November installment after extracting the new agreement from Bentley did the details of his plot take sufficient shape to require review of the early issues.

Three weeks after the request to Morgan, Dickens wrote the often quoted letter (November 3) to Forster: ''I am glad you like Oliver this month [the reference is to Chapters XVI and XVII]—especially glad that you particularize the first chapter. I hope to do great things with Nancy. If I can only work out the idea I have formed of her, and of the female who is to contrast with her.''[19] Rose Maylie does not appear until Chapter XXIX (April, 1838), but it seems likely that Dickens' objective was now clear although the details of his achieving it were as yet uncertain. Dickens' phrasing also implies that his conception of Nancy is a recent one.

In mid-March, 1838, Dickens wrote to Frederick Yates about unauthorized stage productions, indicating that he felt no anxiety about premature revelations: ''I am quite satisfied that nobody can have heard what I mean to do with the different characters in the end, inasmuch as at present I don't quite know, myself.''[20] Not until July 10, 1838 does he declare in a letter to

Bentley: "I have planned the tale to the close."[21] In mid-October he completed the final chapter.[22]

Since the publication of the *Nonesuch* edition of the *Letters of Charles Dickens* in 1938, certainly since the appearance of the first volume of the Pilgrim *Letters* in 1965, the material summarized above has been widely known. Evidence derived from the letters and documents does not disprove the assumption that *Oliver Twist* was conceived from the outset as a novel, but neither does it provide substantial ground for that position. The letters of November 3, 1837 and mid-March, 1838 make it clear that throughout the composition of *Oliver Twist*, Dickens was groping somewhat uncertainly toward his conclusion. The crucial letters are the three of January, 1837 which suggest that "the capital notion" has just occurred to him. In the light of those letters, Morgan's recollection that *Oliver Twist* was to have appeared in the first issue of the *Miscellany* may even be mistaken.

The first issue of *Bentley's Miscellany* in January, 1837 features Dickens as editor, but his contribution as writer, "The Public Life of Mr. Tulrumble, Mayor of Mudfog," does not appear until page forty-nine. Its conclusion is of interest to the question of the conception and plan of *Oliver Twist*: "This is the first time we have published any of our gleanings from this particular source. Perhaps, at some future period, we may venture to open the chronicles of Mudfog."[23] Because neither the first issue nor the prospectus for the *Miscellany* suggests an emergent, extended piece of fiction by Dickens, it seems possible that before the middle of January, 1837, Dickens conceived his contributions to Bentley's publication to be in the vein of *Sketches by Boz*.

One other widely known feature of the serial publication of *Oliver Twist* requires attention before the textual changes for the 1838 edition are examined. In discussing the three interruptions in the sequential appearance of *Oliver Twist* in the *Miscellany*, Mrs. Tillotson notes that the first, in the June, 1837 issue, must be attributed to the death of Mary Hogarth. She explains the omission from the October, 1837 issue as part of the protracted negotiations between Dickens and Bentley over the former's determination to have *Oliver Twist* accepted as the second novel of the August, 1836 agreement. She gives two reasons for the third interruption in the September, 1838 issue: it provided Dickens time to complete the writing for publication in three volumes and it delayed its progress in the *Miscellany* so that sales of the three volume edition would not be hampered by too much of the story having already appeared in the magazine.[24] Mrs. Tillotson also notes that Mudfog articles replaced

Oliver Twist for the latter two interruptions.[25] I do not quarrel with these explanations, but must observe that each interruption occurs at a significant turning point in the development of the novel.

The first interruption, surely primarily occasioned by Dickens' grief, follows Chapter VIII and immediately precedes Oliver's delivery into the care of Mr. Brownlow in the following installment. The second occurs following Chapter XV, preceding the first intervention by Nancy on Oliver's behalf and the return to the town of Oliver's birth and Bumble in the November, 1837 issue. The third interruption occurs in the middle of Chapter XXXIX,[26] preparatory to Nancy's conversation with Rose in the October, 1838 issue. The interruptions of the serial publication of *Oliver Twist*, whatever their causes, came at times when Dickens was working out critical areas in the novel's development. That the interruptions occur at such significant points is consistent with the hypothesis here advanced: Dickens first determined to reverse the typical course of a "Parish Boy's Progress" in order to extend the serial and subsequently found in Nancy a new focus for the novel Bentley reluctantly agreed to accept in partial fulfillment of the August, 1836 contract.

The significance of textual changes which Dickens made in the fall of 1838 for the publication of the three volume edition has unfortunately been misrepresented. In *The Newgate Novel, 1830–1847*, Keith Hollingsworth refers to "minor changes between the magazine version and later editions" but finds the revisions "inconsiderable."[27] Archibald Coolidge in *Charles Dickens as Serial Novelist* indicates that he has found only a "few differences."[28] Since the Clarendon text became available, most critics have followed the lead of Mrs. Tillotson in focusing on the extensiveness of the revision made for later editions, particularly that of 1846. Although Mrs. Tillotson notes that there were substantial revisions of the text of the *Miscellany* and records them accurately, she is primarily concerned with showing that the changes throughout Dickens' editing of the novel were effected to achieve consistency in use of cant terms or in connection with his changing ideas about punctuation and style. Mrs. Tillotson makes one statement, however, which seems even more curious because she does not pursue it. Speaking of Dickens' "respite" because there was no installment in the October, 1837 issue, she states, "Dickens had had longer than usual to consider his installment, and was also now planning further ahead; *the novel had become more than a serial*."[29] The portion which I have italicized is inconsistent with the remainder of her introduction. Even her discussion of obvious changes in Dickens' plans does not fully bear upon her unexpected comparison between a novel and a serial.

Revising in 1838, Dickens deleted or emended more than 260 passages that had appeared in the *Miscellany* in the first eighteen installments. Most of these changes were minor adjustments in word order, punctuation, or language of the "underworld" characters, changes which do not affect the meaning of passages. Some, like the change in the Artful Dodger's height from a dwarfish three feet, six inches to a more respectable four feet, six inches[30] are mere curiosities. A number are related to Dickens' never resolved difficulties in controlling the time frame of the novel.[31]

The most striking changes are those in the divisions of the novel. At the end of the January, 1838 number of the *Miscellany*, which concludes with Chapter XXII, "The End of the First Book" appears.[32] To the reader of the *Miscellany* surely the statement occasioned no surprise. Considered from the perspective of the hypothesis advanced in this essay, what is surprising is the absence of "Book the First" at the beginning of the February, 1837 issue where only "Chapter the First" appears. In *Dickens the Novelist*, Sylvère Monod ignores the early book division of *Oliver Twist* as it appeared in the *Miscellany*, contending that "Dickens contented himself with division into chapters at the outset of his career."[33] Speaking of the difficulties confronting the serial novelist, however, Monod inadvertently lends support to the hypothesis I am advancing:

> Once the novel was provided with a title, one other preliminary decision still had to be made before the first chapter could be written—how the book was to be divided. Into chapters only, or into books and chapters? Dickens' decision had to be made at the very beginning, because, if he wished, for instance, to adopt division into books, the first words to be published, immediately after the title, would have to be "Book the First"; after the first monthly part had appeared, it would already be too late.[34]

Professor Monod misjudges his man, overlooking the fact that Dickens did not begin "Oliver Twist, or, the Parish Boy's Progress" with Book the First. Not until the tenth installment, written three months after he had extracted from Bentley the acceptance of *Oliver Twist* as the second novel of the August, 1836 agreement, is the division into books introduced.[35] The absence of the designation "Book the First" in the *Miscellany*, unless one argues that it is an undetected printer's error, establishes the fact that Dickens significantly altered his plans for *Oliver Twist*. At the very least the introduction and then subsequent deletion of book divisions of unequal length indicates how shapeless were his plans for the work during the early months of composition. Other changes in the text effected for the 1838 edition indicate that the alteration of plans went substantially beyond the question of book division.

The most important changes made for the 1838 edition are the deletions. Some of these have been noted by other critics, others ignored, but
no one has suggested that there is a pattern to the deletions which require
attention. There are fourteen significant deletions. By significant I mean a
deletion of more than several words or a deletion which alters the meaning. Five of these fourteen deletions bear explicitly on the hypothesis that
Dickens did not think of *Oliver Twist* as a novel until sometime after
Mary Hogarth's death in May, 1837 and did not work out his basic plan or
plot details before October of that year. Four of the passages provide circumstantial evidence for the thesis. One provides concrete support. All
five passages appear in the first eight issues, the last one appearing in
Chapter XVII (the November issue). The deletions will be discussed in the
order of their appearance in the *Miscellany* text.[36]

The first such deletion occurs in the first line of the first chapter. The
1838 three-volume edition and all subsequent editions read: "Among
other public buildings in a certain town, which for many reasons it will be
prudent to refrain from mentioning, and to which I will assign no ficti-
tious name . . ." The *Miscellany* reads: "Among other public buildings in
the town of Mudfog . . ."(p. 1). Dickens' only contributions of substantial length to the *Miscellany* other than *Oliver Twist* were three "Mudfog" papers.[37] Robert Colby notes that the use of "Mudfog" at the beginning of the *Miscellany* text suggests "a continuation of *The Mudfog
Papers*," but he does not pursue the point.[38] Dickens' exclusion of the
name "Mudfog" from the 1838 edition at least indicates his desire to dis-
associate the novel from those more satiric and topical pieces. It lends
credence to the hypothesis that when he began "The Adventures of Oliver
Twist" in the *Miscellany*, he was thinking of it as a serial related to that set
of papers. Writing as late as February, 1838, he wrote in the manuscript
"the Mudfog peasantry" (p. 178) but corrected it before publication in
the *Miscellany*. In the course of one year he had concluded that he did not
want to associate Oliver's birthplace with Mudfog.

The second deletion relevant to the hypothesis has greater weight. At
the conclusion of Chapter II, the text of the *Miscellany* reads: "I should
perhaps mar the interest of this narrative (supposing it to possess any at
all), if I ventured to hint, just yet, whether the life of Oliver Twist will be a
long or a short piece of biography." Subsequent editions read: "whether
the life of Oliver Twist had this violent termination or no" (p. 12). Clearly
a three volume novel entitled *Oliver Twist* containing the original passage
would appear absurd. One may argue that the line, initially, was a teaser
for the serial reader. Yet the phrasing and the subsequent deletion of the

passage raises the question whether or not Dickens had himself determined the length of his "biography."

The third deletion is perhaps the most revealing. It conceals a reversal
in design which has gone unnoticed. Chapter VII in the *Miscellany* (May,
1837) concludes: "The blessing was from a young child's lips [Dick] but it
was the first that Oliver had ever heard invoked upon his head; and
through all the struggles and sufferings of his after life, through all the
troubles and changes *of many weary years* he never once forgot it" (p.
44). For the 1838 edition Dickens rewrote the sentence, omitting the
phrase I have italicized. The deleted phrase stands in direct contradiction
to the version of Oliver's life that Dickens began developing in the July,
1837 issue following the interruption of *Oliver Twist* in the June issue. In
a period of only a few months, Oliver is twice freed from Fagin's grasp
and is happily secured in the Maylie household to await passively the
discovery of his fortune. The presence of "many weary years" in the
original text provides strong support for the thesis that Dickens initially
intended Oliver to fulfill a typical "Parish Boy's Progress."

The fourth deletion occurs at the beginning of Chapter XV, one of the
pivotal points in the novel's development. The chapter appears in the
issue of September, 1837, a month preceding the omission of an installment of *Oliver Twist*. It was written while Dickens was battling for the acceptance of *Oliver Twist* as the second novel of the August, 1836 agreement. From the time of his letter of July 14, 1837, in which he first made
the proposal, to the middle of September Dickens used every weapon at
his disposal to force a revised contract from Bentley. In a letter to Forster,
dated 24 September, his exhilaration in the heat of battle is evident. Describing a new offer from Bentley that apparently promised additional
payment, Dickens wrote: "Of course we refused it—a new agreement and
copyright, being the War Cry."[39] A letter of August 18, probably written
just following the completion of the September installment indicates that
Dickens was angry enough to break off all personal contact with
Bentley.[40]

The passage deleted from the *Miscellany* text of Chapter XV is given in
its entirety in the Clarendon edition. The bulk of the passage is devoted to
a rather tiresome, sardonic discussion of the folly of benevolence. Had it
come nearer the end of an installment, one might suspect that it was
"filler" to meet the sixteen-page contractual obligation, but it comes at
the very beginning of the chapter, at the mid-point of the installment.
Only the introductory sentence is directly relevant to the hypothesis. I
quote it only in part:

> If it did not come within the scope and bearing of my long-considered inten-
> tions and plans regarding this prose epic (for such I mean it to be,) to leave
> the two old gentlemen sitting with the watch between them long after it grew
> too dark to see it, and both doubting Oliver's return, the one in triumph,
> and the other in sorrow, I might take occasion to entertain the reader with
> many wise reflections on the obvious impolicy of ever attempting to do good
> to our fellow creatures where there is no hope of earthly reward. . . .

The passage continues at length concluding: "I shall not enter into any such digression in this place: and, if this be not a sufficient reason for this determination, I have a better, and, indeed, a wholly unanswerable one, already stated; which is, that it forms no part of my original intention so to do" (pp. 91–92). It is a curious passage in its entirety, in the part not quoted here stylistically similar to the early chapters of the novel satirizing parish officials. Dickens' mockery of self-interested philanthropists may relate to his own indignation at being treated, as he thought, ungenerously by his publisher. The opening lines here quoted, particularly the parenthetical "for such I mean it to be," sounds very like a throwing down of the gauntlet before Bentley, a declaration that he *is* writing a novel, a warning that Bentley must capitulate.

Mrs. Tillotson draws different conclusions from the same passage. Advancing her contention that the inception of *Oliver Twist* may have been as early as 1833, she states,

> There are certain other references that indicate a long incubation for the
> novel. In chapter XV he speaks, not necessarily ironically, of his "long-con-
> sidered intentions and plans regarding this prose epic"; and in the Introduc-
> tion of 1841 claims that the "conduct and character" of Nancy has been
> "suggested to [his] mind long ago—long before I dealt in fiction—by what I
> often saw and read of, in actual life around me."[41]

These two references are the only textual ones Mrs. Tillotson cites for her "long incubation" theory and they are cited, of necessity, conditionally. The "Introduction" passage argues only for the accuracy of the portrayal of the "conduct and character of the girl." Whether Dickens' assertion in Chapter XV that his plans were "long-considered" is ironic or not is but one of the questions we need to ask. More importantly, how long must Dickens have considered his plans to justify such a claim? To a young writer of twenty-five, four months may meet his requirements for honesty as well as four years. In any event, the declaration that his plans were "long-considered" is less significant than the fact that in the seventh installment of his serial, Dickens chose to declare to his readers (and perhaps Bentley) that *Oliver Twist* was to be a "prose epic."

The fifth deletion is from Chapter XVII which appeared the following month (November, 1837). It is part of an unusually lengthy explanation for leaving Oliver, upon his recapture, in the hands of Fagin while the narrator returns to Oliver's birthplace.[42] In the midst of the third paragraph of the chapter, while addressing his readers on the custom of leaving characters in various dilemmas at the end of each chapter, the narrator adds, "this brief introduction to the present one [chapter] may perhaps be deemed unnecessary." In the *Miscellany*, the text continues:

> But I have set it in this place because I am anxious to disclaim at once the slightest desire to tantalise my readers by leaving young Oliver Twist in situations of doubt and difficulty, and then flying off at a tangent to impertinent matters, which have nothing to do with him. My sole desire is to proceed straight through this history with all convenient despatch, carrying my reader along with me if I can, and, if not, leaving him to take a more pleasant route for a chapter or two, and join me again afterwards if he will. Indeed, there is so much to do, that I have no room for disgressions, even if I possessed the inclination; and I merely make this one in order to set myself quite right with the reader, between whom and the historian it is essentially necessary that perfect faith should be kept, and a good understanding preserved. The advantage of this amicable explanation is, that when I say, as I do now, that I am going back directly to the town in which Oliver Twist was born, the reader will at once take it for granted that I have good and substantial reasons for making the journey, or I would not ask him to accompany me on any account.   (p. 106)

The last sentence, in revised form, was retained. The remainder of the paragraph was deleted for the 1838 edition.

The transparent pose of the historian proceeding straight through Oliver's history "with all convenient despatch" is at best an awkward explanation of Dickens' intentions. Subsequent returns to the town of Oliver's birth are not marred by such self-conscious, mechanical transitions. The declaration "there is so much to do" suggests Dickens' awareness of the complexities before him now that he has extracted the new agreement from Bentley and returned Oliver to the machinations of Fagin.

Chapter XVII, which reintroduces Bumble, must have been written sometime after October 12, 1837,[43] shortly after Dickens requested Morgan to send the first volume of the *Miscellany*. Within the following two weeks, Dickens responded to Forster's praise of the November installment with the previously quoted letter setting forth his expectations for Nancy. That letter, when considered together with the deletions from the *Miscellany* text, would seem to establish the approximate date by which Dickens knew clearly how his serial, now converted into a novel, could achieve a sustaining focus. The deletion from Chapter VII indicates that not until sometime after April did he decide to rescue Oliver from the course on which he had first set him. Not until he was writing the section on Nancy during October, however, does he seem to have been certain that he had a satisfactory character through whom he could express his concern about the cost of public indifference to neglected children. Once Dickens had settled upon Nancy as his principal character for the latter portion of the novel and upon her contrasting figure, Rose Maylie, he was faced with the problem of tying together the disparate strands he had already spun in the *Miscellany*. He may have concocted his melodramatic solution soon after writing to Forster, but there is no allusion to Monks before Chapter XXVI (March, 1838) and no reference to the locket until Chapter XXXVIII (August, 1838).

Of the remaining nine significant deletions from the *Miscellany* text, several lend themselves readily to explanation. A passage in Chapter XXVI, which describes Fagin's behavior upon hearing Toby Crackit's report of the abortive Chertsey "crack" (p. 162), was possibly deleted because it is astonishingly similar to the passage describing Nancy's reaction to the conversation between Monks and Fagin (p. 265). Six other deletions seem to have been made to tone down dialogue or descriptive passages. These include the bathetic lines of Oliver (p. 23) to which G. H. Lewes objected,[44] a trivial thrust at Fang (p. 62), an irrelevant comment on the weather (p. 99), and three passages dealing with Nancy (pp. 121, 130, 131). In the latter Dickens apparently wished to mute suggestions of vulgarity or excessively melodramatic behavior.

Two other deletions are not easily explained. One in Chapter XXI (January, 1838) details the journey of Sikes and Oliver toward Chertsey (p. 137). For the 1838 edition "Twickenham" and the crossing "of a little bridge" are deleted. In further rewriting after the 1841 edition, the name of the "Red Lion Inn" was dropped. That this passage received a strangely disproportionate attention is further evidenced by an addition to the 1838 edition: "here they lingered about in the fields for some hours."

The second curious deletion is in Chapter IX (July, 1837). While Oliver watches drowsily, Fagin inspects his hoard, muttering to himself about capital punishment. The line omitted, "The prospect of the gallows, too, makes them hardy and bold" (p. 52), seems in keeping with the remainder of the passage which Dickens retained: "Ah, it's a fine thing for the trade! Five of 'em strung up in a row; and none left to play booty, or turn white-livered!"

While the deletion of the one line from Fagin's mutterings serves no obvious purpose, the passage is interesting for another reason. It exemplifies a method which Dickens utilized effectively as he extended the serial into a novel. Between June and September as he wrote *Oliver Twist* he prepared several passages with open options to which he could return, if necessary, as he worked out the plot. Among the items which Fagin examines as Oliver watches is a "trinket" with "Some very minute description on it. . . . At length he put it down, as if despairing of success." The 'trinket' anticipates the locket of Oliver's mother. Fagin also examines with particular care a "magnificent gold watch, sparkling with jewels" (p. 51). The passage was written in June, 1837, just before Dickens demanded the new agreement from Bentley. The passage provides pegs upon which he could hang a plot, but is not so explicit as to limit him.

One such passage, however, was too binding, yet Dickens failed to detect it when revising for the 1838 edition. In Chapter XIV (September, 1837) when Mr. Brownlow addresses Oliver in a quite intimidating tone for the purpose of getting the truth about the boy's history, he admonishes: "Speak the truth; and you shall not be friendless while I live." The text of the *Miscellany* and of the 1838 edition contain the clause "if I find you have committed no crime" (p. 86). This clause was not deleted until the careful revision for the 1846 edition. The reason for the deletion seems clear. When writing Chapter XIV, and Chapter IX discussed above, Dickens had not yet conceived of the Leeford will which contains the stipulation that Oliver "in his minority . . . should never have stained his name with any public act of dishonour, meanness, cowardice, or wrong" (p. 351). The first reference to the will does not appear until Chapter XLIX, written sometime after October 2, 1838.[48] At the time of Brownlow's warning to Oliver in Chapter XIV and in the hoard of Fagin of Chapter IX, Dickens may well have had other plans for disclosing Oliver's parentage and developing the theme of virtue triumphant. Brownlow's warning is appropriate to the context of the passage in Chapter XIV, but, in the light of the Leeford will, Dickens must have considered it an awkward tautology.

Another such multiple option passage in Chapter XII (August, 1837) led Dickens into a contradiction which he could have corrected only with difficulty. According to Brownlow and Mrs. Bedwin, Oliver's features are identical to those of the portrait of his mother: "its living copy. The eyes, the head, the mouth; every feature was the same. The expression was, for the instant, so precisely alike, that the minutest line seemed copied with startling accuracy" (p. 72). In the chapter heading of the

Miscellany, Dickens called further attention to the likeness by including "WITH SOME PARTICULARS CONCERNING A CERTAIN PICTURE," which he did not delete until the 1846 edition (p.67). Unfortunately, the reader must also conclude that Oliver looks exactly like his father. The source is Nancy's report to Rose: "That Monks. . . had seen him accidentally with two of our boys on the day we first lost him, and had known him directly to be the same child that he was watching for" (p. 272). Monks has never seen a picture of Oliver's mother nor has he at the time traced Oliver to the workhouse, but, amid all the urchins of London, he knew him "directly." Although Dickens committed such blunders throughout his career,[46] the mistake here was forced on him by the later introduction of the suppressed will and the paranoid, epileptic half-brother. He had so bound himself in the first chapter in which Oliver's mother dies unidentified and in the second chapter where Bumble reports that the Parish offer of a reward for information has gone unanswered that he had no ready means to account for Monks' swift recognition of Oliver.

Another scene to which Dickens did not return also has all the characteristics of the multiple-option method. Any frequent and careful reader of Dickens will find the passage one which whets anticipation. In Chapter XIII (August, 1837), in his first appearance Sikes charges Fagin with being an informer, but is sharply interrupted. Sikes then performs a dumb show of a hanging before he is calmed with liquor. The charge of informing and the dumb show could refer back to Fagin's mutterings in Chapter IX or forward to the hangings Nancy anticipates in Chapter XVI. Because of the confused chronology, it is not clear whether both passages allude to the same hangings. The introduction of the gallows and the return to the hangings twice suggest that Dickens intended to do more with the passages than merely cast a spectre of death over the world of Fagin and his cohorts. This possibility is reinforced by Cruikshank's illustration for the issue.[47] The illustration and the passages lead to the conjecture that between June and September, 1837 he anticipated using the hangings as a vehicle for plot development and subsequently rejected that idea.

The emphasis given here to the several multiple-option passages is intended to demonstrate the number of loose ends evident in the chapters written during the summer and early fall of 1837 as Dickens struggled to develop a plan for his novel which could accommodate the earlier chapters. While their existence *proves* nothing with regard to the evolution of the novel, the hypothesis that Dickens fundamentally altered his plans for the "Parish Boy's Progress" seems a more satisfactory explanation for them than a charge of carelessness.

The significance of the hypothesis I advance can be illustrated by returning to the most trenchant criticism of the structural flaws of *Oliver Twist*, that of Arnold Kettle. Mr. Kettle begins his discussion of the novel by noting that Oliver's awakening in the sanctuary of Brownlow's house in Chapter XII is a "central situation." He describes the first eleven chapters, all but three of which were written before the June omission of an installment, as "an evocation of misery and horror." His argument is that the

> power of the book . . . proceeds from the wonderful evocation of the under-world and the engagement of our sympathy on behalf of the inhabitants of that world. Its weakness lies in Dickens' failure to develop and carry through the pattern so powerfully presented in the first quarter of the novel. . . . The introduction of the plot . . . savours from the very first of a trick.[48]

The hypothesis helps to explain precisely those flaws which most trouble Kettle. The plot is indeed a trick, a conjurer's trick which converts a serial of uncertain length into a novel with the superficial appearance of a unified plan.

Kettle's division of *Oliver Twist* into quarters is also more telling than he seems to have realized. Chapter XII, which he selects as ending the first quarter, was completed during the month that Dickens announced to Bentley his expectation of having *Oliver Twist* accepted as the second novel of their agreement. The second quarter is a new beginning, laying the groundwork for bringing Nancy into the lead role. His choice of Chapter XXXIX as the point of demarcation between the third and fourth quarters seems unusually prescient. The reader of the *Miscellany* encountered Nancy's eavesdropping on the Fagin-Monks conspiracy in August, 1838, but did not discover until October that Nancy would convey the information to Rose.[49] The reader of Chapter XXXIX in book form finds in one chapter what the serial reader discovered over a three month period. The suspension of publication in the September issue of the *Miscellany* may have been related to Dickens' difficulties in working out the details of his ending. That some difficulty existed is indicated by the fact that he did not complete the passage of Nancy's death until early October, 1838.[50] The writing of Chapters XXXIX to XLVII extended over twelve weeks, but Dickens was able to complete the final six chapters in only three weeks.

The assumption that *Oliver Twist* was conceived as a full-length novel offers no satisfactory answer to four insistent questions: 1) Why does no hint of mystery surround Oliver's parentage in the first ten chapters? 2)

Why is the conspiracy between Monks and Fagin so long withheld and so implausible when finally established? 3) Why does the focus shift so drastically from Oliver to Nancy in the latter portion of the work? 4) Why is there such a pronounced alteration in narrative mode following the opening chapters? The hypothesis here advanced offers reasonable explanations.

In Chapter I, although Oliver's mother momentarily arouses the curiosity of the parish surgeon, she is no more than a vehicle for delivering Oliver to the tender mercies of the parish. She dies telling no secrets, delivering no locket, and making only one plea—to be allowed to see her child and die. The presence of the parish surgeon throughout her childbirth and death and the surrounding details of Oliver's birth quite simply do not allow for the conversation which "Old Sally" reports to Mrs. Corney in Chapter XXIV. Had Dickens expected to return to the scene, he surely would not have constricted himself so severely. The plot, perhaps especially because of its elaborateness, appears to be an afterthought, a rejection of the original plan to develop Oliver as a representative ward of the parish in favor of making him heir to a fortune.

The conspiracy between Monks and Fagin is the other element of the plot that does not bear close scrutiny. The suppressed will and the malevolent half-brother subvert the novel more than Dickens could have anticipated. His fascination with the criminal but human qualities of Sikes, Nancy, and Fagin produces extraordinary power and genuine insight which he could not bring to his stage villain, Monks. Although the will was intended to provide the motivation for Monks' absurd and unnecessary attempt to corrupt Oliver, it did not unleash Dickens' creative powers. The contention that the Monks-Fagin relationship was conceived late in composition is supported by the absence of any early scenes foreshadowing the conspiracy first revealed in Chapter XXVI (March, 1838).

According to Nancy's report to Rose in Chapter XL, Monks made inquiries about Oliver after seeing him on the day he is taken before Fang, a scene which appeared in July, 1837. Not until Chapter XXVI (March, 1838), however, does Nancy or the reader know that Fagin's interest in Oliver is rooted in what he blurts out to Nancy: "the boy's worth hundreds of pounds to me" (p. 167). When Oliver is returned to Fagin in Chapter XVI (November, 1837), Fagin greets him with mock graciousness, losing his temper only when Oliver tries to escape. Fagin's behavior does not suggest Oliver's value. Even the anxiety to recapture Oliver depicted in Chapter XIII (August, 1837) arises from his concern that Oliver might provide information to authorities. A person rereading the novel may attribute Fagin's eagerness to the conspiracy with Monks, but a careful reading shows that nothing in Chapter XIII or Chapter XVI supports that assumption. Nancy's intervention in defense of Oliver in Chapter XVI marks the turning point of Dickens' interest in her as principal character, but even in the succeeding issue (December, 1837) there is no certain indication that Dickens has worked out a relationship between Fagin and Monks.[51]

The hypothesis here advanced does not justify Dickens' use of so threadbare a plot, but by accounting for it as a late and hastily considered addition, the hypothesis helps to explain why the plot was so incidental to Dickens' purposes. For all its complexities and coincidences, the plot generates little force in the novel. It is not organically related to any of the novel's principal themes. Once introduced, however, it acts on its own like the Sorcerer's Apprentice, leading Dickens into improbabilities and absurdities such as Monks entrusting his father's will, for "better security" (p. 363), to the safekeeping of Fagin. In spite of the strain the plot places on the reader's credulity, it serves one effective purpose. It enables Dickens to proceed to the portrayal of the generous impulse, the selflessness, and loyalty of Nancy without doing absolute violence to the early chapters of "A Parish Boy's Progress."

Dickens turned his attention from Oliver to Nancy because she alone could exhibit what Dickens was later to call, in the Preface to the 1841 edition, "the principle of Good surviving through every adverse circumstance" (p. lxii). There, of course, he attributes the illustration of the principle to Oliver. Oliver's untutored prayer life, his foreknowledge of how long it will take him to reach the bookseller's shop when he has not been out of Brownlow's house since his arrival there unconscious, his ready preference of death to crime, and total blandness with the Maylies make him an impossible vehicle for what Dickens proclaimed in 1841. In turning to Nancy, Dickens apparently lost all interest in plausibly developing Oliver. As H. M. Daleski argues effectively, the true instrument for revealing the "principle of Good surviving through every adverse circumstance" is Nancy.[52]

The problem of the alteration of the narrative mode of *Oliver Twist* has been discussed by many critics, most recently William Lankford.[53] In the opening scenes, Dickens assumes an intimate relationship with his reader which provides the greatest opportunity for sardonic authorial comments. The narrator's presence is obtrusive, often marked by heavy-handed irony. Only after Oliver flees Sowerberry's establishment is the narrative presence muted. The authorial intrusions which characterize the early chapters disappear, with rare exception, after Chapter XVIII. The narration of the early chapters is akin to portions of the Mudfog articles. Dickens' shift in narrative mode coincides with the decisions which I have argued Dickens made between June and September, 1837 to extend his story into a novel and to turn his focus to Nancy and her contrasting figure, Rose Maylie.

To argue that *Oliver Twist* is the product of a radical change of plans is not to belittle Dickens. The work is, after all, that of a novice, a uniquely talented and ambitious young writer determined to overcome his own "adverse circumstances." James R. Kincaid notes that the reader of *Oliver Twist* is left "with the uneasy suspicion that the book is powerful despite all that Dickens could do to make it conventional and safe, that it represents a triumph of unconscious forces over conscious intentions."[54] With regard to the characterizations of Sikes and Fagin, Kincaid is quite likely correct. The evidence advanced here, however, indicates that many of the problems with which critics of *Oliver Twist* have been occupied are the result of radical and conscious alterations in Dickens' plan for the work. The paradoxes of Dickens the man and the writer continue to astound us. If the hypothesis I advance is valid, it is surely remarkable that he could erect a novel's structure on the foundation of a short serial with such precocious dexterity that those of us who admire his work have found more grist than our mills have been able to grind.

NOTES

1. Sylvère Monod, *Dickens the Novelist* (Norman: University of Oklahoma Press, 1968), pp. 117–120.

2. Arnold Kettle, *An Introduction to the English Novel*, I (New York: Harper & Brothers, 1960), 138.

3. Kathleen Tillotson, ed., *Oliver Twist* (Oxford: Clarendon Press, 1966), p. xv. See also *Essays and Studies*, XII (1959), 87–105. Mrs. Tillotson has attempted to provide grounds for the assumption that *Oliver Twist* was designed as a novel from the outset.

4. Steven Marcus, *Dickens: From Pickwick to Dombey* (London: Chatto & Windus, 1965), p. 55.

5. John Forster, *The Life of Charles Dickens* (New York: Doubleday, Doran and Company, 1928), p. 86.

6. *The Letters of Charles Dickens*, ed. by Madeline House and Graham Storey, I (Oxford: Clarendon Press, 1965), 649–650. Hereafter cited as *Letters*.

7. E. S. Morgan, untitled manuscript of twenty-three unnumbered pages in the University of Illinois collection of the papers of Richard Bentley, p. 23. This document is incorrectly cited by Mrs. Tillotson (*O.T.*, p. xviii). It is not a diary.

8. Morgan, p. 14. Morgan's recollections are also of interest with regard to the subject of George Cruikshank's involvement with the writing of *Oliver Twist*: "I may here remark that this gentleman stated to me emphatically in the course of many conversations I had with him on the subject, in the course of business, that it was to him, Mr. Dickens had been indebted for his introduction to many of the characters that served as prototypes of prominent personages in Oliver Twist: Fagin, the Artful Dodger etc etc; as well as for many suggestions as to the incidents that figure conspicuously in that work" (pp. 14–15). I find no evidence that Cruikshank's possible contribution to the novel contravenes the hypothesis advanced in this study.

9. Morgan, p. 13.

10. *Letters*, I, 682.

11. *Letters*, I, 225.

12. *Letters*, I, 224.

13. *Letters*, I, 227.

14. *Letters*, I, 278.

15. *Letters*, I, 284.

16. *Letters*, I, 308.

17. *Letters*, I, 654. This was the fourth agreement with Bentley. A third agreement had been signed in March which allowed Dickens an additional sum when sales of the *Miscellany* reached 6,000 copies (see pp. 650–651). In March the fourth chapter of "Oliver Twist" was appearing, but the agreement refers to Dickens' contribution as an "original Article," not as a novel.

18. *Letters*, I, 319.

19. *Letters*, I, 328.

20. *Letters*, I, 388.

21. *Letters*, I, 413.

22. *Letters*, I, 441. See letters to Forster and Cruikshank.

23. *Bentley's Miscellany*, I (January, 1837), 63.

24. Tillotson, *O. T.*, pp. xix–xxii.

25. Firm evidence for the dating of the Mudfog articles has not been found. It seems probable that those printed in October, 1837 and September, 1838 were written hastily and specifically for those issues. Both are reports on "The Mudfog Association for the Advancement of Everything" and have no substantive relationship to *Oliver Twist*.

26. Chapter XXXIX in the 1838 and all subsequent editions consists of Chapter the Second and part of Chapter the Third of Book the Third in the *Miscellany*. Chapter the Second appeared in August, 1838. Chapter the Third appeared in October, 1838.

27. Keith Hollingsworth, *The Newgate Novel, 1830–1847* (Detroit: Wayne State University Press, 1963), p. 112.

28. Archibald C. Coolidge, *Charles Dickens as Serial Novelist* (Ames: The Iowa State University Press, 1967), p. 233.

29. Tillotson, *O. T.*, p. xxxv.

30. Tillotson, *O. T.*, p. 47. Hereafter all page references given in the text are to this edition.

31. Oliver's birthday as celebrated at Mrs. Mann's is changed from his eighth to his ninth in three passages (p. 5). When Noah asks Oliver his age, Oliver responds "Eleven, sir" in the *Miscellany*; that is changed to ten (p. 26). The difficulties with Oliver's age are linked to Monks' injunction to Bumble: "Carry your memory back—let me see—twelve years, last winter" (p. 246). Dickens continued to have difficulty with Oliver's age as late as September, 1838. In the manuscript corrected for the October issue of the *Miscellany*, Grimwig refers to Oliver as eleven (p. 279). Other adjustments in time include the extension of the period between his removal from Mrs. Mann and his asking for more from three months to six months (p. 10) and a change in the time he spends picking marks from handerchiefs at Fagin's from "eight to ten days" to "many days" (p. 56).

32. Tillotson, *O. T.*, p. 145. In the *Miscellany* "Book the Second" begins the February, 1838 issue and is completed in the July, 1838 issue, Book the Third beginning in August. For the three volume publication, Dickens removed the book division in favor of consecutively numbered chapters. This decision was perhaps necessitated by the unevenness of length of the three books of the *Miscellany*. Book I is almost half again as long as Book II. Book III is roughly twenty percent longer than Book II and shorter than Book I by the same degree. For the three volume edition, the division is as follows: Volume I (Chapters I–XIX), 331 pages; Volume II (Chapters XX–XXXVI), 307 pages; Volume III (Chapters XXXVII–LI), 315 pages. Chapter XXXVI in the three volume edition is Chapter XXXVII in the Clarendon edition. For the 1846 edition, Dickens divided Chapter XXIX of the 1838 edition into two chapters. See pages 190 and 369–371 of the Clarendon edition for changes in the numbering of chapters.

33. Monod, p. 76. Monod does note the division of *Oliver Twist* into books on p. 119.

34. Monod, pp. 75–76.

35. It is unfortunate that Mrs. Tillotson does not note this fact explicitly in the Clarendon edition where the only allusion to the missing "Book the First" is in her use of brackets for Bk. I in the "Table of Instalments and Chapter Divisions in Different Editions" (p. 369).

36. Most of these deletions were first noted in my unpublished doctoral dissertation "Charles Dickens: In Service of Two Masters," Harvard University, 1961.

37. Dickens did write several other articles for the *Miscellany*. Tillotson notes that "The Pantomine of Life" (March, 1837) and "Some Particulars Concerning a Lion" (May, 1837) were written to fulfill his obligation to provide sixteen pages monthly. (Tillotson, *O. T.*, p. xix). He seems to have written a third article entitled "Mr. Robert Bolton" (August, 1838). This piece was published by George Bentley under the Bentley copyright in 1880 in the collection *The Mudfog Papers*.

38. Robert A. Colby, *Fiction With a Purpose* (Bloomington: Indiana University Press, 1967), p. 324. Also see Marcus, p. 63.

39. *Letters*, I, 312.

40. *Letters*, I, 296–297.

41. Tillotson, *O. T.*, p. xv.

42. The first two paragraphs of Chapter XVII have been discussed by John Bayley as a "brilliant apologia for Dickens' whole creative method" in "*Oliver Twist:* 'Things as They Really Are,'" *Dickens and the Twentieth Century*, ed. John Gross and Gabriel Pearson (London: Routledge and Kegan Paul, 1962), p. 55. Bayley does not take note of the deleted passage.

43. *Letters*, I, 318. See letter to Forster.

44. Tillotson, *O. T.*, p. xxxvi.

45. A letter to Forster indicates that Dickens had dispatched Nancy (Ch. XLVII) by October 2, 1838 but had not yet "sent Sikes to the Devil" (Ch. L). *Letters*, I, 439.

46. For example, in *A Tale of Two Cities* Lucie's wifely virtues during Darnay's incarceration are demonstrated by her "setting aside of his chair and books" (III, Ch. V). Dickens ignored the circumstances of their arrival and presence in France.

47. Tillotson, *O. T.*, opposite p. 50. Note the handbill on the wall.

48. Kettle, p. 131.

49. See note 26.

50. *Letters*, I, 439. Nancy's death occurs in Chapter XLVII. The first portion of what is now Ch. XXXIX was written by July 10, 1838 (*Letters*, I, 413). Letters of late August suggest that he was encountering difficulty working out his intentions. In early September he proposed secluding himself on the Isle of Wight "for Oliver purposes" (Letters, I, 428).

51. Fagin's desire for power over Oliver by involving him in a robbery (p. 126) is often read as anticipatory of the plot with Monks, but is more plausible on the grounds that Fagin advances: the risk of Oliver's escape must be dealt with either by killing him, which is both dangerous and wasteful, or by making him one of the gang through involvement in crime. When Fagin parts from Nancy and Bill (p. 127), however, he muses about Nancy's behavior, then suddenly declares: "The man against the child, for a bag of gold!" Even this line, ambiguous as it is in this context, provides no assurance that Dickens had yet conceived Monks.

52. H. M. Daleski, *Dickens and the Art of Analogy* (New York: Schocken Books, 1970), pp. 72–73.

53. William T. Lankford, "'The Parish Boy's Progress': The Evolving Form of *Oliver Twist*," *PMLA*, 93 (1978), 26–29. Lankford argues that Dickens' modification of his narrative mode is a much more conscious one than I believe the evidence allows.

54. James R. Kincaid, "Laughter and Oliver Twist," *PMLA*, 83 (1968), 63.

In Time and Out:
The Tempo of Life
in *Bleak House*

Patrick J. Creevy

To say that time is an almost constant motif in *Bleak House* is to make no special claims for this novel as a Dickens work. But a mere catalogue of the references (I counted nearly five hundred) is still impressive, and an understanding of the remarkable patterning of the temporal motif adds to one's sense of the novel's powerful dramatic tension. One of the persistent questions that confront the reader of *Bleak House* is whether or not Esther Summerson will gain the confidence she needs to live in time properly—in a Dickensian sense. By this I mean, first of all, simply whether she will come to believe deeply that both meritorious involvement in and unworried relaxation from the tasks time presents us are necessary for the right setting of life's pace—and that a pace set "sweetly" in such a way can have a grace that is spiritually informative. To be, as Inspector Bucket says, both, "game" and "mild," is to be living in accordance with an actually sacred idea of life in time, an idea which suggests, again simply, that time is and is not crucial. The world, for Dickens, can make sense as a vale of soul-making; and so, to begin with, an eager, "game" engagement of the self in time is healthy. The soul should progress. But Dickens insists at least as strongly that such an unrelaxed ego-drive amidst the fever and the fret which always tolls one back only to his sole self is not healthy and is a sign that the sense of time has only testified to gross materialism. So balance, the ability to be, in familiar if paradoxical terms, both in time and out, a self and selfless, is necessary. But that which makes most dramatic and tense that key question regarding Esther's discovery of the right, sacred, informative tempo, is that she lives in a world completely unbalanced, graceless, uninformed. In *Bleak House* it seems that the non-selves who live outside time will never in a healthy way get in, and that the selves who live inside will never gracefully get out.[1]

Self-assertion and self-annihilation never cooperate in a center. The center of Esther's own mind is severely troubled, and so she herself shows strong tendencies toward diffident withdrawal *and* toward worried hyper-activity, but not toward a sweet mean. Dickensian human time is not clock time. One cannot be truly game or mild mechanically or unfeelingly but only tactfully, and this can become seriously difficult; for the tact requires first of all a sure faith in the spiritual meaning of truly graceful behavior. And beyond this, the faith (always the difficult *sine qua non*) needs itself some definite experiential corroboration. Desire needs memory in order for people to begin the spiritually informative, tactfully cooperative dance in living time. Severely troubled Esther needed a mother to rock her gently in her arms and to develop memorably in her the "idea" of sacred tempo. But she did not have this, nor does the bleak world around her provide her with any examples of developed, graceful timing. And so, orphaned, having no center, no experiential good fortune, she fears very much that there is no spiritual meaning in which to believe. And it is this profound uncertainty regarding the nature of life in time which again, I would argue, makes tense the drama of *Bleak House*. The main drama of the novel is represented in Esther's difficult task, which is to develop as best she can the "idea," and in her own nature bring the extremes of self and non-self together, and with abiding faith establish and maintain the tempo in her world.[2]

The present study has four sections. The first deals with characters who for one reason or another will not engage themselves in the living present and also with the dread which makes it so difficult for Esther to be different from them. The second presents characters of the opposite tendency who will not or cannot relax in time, and suggests that Esther is often, for sorry reasons, herself incapable of slowing down. The third attempts to show how Esther, with the help of the amazing Bucket, in a great climax, actually gains the confidence to live gracefully, in time and out, both fast and slow, as she triumphs over her orphan's history. And the fourth takes up the larger providential and eschatological notions which are mentioned, or, perhaps more accurately, questioned in the novel. If this structure is itself too mechanical, it is hoped that it will not give the misleading idea that the elaboration of the temporal motif is without dramatic power. The notions of time in *Bleak House* are for the most part neither distant nor philosophically superfine. The main battles are between mechanism and healthy human (or organic) timing, and between healthy human timing and unhealthy—either sadly balking and uncertain, or hyperactive. But simple or not, these pervasive notions steadily intensify as the narrative develops.

I

When she is informed that Chadband is late for her meal, the devoted Mrs. Snagsby snaps: " 'What's time . . . to eternity?' " " 'Very true,' " Mr. Snagsby says, but adds, " 'Only when a person lays in victuals for tea, a person does it with a view—perhaps—more to time' " (19.235).[3] And Snagsby's point regarding temporal, material responsibility can be considered well taken. Rick Carstone is, of course, at the end of the novel "Beginning" "Not this world" but "The World that sets this right" (65.763). And yet his thorough incapacity for developing a responsible self in this formative world of time has been his undoing. Time *now* is the place where the self discovers its proper identity. Pressing time is *im*pressing, and so Esther observes plaintively, as she recounts Rick's gradual disappearance into a future-dream, that more and more he "was losing himself" (37.466). " 'Is,' " Rick says, " 'is—must be somewhere' " (37.464). But obviously he is never here where the "is" is; and so he rather distractedly confesses, when he is encouraged to enter the world of the present, that " 'There's no now for us suitors' " (37.462).

Harold Skimpole, although Bucket has his real number, is ostensibly just such another. He apparently has no temporally developed self. He says he is a child, he looks like a child, and the one thing he never wearies of is telling those upon whom he depends that he has no idea of time. He is in a way an interesting languorous critic of the worried self tortured by the ticking clock; but the fact that he is not a responsible "I," moving rhythmically, meritoriously in time with human need in this here and now world of exigencies, indicates a serious moral flaw. He speaks of himself "as if Skimpole were a third person" (6.66), and this kind of selflessness throws off human cooperative timing as badly as brutal egotism. Both are refusals to dance. Meals at Skimpole's, not surprisingly, are never served regularly; and when Jarndyce, in the vein of a Mr. Snagsby, offers something of a critical suggestion, Skimpole has a simple explanation: " 'Time is no object here. We never know what o'clock it is, and we never care' " (43.524). Also as Harold, or Skimpole, tinkles the piano keys late into the night, the young company at Bleak House wonder if the unendingly eleemosynary Mrs. Jellyby has finished her long day's work. The grand missionary correspondent is a Christian wonder, but her selfless dedication is destructive of her home as she simply will not exist in local responsible time. For her there is no "now" that is "here." Consequently her children's bodies are "perfect little calendars of distress" (5.57). The dinner hour at Jellyby's is "'nominally . . . five'"; but there the language of appointments is only language, for actually they "'dine at all hours'" (4.39)—no doubt to the continuing material and ultimately spiritual distress of the needy children. And the family maid, who should be a close observer of the temporal order, as she tends the house and cooking fires, is found by Esther exiting a public house, wiping her mouth. She said she had been to "see what o'clock it was" (5.46).

Appointments are highly significant in *Bleak House* because they suggest the possibility of a meaningful concert of responsible selves or of events that might memorably foster confidence; they make believable the claim that life offers more than disrhythmic uncooperativeness or grimly dispiriting abandonment. But if the best hopes are ever realized in the novel, they are realized against a very dark background. And with the chapter, "The Appointed Time," which deals with the combustible Mr. Krook's idea of appointments and time, we come perhaps to sense how dark the *Bleak House* background really is. Krook makes the appointment for twelve o'clock midnight, and this is perfectly absurd. Mrs. Jellyby disheartened Caddy so by occupying until midnight the room that was to be used for the wedding reception that the girl began to disbelieve in meritorious responsibility and loving concert and sat down to cry in the house dust. Midnight is the dark hour in the novel, and more than anyone else's it is Mr. Krook's. Krook is the man of lunatic *eurekas*. "'That was the time!'" (11.128), he exclaims when Snagsby says it was a year and a half ago that Nemo came to the lodgings. But why this ecstatic satisfaction? Krook looks into time and sees absolutely nothing. He has no "idea" at all really, and yet he is disturbingly pleased with his void perceptions. And disturbingly because, first of all, Krook's lunatic unresponsiveness is not really to be dismissed as exceptional but to be admitted as only a pronounced example of that same disorder which leads the whole *Bleak House* world out of step. Krook's uncooperative erasures perhaps could be said in the end to have wiped away the natural idea of cooperation itself and left a *tabula rasa* where the instinct for meaningful concert once read clearly. But then, beyond this, Krook's lunacy may be representative of a still deeper problem; for Dickens also admits with the problematical rag and bottle man the darker, midnight possibility that there is no informative dance for anyone in any case, that we are each in accord with no one and with nothing, that time is a meaningless motion pressing only to nonsensical explosions and that any impression of temporal order we might get is only a grim joke on us. That life in the end is only a Krookian midnight is in fact the possibility that haunts Esther, the potential Exemplar, deep down. Caddy is a miniature of Esther; and Caddy's fear that time is a dark absurdity is the same that troubles Dame Trot, whose mother is, if possible, even more completely absent than Caddy's.

It is both significant and insignificant that the appointed hour is also the first hour of Krook's birthday. He dies seventy-six years, to the day, after he was born. In itself Krook's birthday death truly has no meaning. It is purely accidental and absurd. It only indicates that in this case nothing informative has happened inside the pressure of the round of time. In Esther's room at Bleak House there were "oval engravings of the months—ladies haymaking . . . for June—smooth-legged noblemen, pointing . . . to village steeples, for October" (6.63). This is the round of time, and inside it there must be haymaking while the sun shines, a reaching for life before the approach of the shadow of death, and even a thankfulness for death because it energizes and makes serious all human action. Finally, born of the best moments, there must be faith to point to an extratemporal meaning. Birthdays should be reminders of the preciousness of life in time's round and the occasions of both memory and desire, or, in the end, of faithful relaxation. Also, as they are points in a continuous pattern, they should indicate the psychic continuity of the developing soul. They are the progress reports of the self in time. But then not so for many of the characters in *Bleak House*. Ask Phil Squod how old he is and he can only tell you " 'I'm something with a eight in it' " (26.326). At Skimpole's house the furniture is being sold on his daughter's birthday. Esther Summerson's early memories are only of a "child who lived a life apart, and on whose birthday there was no rejoicing" (18.225). The sense of age has been lost in this world and consequently certain insights into those sacred human needs which our various ages, our spring and fall, give rise to. No one here has any birthday associations with order or with love, and this want engenders in each the sense that perhaps he or she was born only for chaotic lovelessness. Birthdays should bring one back to an original confidence, especially in the meaning of responsiveness and returned response, if not to cosmic mother-love. But the motherless Esther, as she has no healthy memory or desire, nor any temporally developed self, can only look to Ada for a sign of any meaning in a woman's involvement in time. The young Old Dame Durden never danced in the past and is sure she will never dance in the future, so desperately, and fascinatingly, at the stroke of midnight on Ada's twenty-first birthday, she goes to give *her* an inaugural kiss. And this is only one of the many appointments the diffident girl makes for herself with death. She is at this point bleakly convinced that, for her, problematic life will only be a midnight monotony.

There is another birthday to consider, and this is the old girl's, Mrs. Bagnet's. Or perhaps the thing especially to consider, as it brings up again the idea of diffidence in time, is Mr. Bagnet's celebration of it, "according to certain forms, settled and prescribed . . . some years since" (49.587–588). According to form, Bagnet always roasts fowls, and he roasts them strictly by the clock. "'At half-after one . . . To the minute. They'll be done'" (49.588). And on strict clock time they are invariably burned. The cooking fire—or, once again, the whole world of human material need—requires a confident tactful minding. But Bagnet has no confidence at all nor any mind of his own. He has no self. He is a military man, and he looks to the military for the same thing that many do—for a relief from his inadequacy and for a discipline that will provide, in lieu of responsive human tact, at least some kind of timing, at least a march time if never any dance time. Bagnet's troubled friend George is a military man too, and exactly at half-past four when George is to arrive for the birthday, it is "'George! Military time'" (49.590). But birthdays should indeed be the soul's growth reports and should not be celebrated on inorganic military time. The strict punctuality may have its virtues. Jarndyce tells George that he is as regular as the sun. But George himself recognizes it is just "force of habit," and he might have added that in his case it is truly a desperate forcing. George is not at the party to help renew anyone's original confidence, especially in cosmic mother-love.

Of course George is another of Dickens' walking, or as it were here, marching projections of the problems of the diffident, orphaned Esther. When he sees his own mother at Tulkinghorn's, George does not respond in the dance but turns from her, as he has for so long turned from his origins, and looks at an almanac up on the wall. He is "calculating the coming months by it perhaps" (34.427). And indeed as long as he turns his back on the history of love in his life, there is no living future possible for him, only a continuing desperate routine, a calculated time. And motherless Esther too works like a self-doubting trooper and is capable only of frantically complaining, "'How *can* you say [it is] about nothing particular?'" (17.209), when Rick suggests that all work in time *is* about nothing. She can only say: This is the material world. We must march on. She has to agree with Mrs. Badger, who with a mechanical temporal fixation has married all her husbands "'upon the twenty-first of March at Eleven in the forenoon'" (13.157), that the life of the lunatic geologist, Professor Dingo, with his hammering *idée fixe*, is a model of well-spent time. For this girl whose birthdays are a recurring nightmare, time is a regular bleak march to nowhere. And in the end she is no help to the needy Rick, who in a desperate mind turns to the military himself and shows by his frantic behavior even there that he is hopelessly untuned.

The metaphor of the dance, as has been suggested, is extensive in *Bleak House*, but in the pathetic failure of the Turveydrop school, where the uncooperative students must practice their steps in separate rooms, it is perhaps most fully developed. And Dickens' picture of Prince's sad studio only makes the familiar point: that diffidence can never redeem time since it gives no lead to inspiring graceful cooperation. "And thus we danced an hour by the clock" (38.475), Esther says, as she recalls an afternoon spent at the studio; and the poor, disjoined and unrhythmical clock-dancing they do there is nothing but a march of non-selves. Prince, the dance director of *Bleak House*, has a father who "'wouldn't let his son have any name, if he could take it from him'" (14.173). The boy has not entered life's real dance where in response to time-born grief the self gains its glories and where love saves the self and saves the future with a gift for the memory. Instead Prince knows only punctuality. If the unworldly Mrs. Jellyby, in her disregard of the clock, has convinced her children that there is no such thing as meritorious responsibility, and thereby banished the idea of self-respect from her house, the worldly Mr. Turveydrop, with his "handsome gold" watch and his brutal punch-clock concern, has just as unnaturally led his selflessly dutiful child to believe that time is never the dance of love. Prince, as his father's son, waits for Caddy in mechanical clock-time and must timidly confess, when she and Esther come late, that he "'began to fear . . . as it was past the usual time, that Miss Jellyby was not coming'" (14.170). What a bleak sign it is that Caddy and Prince, educated only to disrhythm by their remarkably graceless parents (Esther says "whether I wondered most at Mrs. Jellyby, or at Mr. Turveydrop, I did not know" [30.377]) are the ones who play the music and teach the dance in the heart of London.

II

Quite clearly, though, the "ceaseless working . . . mill of jealousy" (54.645) creates at least as serious a problem as that kind of timidity which never realizes its opportunities for gracefulness. Indeed, the materialistic drive through the night is in some cases carried on with a pure self-

ish energy that astounds. And so while Esther, who looks in the mirror
and is glad she is ugly so her mother can more easily dismiss her, lacks all
conviction, Mademoiselle Hortense is filled with passionate intensity. It
bears repeating that the fact that in this confused world there is brute
egotism as well as sad selflessness, both hot passionate aggression and
timid withdrawal, frenzy and apathy, temporal mania and temporal pho-
bia, does not even begin to indicate any balance has been effected. Rather
it emphasizes the large scale mental fragmentation which results only in
various compartmentalized disrhythms. There is no connection, no dancing in the world's great mind, nor in the mind of any individual. No one is
both game and mild. Everywhere in the separate rooms of *Bleak House*,
impotence is the ghost that haunts the time to relax, or ambition is the
bearer of an unnatural glow.

But the likelihood that the aggressiveness is at least as bad in its way as
the self-effacement, is suggested immediately by the fact that it is at least
as exclusively mindful of the mechanical clock. "... I have to travel all
night," Mr. Rouncewell says to Lady Dedlock, "in order to reach a distant part of the country, punctually at an appointed time in the morning"
(28.355). Rouncewell does seem to know himself and to know what we all
need, perhaps because he does know so well his destination in space and
clock-time. Clocks are, after all, needful things. Lady Dedlock's barter-
ing away of her watch seems to mark the true end of any ambition in her
or concern for her own needs. But what of all the rusty pollution (reminiscent of Tulkinghorn) and the spreading defoliation for which the Ironmaster is responsible? Mr. Rouncewell is a grand, meritorious self, altogether different in his time from his brother George, or from the retreating Esther; but he has achieved his stature temporally, without knowledge
of the sacred "idea." He may know the hour, and he may know himself,
but he does not know men should sleep at night or how to help them to do
so. And it may be really that the Ironmaster's chief function in the novel,
as he is so successful in time, is to show the essential human need for more
than a clock self. In this same connection, nothing is more ridiculous, or
grim, than Mr. Guppy's proposal to Esther. Guppy may be a small fish,
but he is certainly ambitious: "sharpening the carving-knife on the
carving-fork" (9.112), he looks at Esther almost strictly as a hungry ma-
terialist. And when Esther refuses him, saying his offer is "ill-timed and
misplaced," he begs her indulgence in clock time: "'Half a minute,
miss!...a quarter of a minute, miss!'" (9.115). The fact that he quanti-
fies time so and cuts it like so much meat shows that this clock man is spiritually uninformed, that he does not know that the heart's needs arise
spontaneously in living time and that love is not amenable to drive.

And of what can the Dedlock's grand horologe inform Mr. Tulking-horn besides the hour? "If it said now, 'Don't go home!' What a famous clock hereafter . . ." (48.582). But the rich man's showpiece has only provided Tulkinghorn with some disciplinary information, the number of minutes till ten. It can speak nothing now to his needs for life and sets him only gracelessly on his competitive course. "What does it mean?" (48.585), the narrator asks, when after the murder the clock bell tolls out ten o'clock. Two driving selves have come into deadly confrontation; and what, as it tolls out its unhelpful noise, can the clock reveal except its own failure as a conductor of human rhythm? Indeed the clocks themselves seem to ring out competitively. Each one's bells only jar with all the other jarring bells in town, "the metal voices, near and distant, resounding from towers of various heights, in tones more various than their situations" (32.400). Mechanical temporal arrangements are seen as only so many sectarian arguments in an absurd dispute. Clock time, unless it rings from a steeple which really indicates a meaning above time, and which obviates competitive frenzy, is always "a clangour about nothing" (32.392).

There are other examples of aggressive, mechanical drivers who would, in the confined, strictly time-bound world, exercise complete dominion. And they sometimes in their brute clangoring about nothing can make a Rouncewell or a Guppy seem altogether relaxed. Certainly the incredible Mrs. Pardiggle cannot escape our notice here. She has such a "mechanical way of taking possession of people" (8.99); and, because she does not understand fatigue, she will not cooperate with a soul. "'I do not understand what it is to be tired; you cannot tire me if you try!'" (8.96), she says; and she announces with tremendous worldly self-satisfaction in time *now,* "'I am here again'" (8.98). This is the present tense confidence of the bully, which, like all materialistic "success," has a way of maintaining itself not upon any sacred idea but comfortably upon absurd or unhealthy principles. The bully, to put it bluntly, can beef up in time on pure bull. Which brings us straight to the vessel Chadband who, although he is late for dinner once, is for all practical purposes there now where the food *is*; and if Jo thinks that Chadband is there to respond to him with the grace of a dancing love, Jo is sorely mistaken. Of his "Terewth" he says to the boy, "'I say to you that I will proclaim it to you, whether you like it or not; nay, that the less you like it, the more I will proclaim it to you'" (25.321). So much for relaxed cooperation. Chadband is a fat self who would, strictly in the bleak sense, "partake" of life. As spiritual as a blackmailer, he comes with terrible timing to prey upon Sir Leicester.

"Why," he asks, "are we now in the mansions of the rich and great, my friends? Is it because we are invited? Because we are bidden to feast with them, because we are bidden to rejoice with them, because we are bidden to play the lute with them, because we are bidden to dance with them? No. Then why are we here, my friends? Air we in possession of a sinful secret, and doe we require corn, and wine, and oil—or, what is much the same thing, money—for the keeping thereof?" (54.643-644).

So many of the most important themes in the novel are brought together in this laughable but deadly bombast: the Dedlocks' selfish aristocratic exclusion; the material envy of other *selves*; the mockery of music and dance, or human timing; food; money. The materialistic disease which throws off the sacred tempo of human life stands revealed in the witness of the vessel's perfect tactlessness. Chadband is the flesh and blood of the strictly time and space-bound ego. He is a man of "dimensions"; and his effect on Jo, whom he should as a preacher be leading into the informed and informative dance, demonstrates how disconcerting and divisive and essentially inhuman his temporal attitude is. The boy, the narrator says, "Would rather run away from him for an hour than hear him talk for five minutes" (25.323).

And beyond the wholly insensitive brutes, there are the downright killers, such as Vholes, the predator, the cat by the mouse hole, who professes familial altruism and yet who loves his three daughters no more (and his self no less) than the phony Skimpole does his. And Vholes never relaxes. "'I am to be found here,'" he says to Rick, "'day by day . . . and term-time or vacation makes no difference to me'" (39.485). The predator in his grinding materialism is always at the wheel, for there is only so much space to be gained and only so much time to gain it in. Black Vholes, who says that he believes in no fond memories and never holds out future-hopes, lives strictly in the material now. Just as he rushes the frantic Rick back to London, so he continuously tolls back worried selves to a single bleak idea. He never steps out of driving time. He is like the pure materiality of corporal death itself, which has none of the various rhythms of life but, as is shown in the case of poor Jo, labors "all round the clock" and "drags over stony ground" (47.570).

Of course—and now we go even beyond Vholes to the violently homicidal—the epitome of unrelaxed egotism is Hortense. She has no "idea" of anything except Hortense, and she is more than hungry to see herself in the mirror. When she is arraigned by Bucket she comes in "with something in her dark cheek beating like a clock" (54.647). She is frenzied inside time, and she seems to laugh at the whole idea of spiritual significance when she mocks her "angel" Bucket for not being able to bring back Sir Leicester from the as good as dead. In the tight, worldly arena with

Tulkinghorn, driving restlessly for territory in a limited space, she says she will come as his antagonist "'again . . . And yet again. And yet again. And many times again. In effect, for ever!'" (42.519)—that is, until death. She is nothing but relentlessly ferocious; and in her quick frustrations she surely shows that the need to escape the pressure of time, to relax and to sleep, is as important as to find *in* the pressure of time one's proper shape.

But finally Esther too, though she indeed can be part of the sad "we" at the Turveydrop school, and though it would obviously be a mistake to call her an enormous self, let alone a killer, is one who "hovers." "' . . . I am only going away to come back to-morrow,'" she says to the newly situated Rick and Ada, "' . . . I shall always be coming backwards and forwards, until Symond's Inn is tired of the sight of me'" (51.614). This is gentler certainly than Mrs. Pardiggle's fierce obtrusiveness, yet it is surely over-watchful; and when Esther confesses she is "hovering about" her darling (51.616), we connect her immediately with Hortense, who is said several times to be hovering about, and with Guppy, who "hovers" over Esther herself with his knife and fork. Esther may not have much; but she would—especially as there may really be no "right world" anywhere— drive disrhythmically to possess here what she can, or rather hang in sleepless suspension over what she cannot.

III

So we can see the novel in Esther. She is one who at points thinks of escape into a redeeming eternity yet who cannot in the meantime articulate a faith. She is neither a developing self nor a real saint. Her father is Mr. No One, who, like his daughter, works with a grim regularity in the night and who for no reason gets his job done on time (and who also escapes into the timeless through opium supplied by Alan Woodcourt). Her mother is the high and mighty but frighteningly restless Lady Dedlock, and nearly the last words Esther has from this lofty Someone are, "'I have no purpose but to die'" (59.710). Everything is loaded on Esther's back; and it is she, the child of the division of self and selflessness, who must if the change is ever to occur, redeem the sacred idea of life as maternal or parental love.

But she has absolutely no working position. She cannot move into the future but only spins on day after day. She has no informative memory or informed desire. The "wind . . . wandered in the dark," she says, "like my memory over my life" (8.85). She recounts how, after she finally met and spoke to her, her mother's voice "made an enduring impression on my memory." But pathetically she laments that this was the voice "which in my childhood I had never learned to love and recognise, had never been sung to sleep with, had never heard a blessing from, had never had a hope inspired by . . ." (36.451–452). Without an inspiring, memorable blessing to move her forward, or a loving musical rhythm to ease her into deeply faithful relaxation, she cannot know healthy human timing. "I have ever since connected the feeling with that spot and time" (31.380), she says, as she remembers the point in her history just before her illness and after which she said she knew she never would be the same. But the memory was primarily of "a lurid glare" which "overhung the whole dark waste" (31.380) of London, and the turn in her history, after the establishment of this dark impression, was only into disease and deeper loss. "I have a very indistinct remembrance of that night melting into day, and of day melting into night again" (31.391), she recalls vaguely, as she tries to describe her complete loss of natural rhythm in the depths of her unnamed disease. Later the mechanical, material Tulkinghorn succeeds, as he hovers over Lady Dedlock, in "closing up her view of the night as well as of the day" (48.579); and mother and daughter, separated terribly, suffer alike from the loss of a sense of time. Whether Esther, as she emerges from the depths of what she calls her "inexplicable agony" (35.432), will be more fortunate in time than her mother and discover some purpose other than to die is only another version of the central question regarding her discovery of the sacred idea of tempo.

Esther falls in her terror into what she calls a "great black space" (35.432); and perhaps nothing is more like her dread than that which Emily Dickinson describes in lines perfectly expressive of the feeling that for the soul in great fear all changes in space have been arrested and saving time has ended: "when all that ticked has stopped, and space stares all around." In Esther's "great black space" there are "colossal staircases" (35.431) leading nowhere. She says, "I had never known before how short life really was, and into how small a space the mind could put it" (35.431); but she can compress her time so because it has never been developmental. Her memory is a blank, and her future will correspond. In her nightmare all the years of her life are melted together; she says that "the way in which these divisions of time became confused with one another, distressed my mind exceedingly" (35.431). The distressing thing is that when it is all brought before her as a bleak unit, without the false divisions of the years, she realizes that she has never gone anywhere, because she has never had anything to spring from.

After her disease has passed physically, but before she has emerged into any kind of real health, Esther reviews her life again and decides that she must turn to the one bright light that has shone for her. She asks, in clock time, for John Jarndyce's letter and then consents to the idea of his proposal. Having come to this light, she says she saw "the close of the benignant history I had been pursuing . . ." (44.538). Esther, in her great fear of being lost altogether, closes her history before it really has begun, and, though she thinks she has chosen best, she knows, somehow, that she has expelled herself unnaturally from hopeful human time. She remains sadly estranged, "as if something for which there was no name or distinct idea were indefinitely lost to me" (44.538). And it is moving to hear her from her great black space say no to Alan Woodcourt, and, with the prospect of the autumnal Jarndyce before her, tell him that she, in her springtime, has "'nothing in the world to desire'" (45.549). Her history is over; she will take the flowers which Alan had once left her as a precious memento of his true affection and, hopelessly annihilating both memory and desire, burn them.

Very strangely, but perhaps understandably in this case, Esther had touched the flowers to the lips of the sleeping Ada before she destroyed them. Her feeling of self-worth is so feeble that she cannot even bid her own opportunities farewell. She has removed herself almost completely from the ground on which direction is discovered. In what must be considered one of the most powerful sequences in nineteenth-century fiction, however, Esther, with the help of Bucket, who knows himself very well, will drive across her whole life in the dark night and, at the end, confront the question of her real worth and proper direction. And she will call for Alan Woodcourt to be there "now" to help her at the most memorable and frightening moment.

But to begin with, though Bucket plays the flute by ear and not mechanically, is a genius of detective tact, is responsive in time, and is no stiff allegorical figure, he nevertheless has his inadequacies. He is no lover for one thing; his bedroom graces include stuffing the sheet into his wife's mouth. Also, although the fact that Bucket has been working on this "beautiful case" "'morning, noon and night'" (53.631) does not at all indicate that he is a driving machine, but simply that he is responsive to the exigencies of life, he still does view life as a "case." "'I am damned if I am a-going to have my case spoilt . . . or anticipated by so much as half a second of time, by any human being in creation'" (54.643), he swears, as he points the living finger. But perfect timing for Bucket is merely perfect gamesmanship. Although he knows how to relax as a human being must, he relaxes primarily as a sportsman does. "Refreshed by sleep, Mr. Bucket rises betimes in the morning, to prepare for a field-day" (54.636). Significantly Dickens disrupts the straight timing of "the chronicle" now to go back to the night before, when the old girl, Mrs. Bagnet, who does not see life as a case, or the time for action as a field-day, responded to crying human need by racing through the night to get Mrs. Rouncewell. If Bucket had acted this soon and not been so game for "the weapon," he might have saved Lady Dedlock's life. In addition to this it is strictly to his watch that he rather blithely attends as Sir Leicester lies stricken by the news of his lady's lost reputation.

But Bucket can and does come truly alive. When he does see that Lady Dedlock has fled and knows a life is at stake, he immediately vows " 'Not a minute must be lost' " (56.670). He takes the money for expenses, but he is aware that the idea of time as money is beginning to change into an altogether different concept. Soon an hour is " "worth a thousand pound" " (56.673) he says, suggesting that he knows life at its heart is no monetary matter. Finally it is his greatest wisdom that he knows that in this venture he must complete his nature, become more than the perfect temporal tactician, and attend to this situation more than gamely or dutifully. Alan Woodcourt says to Esther that she makes duty "sacred"; and so Bucket too, as he knows that the situation calls for substantiation of the sacred meaning of time itself, says " 'I want Miss Summerson' " (56.672).

More importantly, the cooperation of Bucket and Esther should work for the completion of Esther's nature. Bucket knows his own name, no doubt about that; in his perfect confidence he is so effective in space and time that the narrator attributes to him something of a semi-divinity and says, not altogether sarcastically, that "Time and place cannot bind Mr. Bucket" (53.626). Bucket is living self-assurance. He is the self in time at its best. Thus he could be the one to bring Esther, and he seems eager to bring her, to her proper ground, where she must learn the sacred meaning of opportunity, or how confidently to get out of the world of time simply by going so far in.

When he first arouses her, Esther cannot make out Bucket's "plan." She can see that it is past one "by the clock against the wall" (57.675), but has no clear understanding of what she is to do, or be, or of what time it is on the clock of human need. So " 'that it ends well . . . Miss,' " Bucket says; and Esther replies " 'I pray to Heaven it may end well!' " (57.675). But at this point no one is possessed of any teleological certainty, or more particularly, of the faith that the well-timed response is, in any large sense, informative. Time and again Esther is frightened by the sounds of "the monotonous wheels . . . whirling on" (57.678). Only dreary uniformity stretches out endlessly in her mind's view and review of her existence. "If I ever thought of the time I had been out," she says, "it presented itself as an indefinite period of great duration; and I seemed, in a strange way, never to have been free from the anxiety under which I then laboured" (57.687). Endless anxiety—but Bucket, who never slackens in his purpose, which is to reunite the two halves of a broken meaning, tells her " 'You're beginning to get more yourself now . . .' " (57.679). He is bringing her to the point of almost unbearable heartbreak and love, to an unforgettable new "now," in which she must act responsibly but also as witness to the deep meaning of the rhythms and the tact of human love. " 'The naturalest way is the best way, and the naturalest way is your own way' " (57.682), he tells her as he asks her to make the important inquiries in this extraordinary case. Everything depends upon her blessing the action in the natural way, with graceful and loving timing. " 'You're a pattern, you know, that's what you are,' " says Bucket, " 'you're a pattern' " (59.704). But we remember how Bucket created Snagsby's personality for him, and we wonder if this is similar fabrication. What is Esther, and what is the right timing, the proper pattern for life? " 'My dear,' " Bucket informs her now, " 'when a young lady is as mild as she's game, and as game as she's mild, that's all I ask . . . She then becomes a Queen, and that's about what you are yourself' " (59.704). Bucket says it plainly then: that if someone is out of time and in, deeply, faithfully relaxed and yet ready in time for action, a veritable selfless self—that person is of central importance in her world. She sets the pace. But inside Esther there is a Guster, a girl of fits and frights who must be calmed, assured. Esther convincingly has to pacify her own fitful self and find out in her own heart where she must, as a loving, meritorious self, go now. Alan Woodcourt, with miraculous but symbolically perfect timing, is there by her side. She could cry in thanks to find him, she says, "after my feverish wandering journey, and in the midst of the night . . . " (59.705). " 'Don't leave me now!' " (59.7112) she pleads with him, as she goes into what for her is the most profound darkness. She will find there unspeakable grief, no doubt—and informative love?

IV

The fact that Esther says she must now "proceed to other passages" (60.714) in her narrative is not necessarily indicative of frantic uncertainty or of essential timidity. It perhaps shows more a healthy retreat from morbidity. But the question as to whether her journey to the heart of experience has ended well, has finally given her some extra-temporal idea, is still to be answered. The teleological question as to the first purpose of the human experience of life in time is one that lies behind many of the problems the novel dramatizes. It is touched upon directly frequently enough, though it must be said that the question is never easily contained by a religious answer. Jarndyce preaches a providential message on several important occasions. "'Trust in nothing,'" he says to Rick, "'but in Providence and your own efforts. Never separate the two, like the heathen waggoner'" (13.162). Live in time and keep an eye to the extra-temporal. Be active and also patient, yourself and God's child too. At times Jarndyce can convince the temporally worried Esther. "I neither worked nor thought, any more, that night," she says of a time he had come to relax her, and "I opened my grateful heart to Heaven in thankfulness for its Providence . . . and fell asleep" (17.214). But Esther also in a compulsive "burst of gratitude to the providence of God" (36.449) can express thanks for her deforming scars! Her sense of a divine intention here is nothing but the unhealthy fruit of her own history of trauma. What is more, Jarndyce, who is the one who introduces from the Bible the inevitable "'there is a time for all things'" (24.302), seems too often to be a man of stock phrases. "'Leave all else to time, truth, and steadfastness'" (24.303), he says, but his proverbial wisdom is not always mightily convincing.

Of course Miss Flite, who waits religiously in time for a discernible judgment, is an extremely important figure in this connection. Whether she is mad or not is significantly questionable, but her eschatological expectations, which are based upon the faith that right rhythm is divinely sanctioned and cannot be denied in the world, are never fulfilled. Also, interestingly, there is this from Jarndyce regarding Flite's visit to the sick Esther: "'Little Miss Flite . . . made nothing of walking down here— twenty miles, poor soul, in a pair of dancing shoes—to inquire. It was Heaven's mercy we were at home, or she would have walked back again'" (35.437). They were there to respond rhythmically to the selfless and yet meritorious labor of love of the faithful lady in dancing shoes, and so she did not return with a broken heart and a broken faith in the sacredness of loving rhythm. But even here in the successful dance, things were a half-step from disaster; so maintenance of faith in the *eschaton*, or in the "now" as suggestive of purpose, seems rather hazardous.

Little Jo, who is said to "listen to . . . music" with the "animal satisfaction" (16.199) of a dog, looks up to the cross atop St. Paul's for a sense of direction in time. He sees "everything moving on to some purpose and to one end" (19.244), but he knows "nothink" of where to move himself or of what is to be learned from responding: "one might suppose that sacred emblem to be, in his eyes, the crowning confusion of the great, confused city . . ." (19.243). When the boy dies, just before he can say the "Thy name" of the Lord's Prayer, the narrator complains that "if the Chadbands, removing their own persons from the light, would but show it thee," "there is a history" (25.323) which could save even those like you. Christ's sacred history as a temporal pattern, the example of his glorious involvement in and his sure detachment from pressing, grieving time, could save. Time is the place of *heilgeschichte*—if we only knew. And yet our ignorance of the eternal pattern does not invalidate it, and the narrator does praise it *sub specie aeternitatis*. It is a rhythmic guide and an inspiration for all time. But Jo only sees it in the humanity of Woodcourt, and for all the quasi-theological suggestion in the novel, the human reflection of the pattern is the best there really is to go on. The "noble history" (36.442) of Woodcourt's "generous and gallant deeds" (36.442) aboard the sinking ship touches Esther deeply. Alan's gallant, generous history is the very pattern of self-realizing human selflessness, and those whom he saved "fell down at his feet" and "all but worshipped him" (36.442). And now for Esther he is there again to give her what does seem to be the very best she could have to go on, and the sacred is "all but" laid bare.

————————

Jarndyce says, perhaps this time with a wisdom that can be trusted, that "'All generous spirits are ambitious . . . but the ambition that calmly trusts itself to such a road, instead of spasmodically trying to fly over it, is of the kind I care for. It is Woodcourt's kind'" (60.717). The selfless self who in his generous ambition can both work and sleep, like Alan Woodcourt, is alive; and the way he moves, with continuing and spontaneous awareness of need, is the way men should. But finally, the fact that Woodcourt is a largely absent figure, who Esther can believe is her lover only after her long and painful detention out of time, indicates the degree to which the *Bleak House* world is one in need. The best hopes are indeed only realized against dark backgrounds here. And how extensively they are realized is uncertain. It seems Dickens would have us consider realistically (which is not necessarily to say completely pessimistically) the distance that Esther's influence might extend beyond the new Bleak House. But surely we are to believe too that, at least as far as her familial and familiar social domain extends, she will be the pattern, the game as well as mild Queen, and that finally she *has* come, through time's intense pressure, to understand as best we can the sacred idea of tempo.

NOTES

1. For a brief introductory study of Dickens' concern with time, the reader should see George Ford's "Dickens and the Voices of Time," *Nineteenth-Century Fiction*, 25 (1970), 428–448. Ford also includes here a helpful list of general studies of the problem of time and of Victorian ideas of time. More recently John R. Reed, "Freedom, Fate, and the Future in *Bleak House*," *CLIO*, 8 (1979), 175–194, has argued effectively that the double narrative can be seen as a free will versus determinism debate, with Esther standing clearly for free human participation in the aid of a divine scheme. Reed insists, it would seem correctly but also without enough sense of trouble, that ideas of Christian history prevail in the novel.

2. Of all the recent revaluations of Dickens' characterization of Esther, Alex Zwerdling's "Esther Summerson Rehabilitated," *PMLA*, 88 (1973), 429–439 must be included among the most able. Zwerdling also provides a list of other "useful studies of Esther Summerson along psychological lines." The reader might well consult too, for a truly impressive survey of the deadly background against which Esther must stand up for life, Garrett Stewart, "The New Mortality of *Bleak House*," *ELH*, 45 (1978), 443–487.

3. All textual references are to the Norton Critical Edition of *Bleak House*, ed. George Ford and Sylvère Monod (New York: 1977).

Bleak House and the Playhouse

H. Philip Bolton

Jo, the poor crossing sweeper of *Bleak House*, has often been reborn upon the stage. Every year since about 1835, at least several and often many of the more than 700 "Dickens plays" have been produced. What one critic calls the "Dickens deluge"[1] has abated somewhat during the twentieth century, as popular theater itself has declined, but a steady trickle continues even today, and a "Bleak House" has been performed in London as recently as April of 1977. Of course when we look up from the play texts and out from the playhouses to the larger worlds of the movies, radio, and television, we find characters aplenty from Dickens.

The bibliographers of theatrical adaptations of Dickens[2] show evidence of more than forty British and American staged versions of *Bleak House*. Such a great many plays derived from the book that Malcolm Morley, the best of the catalogers of Dickens plays, could not unearth them all; the list after this article adds a few plays.[3] This great wealth of theatrical response to the novel confirms the latent theater that many critics[4] have sensed generally in Dickens and even particularly in *Bleak House*, which is so very unplaylike a novel in sheer bulk and multiplicity of interests.

Plays made from novels identify those scenes, characters, and events that playwrights calculated would be most powerful on stage. When many staged versions of a novel arise, a consensus about what elements are successfully dramatic and theatrical may emerge. We must only beware any degenerative tendency in a series of dramatic adaptations for a study especially of the more popular productions to prepare us to explain certain elements in Dickens's novel-writing craft.

At first *Bleak House* plays outrage people and even incur censorship; later the outraged sensibility becomes absurd and the whole affair is subject to burlesque. Tastes change. The *Bleak House* plays start in 1853 and 1854 with "serious" and disturbing versions at the Pavilion, City of London and other theaters. But this series of related stagings of *Bleak House* does tend to degenerate, more than twenty years after the novel first appeared, into burlesques at the Surrey and Greenwich theaters. Also notable in the twentieth century are schoolroom plays and occasional amateur productions. A substantial group of these playwrights have reached a kind of consensus about the basic appeal of the book. Especially certain nineteenth-century dramatists agree with each other.

Both Morley and Fawcett emphasize most, among the *Bleak House* plays, the group of productions in 1876 and 1877 which—twenty-three years after the novel's first publications—focus on Jo the orphan. But the Cockney crossing sweeper was obviously important to playwrights as early as the first week of June, 1853, four months before the novel was complete.

Theatrical events surrounding the novel during the week of Monday, May 30 to Monday, June 6, are highly suggestive. In that week the sixteenth installment of Dickens' novel appeared, and interest in the story probably reached a monthly high point. But events in chapters fifty through fifty-three could not have influenced the two staged versions of *Bleak House* licensed and produced at that time. Rather, both plays were based upon the novel so far as it had proceeded in the May issue, the fifteenth, to slightly more than three-fourths of its full length. In fact, many plays based on the novel end with events in chapter forty-seven, in which Allan Woodcourt and Miss Flite take the dying orphan to Trooper George's Shooting Gallery, where Jo breathes his last, "moves on" for good. Jo is

> Dead, your Majesty, Dead, my lords and gentlemen. Dear Right Reverends and Wrong Reverends of every order. Dead, men and women, born with Heavenly compassion in your hearts. And dying thus around us every day (XLVII, p. 705).[5]

On Tuesday, May 31, the Lord Chamberlain received from the management of the City of London Theatre a manuscript titled simply "Bleak House," and evidently composed in haste by John H. Wilkins. In Act I, two scenes are numbered "iv," for example. The play aims at the cheapest, easiest thrills. Woodcourt warns in Act II, scene ii, that Kenge, Carboy, and Mme. Hortense are going to kidnap Esther—a severe twist on the original Dickens. The play ends with Jo's death on stage. William Bodham Donne, then acting as Kemble's deputy Examiner of Plays, has initialed the manuscript beside the notation "License issued June 1"—only the day after he received it, and with great bureaucratic despatch and no apparent censorious qualms.

There was reason for Donne's haste. Another and a competing theatrical management, at the Pavilion Theatre, was evidently pressuring him for immediate permission to produce another play based on *Bleak House*. On Saturday, June 4, Elphinstone and Neale of the Pavilion submitted to the Examiner of Plays a manuscript titled somewhat more pretentiously "Bleak House; or, The Spectre of the Ghost Walk," by George Dibdin Pitt. Mr. Pitt's play has been more nearly labored over than was the City of London version. A note on the first page of Act II, by J. C. Morgan, prompter at the Pavilion, reminds the Examiner—halfway through his dreary duty—that this matter is "intended for representation on Saturday, June 4, 1853"—which was that very evening. Habitually prompt as Examiner, Mr. Donne must have felt exasperated to be urged to hurry to license Pitt's play. And midway through the first scene, the text breaks off with the following note:

> Having received information that an offense has been given by Mr. Dickens in the [illegible] . . . of the Inquest, as making it too ludicrous I have left that scene out of this version and interwoven the Witnesses in the Death scene—this is also will be [*sic*] the only version in which Capt Hawdon is Resuscitated and is the Ghost of himself—
> the Lord Chamberlain has I understand instructions to suppress any Comic Coroner's Inquest, as in the Work—
>
> G.D.P.

Pitt knows about and is competing with another theatrical version of the story that is about to appear—probably the play at the City of London. Dickens has evidently seen a script, or heard about a script, or attended a rehearsal or performance of a *Bleak House* play, and has pressured Pitt, whose very syntax collapses with his haste to appease the Inimitable and propitiate the censor. Despite such hardships, this version of the play is at least more original than its City of London competitor. We get to watch Hawdon overdose himself with opium and have terminal convulsions, all to appropriate music. Needless to say, Pitt has been free in his treatment of Dickens' original idea. However, just like the City of London "Bleak House," this play ends with Jo's death. About the power of that element of dramaturgy the hacks agreed with each other and with Dickens. The Pavilion version beat the City of London version to the boards, opening on schedule on June 4, and appearing before its license was officially sent on June 6. All the while, the last installments of the novel existed mostly in Dickens' mind.

The evidence of various documents in and related to the Lord Chamberlain's collection of plays thus suggests a rush to production in May and June of 1853—as if the managers and house writers of two theaters sensed theatrical gold in *Bleak House*. As these first two and several later plays indicate, this precious vein was the life and death of Jo the orphan. Playwrights have tended to select that story from among the others in the novel. The urchin's death in Dickens' fifteenth installment especially excited the hacks and managers to dream of full houses and full coffers. In that collective fantasy of the play, these merchants in imagination calculated, Jo the orphan was sensational; his death would prove outrageously enjoyable. It would afford the luxury of tears. And when Jo had left the novel, in May, at least two theatrical managers felt they could then serve their audiences with the latest fare from Charles Dickens. So far as the playwrights were concerned, the fates of the remaining characters were incidental and would work out according to pat formulae. Only Jo truly mattered.

Jo mattered to the ordinary playwrights of London, and to official London. Pitt had heard that the Lord Chamberlain had received instructions not to tolerate "any Comic Coroner's Inquest," and these orders could not have come from Dickens. Apparently some dangerous satire of the authorities lurked in this scene; apparently it expressed bitterness too deep for some to trust upon the stage. Yet touching even more on a public nerve than the absurd Beadle and Coroner debating Nemo's death was the far more bitter death of Jo the mere child. In the third version of "Bleak House" to appear in London theaters, Jo's death scene is omitted because the Lord Chamberlain has censored it. A Permit for production was issued to the Strand on May 29, 1854. This version, by an author whose name is illegible to me, appears in *The Register of the Lord Chamberlain's Plays* with the following instructions:

> Omit all oaths & act II, sc. 4.
> *Allan* Can you say what I say, Joe?
> *Joe* Anything you say, Sir, for I know it will be good.
> (*Allan whispers to him*) 'Our Father,' yes Sir, that's very good.
> (*Allan whispers again*) 'In Heaven,' yes Sir the lights a coming.
> (*Allan whispers again*) Hallowed by thy name. (Falls back dead)
> . . .
>
> [signed] Wm Bodham Donne

The only part of this notation truly typical of the treatment contemporary plays received at the hands of the censor is the phrase "omit all oaths"; otherwise the censorship is unusual. The offense must have had something to do with presenting the sacred on a secular stage. In any case, the manner of Jo's death disturbed Victorian minds.

Suffering children provided powerful images. They had successfully appeared on the London stage long before Dickens invented Jo. From March 1838 to March 1839, *Oliver Twist* had inspired at least eleven London stage versions of the adventures of a waif. And from July 1838 to July 1839, *Nicholas Nickleby* had inspired at least six London plays presenting the misadventures of children. Oliver displayed his kinship to Smike when they appeared—sometimes as twin bills—at the Surrey, City of London, and Adelphi theaters in plays by C. Z. Barnett, Edward Stirling, George Almar, J. Stirling Coyne, and D. Pitt. More than ten years before he came to write *Bleak House*, Dickens had known about these productions—deploring some, enduring others, and enjoying a few. The creator of Jo understood full well the pathos of the dying child.

After the first four productions of *Bleak House* plays—at the City of London, Pavilion, Lyceum (New York), and Strand—the managers and playwrights turned their attention elsewhere for twenty years. In the interim, however, Dion Boucicault succeeded on the stage with "Smike" (1858), and the tradition of the stage orphan did not die when Dickens passed away in 1870. Circumstances were propitious for the next episode in the history of the stage versions of *Bleak House*, as Morley had told it. Twenty-two years after the first publication of the novel, in California, on the strength of her unexpected success as Jo in a supporting role in a play called "Chesney Wold," Jennie Lee convinced her husband, J. P. Burnett, to write a play that would star her as the orphan Jo. No less an authority than Dion Boucicault advised this. Burnett did his duty, and "for something like a quarter of a century *Jennie Lee as Jo* was familiar billing the world over.... Other characters in the drama, particularly the men, were in the nature of caricatures in respectful attendance; the limelight was all on Jo."[6] Burnett's play was never published, but was obviously a very effective piece of melodrama in which music milked every drop of pathos from the dying crossing sweeper.

Burnett had many months to ponder his play before he presented a text to the Lord Chamberlain. Even his considered and "fair" copy is emended. Many lines in the closing scene have been cut for the sake of economy; but on the very last page of the manuscript, after "Our Father which art in heaven," the words "hallowed be thy name" are almost blacked out in heavy spiral lines—apparently by Burnett, who was nervous about the Examiner's reaction. Burnett dared to leave only the first line of the prayer. But sure enough, even in February of 1876, more than five years after Dickens' death and twenty years after the last previous censorship of the play, Donne's successor as Examiner lists Burnett's

"Jo" in *The Register of the Lord Chamberlain's Plays* with the following instructions about the orphan's death: "Omitting last scene the words 'Our Father—which art in heaven.'" The censor would not even accept the proffered compromise of Jo's speaking only one line from the prayer.

Nor was this all. Jennie Lee had such a great success that seven imitations of her "Jo" ran in or near London during 1876. Several individual Jo-plays appeared at several theaters, so that the waif was both immortal and omnipresent. We might say that Jo became a kind of minor popular deity, associated—for all the Examiner might do—with sacred wording.

Yet surprisingly, both the manuscript and printed versions of Lander's "Bleak House; or, Poor 'Jo'" (produced at the Pavilion in March) end with the words of the Lord's Prayer, which the Examiner did not forbid. Perhaps he did not read this version. Perhaps he had discovered that he was mistaken to think any harm existed in the scene. Perhaps, between licensing Burnett's version on February 17 and Lander's on March 20, the censor resigned himself to the inevitable mass worship of Jo.

For Rhoyds's version at the Greenwich Theatre has Jo die with the words "Forgive me and take me home" (an obvious compromise). Thorne's version at the Alexandria Opera House, Sheffield, omits any prayer but has Jo die in Woodcourt's arms at the play's final moment. Price's version at the Theatre Royal, Coventry, has Jo die speaking some of the Lord's Prayer at Esther's prompting. Wylsone's version at the Victoria ends with Jo praying silently while he dies. The Lord Chamberlain has no record of the Hazleton or Hurst versions at the Britannia and Surrey theaters, but in a collection of manuscripts derived from the Britannia, Hoxton, there survives a "Jo" by J. B. Johnstone which was apparently never produced, quite possibly because the managers of the Britannia preferred Hazleton's version. Johnstone has Jo die without benefit of the Lord's Prayer. And his play apparently died without production.

As if all this "Jo-mania" were not enough—and because it was entirely too much—burlesques of the Jo plays appeared in May and October of 1876. Green and Allen wrote "Jo v. Jo," produced at the Surrey on October 9. The poor Examiner (the only person in London required to read all the "Jo" scripts) must have greeted this irreverent spoof with some relief. In staging it, the Surrey probably ridiculed its own "serious" production of "Poor Jo" by Terry Hurst, for this co-authored burlesque includes a theatrical manager searching for an actor to play Jo. The enterprising Philander Patterdash seeks out a genuine crossing sweeper, "Old Jo," whom he at first engages to play the part, calculating that his theater may thereby "out-Jo" the other houses. But his girlfriend, an aspiring actress disguised as "Young Jo," convinces him that she would be better in the role. She does this by reciting familiar lines from the novel. Her imitation seems so much more "real" than "Old Jo's" genuine Cockney to the befuddled Philander that he hires his girlfriend on the spot, not recognizing her until she doffs her disguise.

Though it is a piece of fluff, "Jo v. Jo" suggests some reasons for the Jo-mania of 1876. It opens with a song:

> Trade is looking very bad
>   There's no brooms now to be had
> And from nobody a Copper can we squeeze
>   Through the foreign loans and stocks
>   People can't afford a box
> At the Op'ra or what is worse
>   To us a box of our Fuzees
> What on earth are we to do?
>   It's no wonder we look blue
> We have lived on cold roast chicken for a week
>   And the worst of all things is
>   We have scarcely tasted fizz
> And to Chablis or Sauterne we're almost strangers so to speak
>
> Oh Oh—will you kindly tell us what on earth we are to do.

The protest against the sufferings of the poor that may well have frightened the Examiner in Jo's death, in 1854, appears in a remarkably serious form in the "unserious" "Jo v. Jo." Green and Allen take as their premise the idea that the sufferings of the real people of London cannot be adequately illustrated in the person of one dying boy. Jenny, one of these "real" people, says of the "real" sweeper: "There's my old Jo as cross as his crossing." If times were bad, people probably enjoyed feeling sorry for a waif who had it even worse than then they did. Green and Allen have Young Jo enter and sing:

> I'm a merry crossing Sweep-ah
>   With my broom myself I keep-ah
> And than me no cove is deep-ah
>   For at every move I'm fly.

Green and Allen have the "real" street people dislike this streak of complacency in the "phony" Jo. (Sentiments are changing.) The two Joes fight with their brooms for swords. According to Morley, Green and Allen "sadly misfired."[7] The failure suggests how seriously Victorian audiences took their crossing sweepers, and how sweet tears were more powerful than bitter guffaws.

While also testifying to the importance of Jo, this spoof is an early hint of the coming degeneration in the sequence of Jo plays. There were four

more on the theme in the next two years in London, and then three more
derived from *Bleak House* in the decade of the eighties. J. Palgrave Simpson's "Lady Dedlock's Secret," which Frederick Kitton thought a good
play,[8] does not focus strongly upon the crossing sweeper, and ends with
Lady Dedlock's death, not the orphan's. In 1892 Hughes and Bickley can-
nibalized large chunks of Lander's version, including Jo's deathbed reci-
tation of the Lord's Prayer. Jennie Lee also continued to play her version
of Jo through the last decade of the century, and even beyond; but now
George Bernard Shaw grew irritated with dramatized Dickens generally,
and Burnett's version particularly.

> . . . somewhere between the drying of the Flood and the advent of Ibsen—
> Bleak House shared the fate of most of Dickens's novels in being 'adapted
> to the stage.' The absurdity of the process is hardly to be described, so
> atrociously had these masterpieces to be degraded to bring them within the
> competence of the theatre; but the thing was done somehow; and the Artful
> Dodger, Smike, Micawber, Peggotty, and Jo were born again as 'famous
> impersonations,' . . .

Of Burnett's "Jo" Shaw says:

> . . . truly the spectacle is an astonishing one, . . . Imagine the poor patheti-
> cally ridiculous Guster not only condemned to mere knockabout buf-
> foonery, but actually made to fall down in a *comic* epileptic fit on the stage!
> Buckett has his psychology considerably complicated by the fact that the
> author has rolled him up with Mr Jarndyce and the Cook's Court police-
> man; so that there are three characters in one person, a trinitarian expedient
> which presents an absolutely insoluble problem to the actor. . . . On the
> stage, one perceives, Dickens was impossible because he was infinitely too
> poetic, too profound, too serious, too natural in his presentment of things—
> in a word, too dramatic for the theatre of his day. Not that I shall allow any-
> one to persuade me that Jo was ever anything more than a third-rate work at
> any period of our stage history; but it must have been much more highly
> esteemed when it was first perpetrated than it is now, even by an audience in-
> vited at 'cheap summer prices,' and so carelessly catered for, that in the
> scene in which Guppy explains to Esther Summerson that what she takes for
> smoke is a London fog, we are treated to the most brilliantly sunshiny front
> cloth the scene-dock of Drury Lane affords.

Careless production was one problem in the 1896 version of "Jo." But
the taste on which Burnett's play had depended was withering; and indeed, Shaw did his best to kill it. Nevertheless, G.B.S. had a certain
grudging respect for the main character of the play.

> All that can be said for Miss Jennie Lee's Jo nowadays is that if the part
> had been left between herself and Dickens, something credible and genuine-

ly moving might have come of it. But Mr Burnett has carefully laid out his lines and stage business for the crudest and falsest stage pathos and stage facetiousness. Jo is one moment a cheeky street arab, and, the next, is directly expressing, to slow music, not the darkened ideas of Jo, but Mr Burnett's version of the compassionate horror roused in the social and political consciousness of Dickens by the case of Jo and his fellow-outcasts. Dickens himself is not wholly guiltless of this: in the novel one or two of Jo's speeches are at bottom conscious social criticisms; but it is not the business of the dramatist to develop a couple of undramatic slips in a novel into a main feature of the leading part in a play.[9]

The reformist, sentimental, and melodramatic tastes for such plays were fading rapidly. Shaw rejects Burnett's play but also condemns Dickens' dramatic craft. To Dickens and his contemporaries, the pathos in Jo was acute. To Shaw and many of his contemporaries, such feelings of pity were mere sentiment. With the fading of the theatrical taste for melodramatic emotions came the fading of true appreciation of "Dickens plays"; and to some degree truly felt reaction to Dickens' very novels may also have diminished. In rejecting certain theatrical conventions, we moderns have tended without meaning it to reject also certain of Dickens' novelistic assumptions.

During the first decades of the twentieth century, a last few professional versions of *Bleak House* appeared on stage. Thereafter it began a shadowy theatrical existence in the schoolroom plays of Fanny Johnson, Horace B. Browne, W. H. Skeen, and Daisy Melville Vance—passing from the context of entertainment to that of instruction. None of these brief sketches focuses on Jo, who is dying out. He has but flickered to life again in Jones-Evans's "Death of a Lawyer." This play, focused on Tulkinghorn as a kind of tragic villain, has been broadcast as a radio drama in Australia—without the part of Jo, for whom there wasn't time. But Jones-Evans includes the waif in his script because, he says,

> Jo is DRAMA (a splendid part for a young girl or boy actor) and has nothing to do (so far as I am concerned) with sociological conditions. As a dyed-in-the-wool actor, I regard him (I also feel Dickens did too) as a highly desireable vehicle from the viewpoint. So, with all the arrogance of an artist, made him a *must* as a *tear-jerker*.[10]

Here then is the theatrical motive for including Jo in the play: to move the audience, to make them cry. Jones-Evans is as competent as a playwright as any who has dramatized Dickens. As a proponent of the Lyceum-school of entertainment which, as he knew it, was much closer to the theater of Dickens' time than is most London stagecraft today, Jones-Evans speaks with a certain authority of the theatrical potential in *Bleak*

House. His purpose is to move the audience; Jo is a sure means to that end. Jones-Evans believes what J. P. Burnett and Dion Boucicault understood: Dickens' Jo is the emotional center of the novel. When he dies, the playwrights go immediately to work. When there is a rage for plays based on the novel, most focus on Jo. The waif is the heart of this book, the dramatizers and their enthusiastic audiences seem largely to agree. They thereby indicate the function of Jo in the novel. He is an "emotive" character in a specifically melodramatic nineteenth-century sense.

In the melodrama, or "melody-drama," occasional music heightened and emphasized the emotional effect on the audience of the characters and their situations. Certain tunes were also a kind of "signature" for important characters about whom the audience was to have certain highly stylized feelings of pity, or hatred, or contempt. Burnett carefully used music to try to control his audience's reaction. His manuscript of "Jo" indicates where the author hoped to achieve by music the strongest response in the playgoers. A circle with a dot at its center—and sometimes a line through it or two lines underneath it—was the standard mark for music; and Burnett has carefully used this symbol together with instructions like "Jo's music kept up till drop," and "Jo's tremulo hurry," Burnett's script thereby gives evidence of the dominant intended effect of certain dramatic devices and characters—the suffering child, the lady with a past.

Moreover, Dickens' and Burnett's methods are similar insofar as both are interested in striking effects more than orderly construction. Both seek the most efficient way of moving an audience more than the most elegant way of working out a plot. Both contemporary to and twenty years later than the novel's first publication, plays based on *Bleak House* strongly indicate that Jo proved to be Dickens' most effective single instrument toward the end of tear-jerking.

FIGURE 1
Fanny Janauschek as Lady Dedlock.
By permission of The Billy Rose Theatre Collection / The New York Public
Library at Lincoln Center / Astor, Lenox, and Tilden Foundations.

After which, at 8.15, will be presented a New Drama, in Three Acts, by
J. P. BURNETT, entitled

" JO "

Adapted for the Stage from CHARLES DICKENS' well-known Novel,

BLEAK HOUSE.

CHARACTERS.

Sir Leicester Dedlock   (Sir Leicester is twenty years full measure older
   than my lady; he has a twist of the gout now and then, and walks a
   little stiffly, but is of a worthy presence, ceremonious and stately)
                                                   Mr EDWARD PRICE
Mr Tulkinghorn   (rusty to look at, of the old school, surrounded by a
   mysterious halo of family confidences, an oyster of the old school whom
   nobody can open)   ...   Mr FLOCKTON
Mr Snagsby   (a mild, bald, timid man, with a tendency to meekness
   and obesity)   ...   ..   Mr J. B. RAE
Mr Chadband   (a large yellow man, with a fat smile and a general
   appearance of having a good deal of train oil in his system)
      ..   ..   Mr C. WILMOT
Mr Guppy   (a young man of the name of Guppy)   Mr CHARLES STEYNE
The Coroner   ...   .   Mr BENBROOK
Policeman   ...   .   Mr JOHNSON
The Beadle   ...   .   Mr HARCOURT
Mr Bucket   (Inspector Bucket of the Detective—a stoutly-built, steady-
   looking, sharp-eyed man of about the middle age, with an attentive
   face)   ...   Mr J. P. BURNETT
Jo   (very muddy, very hoarse, and very ragged; " I don't know nothing,
   I don't, but he wos werry good to me he wos ")   Miss JENNIE LEE
Lady Dedlock   (she has beauty still, a fine face and elegant figure—she
   is perfectly well-bred)   ...   Miss LOUISE HIBBERT
Esther   (our Little Woman—Dame Durden)   Miss NELLY HARRIS
Mrs Rouncewell (a fine old lady, handsome, stately, wonderfully neat)
    ..   ...   .   Miss ROBERTSON
Jenny   ...   .   Miss VERNON
Rosa   (dark-eyed shy village beauty)   Miss NORRIS
Guster   (a lean young woman from the workhouse, who has fits, which
   the Parish can't account for)   ..   Miss KATE LEE
Mrs Snagsby   (she manages the money, and acknowledges no respon-
   sibility as to what she thinks fit to provide for dinner)   Miss STEELE
Hortense (My Lady's maid, a Frenchwoman of two and thirty, a large-
   eyed brown woman with black hair, with a feline mouth and a general
   uncomfortable tightness of face)   Miss DOLORES DRUMMOND

FIGURE 2A
Program Notes for the Globe Theatre production of J. P. Burnett's
"Jo," in February 1876. *Dramatis Personae*. "Sir Leicester Dedlock"
(Edward Price) wrote his own "The Life and Death of Jo," produced at
the Theatre Royal, Coventry, in May 1876.

Act I.

Scene 1.—**Room at the Sol's Arms—The Inquest**—" He wos werry good to me, he wos."

Scene 2.—**Street near Piccadilly**— "The Young Man of the name of Guppy."

Scene 3.—**Chesney Wold**—" My Lady at home. "

Scene 4.—**Jo's Crossing**—" She axed me to show her all them there places."

Scene 5.—**Potter's Burial Ground, Russell Court, Drury Lane**— " She guv me a sovereign, and then hooked it."

Act II.

Scene 1.—**Back Parlour at Mr Snagsby's—Mr Bucket's instructions**— " You're to move on."

Scene 2.—**Jo's Crossing**—" Moving on. "

Scene 3.—**Chesney Wold**—" I am your mother, your guilty, conscience-stricken mother. "

Mr Tulkinghorn and My Lady's Maid—" In all these years I never heard the step upon the Ghost's Walk more distinct than it is to-night."

Act 3

Scene 1.—**Chesney Wold**—Springing a mine—Mr Bucket presents his lodger and his evidence.

Scene 2.—**Cook's Court, Lincoln's Inn**—" Moving on. "

Jo and Guster—" I'm a moving on, sir.' Mr Bucket does his duty.

Scene 3.—**TOM-ALL-ALONE'S—Death of Jo**—" The carts shaken all to pieces."

The Light is come upon the Dark Benighted Way.

The New Scenery painted expressly for this production by Mr W. BRUCE SMITH, realising the exact spots mentioned by CHARLES DICKENS in the novel of " Bleak House," and the original illustrations by PHIZ.

Costumes by Mr HARRISON.   Stage Appointments by Mr LYONS.
Perruquier, Mr CLARKSON.

The Orchestra, under the direction of Mr EDWARD SOLOMON, will perform the following selection of Music :—

OVERTURE	...	" La Couronne d'Or "		Herman
OVERTURE	...	..	" Bleak House "	...	Edward Solomon
WALTZ	...	...	" Doctrinen "		...	Strauss
QUADRILLE	...	...	" Vagabond "		Coote

NOTICE.

Mr. F ANCIS FAIRLIE has much pleasure in announcing that on EASTER MONDAY NEXT (April 17th), Miss **ADA CAVENDISH** will commence an engagement at this Theatre, when will be produced " **MISS GWILT**," a Drama in Five Acts, by WILKIE COLLINS, altered by the Author, for production on the Stage, from his Novel of " **ARMADALE**." The Play will be produced under the Author s direction, with a Powerful Cast, and completely New Scenery and Appointments.

FIGURE 2B
Program Notes for "Jo" (continued). *Scenario.*

FIGURE 3

Jennie Lee.
By Permission of The Billy Rose Theatre Collection / The New York
Public Library at Lincoln Center / Astor, Lenox, and Tilden Foundations.

FIGURE 4

Jennie Lee as Jo in a New York City production, *circa* 1881, probably at the Fourteenth Street Theater, or at Haverly's in Brooklyn.

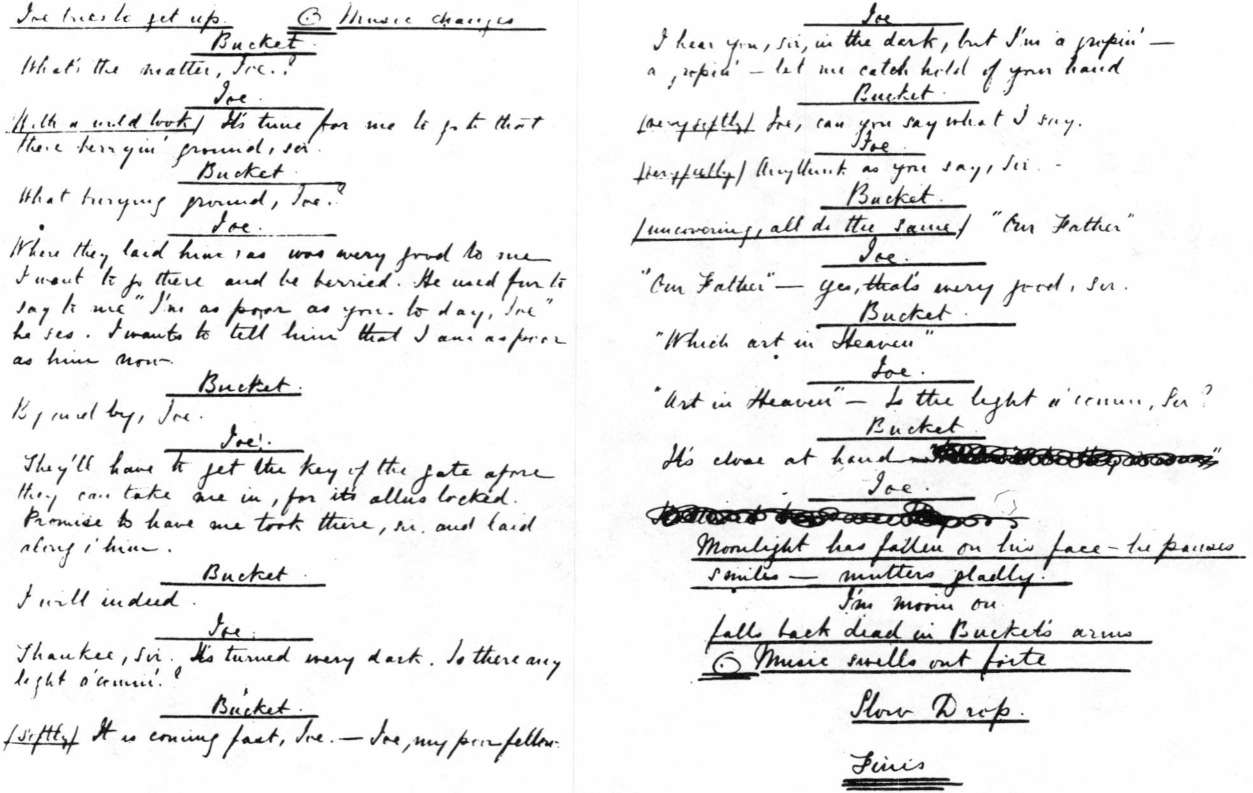

FIGURE 5

The last two leaves of Burnett's manuscript of "Jo," showing marks for
music, as well as an attempt to appease the censorship of the Examiner of
Plays by omitting part of the Lord's Prayer.
By permission of The British Library.

Concluding with Special Edition of CHARLES DICKENS' "BLEAK HOUSE," Dramatised for Little NELLY HOWITT, entitled **POOR.**

POOR, JO.

"He wos wery good to me, he wos."
JO, in "BLEAK HOUSE."

Only a waif on the waters of Life;
His existence ignored in the world's busy strife;
Homeless and hungry, neglected, forlorn,—
But a type still of thousands that daily are born,
Rough in his language, his manner as well;
Of father, or mother, or friends he can't tell.
Born of the outcast, and cradled in woe,
In this little starved creature we find

All day he toils at a crossing for bread,
At night in some doorway that's bleak rests his head,
If rest it be called, in the desolate street.
With his slumbers disturbed by the man on the beat,
Heart-broken—tired—for pity he prays;
But "Move on" is the order, and he obeys.
So stern is the law, and hard him upon,
Sad child of the gutter, he still must MOVE ON.

Mr Tulkinghorn, a Solicitor, ...	Mr H. ASHLEY
Mr Chadband, ...	Mr H. HILL
Inspector Buckett, ...	Mr T. C. HOWITT
Nemo, a Mystery, ...	Mr LESLIE SCOTT
Richard Carstone, ...	Mr M. LOVE
Mr Snagsby, ...	Mr H. CREAMER
Sir Leicester Deadlock, ...	Mr BRANDON
Jo, the Crossing-Sweeper, ...	Little NELLY HOWITT

The performance of this child is simply marvellous. Her conception of Dickens' little waif is truly artistic and natural.

Lady Deadlock, ...	Miss ADA DOWSING
Esther Summerson, ...	Miss K. HILL
Mrs Snagsby, ...	Miss CREAMER
Hortense, ...	Miss M. STODDART
Mrs Rouncewell, ...	Miss JESSIE SMEATON
Guster, ...	Petite MARIE VERONA

FIGURE 6

Detail of a program for a production of "Poor Jo" at the Royal Princess, Edinburgh, May 1882.

By permission of The Billy Rose Theatre Collection / The New York Public Library at Lincoln Center / Astor, Lenox, and Tilden Foundations.

HANDLIST OF BLEAK HOUSE DRAMAS

TITLE(S) AND NUMBER OF ACTS [in square brackets appear variations in wording.]	AUTHOR(S)	PERFORMANCE(S): THEATRE(S), PLACE(S), DATE(S) (Unless otherwise indicated, the place is London.)
1. Bleak House; or, the Wandering Spirit [Spectre] of the Ghost Walk (2)	George Dibdin Pitt	Pavilion 4 June 1853; Marylebone 4 July 1853
2. Bleak House (4)	Austin Lee and/or John H. Wilkins	City of London 6 June 1853
3. Bleak House (4)	John Brougham	Wallack's Lyceum, NYC 10 Oct to ca 13 Nov 1853; Arch Street Theatre, Phila, PA 15 Nov 1853; Burton's Tripler Hall, NYC 11 July 1859
4. Bleak House; or, The Ghost Walk (2) [The Adventures of Jo the Crossing Sweeper]	Unknown	Strand 29 May 1854; Bower Saloon, Stangate 2 Sept 1854
5. Chesney Wold (4 or 5) [Lady Dedlock and Hortense] [Bleak House] (4)	Henry Randle and/or Fanny Janauschek	Ford's Grand Opera House Baltimore, MD 22 Feb 1873; Boston Museum, Boston, MASS March 1873; Booth's, NYC 23 Feb to 14 March 1874; California Theatre, San Francisco, CA 7 to 18 June 1875; De Bar's Grand Opera House, St. Louis, MO 1875; Productions in Cleveland,

HANDLIST OF BLEAK HOUSE DRAMAS

WARRANT FOR ASSERTING EXISTENCE, PUBLICATION DATA, REMARKS (The ms. # refers to the Lord Chamberlain's plays. Titles of standard reference works appear only in the first reference to each.)

Ms. 52940M. Morley. The version first produced. Not published. James W. Elphinstone and Frederick Neale managed the Pavilion and therefore almost surely did not write the competing play at the City of London (#2), as Nicoll indicates.

Ms. 52940K. The version the Lord Chamberlain first received and licensed. Not published. The manuscript gives Lee as author; but Morley gives Wilkins as "dramatist in ordinary" to the City of London.

Odell in *Annals of the New York Stage*; Sherman in *Drama Cyclopaedia*; Ireland in *Records of the New York Stage*; Brown in *A History of the New York Stage*; Hughes in *History of the American Drama*; Morley. Not published. The first play based on the whole novel. Boucicault helped to produce it; Laura Keene played Lady Dedlock. It may also have played Boston.

Ms. 52947R. Morley; Nicoll. The first version censored. Not published. The Stangate production had the alternate title indicated.

Ms. in Houghton (Harvard) Theatre collection; Odell; Brown; Pierce; Morley; program at Lincoln Center; U.S. copyright (#12639) to Frederick J. Pillot (Janauschek's husband) on 14 Nov 1876, for "Lady Dedlock and Hortense," authored by Janauschek. Not published. Henry Randle holds no U.S. dramatic copyright, but may have played Jo in Boston in 1873 and is alleged author of "Chesney Wold" starring Janauschek in program at Lincoln Center and in review of #27 in Houghton Collection. 2/8454

In the Baltimore production, "Jo, who thinks that name quite long enough for him," was played by "Miss L. Rich." In California Jennie Lee played Jo, which led to #7 by Burnett. This derivative play in turn had a great many imitations. See below.

The first production in Baltimore had the title "Chesney Wold," as did the New York premiere at Booth's in 1874. But the *New York Times* advertises "Lady Dedlock and Hortense" for that same Booth's (1874) production; so two titles referred to one production. In Nov. 1877 the Broadway played "Lady

TITLE(S) AND NUMBER OF ACTS [in square brackets appear variations in wording.]	AUTHOR(S)	PERFORMANCE(S): THEATER(S), PLACE(S), DATE(S) (Unless otherwise indicated, the place is London.)
5. Chesney Wold (4 or 5) [Lady Dedlock and Hortense] [Bleak House] (4) (cont.)		New Orleans, Providence, & Canada; Boston Theatre, Boston, MASS 30 Oct to 11 Nov 1876; Academy of Music, Buffalo, NY 1876; Broadway, NYC 17 March 1877; Boston Theatre, Boston, MASS 2 to 16 April 1877; Broadway, NYC 12 to 23 Nov 1877; De Bar's, St. Louis, MO 1877; Hooley's, Chicago, IL 2 March (1878?); Globe, Boston, MASS 1879; Park, Boston, MASS 9 Feb 1881; Booth's, NYC 15 to 19 March 1881; Park, Boston, MASS 30 April 1881; Union Square, NYC 24 Oct 1881; Windsor, NYC 21 Nov 1881; Park, Brooklyn, NY 13 & 16 Dec 1881; Windsor, NYC 22 & 23 Nov 1882; Third Avenue, NYC 22 Dec 1882; Grand Opera House, NYC 19 & 24 Nov 1883 & 14 Jan 1884;

WARRANT FOR ASSERTING EXISTENCE, PUBLICATION DATA,
REMARKS (The ms. # refers to the Lord Chamberlain's plays. Titles of
standard reference works appear only in the first reference to each.)

Dedlock and Hortense'' on the 12th and "Chesney Wold" on the 21st and
23rd. These were variant plays or merely variant titles. The *Times* and Brown
refer to productions in 1881, 1884, & 1886 as "Bleak House," which became
the preferred title.

There were more than forty productions of these "Bleak House" plays over
a period of twenty years. Like the title, the text may have varied. But I here
show all plays featuring Janauschek, who played Lady Dedlock and Hortense
as twin roles for fifteen years, with a wide variety of actresses playing Jo. Her
success inspired several other plays—see #'s 19, 27, 29, 34, 35.

TITLE(S) AND NUMBER OF ACTS [in square brackets appear variations in wording.]	AUTHOR(S)	PERFORMANCE(S): THEATER(S), PLACE(S), DATE(S) (Unless otherwise indicated, the place is London.)
5. Chesney Wold (4 or5) [Lady Dedlock and Hortense] [Bleak House] (4) (cont.)		Star, NYC 5 to 12 May 1884; Grand Opera House, Brooklyn, NY 12 to 19 May 1884; Wahle Opera House, Buffalo, NY 1884; Park, Boston, MASS 1 Dec 1885; Grand Opera House, NYC 5, 6 & 8 Jan 1886; Windsor, NYC 5 & 7 Oct 1886; Grand Opera House, NYC 7 to 12 Feb 1887;
		Chestnut Street, Phila, PA 14 Feb 1887; Theatre Comique, NYC April 1887;
		Boston Museum, Boston, MASS 30 April into May 1888; [Cincinnati] Sept 1888;
		Albaugh's Grand Opera House, Washington, DC 8 Sept 1890; Miner's (?) or People's (?), NYC 11 May 1891; DeGive's Opera House Atlanta, GA 4 Jan (1892?); Coates Opera House, Kansas City, MO 29 Oct 1893; People's (?) NYC 2 Aug 1894; Bowery, NYC 13 Aug 1894

WARRANT FOR ASSERTING EXISTENCE, PUBLICATION DATA, REMARKS (The ms. # refers to the Lord Chamberlain's plays. Titles of standard reference works appear only in the first reference to each.)

The Chestnut Street, Philadelphia, version in 1887 featured Janauschek and "Poor Joe, a waif and street sweeper," impersonated by "Miss Lavinia Shannon."

"Bleak House" at the Boston Museum in 1888 starred Janauschek. In *Old Boston Museum Days*, Kate Ryan describes herself playing Esther to Janauschek's Lady Dedlock. A program at Lincoln Center gives "Miss Miriam O'Leary" as "Jo, a waif of the streets."

Lazenby, in "Stage Versions of Dickens Novels in America," says that Janauschek abandoned "Bleak House" in 1888. Jane Coombs played Lady Dedlock in Cincinnati in 1888 and in Washington in 1890. Morley puts Coombs in both Hortense and Lady Dedlock at Miner's in 1891; but Brown says the house was in ruins then.

Coomb's play is not identical to Janauschek's. Lazenby suspects that Coomb's play derived from Simpson's (#6); but Hortense, whom Coombs often played, is missing from Simpson's version.

TITLE(S) AND NUMBER OF ACTS [in square brackets appear variations in wording.]	AUTHOR(S)	PERFORMANCE(S): THEATER(S), PLACE(S), DATE(S) (Unless otherwise indicated, the place is London.)
6. Lady Dedlock's Secret (4)	John Palgrave Simpson	Amphitheatre, Liverpool 18 March 1874; Opera House, Aberdeen 3 April 1874; Theatre Royal, Windsor 28 Nov 1883; Opera Comique 26 March 1884
7. Jo; or, Bleak House (3)	J. P. Burnett	Prince of Wales, Liverpool 8 Nov 1875; Globe 21 Feb 1876; Westminster Acquarium Easter, 1876; Globe 11 Sept 1876 to spring 1877; Gaiety 1879; At "all the principal theatres in the provinces," says Pascoe; Fourteenth Street (Haverly's) NYC 29 Aug 1881; Haverly's, Brooklyn, NY 27 Sept to 2 Oct 1881; Baldwin, San Francisco, CA 7 Nov 1881; Strand 18 Feb 1885; Travelled to Australia, South Africa, India, China; Drury Lane 13 May 1896;
		Lyric 7 Feb 1921

WARRANT FOR ASSERTING EXISTENCE, PUBLICATION DATA,
REMARKS (The ms. # refers to the Lord Chamberlain's plays. Titles of
standard reference works appear only in the first reference to each.)

Kitton; Eldredge in *Stage Cyclopaedia*; Morley; Nicoll; Fawcett. London and
New York: French (#1822), n.d. Kitton thought this a good play and Morley
notes it. Not in the Lord Chamberlain's plays.

Ms. 53162B. Kitton; Odell; Brown; Eldredge; Broadbent in *Annals of the
Liverpool Stage*; Pascoe in *The Dramatic List*; Morley; Pierce; Nicoll. Not
published. The most famous version; it ran for six months and over 100 performances at the Globe, starring Jennie Lee as Jo. The series of performances
shown here is highly incomplete.
The *Athenaeum* for 26 Feb 1876 says,

> Miss Jennie Lee, a young lady known principally in burlesque, plays the
> part of Jo with a realism and a pathos difficult to surpass. . . . in get-
> up and in acting the character was thoroughly realized; and the hoarse
> voice, the slouching, dejected gait, and the movement as of some hunted
> animal, were admirably exhibited.

"Jo" was widely imitated. See #'s 8, 9, 10, 11, 13, 14, 15, 16, 17, 20, 21, 22,
23, 24, 25, 26, 27, 31, 32.

In her eighties, Jennie Lee played Jo one last time at the Lyric to raise money
for a children's hospital.

TITLE(S) AND NUMBER OF ACTS [in square brackets appear variations in wording.]	AUTHOR(S)	PERFORMANCE(S): THEATER(S), PLACE(S), DATE(S) (Unless otherwise indicated, the place is London.)
8. Bleak House; or, Poor Jo (3 or 4)	George Lander	Pavilion 25 March 1876; Elephant and Castle 8 April 1876; Globe 19 Aug to ca 10 Sept 1876; Marylebone 1876; [London] 1890
9. Joe, the Waif of the Streets	Richard H. Cox	
10. Jo the [Only a] Waif; or, The Dedlock Mystery (2)	Herbert Rhoyds	Greenwich 24 April 1876; Topeka, Kansas 1890
11. Bleak House; or, Poor Jo [the Crossing Sweeper] (2)	Eliza Thorne	Alexandria Opera House Sheffield 28 April 1876
12. Only a Waif; or, The Dedlock Mystery	Unknown	Greenwich 4 May 1876
13. The Life and Death of Joe (4)	Edward Price	Theatre Royal, Coventry 15 May 1876
14. Dickens' Jo; or, The Dedlock Disgrace (3)	John Wylsone	Victoria 12 to 25 Aug 1876
15. Jo	Frederick Hazelton	Britannia, Hoxton 13 Sept 1876

WARRANT FOR ASSERTING EXISTENCE, PUBLICATION DATA, REMARKS (The ms. # refers to the Lord Chamberlain's plays. Titles of standard reference works appear only in the first reference to each.)

Ms. 53163Q. Kitton; Eldredge; Morley; Pierce; Fawcett; program at Lincoln Center. London: Dicks (#288), ca 1883.

Pierce. U.S. copyright (#4902) to Edward T. Anthony in San Francisco, 22 April 1876. Not published. Gagey in *The San Francisco Stage* mentions no such play. Lazenby suggests it was never produced.

Ms. 53166F. Eldredge; Sherman; Pierce; Nicoll; Fawcett. Not published. Clara Dillon played Jo at the Greenwich.

Ms. 53165M. Eldredge; Pierce; Morley; Nicoll. Not published.

Morley; Nicoll. Not published. A burlesque of the Rhoyds play (#10).

Ms. 53166D. Morley; Nicoll. Not published. With Jennie Lee, Price had earlier played Sir Leicester Dedlock at the Globe. Here Clara Dillon joined him to play Jo, moving from the Greenwich (#10).

Ms. 53170E. Nicoll. Not published.

Morley; but not in the Lord Chamberlain's Plays, Nicoll, nor the Pettingell collection, which derived from the Britannia. Not published See # 16.

TITLE(S) AND NUMBER OF ACTS [in square brackets appear variations in wording.]	AUTHOR(S)	PERFORMANCE(S): THEATER(S), PLACE(S), DATE(S) (Unless otherwise indicated, the place is London.)
16. Jo	J. B. Johnstone	
17. Poor Jo (2)	Terry Hurst	Surrey 1876
18. Jo v Jo (1)	Frank W. Green & Oswald Allen	Surrey 25 Sept to 9 Oct 1876
19. Poor Little Jo	G. Murray Wood	Park, Camden Town 2 July 1877; Park, NYC (?) 1877
20. Poor Jo (5)	Benjamin Edward Woolf	[Boston] 11 Dec 1876; Union Square, NYC 23 July to 11 Aug 1877; Academy of Music, NYC 11 Dec 1879; Aberle's, NYC 19 Jan 1880; [Chicago] ca 1880
21. The Dedlock Secret (4)	Frank Carlos (Frank Carlos Griffith)	
22. Tom All Alone [Alone's] (4)	Henry A. Weaver	Booth's, NYC 11 March 1878; Bowery, NYC 19 April 1878; Wood's (Broadway), NYC 26 Nov 1878

WARRANT FOR ASSERTING EXISTENCE, PUBLICATION DATA, REMARKS (The ms. # refers to the Lord Chamberlain's plays. Titles of standard reference works appear only in the first reference to each.)

Pettingell ms. Probably from Britannia papers. Not in the Lord Chamberlain's plays nor Nicoll. Not published. See # 15.

Kitton; Pierce; Fawcett; not in Nicoll, Morley, nor the Lord Chamberlain's plays. Not published.

Ms. 53172C. Eldredge; Morley. Not published. A burlesque of #17 and other Jo plays.

Pierce; Morley; Fawcett; Nicoll. Not in the Lord Chamberlain's plays, Odell, nor Brown. Not published. The NYC production may be a ghost.

Brown; Morley; Odell; Sherman; Lincoln Center File. Not published. The Union Square production starred Mary Cary as Jo, using—reports Lazenby—Negro rather than Cockney dialect.

U.S. copyright (#14263) to F. Carlos in Boston, 22 Dec 1876. Pierce. Hixon & Hennessee in *Nineteenth Century American Drama* mention this author but not this play. Not published.

U.S. copyright (#21601) to Henry A. Weaver on 9 Feb 1877; Pierce; Morley; not in Odell nor Brown. Not published. Lazenby reports that the boy actor H. S. Wood played Jo.

TITLE(S) AND NUMBER OF ACTS [in square brackets appear variations in wording.]	AUTHOR(S)	PERFORMANCE(S): THEATER(S), PLACE(S), DATE(S) (Unless otherwise indicated, the place is London.)
23. Poor Jo	Henry Davenport	Royal, Southampton 25 Feb 1878; Royal Princess, Edinburgh May 1882
24. Joe the Poor Waif; or, The Mystery of Chesney Wold	Kessie Wood	Rotunda, Liverpool 4 July 1881
25. Move On; or, Jo the Crossing Sweeper [Outcast] (3)	James Mortimer	Grand, Islington 1 Sept 1883; Lyric 5 July 1892
26. Bleak House (4)	George A. Hughes & A. Charles Bickley	Grand, Walsall 28 Sept 1892
27. Bleak House; or, Events in the Life of Jo	Oswald Brand	Grand, Islington 1 June 1903
28. Bleak House	James Stillwell & Wilfred Benson	Royal, Margate 23 & 26 Nov 1903
29. Bleak House (4)	A. Hale	
30. The Philanthropist	Fanny Johnson	
31. Poor Joe	Unknown	Holloway Empire 3 March 1911

WARRANT FOR ASSERTING EXISTENCE, PUBLICATION DATA,
REMARKS (The ms. # refers to the Lord Chamberlain's plays. Titles of
standard reference works appear only in the first reference to each.)

Eldredge; Pierce; Morley; Nicoll; Fawcett; Lincoln Center File. Not published.
Miss Woodyer played Jo in Southampton. Nelly Howitt played the urchin in
Edinburgh.

Eldredge; Pierce; Morley; Nicoll; Fawcett. Not published. Possibly related to
#19. Kessie Wood played Jo.

Kitton; Eldredge; Morley; not in the Lord Chamberlain's plays. Not published.
Lyric revival titled "Jo the Outcast."

Ms. 53508K. Morley; Nicoll. Not published. This version cannibalizes Lander's
(#8).

Eldredge; Pierce; Morley; Pettingell collection (where Arthur Williams tipped in
cast list); Fawcett. Not published. Kate Brand played Jo. Review in Houghton
(Harvard) Theatre collection alleges that the play derived from Henry Randle's
"Chesney Wold" (#5).

Eldredge; Pierce; Morley. Clipping in Houghton (Harvard) Theatre collection.
Not published.

U.S. copyright (#8422) to Mrs. Edmund Maurice, London, on 26 April 1906.
Not published.

In *Dramatic Scenes from English Literature*. London: Arnold, 1903, pp.
149–161.

Morley. The last professional production that Morley notes. Not published.

TITLE(S) AND NUMBER OF ACTS [in square brackets appear variations in wording.]	AUTHOR(S)	PERFORMANCE(S): THEATER(S), PLACE(S), DATE(S) (Unless otherwise indicated, the place is London.)
32. Poor Jo	Peter Davey	Royal County, Kingston-on-Thames 8 April 1912
33. Mr George's Shooting Gallery	Horace B. Browne	
Mrs Snagsby's Guests	Browne	
Mr Guppy's Proposal	Browne	
34. [The Great] Lady Dedlock (4)	Paul Kester	[United States] Autumn 1923; Ambassador, NYC 31 Dec 1928 to Spring 1929
35. Lady Dedlock's Secret (3)	Jerome Lejay Collamore	
36. Bleak House (3)	W. H. Skeen	
37. Breaking the News	Daisy Melville Vance	
Inspector Bucket	Vance	
38. Lady Dedlock's Secret	Miss Evans	
39. Bleak House	Tom Mason	Palmer's Green 1936
40. Bleak House	Robert Wetzel	
41. Bleak House (3)	Gladys Waterer	Broadstairs Dec 1950

WARRANT FOR ASSERTING EXISTENCE, PUBLICATION DATA, REMARKS (The ms. # refers to the Lord Chamberlain's plays. Titles of standard reference works appear only in the first reference to each.)

A typescript in the Pettingell Collection. Not published.

In *Short Plays from Dickens: for the Use of Amateurs and School Dramatic Societies*. London: Chapman & Hall, 1908, 1916, pp. 162-174.

Ibid., pp. 157-161.

Ibid., pp. 151-156.

U.S. copyright to Paul Kester on 19 April 1920; Morley; Sherman. Not published. *Best Plays of 1928-1929*. Forty performances 1928-1929.

U.S. copyright to Helena Benedict Collamore in Pasadena, CA, on 8 Dec 1924. Not published.

One of a series, *Scenes from Dickens*. London: French, 1924, 1927. Includes "Lady Dedlock's Secret," "Breaking the News" (re: Jellybys), & "Discipline" (re: Trooper George).

Morley, N.P.: Unknown, 1935. "A snippet," says Morley.

Ibid., another "snippet."

Morley. N.P.: Unknown, 1936.

Morley. Amateur production. Not published.

U.S. copyright 15 Dec 1949. TV serial.

Dickensian notice (Dec 1950); Morley thought this Dickens Festival production "first class."

TITLE(S) AND NUMBER OF ACTS [in square brackets appear variations in wording.]	AUTHOR(S)	PERFORMANCE(S): THEATER(S), PLACE(S), DATE(S) (Unless otherwise indicated, the place is London.)
42. Bleak House (3)	Emlyn Williams	[Cardiff & Edinburgh] Aug 1952; Ambassador, NYC 1952; Bijou, NYC 20 April to 8 May 1953; Great Northern, Chicago, IL 15 April (1954?)
43. Dickens' Bleak House	Paul Gregory	
44. Bleak House (3)	John Patrick (John Patrick Goggan)	[New York] Fall (1955?)
45. Lady Dedlock's Secret	Walter Carl Brown	
46. Scenes from Bleak House	Jane Bacon	Portland Hall, London Polytechnic 30 April 1959
47. Death of a Lawyer (3)	Eric Jones-Evans	On radio, Australia 10 Sept 1961; Radio New Zealand Nov 1961; Radio South Africa Dec 1961; Plymouth 12 May 1970; Radio South Africa March 1976; Stanford, Lincolnshire Nov 1976; Malta June 1977
48. Bleak House	Unknown	Royal Court Spring 1977

WARRANT FOR ASSERTING EXISTENCE, PUBLICATION DATA, REMARKS (The ms. # refers to the Lord Chamberlain's plays. Titles of standard reference works appear only in the first reference to each.)

Fawcett; Lincoln Center File; *Best Plays of 1952–1953*. Not published. A one-man show. At the Bijou it ran 24 performances. Kronenberger says, " . . . impersonating thirty-six Dickens characters . . . if the result was scarcely *Bleak House*, it was often pleasant."

U.S. copyright 31 Dec 1953. Movie version.

U.S. copyright 25 April 1951; Morley; Lincoln Center file.

U.S. copyright to Walter Carl Brown on 17 Dec 1959. A TV play.

Dickensian notice (1959).

Morley. Southampton: Wilson, 1962. Available through French.

Confirmed by Royal Court personnel.

NOTES

1. F. Dubrez Fawcett, *Dickens the Dramatist: on Stage, Screen, and Radio* (London: Allen, 1952), ch. iv.

2. Dorothy Pierce, "Special Bibliography: The Stage Versions of Dickens' Novels," *Bulletin of Bibliography*, Jan. 22, 1937, 10; May 8, 1937, 30–32; Sept. 13, 1937, 52–54. Malcolm Morley, in a series of articles details professional productions in England and the United States before 1940, *The Dickensian*, 38–53 (1942–1957), *passim*. See also Clive Hurst, *Dickens Playbills in the Bodleian Library* (Oxford: Oxford Microforms, 1981).

3. The list derives from Pierce, Morley, and the *Catalogue of Additions to the Manuscripts: Plays Submitted to the Lord Chamberlain* (London: Trustees of the British Museum, 1964). See also *The Register of the Lord Chamberlain's Plays*, or the "Day Books." These and the manuscripts themselves tell us when a play was submitted, by whom it was read, when it was licensed, and whatever was suppressed. Also invaluable is Allardyce Nicoll, "Hand-List of Plays: 1850–1900," *A History of England Drama 1660–1900*, vol. V (Cambridge: Cambridge University Press, 1946), pp. 229–850. See especially Morley, "*Bleak House* Scene," *The Dickensian*, 49 (1953), 175–182. The "Handlist of *Bleak House* Plays" appended to the present article is certainly not the last word on such works.

4. Thomas Edgar Pemberton, *Charles Dickens and the Stage* (London: George Redway, 1888). S. J. Adair Fitzgerald, *Dickens and the Drama* (London: Chapman and Hall, 1910). J. B. van Amerogen, *The Actor in Dickens* (London: Cecil Palmer, 1926). Fawcett, *op.cit.* Earle Davis, *The Flint and the Flame: The Artistry of Charles Dickens* (Columbia: University of Missouri Press, 1963). Robert Garis, *The Dickens Theater: A Reassessment of the Novels* (Oxford: Clarendon Press, 1965). William F. Axton, *Circle of Fire: Dickens' Vision and Style and the Popular Victorian Theater* (Lexington: University of Kentucky Press, 1966). David Parker, "Dickens's Archness," *The Dickensian*, 67 (1971), 149–158.

5. *Bleak House*, ed. Norman Page (New York: Penguin, 1977).

6. Morley, "*Bleak House* Scene," *The Dickensian*, 49 (1963), 178.

7. *Ibid.*, p. 180.

8. *Dickensiana: A Bibliography* (London: G. Redway, 1886), p. 379.

9. Shaw, *Our Theatres in the Nineties*, vol. XXIV of *The Collected Works of Bernard Shaw* (New York: Wise, 1931), pp. 140–143.

10. Unpublished letter to author.

A Tale for Two Dramatists

Richard J. Dunn

In his "The French Revolution as *Theatrum Mundi*," Joseph Butwin does not mention either Carlyle or Dickens but shows how the first historians of the French Revolution often spoke of it as a play. Butwin also points out how participants in the revolution were aware that their world had become a theater.[1] That Carlyle's and Dickens' works often regard revolutionary figures as actors, describe crowds of people as engaged audiences, and treat many historical events as performances is evident to any reader of *The French Revolution* and *A Tale of Two Cities*. As Michael Goldberg has said, the dramatic mode of these books is a natural stylistic concomitant of the writers' view of the revolution as a process working itself out in moral terms.[2] For Carlyle and Dickens the French Revolution was indeed a great drama, and each attempted to write about it dramatically. I am aware that subject matter was not the sole determinant of style for either author, but in this paper I want briefly to consider how each regarded the revolution as a great drama yet also took into account the grave dangers of mere theatrical performance in the revolution.

There is, as Carlyle especially recognized, an essential duplicity in the words "drama," "theatrical," "actor." Throughout his works he, on the one hand, celebrates history as cosmic drama and insists upon action and articulation as primary modes of heroism. On the other hand, he scorns the merely histrionic and artificial, the masquerading and mimicry of a people unable to enact their true roles. In his history of the French Revolution Carlyle stresses the distinction between significant and insignificant drama, meaningful and ineffectual action. He describes the uprising as a great dramatic event, "a great Phenomenon . . . a *transcendental* one, overstepping all rules and experience; the crowning Phenomenon of our Modern Time."[3] Much was only noise and chaos, and, as Carlyle remarks, the Bastille seemed to fall by miraculous sound. Noisy phases of fever-

117

frenzy burst forth in Carlyle's account, but he argues that the frenzy burns itself out so a new order may arise. Behind this claim is Carlyle's faith in the irrevocable word, the action completed. "What," he asks, "is this Infinite of Things itself, which men name Universe, but an Action, a sum-total of Actions and Activities?" (III, iii, 183). Such might serve as the definition of a superb play, for that also is a sum of actions, unified by some sort of meaning. In Carlyle's great life drama, heroic speech and action are both enactments of transcendental faith. To Carlyle's thinking, the quality of the play is the thing to be watched. Imposture, masquerading as the real thing, is the great evil, and the penultimate paragraph of Carlyle's history celebrates a fiery purging of Imposture—"one red sea of Fire, wild-billowing, enwraps the World." So describing the result of the revolution, Carlyle maintains his moral that "all grows and seeks and endures its destinies" (III, i, 103).

So much for the grand outcome. Along the way Carlyle often attempts to distinguish true from false, genuine human drama from artificial and mechanical performance, meaning from nonmeaning. He is most self-conscious of this effort about half way through his history, in the chapter titled "Symbolic." He begins the chapter pointing out the naturalness of all symbolic representation: life, says Carlyle, is the act and word striving to make visible a "Celestial invisible Force." How best to do it? "With sincerity if possible; failing that, with theatricality, which . . . also may have its meaning."

For an author ever so vigilant against sham and so impatient with mere performance—those wearers of costumes and dancers on ropes—Carlyle here seems surprisingly tolerant in his recognition that often we have "Imagination herself flagging under the reality; and all noblest Ceremony as yet not grown ceremonial but solemn, significant to the outmost fringe." His reasoning seems to be that intent may be sincere even when the performance or ceremony is questionable. "No Nation," he continues, "will throw by its work, and deliberately go out to make a scene without meaning something thereby." Moreover, "no scenic individual, with knavish hypocritical views, will take the trouble to *soliloquize* a scene." He grants that "scenic exhibition" is more natural to French than to English people, and he postulates that the "theatricality of a People goes in a compound ratio: ratio indeed of their trustfulness, sociability, fervency; but then also of their excitability, of their porosity, . . . or say, of their explosiveness, hot-flashing" (II, i, 47–48). Viewed in this way, much human theatricality is pardonable for Carlyle, because he regards it as "the passionate utterance of a tongue with which sincerity stammers; of a head with which insincerity babbles,—having gone distracted." Yet contrasting all these pitiable performances are what Carlyle reveres as "unpremeditated outbursts of Nature. . . emitted from the great everliving heart of Nature herself: what figure *they* will assume is unspeakably significant" (II, i, 49).

The sound and fury of revolution often seem to lack significance; confusion and destruction seem to reign in Carlyle's description of the revolutionary cycle as the violent, seldom satisfactorily articulated overthrow of insincerity and imposture. But the great drama is apocalyptic, and in conclusion Carlyle celebrates the end of the "dominion of IMPOSTURE" with "the images all run into amorphous Corinthian brass" (III, vii, 323). The Biblical suggestion is apt, for in making his point about honest human performance, Carlyle throughout has opposed the hypocritical and deceitful, the evil of sham. To see and to act only in part but out of good faith is the most that can sometimes be accomplished in a tumultuous time, and thus Carlyle well may write with a hint of the forebearance Paul recommended to the Corinthians. I realize that wrath more than forebearance characterizes Carlyle's apocalyptic voice, for he pulls no punches in damning the Empire of Imposture—"ha! what see I?—all the *Gigs* of Creation: all, all! Wo is me! Never since Pharoah's Chariots, in the Red Sea of water, was there wreck of Wheel-vehicles like this in the Sea of Fire. Desolate, as ashes, as gases, shall they wander in the wind" (III, vii, 322).

To Carlyle, then, the grand phenomenon of the French Revolution was a spectacular dramatic event in human history. Its violence may point up the hazard of spontaneity, but its lesson is clear: "the beginning of man's doom is, that vision be withdrawn from him; that he sees not the reality, but a false spectrum of the reality" (III, iii, 138). The dramatic struggle his book presents is one of anarchy (revolutionists acting without clear vision) versus an intolerable posturing authority. At this level the opposition is absolute, and the play as clear-cut as melodrama. But in the world view of Carlyle there is more complication through a sense of tragic division between mere human theatricality and the "everliving Heart of Nature." Strain between artifice and truth remains evident in Carlyle's concluding prophetic statement:

> For whatsoever once sacred things become hollow jargons, yet while the Voice of Man speaks with Man, hast thou not there the living fountain out of which all sacrednesses sprang, and yet will spring? Man, by the nature of him, is definable as "an incarnated Word." Ill stands it with me if I have spoken falsely: thine also it was to hear truly Farewell.   (III, vii, 323)

The curtain is down but the curtain speech reverberates with the philosophy behind Carlyle's own performance as he concludes self-consciously (almost like an actor stepping to the front at the end of a play) and sincerely to underscore the value of the transcending word.

In *A Tale of Two Cities* the sense of performance, especially in the dramatic climax, is often more overt than any philosophy behind it. Dickens came to the novel fresh from amateur theatricals; the idea for the rebirth theme comes from the stage as well as from urgencies in his private life. As Sylvère Monod has said, Dickens in *A Tale of Two Cities* had an actor's sense of participating in a chosen role.[4] Other commentators have noticed many of the novel's dramatic devices—G. Robert Stange thinks highly of Dickens' use of tableaux, and he discusses a number of the scenic and picturesque elements.[5] John Kucich acknowledges the book's serious application of melodrama[6]; K. J. Fielding regards the *Tale* as Dickens' attempt at romantic tragedy.[7]

Rather than to point again to many of the dramatic devices and consider their effectiveness, I want to indicate how *A Tale of Two Cities* incorporates Carlyle's sense of the greater drama, the revolution as a "great Phenomenon." Consider, first, that letter in which Dickens discusses the kind of book he is writing. He speaks of

> a *picturesque* story, rising in every chapter with characters true to nature, but whom the story itself should express, more than they should express themselves, by dialogue. I mean, in other words, that I fancied a story of incident might be written, in place of the odious stuff that is written under that pretense. . . .[8]

It is questionable whether Dickens was more dramatic here than in some other novels, but he certainly was more austere in style.[9] The key issue is his commitment was more austere in style.[9] The key issue is his commitment to characters "true to nature." In this he directly follows Carlyle, for his insistence upon truth to nature reiterates Carlyle's stress upon sincerity. In having story dominate character, Dickens also follows Carlyle by writing history with a controlling thesis about the tide of events cumulatively enforcing a lesson. The sum of events, greater than any of those innumerable biographies Carlyle elsewhere defined as history, is more important than the story of any character caught up in those events, even than the romantically tragic story of Sydney Carton.

For Dickens, as for Carlyle, there is meaning and connectedness in the scheme of things. Proof of that in *A Tale of Two Cities* depends mainly upon the Carton–Darnay–Manette domestic story where coincidence figures so prominently. Cringe though many readers do because of the sentimental and melodramatic aspects of this story, we should keep in mind Dickens' larger purpose. In the same letter describing his determination to write picturesquely with character subordinate to event, he indicated distaste for "odious stuff . . . written under the pretense" of being significant. Taken with the praise his preface gives to Carlyle's history, this statement must be taken as a sign of Dickens' seriousness, and his intention to set his work apart from popular theater concurs with Carlyle's expressed scorn for mere theatricality.

That Dickens was serious indeed is evident by the opening of his third chapter where he ponders "the wonderful fact . . . that every human creature is constituted to be that profound secret and mystery to every other." The death of a loved one, especially, reminds him of "the secret that was always in that individuality."[10] This is one of Dickens' most overt Carlylean statements, not only because it employs Carlyle's rhetorical tactic of stressing the wonder of facts but particularly because it respects an essential incommunicability of "innermost personality." As in earlier novels which acknowledged the power of the uncanny, Dickens here in his third chapter speaks of darkly clustered houses, each enclosing its own secret and containing an awfulness contrasting the triviality of much public life. *A Tale of Two Cities* pictures many public spectacles—the spilling of the wine, the collapse of the Bastille, the sharpening of the knives, the dancing in the streets, and the scenes in court—but we need to remember that this book also remains sensitive to a buried life, to inarticulate and mysterious depths. Carlyle, discussing natural and symbolic expression, had spoken of the celestial force invisible within, and early in *A Tale of Two Cities* Dickens acknowledges a similar resource.

Granted, much of the revolution, as traced in the novel, has no respect for secrets. The ciphers in the woman's knitting become an executioner's list of victims; more ironically, Dr. Manette's secret manuscript turns into the death sentence for his son-in-law. The chief keeper of secrets, Sydney, goes to his death with what some in the crowd might recognize as a sublime and prophetic face, but his famous last words, conveyed to us by a fellow-victim, are appropriately after the fact of his heroic action. The words but not the action remain problematic. Their effect upon both immediate and future audiences contrasts the definitive quality of Sydney's sacrifice. The final scene, then, is most literally a translation of word into deed, act into meaning, and it epitomizes behavior Carlyle hailed as heroic.[11]

Study of the various courtroom scenes and of a number of other performances in *A Tale of Two Cities* would indicate that Dickens was very aware of the history presenting itself as drama and of people coming across as poor players. Recall, for example, how the road-mender seeking sanctuary with the Defarges fears Thérèse as he foresees her continuing her knitting "until the play is played out" (II, xv, 203).

Without Dickens' underlying and explicitly Carlylean sense of a substantial inarticulate life, the novel would at best be pathetic in its statement about the French Revolution. There is no question that many of the narrative devices are melodramatic and sentimental in the most pejorative senses of those terms, but we should take the melodramatic structure seriously. Melodrama, as a technique, is usually oversimple and often mechanical. So, too often, is the idea of revolution. As John Kucich says, "the purely mechanical quality of [the revolutionaries'] imitative violence is underscored by the ominous note of historical destiny in this novel."[12] Carlyle had spoken of revolution as a violent kind of growth toward a destiny, and so too does Dickens finish with a sense of the revolution's grand accomplishment. His final chapter starts with the familiar passage about the tumbrils rumbling on through the Paris streets and on through history. He warns of a horror that may return if humanity is ever again so crushed out of shape, and Dickens continues with an echo of the final passage of Carlyle's book, once more treating the French Revolution as the overthrow of imposture:

> Six tumbrils roll along the streets. Change these back again to what they were, thou powerful enchanter, Time, and they shall be seen to be the carriages of absolute monarchs, the equipages of feudal nobles, the toilettes of flaring Jezebels, the churches that are not my father's house but dens of thieves, the huts of millions of starving peasants! No; the great magician who majestically works out the appointed order of the Creator, never reverses his transformations. . . . Changeless and hopeless, the tumbrils roll along.   (III, xv, 399–400)

"Time" to Dickens' thinking, and indeed in many an earlier Dickens fairy tale, is certainly a "powerful enchanter," but here Dickens sounds a more serious Carlylean note of respect for time as a scope of dramatic action, a theater for history. Note especially his metaphors of performance when he speaks of the royal carriages, equipages, toilettes. With the elaborate props, the former rulers of France seemed always to present themselves as performers. As surely as the conclusion of *The French Revolution* describes the fiery consumption of thrones, mitres, pretentious "Wheel-vehicles," so too does Dickens here envision the transformation of sham.

But rather than append an epilogue as had Carlyle when using the "Voice of a Man" speaking with "Man" to defy hollow jargons, Dickens adds the "sublime" example of Carton's death. I have already nominated Carton as an exemplary Carlylean hero, one who achieves the satisfaction of sincere action. A slight emendation of his famous last thoughts may therefore be in order to underscore my point: "It is a far, far better thing I do than anything I have ever said."

I have looked at a few important connections between *The French Revolution* and *A Tale of Two Cities* to suggest the authors shared not only assumptions about the historical event's instructive importance but also about it as an occasion for enacting what Carlyle valued as human "trustfulness, sociability, fervency" on a stage remarkable for more explosive and terrifying theatricality. A separate study might focus more on the performances of Carlyle and Dickens themselves, for both were chief actors as narrators. I have dwelt more on what they seemed to be up to than on the quality of what they achieved. Opponents of mere theatricality in the conduct of private and public life, both Carlyle and Dickens nonetheless employed a number of theatrical devices as they responded to the profound drama of the French Revolution. Flaws in their productions may be evident, and evidently may be accounted for in a number of ways. But Carlyle and Dickens deserve applause as melodramatists. Both presented their subjects with the polemic intention common to melodrama; both centered their attention in those realms of social and public action that are the subject locales of melodrama. And, as Robert B. Heilman in his study of melodrama as complementary to tragedy says, it is natural for melodrama to ally itself with history. We certainly too often dismiss melodrama as a matter of shock effects, but as Heilman reminds us, melodrama also quite legitimately traffics in ideas and makes use of fundamental concepts and values.[13] As two dramatists, Carlyle and Dickens were melodramatists, pointing out extremes but remembering also to value humanity and to be wary of posturing performance.

NOTES

1. Joseph Butwin, "The French Revolution as *Theatrum Mundi*," *Research Studies*, 43 (1975), 141-152.

2. Michael Goldberg, *Carlyle and Dickens* (Athens: University of Georgia Press, 1972), p. 119.

3. *The French Revolution* (London: Chapman & Hall, 1896), I, Bk. vi, 212. Further citations are included in the text and are from this edition.

4. Sylvère Monod, *Dickens the Novelist* (Norman: University of Oklahoma Press, 1968), p. 453.

5. G. Robert Stange, "Dickens and the Fiery Past: *A Tale of Two Cities,*" *English Journal*, 46 (1957), 381-390.

124   DICKENS STUDIES ANNUAL

6. John Kucich, "The Purity of Violence: *A Tale of Two Cities,*" *Dickens Studies Annual: Essays on Victorian Fiction*, 8, Michael Timko, Fred Kaplan, and Edward Guiliano, eds. (New York: AMS Press, 1980), pp. 119–138.

7. K. J. Fielding, *Charles Dickens: A Critical Introduction* (London: Longmans, 1965), p. 201.

8. *The Letters of Charles Dickens*, ed. Walter Dexter (London: Nonesuch Press, 1938), III, 118.

9. Robert Alter remarks,

> By dramatically translating this notion of inevitability into the irreversible progress of violence in the life of a nation, Dickens, who is usually anything but an austere writer, gives this novel a kind of oblique reflection of the stern grandeur of the Greek tragedies. . . ."The Demons of History in Dickens' *Tale,*" *Novel*, 2 (1969), 142.

10. *A Tale of Two Cities* (Harmondsworth: Penguin, 1970), I, iii, 44. Further parenthetical citation of Book, Chapter, and page numbers are from this Penguin edition.

11. The code for heroic action is most evident in the stress upon anti-self-consciousness in *Sartor Resartus* and in the enumeration of characteristic qualities in *Heroes and Hero Worship*.

12. Kucich, p. 129.

13. Robert B. Heilman, *Tragedy and Melodrama* (Seattle: University of Washington Press, 1968), p. 76.

The Duplicity of Doubling
in *A Tale of Two Cities*

Catherine Gallagher

For the past several years readers have been discovering that Victorian novels can be as ironically self-reflective as any novels. Now that they are expected to, Thackeray, Dickens, and George Eliot reveal the fictitiousness of their fictions, the constructed nature of their constructions, the wordiness of their worlds, as regularly as do Proust, Joyce, and Virginia Woolf. One of the primary techniques of Victorian self-reflectiveness that has lately attracted attention is the insertion into the novel of analogues for novelistic narration, analogues that expose the constructing operations of the narrator even as he or she pretends to be passively mirroring an objective reality. Several of the essays in this collection call our attention to such analogues in *A Tale of Two Cities* and explain how, in themselves, they reveal the methods and intended effects of the narrative. This essay also addresses the topic of narrative analogues; however, it investigates not so much what the novel reveals in the creation of such doubles as what it conceals.[1]

Moreover, this essay links the question of what the narrative conceals by providing doubles for itself to the issue of the connection between the novel and the social phenomena it purports to represent. Like all historical novels, *A Tale of Two Cities* advertises itself as a record of events that had their own separate existence outside of the novel. And like realist novels in general, it can accommodate a greal deal of self-referentiality without relinquishing its claim to represent an independent reality. Indeed, *A Tale of Two Cities*, like many nineteenth-century novels, often achieves its self-reflectiveness just by calling attention to itself as mere representation. By presenting itself as simple representation, a thing whose very thingness is secondary or epiphenomenal, the novel conceals an aspect of itself; it conceals the fact that it is itself a kind of social practice. By drawing its content from social phenomena that are at once independent realities and analogues for novelistic narration, the novel gets us to focus alternately on what it is *about* and on how it accomplishes its representational effects. In the very act of giving us these alternative perspectives, the novel obscures its deeply social roots and functions. But the critic can uncover what the novel seeks to bury if she refuses to limit herself to the perspectives of the text itself, if she is willing to regard the novel as one among a number of historical phenomena, to investigate the separate but competing social functions of the novel and the phenomena it takes as its dark doubles.

The issue of analogues, metaphors, or doubles for narration and the issue of the social functions of fiction, then, are dealt with here as a single issue, an issue inseparable from larger topics in nineteenth-century social history. To demonstrate this unity, I will discuss three social phenomena that the narrative takes as analogues for itself precisely because they are in competition with the novel. The English public execution, the French Revolution, and the crime of resurrection, or grave-robbing, are all internal analogues for the novel, but they are more than that; they are additionally alternatives to it, for they accomplish many of the novel's functions. By using them as internal, contrasting doubles for itself, by attempting to incorporate them, the novel tries to clear a space for itself, differentiate itself from the social and supersede it.

All of these phenomena—English public executions, the French Revolution, and the crime of resurrectionism—are presented in *A Tale of Two Cities* as monstrous violators of the realm of the private. As such, all might seem to threaten the very foundations of the nineteenth-century novel, a genre that grows out of and depends on a high valuation of the private and domestic realms. However, as violators of the private, these phenomena might also be said to *resemble* the novel, whose most basic task, as Dickens formulated it in the following well-known passage from *Dombey and Son*, was the exposure of the private.[2] Here is the narrator of *Dombey and Son* invoking himself: "Oh for a good spirit who would take the house tops off, with a more potent and benignant hand than the lame demon in the tale, and show a Christian people what dark shapes issue from amidst their homes. . . . "[3] This longing for exposure and revelation, for the transgression of the very public/private boundary created and valued by the novel, can be detected everywhere in Dickens' novels. The wish to take the house-tops off, to render the private observable, is the wish informing the very existence of the omniscient narrator.

But the quotation from *Dombey and Son* presents this activity of the exposure of the private in two lights, one flattering and one very unflattering. Even as the narrator suggests that exposure can be the work of a good spirit, expelling hidden evils and creating light and order, he reminds us that it is nevertheless a transgression, and, consequently, within the novel's structure of values, akin to the work of a demon. How can the novel conceal this side of its own need to reveal and expose; how can the novelist reassure himself and his readers that he is in league with the good spirit, that his operations are benign? One way to suppress the fear that novelistic omniscience verges on the demonic is to provide, within the novel, an alternative version of the will to omniscience, one that is clearly destructive, preferably murderous or ghoulish, so that by contrast, the narrator's activities will seem restrained and salutary. Execution, the Revolution, and resurrectionism perform precisely this function in *A Tale of Two Cities*.

Consider, for example, the public execution, and consider it, for a moment, independently of the novel to get a sense of why Dickens was attracted to it. No event was better suited to render the private public, to expose the intimate in the interests of public order. In its most obvious sense, this would be true of all public executions, for by definition they expose to full public view a moment that was becoming more and more intensely private as the nineteenth-century wore on, the moment of fatal suffering and death. That exposure should remind us of the historical links between public executions and those other ritual inversions of public and private: human sacrifice and carnival. Furthermore, when we consider the physical details of hanging, the type of execution used in England seems calculated to maximize the exposure of the dying victim. The erection of the penis and the evacuation of the bowels are among such details, and hanging, up until quite late in the Victorian period was a slow-working method; the drop was short, and the body was left, fully visible, to writhe and strangle for many minutes.[4]

Moreover, as Dickens reminds us in *A Tale of Two Cities*, some crimes were punishable by even more intrusive forms of exposure. One of our earliest views of Charles Darnay renders him, through the ogreish anticipation of the crowd at his trial, a man literally turned inside out:

> The sort of interest with which this man was stared and breathed at, was not a sort that elevated humanity. Had he stood in peril of a less horrible sentence—had there been a chance of any one of its savage details being spared—by just so much would he have lost in his fascination. The form

that was to be doomed to be so shamefully mangled, was the sight; the immortal creature that was to be so butchered and torn asunder, yielded the sensation.[5]

Treason, you will recall, is the charge, and the penalty is an almost unimaginable mixing up of specular awareness and intense interiority, as the live sufferer is forced to watch the breaking open, pulling out and destruction of his own insides. To emphasize the extent of its violation, Dickens includes the full sentence:

> "Ah!" returned the man, with a relish; "he'll be drawn on a hurdle to be half hanged, and then he'll be cut down and sliced before his own face, and then his inside will be taken out and burnt while he looks on, and then his head will be chopped off, and he'll be cut into quarters. That's the sentence." (91)

In these fairly obvious ways, then, the public execution, especially when accompanied by torture, can be seen as a nightmare of transparency, of publicly displaying what is hidden, intimate, secret, in the interests of creating social order and cohesion. Here is a collective longing for omniscience and power taking the most savage form imaginable. Here it is not just the walls or rooftops of the house that are ripped away, but the walls of the body itself. And thus Dickens' appalled references to several brutal executions at the outset of the novel establish the crucial differences between such practices and the novel's own will to transparency. Compared to the awful executions mentioned in chapter one and to Damiens's execution recounted later in detail, the novelist's methods of exposing the intimate are safe, sane, sanitary, and benevolent. They are safe because they do not entail that reversibility of violence dramatized in *A Tale of Two Cities*. As Michel Foucault has argued, penal reformers of the eighteenth and nineteenth centuries (and Dickens was such a reformer) feared that a population exposed to such a violent theater of punishment would become a violent population.[6] This note is sounded early in *A Tale of Two Cities*, where we learn in the first chapter that the hangman's seemingly arbitrary activities only contribute further to the disorder and violence that can easily turn against the State, and keep turning and turning as they do in Dickens' portrayal of the French Revolution.

In contrast, the novelist may pry, spy, and expose the secret, the personal, but he manages to do these things while maintaining both propriety and privacy. Indeed, the very production and consumption of novels, as well as their contents, perpetuate the idea that the private can be made public, brought to light, and yet still be kept private.[7] In this sense,

Dickens' work as a novelist is of a piece with his work in reforming the law. The public execution, he argues, should give way to a procedure relying on a few witnesses and a lot of paperwork. As Dickens describes the procedure in a letter to the *Times* in 1849, the multitude of the crowd would be replaced by a multitude of pieces of writing:

> To attend the execution I would summon a jury of 24, to be called the Witness Jury, eight to be summoned on a low qualification, eight on a higher; eight on a higher still; so that it might fairly represent all classes of society. There should be present likewise, the governor of the gaol, the chaplain, the surgeon and other officers. All these should sign a grave and solemn form of certificate (the same in every case) on such a day on such an hour, in such a gaol, for such a crime, such a murderer was hanged in their sight. There should be another certificate from the officers of the prison that the person hanged was that person and no other; a third that the person was buried.[8]

As in the novel itself, in the private execution, as Dickens called his imagined punishment, that which is private is given over to the power of the public, but the public executes its power privately.

Thus, the very form of the novel defines itself against the public execution, not only in spite of, but also because of their resemblances. This is especially true in *A Tale of Two Cities*, which establishes the public execution as one of its founding abominations. To take the public execution merely as a point of departure, however, is to ignore some of the more subtle ways in which the novel incorporates and depends on the institution of the public execution. To explore these further connections, I will need to discuss not the general institution of public executions, but certain peculiarities of English public executions. Thus far I have been talking as if the execution, both inside and outside the novel, consisted merely in the forcible exposure of the intimate sensations of the condemned person's body, but the English execution did two other things particularly well that the novel was supposed to do: it retrospectively narrated an individual life while it simultaneously created a sense of social cohesion and totality.

English executions differed from those of other nations in the degree of activity allowed the victim and his opportunities for autobiographical representation. The victim's first such opportunity was his trial, but many opportunities succeeded condemnation. There was, for example, the theatrical opportunity provided by the prison chapel service that took place on the Sunday before the execution. Here the Ordinary of Newgate, the prison chaplain, would deliver a sermon, not only to the condemned, but also to the crowds of people who would bribe their way in to see the condemned. Because they had an audience, the prisoners were very often rowdy during this service, intent on expressing themselves, and the Ordinary's record is crowded with complaints: Christopher Freeman, we learn, "behaved very undecently, laughed and seemed to make a mock of everything that was serious and regular." And Ann Mudd, the account tells, "Used to sing obscene songs, and talked very indecently," while Christopher Rawlings in the days before he was hanged busied himself in chapel by cutting off the tassels of the pulpit cushion.[9] In addition to these small examples of self-dramatization, each condemned prisoner in Newgate was required to go through an autobiographical exercise. He was required to assist the Ordinary in making an *account* of his life. And there were frequently extraordinary struggles over these accounts. In the first place, the Ordinary as narrator often had difficulty subduing his rebellious characters. They would not always go along with his version of the plot. A historian of Newgate tells us,

> The Ordinary not only liked to have positive statements of guilt to the particular crime, but assent to a general range of immoral conduct. A story was told about Lorraine [an eighteenth-century Ordinary] and a young pickpocket about to be hanged. The Ordinary, expecting to hear the lad explain his sinful life in terms of Sabbath-breaking, lewd women or drink, was surprised when the boy insisted that he was innocent of them all, particularly the first since as a pickpocket he could never afford to miss a Sunday.[10]

In the second place, prisoners often wanted to sell their stories to higher bidders outside the prison walls. They wrote their own manuscripts in secret and smuggled them out to high-paying publishers. Other prisoners simply tried to keep their secret until they were on the scaffold, where their last speech would reveal all. But even before they got to the scaffold, in the days when hanging took place at Tyburn, there were ample opportunities for making speeches about one's life. The procession sometimes made several pub stops and stops to visit friends;[11] the condemned would get down and drink and talk over old times. Both during these stops and during other parts of the journey, the condemned gave blessings, kissed their children goodbye, cursed people, etc. Executions, in short, could turn into enacted autobiographies, which were supplemented by the many accounts of the life and crimes of the condemned that were being sold all along the route and at the place of execution. Such life histories of criminals were, of course, the immediate ancestors of the novel.

English executions were also unique in the extent to which they obscured the power of the State.[12] They seem staged to create the illusion that a total society, not a single class or government, was executing a felon. What is more, in the eighteenth and nineteenth centuries, the people were not content to be represented symbolically through the crown at these events, but turned out themselves in huge and generally disorderly crowds that were nevertheless socially differentiated. Indeed, we might argue that, in a time when a sense of social totality was becoming increasingly difficult to achieve, the public execution was a reassuring representation of wholeness. Nowhere else would all strata of society display themselves in such numbers. Tickets were sold, and the wealthy would pay high prices for gallery seats. At public executions one could see the differentiated but nevertheless cohesive whole of eighteenth- and nineteenth-century England.

The public execution, then, in addition to enacting a personal narrative also provided a synoptic view of society; the very two things the novel prided itself on doing. Indeed, the connection between the novelistic synoptic vision and the public hanging is explicit in a few of Dickens' novels. A famous early example of this connection is the death of Bill Sikes in *Oliver Twist*. Sikes's death admittedly is not technically an execution, but that makes it all the more revealing for my purposes, for it perfectly reproduces the submergence of the state in the English execution. It is the whole population of London, and not just the police, that brings Sikes to bay and causes him to hang himself—Sikes is on a rooftop attempting to let himself down, with a rope, into a ditch:

> The crowd had been hushed during these few moments, watching his motions and doubtful of his purpose, but the instant they perceived it and knew it was defeated, they raised a cry of triumphant execration to which all their previous shouting had been whispers. Again and again it rose. Those who were at too great a distance to know its meaning, took up the sound; it echoed and re-echoed; it seemed as though the whole city had poured its population out to curse him.
>
> On pressed the people from the front—on, on, on, in a strong struggling current of angry faces, with here and there a gathering torch to light them up, and show them out in all their wrath and passion. The houses on the opposite side of the ditch had been entered by the mob; sashes were thrown up, or torn bodily out; there were tiers and tiers of faces in every window; cluster upon cluster of people clinging to every house-top. Each little bridge (and there were three in sight) bent beneath the weight of the crowd upon it. Still the current poured on to find some nook or hole from which to vent their shouts, and only for an instant see the wretch.[13]

This is the only time in the novel that the divided world of the metropolis achieves wholeness, for Harry Maylie and Mr. Brownlow are parts of the mob, which also includes the poor and the criminal. As in *Dombey and*

Son, the roof-top here is the perch of omniscience, but the synoptic moment is created and perceived only in the seconds before hanging.

Dickens also uses the moment of execution as the synoptic moment in *A Tale of Two Cities*. Here again the omniscience gained in the moment of Sydney Carton's execution, a prophetic vision giving us a chronological panorama extending several generations into the future, is synonymous with the narrator's omniscience.

In sum, Dickens uses the public execution as a method of defining, by contrast, the innocence of his own longing for transparency and omniscience. However, he then incorporates the conventions of representation of the English execution into his narrative to achieve some of his most typically novelistic effects: the retrospective of Sydney Carton's life, for example, and the prophetic synopsis of its close. This incorporation, indeed, is an effort to absorb the functions of the public execution and circumscribe them within the novel. In the same letter to the *Times* in which Dickens requested that the crowd be replaced by its representatives (eight men from each social class) at executions, he expressed his hostility toward the theatrically autobiographical character of public executions. He recommends that all elements of public entertainment be suppressed:

> [The] execution within the walls of the prison should be conducted with every terrible solemnity that careful consideration could devise. Mr. Calcraft the hangman . . . should be restrained in his unseemly briskness, in his jokes, his oaths, and his brandy.[14]

Moreover, even journalistic accounts publicizing the condemned are to be disallowed:

> From the moment of a murderer being sentenced to death, I would dismiss him to dread obscurity. . . . I would allow no curious visitors to hold any communication with him; I would place every obstacle in the way of his sayings and doings being served up in print on Sunday for the perusal of families.[15]

The novelist, alone, it seems, should be able to appropriate, through representation, the functions of the execution.

In the paradoxical nature of its relationship to public executions—the way it at once uses them as a point of departure and contrast to itself and also incorporates them to achieve its own internal purposes—*A Tale of Two Cities* resembles a second historical phenomenon that is analogous to novelistic narration: the French Revolution. Like the narrator, the revolutionaries take the outrages of public execution as founding events, events that are to justify them and differentiate them from the Old Regime. The execution of Damiens and that of the Marquis's assassin are particularly important in this regard. Finally, however, the Revolution becomes even more dependent on the public execution than the Old Regime had been. If the public execution is a nightmare of omniscience, of the exposure of the private to public scrutiny, then the Revolution is that nightmare amplified a thousand times. And this amplification can be seen and felt not only in the multiplication of executions but also in the numerous invasions and expositions of the private that characterize the Revolution from the outset and link it closely to the method of narrative omniscience.

The secret brotherhood of the Jacquerie resists the intrusion of royalist spies, but it also creates itself through spying, through the surveillance and exposure of dark things and private things. "Do you make a show of Monsieur Manette?" asks Mr. Lorry of Defarge when they discover the three Jacques "looking into the room" of the distraught doctor "through some chinks or holes in the wall." "I show him, in the way you have seen, to a chosen few" (68), replies Defarge. Indeed, the intrusive stare characterizes most personifications of the incipient Revolution. One such personification is Madame Defarge, who always "looks steadily" at the people she enters in her knitted record. It is the stare that differentiates her from other denizens of St. Antoine:

> So cowed was their condition, and so long and hard their experience of what such a man [as the Marquis] could do to them, within the law and beyond it, that not a voice, or a hand, or even an eye was raised. Among the men, not one. But the woman who stood knitting looked up steadily, and looked the Marquis in the face. (143)

A second personification of the embryonic revolution is the Gorgon, who, we are told, "surveys" the country house of the Evremondes, turning the Marquis to stone. Whereas the Gorgon of mythology is a creature who kills by being looked at, the Gorgon-Jacquerie kills its victims by looking at them. By inverting the myth here, Dickens merely emphasizes the significance of the stare.

Once the Revolution establishes itself, the stare becomes a national characteristic. A whole population practices surveillance on itself, a surveillance that ultimately destroys. When Darnay returns to France, he encounters, we are told several times, a "universal watchfulness" that the narrator finds particularly abhorrent, just as he deplores the exposure of the domestic encoded in the law demanding that all the names of the inhabitants of a residence be listed outside on the front of the house. Indeed, these demands for transparency, for the exhibition of the private, are excessive. It is as if the Revolution had inspired every citizen with a need to rip away the house-tops, to expose the interior, in short, to commit the transgressions of the omniscient narrator.

Both the Revolution and the Dickens narrator need to transgress against the private, and, to justify their transgression, they must create a belief that dark things (plots, conspiracies, vices) lurk everywhere, needing to be revealed. The belief in secrets creates the need to expose, but the need to expose is reciprocally dependent on the invention of secret plots. The French Revolution was uncannily like a Dickens novel in this regard: the invented hidden plot justifies the will to omniscience.

Dickens, of course, did not invent this characterization of the French Revolution, which had already been represented, by anti-revolutionaries and revolutionaries alike, as a practice of excessive exposure. In his *Reflections on the Revolution in France*, for example, Edmund Burke characterizes revolutionary thought as a process of unmasking, unclothing, stripping away symbolic drapery:

> All the decent Drapery of life is to be rudely torn off. All the superadded ideas, furnished from the wardrobe of a moral imagination, which the heart owns, and the understanding ratifies, as necessary to cover the defects of our shivering naked nature, and to raise it to dignity in our own estimation, are to be exploded as a ridiculous, absurd, and antiquated fashion.[16]

And Carlyle, whose constant concern is with the making and unmaking of symbols also notes the rending and discarding of the old symbolic vestures in revolutionary activity. The revolutionary symbols that replace the symbols of the Old Regime, moreover, are often symbols representing the pulling away of symbols: the destruction of the Bastille, decapitated heads of aristocrats, the guillotine itself.

These representations of the Revolution as exposure, we must note, were also the self-representations of the Revolution, especially just before and during the time of the Terror. The Terror explicated the Revolution's insistence on transparency and its corollary invention of hidden plots. Revolutionaries had always expressed a great deal of anxiety about secrets, about privacy itself and about language in general, which they saw as a primary tool of deception. There were constant demands for the perfectly expressive and revealing word. And as Radicals gained more and more power, they predicated the very survival of the Revolution on, as a historian of the Revolution puts it,

> transparency between citizen and citizen, between the citizens and their government, between the individual and general will. . . . This kind of trans-

parency gave meaning to the civic oath and to the revolutionary festival, both of which depended on enthusiastic adherence, i.e., on the abolition of distance between citizen and citizen and between individual and community. Community, in essence, *was* this transparency between citizens.[17]

This was the mentality that led, during the Terror, to the institutionalization of public vigilance, denunciation, and decapitation, the essence of the revolutionary experience as we see it depicted in *A Tale of Two Cities*. The idea that secret plots were lurking everywhere was, of course, necessary to justify this vigilance, and the more transparent the community became, the more nefarious must these plots be, for authorized enclaves of privacy had been wiped out. The fact that these plots were invisible, even given this new transparency, was proof of their pernicious purposes. Thus when Saint-Just denounces Danton, whose crime is the concealment of a network of plotters, he stresses the fact that guilt is proved by the burial of evidence: "You will recognize," he exclaims, "the sure signs of the party opposed to the Revolution, the party which always conceals itself."[18] In other words, the fact that you cannot see it proves that it is there. How can it be a plot if it is not hidden?

The resemblances to Dickens' novels, with their insistence on omniscience and their concomitant need for someone always to be hiding something, are obvious. Moreover, these characteristics are not unique to Dickens; it is practically a *donnée* of nineteenth-century realist fiction that the real is beneath the surface, a hidden network of connection that must remain at least partially hidden if the novel is to continue. When full transparency is achieved, the novel ends. When we know all the connections between the Evremondes, the Manettes and the Defarges, the novel no longer has a *raison d'être*. On his late-night ramble through Paris, just before he goes to La Force to change places with Darnay, Sydney Carton hears the final revelation, makes the final connection between Madame Defarge and the Evremondes. At that moment there is nothing left to be learned; the novel, like Carton, has reached the threshold of full execution. It must end, for its continuation is as dependent on the discovery of plots as is that of the revolution itself.

It was just such an end to their own *raison d'être* that the Radicals feared, and thus they set themselves the task of the infinite invention and discovery of plots. Hence the Revolution reminds us of that reluctance to end that so often characterizes the Victorian novel. Revolution is opposed to resolution: it is a kind of fiction in which ultimate climax must be always deferred. Saint-Just comments on the infinitude of the structure he is creating: "One speaks of the highpoint of the revolution; who will fix it, this highpoint? It is moving."[19]

But novels, of course, must bring themselves to an end; they must move more or less purposely, willfully toward resolution. *A Tale of Two Cities*, indeed, emphasizes this difference between itself and the revolution by merging is own execution, its own ending, with Carton's execution and thereby stressing the voluntariness of its close. And this impulse toward resolution is only one of the most obvious ways in which the novel distinguishes its own practices from those of the Revolution. The differences are, after all, the point of the comparison. The Revolution, like the public execution, is a double for the narration itself in all of the ways I have just detailed. But like the other doublings in this book, indeed like splitting and pairing in general, the doubling of the methods of novelistic narration with the methods of the Revolution is a protective device. Sydney Carton saves Charles Darnay by a set of resemblances and differences that allow the displacement of one by the other. Earlier, in the London trial episode, casting suspicion on Sydney Carton draws off suspicion from Charles Darnay. Similarly, the presence of the Revolution as a double of the novelistic narration exculpates the narration. By depicting this excessive, malignant, demonic version of the will to transparency, the Revolution, the novel discovers itself to be, in comparison, moderate, benign, even angelic.

Thus we are never confused about whether the novel is for or against the protection of the domestic enclave it exposes. The novelist makes his revelation of the private in the name of the private and for the sake of the private. The Revolution is a specific attack upon the private by means of exposure. In contradistinction, the novel seems to represent the repulsion of that attack. We do not readily suspect the narrator of exercising or desiring any excessive power over his universe or over us. The narrator sees and detects, not for his own profit (like the many spies in the book), but supposedly for the profit of the good people he spies on.

His detection resembles the businesslike spying of Jarvis Lorry. As Lorry interrogates Miss Pross about Doctor Manette's past, he reminds her that he and she are "both people of business" (127). And at several other points during their interview, he recalls her to a sense of his serious but benign intentions. "I don't approach the topic with you out of curiosity, but out of zealous interest," he assures her; and he continues, "a doubt lurks in my mind, Miss Pross, whether it is good for Doctor Manette to have that suppression always shut up within him. Indeed, it is this doubt and the uneasiness it sometimes causes me that has led me to our present confidence" (129). Both the revolutionaries and Jarvis Lorry are intent on discovering the secret of Doctor Manette's imprisonment, yet Jarvis Lorry's prying seems pure and benign to us. We have no trouble believing him when he tells us it is for Doctor Manette's good. Similarly, we are sure that what the narrative as a whole reveals, it reveals for the good of the exposed. We do not suspect the narrative, and we do not suspect it because its double, the Revolution, so theatrically exhibits all the suspicious behavior associated with compulsive prying.

The Revolution exhibits this behavior theatrically, and Jerry Cruncher, the resurrection man, exhibits it surreptitiously, drawing off and disposing of any residual uneasiness we might feel about the narrator's discreet and businesslike procedures. The crime of resurrectionism, as A. D. Hutter has shown elsewhere in this volume, is the clearest and the most elaborate of the narrative's dark doubles for itself. Hutter has pointed out that Jerry's job is like the narrator's in that both dig up the past and uncover buried mysteries. Jerry's work is also like the narrator's, however, in that both expose the private place. Robbing a grave is, after all, yet another version of pulling off a roof-top. And, indeed, the crime of resurrectionism was often represented as the ultimate violation of privacy, the privacy of both the dead and the family. It was a crime against family sentiment, the very foundation of the domestic. This is particularly clear when the robbing of a woman's grave is reported. The following account of the activities of Edinburgh medical students illustrates the depth of popular feeling on this subject:

Rosyth was the scene of another tragic story in which Edinburgh students were concerned. They had learned of the death of a beautiful young bride in her first childbirth. Insensible to all considerations save the gratification of their passion for dissection, they had made it a matter of competition who should obtain possession of the body of the village belle. The party that reached the spot first set to work with all speed and soon had the body unearthed and stripped preparatory to placing it in the sack for removal. They had paused for a moment to admire the perfect proportions and fair skin of the female form divine that lay before them when the sound of a dog howling in distress fell on their ears. Presently the light of a lantern warned them that someone was approaching, and without waiting to put the body in the sack and shoulder the burden, they seized it by the heels and fled, dragging it along the ground behind them. When they reached the sea wall beyond which their boat lay in readiness at the edge of the tide, the woman's long, golden hair, which in life had reached below her knees when uncoiled, and loosened in the exhumation had trailed out as the body was drawn along, became entangled among the rough, projecting stones, and stayed their progress. Tugging violently, they overcame the obstruction and reached the boat with their freight, but in their tugging some of the golden tresses and part of the scalp had been torn away, and were left entangled in the sea wall. The husband, who had been alarmed by the uneasy howling of his dead wife's pet, and had set out to assure himself that her grave had not been disturbed, was diverted from his first intention by the sound of the students' hurried flight and turned in pursuit. When he came to the sea wall the faithful animal, which had followed him, scented these remains and stood barking excitedly over them. By the light of his lantern he recognized the fair hair that but a year before had been garlanded with orange blossoms and now brought him confirmation of his worst fears. As the students drew away from the shore, congratulating themselves on having beaten their competitors, he stood upon the wall holding to his quivering lips all that was left to him of his bride, so beautiful even in death, and calling down the vengeance of Heaven on the violators of her last sanctuary.[20]

What strikes one immediately about this powerful little narrative is the ingenuousness of the writer's claim that the medical students are "insensible to all considerations save the gratification of their passion for dissection" even as the very next clause in the sentence stresses the overtly sexual dimension of this passion. The passion for dissection, which leads to resurrectionism, is so closely associated with sexual violation in the narrator's mind that he assumes the former entails the latter. Nor does the narrator seem aware that there is any tension between his conventional, romantic language and the fact that the abducted woman is a corpse. We are, for example, left with the standard sentimental image of the young husband pressing his stolen bride's "golden tresses" to his lips, and are expected not to flinch at the bizarre detail that bits of scalp are dangling from those tresses. Such discordant elements are only conceivable within an ideology that already, in some sense, conceives of the domestic woman as so immobile, passive, and sequestered that she is already dead and buried. In violating her grave, the resurrectionists transgress against the culmination of her privacy, the perfection of her feminine being; they are "the violators of her *last* sanctuary."

Much less violent, of course, is the sort of violation practiced by the novel, but we should remember Miss Pross's complaint that ever since the Resurrection of the Doctor, that is, since the opening of the novel, "hundreds of people who are not at all worthy of Ladybird [have] come here looking after her" (125). We are, of course, supposed to see Miss Pross's complaint as absurd and fantastic; Lucie's sanctuary has been invaded, not by hundreds of people, but by half a dozen; she has only three men desiring her body, not throngs. Nevertheless, our first tour of the Manettes' home is conducted in a strangely guilt-ridden fashion. Mr. Lorry, who had previously "resurrected" the doctor, arrives at their

"secluded" retreat when no one is home, and, with a strong consciousness of his own (licensed) invasiveness, wanders from room to room,
allowing the narrator to comment on what each room reveals of the inhabitants, especially of Lucie. Later we see this tour as part of Lorry's attempt to retrieve the doctor's past, an attempt at yet another benign resurrection. Nevertheless, the slight taint of prying remains attached to our
introduction into Lucie's house, giving a certain limited credence to Miss
Pross's alarm: we are the "hundreds of people."

Jerry Cruncher's domestic establishment provides a comic inversion of
this suppressed connection between the crime of resurrectionism and the
exposure of the domestic. Jerry, whose acts of exposure are themselves
clandestine, can tolerate no revelations within his own household. He
continually abuses his wife for praying, for communicating with a potentially interfering Being. He tries to beat his wife into protecting his privacy, into concealing it from an omniscient gaze. The outlandishness of
Jerry's claim to speak in the name of privacy and the inviolability of the
family circle overshadows the illegitimacy of the narrator's similar claim.

Of all the doubles for novelistic narration in *A Tale of Two Cities*, then,
the crime of resurrectionism is in many ways the most comprehensive.
And, of course, it is also a close relative to the two other doubles I have
discussed here, providing historical as well as metaphorical links between
them. Hutter mentioned its connections to the French Revolution's secu-
larism and anti-historical impulses as well as its parodic relationship to
the theme of *liberté*. Another of its connections to the Revolution is simply the historical fact that that event brought in the method of teaching
anatomy that first created the lucrative market in bodies in England and
Scotland.

But there is yet another link between the Revolution and the crime of
resurrection established through their common association with execution. Like the Revolution, resurrection destroys the distinction between
the innocent and the guilty. It demands the exposure alike of those who
deserve it and those who do not. Prior to the English Anatomy Act of
1832, the only bodies legally available for dissection were those of executed criminals. To be dissected was to be treated like a criminal; indeed,
it was to be treated like the worst kind of criminal. Even hardened con-
victs on their way to the gallows begged not to be sent to the Surgeons.
One Vincent Davis, for example, who was hanged at Tyburn in 1725 for
killing his wife, exclaimed on arrest, "I have killed the best wife in the
world, and I am certain of being hanged, but for God's sake, don't let me
be anatomised!"[21] Dissection was a fate then reserved only for the most

despised or unfortunate of the condemned. But the resurrection men broke through this reservation. Treating the bodies of the most innocent like those of murderers, they provided a postmortem Reign of Terror.

Resurrection, then, as a double for omniscient narration, is both historically and metaphorically linked to those other narrative analogues, revolution and execution. Indeed, by its wealth of associations it seems to absorb the others. But at the same time, resurrection is in competition with both execution and revolution. An executed body, after all, did not need to be resurrected; it was free to the surgeons for public dissection. And, of course, the punishment for drawing and quartering, as Jerry interestedly points out, "spiles" the body. Spoils it, that is, for dissection by dissecting it alive. Jerry greatly resents this destruction of prospective "scientific goods." But he resents even more the surplus of bodies created by the Terror. When he renounces the trade of resurrectionism, he explains to Jarvis Lorry, "A man don't see all this here goin' on dreadful round him, in the way of Subjects without heads, dear me, plentiful enough fur to bring the price down to porterage and hardly that, without havin' his serious thoughts of things" (337). Behind Jerry's conversion from grave robber to grave digger is the understanding that revolutionary society would ruin his trade. A society not based on family sentiment, the respect for privacy, and the sanctity of the domestic would flood the market with bodies, and the "honest tradesman" would be out of business. Resurrectionism, like the novel, needs the respect for privacy it violates; it relies on having things buried.

Resurrection, then, gives us an analogue for narration, but also a double for the antagonistic, competitive relationship between the novel and its analogues. Neither the novel nor the resurrectionist could survive in a society where exposure was cheap, plentiful, even, God forbid, free. How can the honest tradesmen, the resurrectionist and the novelist, thrive in a society that turns itself inside out? Resurrection, then, is more than just *another* double for narration; it also doubles the novel's competitive relationship to the theatrical doubles (execution and Revolution) that we examined earlier.

The displacement of resurrection by execution is an inverted version of the displacement of execution and Revolution by the novel. And inversion, of course, is the point. One of the neatest tricks of *A Tale of Two Cities* is its creation of the illusion that a theatrical society is displacing the honest tradesman; whereas, of course, the opposite was the case: the honest tradesman, the novelist, privately selling his discreetly packaged revelations of the private, was displacing the theatrical society. And he could only do so by advertising the inviolability of the private. Thus, the narrator's only first-person statement can be read, not as a poignant lament about the ultimate inaccessibility of one's intimates, but as a reassurance that the private will always be there and yet will always be just beyond our full comprehension:

> A wonderful fact to reflect upon, that every human creature is constituted to be that profound secret and mystery to every other. A solemn consideration, when I enter a great city by night, that every one of those darkly clustered houses encloses its own secret; that every room in every one of them encloses its own secret; that every beating heart in the hundreds of thousands of breasts there, is in some of its imaginings, a secret to the heart nearest it! Something of the awfulness, even of Death itself, is referable to this. . . . My friend is dead, my neighbor is dead, my love, the darling of my soul, is dead; it is the inexorable consolidation and perpetuation of the secret that was always in that individuality, and which I shall carry in mine to my life's end. In any of the burial-places of this city through which I pass, is there a sleeper more inscrutable than its busy inhabitants are, in their innermost personality, to me, or than I am to them? (44)

The quotation, which connects the narrator and the resurrection man by equating the domestic with the grave, posits a perpetual scarcity of intimate knowledge, and thereby raises the value of the revelation of the private, insuring a continued demand for the honest tradesman's goods.

As a double for both novelistic narration and the antagonistic relationship between novelistic narration and its doubles, resurrection is very revealing. Indeed, for the purposes of this essay, it is almost too revealing; this essay began with the premise that doubling is primarily a method for protecting and concealing, and yet here resurrection seems to be revealing the fact that the novel is actually in competition with the social practices it represents.

This revelation, however, is anything but automatic; it can be reached only by stripping away, with the aid of other historical materials, layers of concealment. The most proximate layer is the inversion just referred to: the inversion by which the private tradesman gets replaced by the theatrical society instead of, as in the case of the novelist, replacing that society. But even this inversion is screened from view by yet another act of doubling in which the theme of resurrection itself becomes an explicit double for doubling. That is, we do not see that resurrection is an ironic double for the competition between the novel and other social practices because the narrator introduces it as already doubled: it is the explicit ironic inversion of transcendent Resurrection with a capital "R" in the stories of Manette, Darnay and Carton. Resurrection comes into the novel, as it were, pre-paired with the very operation the novel advertises as its explicit analogue: benign Resurrection, which saves Doctor Manette, Charles Darnay, and Sydney Carton, which recalls to life, recollects the past, redeems the present and the future.

This explicit doubling of resurrection does two things. First it creates an illusion of candid self-referentiality: a book so explicit about its structure must have nothing to hide. What, after all, could be more honest than calling attention to one's own duplicity? Second, by explicitly pairing resurrectionism with the benign, angelic side of the will to omniscience, the narration controls and limits the similarities we will see between resurrection and the novel. Specifically, it suppresses the insight we have gained only by going outside the novel: the insight that the novelist and the resurrection man are both, out of self-interest, antagonistic to the theatrical society.

A Tale of Two Cities, then, not only gives us doubles of narration to draw suspicion away from itself, but it also gives us a double of doubling so that, if we restricted ourselves to the text, we could not possibly be suspicious of that method. Consequently, in *A Tale of Two Cities* we have a clear illustration of how omniscient, novelistic narration came to replace certain social practices of an earlier, more theatrical society by temporarily assuming some essential functions of those practices and then making itself an explicit contrast to them. Of all nineteenth-century novelists, Dickens may have been the most aware of the close bond between his own works and the more public and theatrical practices they were replacing. That may, in fact, be why we find in his work the cleverest mechanisms of concealment. The mechanisms need to be clever, for the thing being concealed is, in some ways, very obvious. The novel does not just record a social transition; it enacts one.

That transition was perhaps most powerfully enacted, paradoxically, on the Victorian stage itself, where Dickens, in the last years of his life, added a new item to his repertoire of public readings. He began doing the murder of Nancy and death of Bill Sikes from *Oliver Twist*, and he reported that the performances bore a strong resemblance to public executions: "There was a fixed expression of horror of me, all over the theatre, which could not have been surpassed if I had been going to be hanged. . . . It is quite a new sensation to be executed with that unanimity."[22] How can this final institutional exchange be explained? Was Dickens giving back to the public, theatrical realm much of what he had appropriated from it? Were these readings public confessions, disclosures of the novelist's guilty connection to the phenomena he was displacing, as well as acts of reparation?

In answer to the first question, it must be pointed out that Dickens is here entering the realm of the theatrical, but only, after all, to modify it in the direction of the novelistic. His readings in general made a peculiarly non-theatrical use of the theater: with most of the stage darkened and draped, the solitary reader stood at the velvet-covered lectern reading the already familiar stories. No characters appeared, no scenes became visible; all was represented in words, realized only privately through the imaginative effort of each of the thousands of hearers. No theater could have been less like that normally experienced by Victorian theater-goers, who, amid noisy and unruly crowds, generally witnessed almost wordless productions of spectacular materiality, such as the real horses and chariots raced on conveyor belts in Victorian productions of *Ben Hur*. Given the nature of Victorian theater, when Dickens takes the stage to read his novels, we might say that he is blotting out the theatrical, making the stage a huge blankness to accommodate the resonating words of the novel. Far from being a capitulation to theatrical modes of representation, then, Dickens' readings can be seen as further acts of appropriation and displacement.

From this understanding of the readings in general, we may be able to derive the meaning of the violent *Oliver Twist* performances, which Dickens thought bore such a strong likeness to public executions. As in all of Dickens' readings, the performance called attention to its novelistic representational mode; there was no stage illusion. The simulated self-execution of Sikes took place only in the private space of the hearers' minds, while the shared experiences were of Dickens' voice and the spectacle of his self-presentation as narrator. The revelation here is of the novelist, not of the executed. In his performance, Dickens does not directly pretend to be Bill Sikes; he does not even take the risk of identification taken by a normal actor. Instead, Dickens plays the novelist, exposes himself as novelist. It is the anonymous revealer who is here revealed. Consequently, in these performances, the novelist proves that he is willing to expose himself, and his exposures of others are thus justified. He is no furtive resurrection man, but a self-presenting representer.

Like Sydney Carton and Christ himself, the good Resurrection Men, Dickens experiences the execration of the crowd only as the self-conscious representer of another, but in Dickens' case the knowledge of the merely representational nature of the performance is, apparently, shared by performer and audience. However, underneath this self-conscious and candid representing that constantly calls attention to its mediations, a real self-execution was secretly taking place. For Dickens had been told by his doctor and many of his friends that he was bringing his illness to a fatal crisis by performing the violent readings from *Oliver Twist*. And yet he willfully continued the performances even though he seems to have believed they would kill him. Concealing this self-executing Dickens is his criminal double, the self-executing Sikes. Far from being a public execution, these readings, which are the representation of a public-execution, are also its inversion, the final triumph of the novelistic. No one's death is exposed here. Someone is dying, but only secretly, while the crowd's attention is focused on the duplicitous representation of the death of the double.

Indeed, Dickens uses the same methods of revelation and conealment when, in the guise of longing for the cessation of these performances, he longs for his own death and the final blankness of the theater. In a sentence that necessarily conjures the ghost of Sydney Carton, he writes of his last readings, "'Like lights in a theater, they are being snuffed out fast,' as Carlyle says of the guillotined in his Revolution. I suppose I shall be glad when they are all snuffed out."[23]

NOTES

1. For the seminal discussion of the novel's internal uses of the institutions it competes with, see D. A. Miller, "The Novel and the Police," *Glyph*, 8 (1981), 127–147.

2. For a full discussion of the novels' relationship to the public-private opposition, see D. A. Miller, "Discipline in Different Voices: Bureaucracy, Police, Family, and *Bleak House*," *Representations*, 1 (Winter, 1982), 59–89.

3. *Dombey and Son* (London: Chapman & Hall, n.d.), p. 739.

4. Horace Bleackley and Lyn H. Lofland, *State Executions Viewed Historically and Sociologically*. (London: Chapman & Hall, 1929), p. 311.

5. *A Tale of Two Cities*, ed. and intro. George Woodcock (Harmondsworth: Penguin, 1970), p. 93. All subsequent quotations from the novel are from this edition, and page numbers will be given in the text.

6. See *Discipline and Punish; the Birth of the Prison*, trans. Alan Sheridan. (New York: Vintage Books, 1979), pp. 32–103; and Michael Ignatieff, *A Just Measure of Pain; The Penitentiary in the Industrial Revolution, 1750–1850* (New York: Pantheon, 1978), *passim*.

7. Miller, "Discipline in Different Voices."

8. Dickens, "Letters to the Editor of the *London Times*" (13 November 1849) vol. 22, *Collected Works* (New York, 1892), 242.

9. P. Linebaugh, "The Ordinary of Newgate and His Account," *Crime in England 1550-1800* (London: Methuen & Co., 1977), pp. 251-252.

10. Linebaugh, pp. 257-258.

11. Bleackley and Lofland, pp. 291-292; August Mencken, ed., *By the Neck: A Book of Hangings* (New York: n.p., 1942), p. 250.

12. Thomas Laqueur, "Politics as Carnival in Hanoverian England," Humanities Institute, Stanford University, 12 Sept. 1982.

13. *Oliver Twist* (New York: Penguin, 1966), pp. 450-451.

14. Dickens, "Letters to the Editor," *loc. cit.*

15. *Ibid.*

16. *Reflections on the Revolution in France*, ed. Thomas Mahony (Indianapolis: Bobbs-Merrill, 1955), p. 87.

17. Lynn A. Hunt, "The Rhetoric of Revolution in France," forthcoming in *History Workshop Journal,* (Spring 1983).

18. Quoted in Hunt, *op.cit.*

19. Quoted in Hunt, *op.cit.*

20. Recounted in Cecil Howard Turner, *The Inhumanists* (London: Alexander Ouseley, 1932), pp. 92-93.

21. Turner, p. 50.

22. Quoted in Edgar Johnson, *Charles Dickens; His Tragedy and Triumph* (New York: Penguin, 1979), p. 556.

23. *Ibid.*

Charles Darnay and Revolutionary Identity

Edwin M. Eigner

Since this essay is in some senses a continuation of a piece I published in *Dickens Studies Annual*, 11,[1] and since that piece contains the framework within which the following argument must be understood, I shall begin, as the RSC does at the beginning of each act of *Nicholas Nickleby*, with a brief recapitulation. The controlling idea in the first paper, as in this one, is that from as early as his own version of *Nicholas Nickleby* in 1838, Dickens structured each of his novels on a form of popular entertainment called the Christmas or Easter Pantomime.

Dickens' Pantomime is not to be confused either with the sort of thing Marcel Marceau does or with the cheap entertainments called pantomimes or pantos which are staged these days in England every Christmas season, although both are descendants.[2] The Regency and Early Victorian Pantomime which influenced Dickens was a highly stylized affair, always in two parts. In the first and relatively realistic scene, a pair of young lovers would have their romantic plans frustrated by three characters: the girl's avaricious or weak father, a wicked or foppish lover whom the father favors, and a blundering comic servant. When the wicked lover seems about to triumph, a benevolent spirit out of Mother Goose or the Arabian Nights or some other fantasy appears and changes each of the characters into one of the figures from the English development of the *commedia dell arte* Harlequinade. The girl becomes Columbine, the boy she loves becomes Harlequin, the father is changed to Pantaloon, the wicked lover is transformed to a figure called Dandy Lover, and the servant becomes Clown, who is the ancestor of Charles Chaplin and the circus and rodeo clowns of today. These transformations give the young lovers another chance, with the odds in their favor this time, for Harlequin is nimbler than his enemies and he is aided by a magic bat or slap-stick. He is also the beneficiary of the actions of Clown, who either intentionally or inadvertently betrays his masters, Pantaloon and Dandy Lover, and saves the

147

young people. This is done at his own expense, not only because he receives blows from his master but, frequently, because he is himself in love with Columbine.

My argument is that most Dickens heroines find themselves surrounded by four would-be lovers, who correspond to the four male figures in the Harlequinade. She always has a father or a father figure who gets her into trouble, sometimes by selfishly exploiting her, as in *Nicholas Nickleby*, but more often unintentionally, as with Dr. Manette in *A Tale of Two Cities*, or at least without any consciously wicked intention. I make this last qualification because there is frequently the suggestion, as with Manette again, that the father's feeling for his daughter is not purely parental and that he views her favored lover, Charles Darnay in this novel, with more than a touch of sexual jealousy. Consciously, Manette means nothing but good for Charles, and he is sincerely active in his attempts to free him, but the efforts fail, after all, and it is, of course, Manette's testimony, written in the Bastille, which condemns Charles.

The heroine has also a wicked lover, whose principal crime is usually an aspiration to rise in the social world by unfair or crass means until he achieves the bliss of winning her. Lawyer Stryver of *A Tale of Two Cities* is a weak embodiment of this figure from the Dickens Pantomime. A more recognizable wicked lover is Carker the Manager of *Dombey and Son* or Uriah Heep of *David Copperfield*, of whom George Orwell writes:

> Considering how Heep's general lowness—his servile manners, dropped aitches and so forth—has been rubbed in throughout the book, there is not much doubt about the nature of Dickens's feelings. Heep, of course, is playing a villainous part, but even villains have sexual lives; it is the thought of the "pure" Agnes in bed with a man who drops his aitches that really revolts Dickens.[3]

Stryver is like these wicked lovers because he perceives the heroine as the reward, not as the means of his elevation—he is rather proud, in fact, of his decision to please himself and marry a poor girl. He is also like the others in that his shouldering self-assertiveness and vulgar determination to rise in life represent or reflect a chief evil which the novel exposes. From one point of view, at least, social mobility at any price is what the French Revolution is all about.

Stryver is typical of this figure once again in that he employs, in a virtual slave capacity, the most dissipated and improvident of all the characters of the novel, a personage whom no one regards seriously and from whom no one ever expects anything, but who, like the Clown in the Harlequinade, always performs the essential action which saves the heroine. It was this character, developed from Newman Noggs of *Nicholas Nickleby*,[4] through Micawber of *David Copperfield*, and finding most serious expression in Sydney Carton of *A Tale of Two Cities*, which I concentrated on in my paper of last year, arguing that since he possessed the Saturnalian or sexual energy which belonged in the Pantomime Harlequinade to Clown rather than Harlequin, he was able to act where the romantic lover, from whom one would naturally expect action, was powerless.[5] David Copperfield cannot save Agnes from Uriah Heep, but Micawber can. In *Great Expectations*, where for the first time Dickens did not provide an adequate clown figure, the heroine is not rescued and actually marries and is bedded by the wicked lover. And in *A Tale of Two Cities* it is the unregarded Sydney Carton who can act decisively in the crisis, while his much more successful and substantial rival, Charles Darnay, has been powerless, powerless not only to defend himself from the revengeful fury of the revolution, but also impotent to protect his family, to avoid being caught in the machinations of his wicked uncle, to benefit the starving peasants on his French estate, and, perhaps most significantly, to carry out the first charge of his life, laid upon him by his mother when he was a boy, to find and care for the sister of the raped girl, Madame Defarge, who has little trouble finding and taking care of him.

It is this figure, the romantic lover, on whom I wish to concentrate this time, for just as Sydney Carton was the least funny and the most significant of Dickens' Clowns, so Charles Darnay is the most heavy-footed and, certainly to this point of the author's career, the most problematic of his Harlequins.

Readers and critics, until recently, at any rate, have found Dickens' romantic heroes among the least interesting of his characters, and Darnay is certainly no exception in this regard. He has differed from the other heroes who end up with the girls, however, in that, from the beginning, and in spite of the facts that his manners are impeccable and usually calculated not to give offense, he has inspired animosity both from those within the novel and those outside it. If we could forgive the wicked Marquis de St. Evremonde anything, perhaps it would be for what Albert Hutter, in a brilliant essay, calls his "murderous impulses towards his brother's child,"[6] for Charles holds himself morally superior to his uncle and openly rejects everything the latter stands for. This is, I believe, the only time in the novel he takes such a tone. Nevertheless, it is understandable, I suppose, that Madame Defarge and the revolutionaries should see Charles, whether mistakenly or not, as their enemy, the symbol of their oppression. Even the Old Bailey crowd in England can perhaps be excused for their disappointment at not getting to see him half-hanged, then taken down and sliced before his own face, then have his insides burnt while he looks on, then have his head chopped off, and then have his body cut into quarters. Maybe there is not anything personal in this. One could not hope, moreover, that Charles would be especially popular with his English romantic rivals. It is to be expected, therefore, that Stryver should "believe there is contamination in such a scoundrel"[7] and that Carton should simply "hate the fellow."[8] Nor should we be surprised at the negative feelings of those millions of readers who have identified with Carton and felt his rejection by Lucie as if it were their own. Even Charles is quick to excuse his father-in-law for condemning him and his descendants "to the last of their race."[9] It's what he's come to expect. Nevertheless, some of the dislike for Darnay goes beyond the explanations provided.

Less than a month after the last chapter of the novel was published, James Fitzjames Stephen wrote to express his contempt for this coward who "thought he had better live by his wits in London than have the responsibility of continuing a landowner in France,"[10] and Lawrence Frank, a recent interpreter, sees Charles as a self-deceiver, who "lives 'unknown in England,' where he is 'no Marquis': unknown to his tenants in France, unknown to his wife, unknown, finally, to himself."[11] In the centennial year of Dickens's death, 1970, the French critic Sylvère Monod noted the "unusually unanimous critical feeling against" Darnay, citing the condemnations of John Gross, K. J. Fielding, and Edgar Johnson. He concludes the summary with his own conviction that while Dickens identified Darnay with himself, "lending him his own leaning towards 'The Loadstone Rock'," he did not give Darnay "more than .01 percent" of his own vitality.[12]

Jack Lindsay was, I believe, the first to note this identification of Dickens with Darnay when he pointed out that the latter "has the revealing initials Charles D."[13] Charles's real name, Evremonde, has also been seen as significant, but in an almost opposite way. Robert Alter believes it suggests the character is "a sort of Everman,"[14] and Elliot Gilbert, in a paper delivered at the 1982 Santa Cruz Dickens Conference and printed in the present volume, calls the name "a multi-lingual, two-cities pun on 'everyman' or 'all-the-world.'"[15] At another paper delivered at the same conference, Garrett Stewart emphasized the sudden grammatical shift into the first person plural in Book the Third, Chapter 13. The reader, as Stewart suggested, is virtually "conscripted" to accompany the drugged Darnay as the coach takes him, Mr. Lorry, Dr. Manette, and the two Lucies away from the danger of Paris.

Perhaps these insights, beginning with Alter's, provide clues to Darnay's unpopularity. If Dickens wants to identify such a character with himself, that is one matter; but if he is going to try to force us to accept such an identification, that is something else again. But why should we object? Charles is good-looking, well-born, well-bred, well-educated, intelligent, fortunate in both life and love. If he does not have Charles Dickens' vitality, he at least has his industry, and if the aristocratic Fitzjames Stephen wants to call schoolteaching "living by one's wits," why should literary critics, who are most of them schoolteachers themselves, want to share the contempt?

I think an answer to this question and also to the question of why Charles is so disliked within the novel may lie in the way this hero regards himself. Darnay's self-contempt is not so Byronically obvious as Carton's, but I suspect it is deeper and more difficult to transcend, at least by his own efforts. Think, for instance, of the meek way he accepts Carton's insolence after the English trial and the modest way he presses his claim to Lucie when he asks her father not to oppose his courtship.

> I have felt [he says], and do feel even now, that to bring my love—even mine—between you [and Lucie], is to touch your history with something not quite so good as itself.[16]

At the level of the book's religious allegory, he is, of course, Everyman, suffering from original sin. In this regard, Taylor Stoehr has written that "Darnay's guilt appears to be hereditary."[17] Albert Hutter and Lawrence Frank, moreover, in articles previously cited, have both argued convincingly that he is guilty also of a kind of parricide, having imagined or willed the death of his father's twin brother, the evil Marquis, just hours or perhaps minutes before the latter's murder. But one does not need a Christian or a Freudian interpretation to understand the guilt feelings of a man who was told by his mother when he was two years old that unless he can find and reconcile the needle-in-a-haystack sister of the peasant girl his father had wronged, "atonement would one day be required of him."[18] Moreover, guilt is a speciality of the romantic hero in Dickens' later novels.

In the essays he wrote about the Pantomime at various pionts in his career, Dickens had interesting things to say about most of the figures, but Harlequin was described only as an ordinary man "to be found in no particular walk or degree, on whom a certain station, or particular conjunction of circumstances, confers the magic wand."[19] In other words, he is lucky enough to be loved by Columbine, and this luck seems to be the one most significant aspect of the character Dickens derived from Harlequin. Two years after the publication of the essay in question, when he was driving towards the conclusion of *Nicholas Nickleby* and setting up what I believe to be the first pantomime within his fiction, Dickens had pantaloon-wearing Ralph Nickleby say of his Harlequin nephew, "There is some spell about that boy.... Circumstances conspire to help him. Talk of fortune's favours! What is even money to such Devil's luck as this?"[20] Thus began, if it did not begin even earlier in *Oliver Twist*, a line of Dickens heroes who narrowly escape death in war or by plague or shipwreck or attempted murder or who are selected arbitrarily to become gentlemen, while the Uriah Heeps and Orlicks eat their hearts out. In *The Frozen Deep*, the Wilkie Collins–Charles Dickens play which inspired the writing of *A Tale of Two Cities*, Richard Wardour, the model for Sydney Carton, says contemptuously to the man whom he has not yet recognized as his rival but for whom he will ultimately sacrifice his own life, "You have got what the women call a lucky face."[21] And Carton himself regards Charles Darnay similarly when he reflects, "I thought he was rather a handsome fellow, and I thought I should have been much the same sort of fellow if I had had any luck."[22]

Charles is, of course, not only lucky in his face and in love and in his Harlequin knack of always getting out or being gotten out of the deadly scrapes he finds himself in, he is also extremely lucky in his birth as compared to his starving French countrymen. This last mentioned aspect of his luck, moreover, is what relates him most closely to other Dickens heroes and to the guilty feeling heroes in a number of important nineteenth- and twentieth-century novels. Previously, in an article called "Faulkner's Isaac and the American Ishmael,"[23] I dealt with a recurring relationship in American fiction between one man, who has inherited because he was lucky enough to have been born white, and his disinherited brother, no less a man than he, but of a different race. The Biblical story this relationship was always intended to bring to mind was, of course, that of the young Ishmael, who was cast out into the wilderness, deprived both of material prosperity and of his share in the Covenant because he was replaced by his younger brother Isaac, who had the luck to be born legitimate. I was especially interested in the fact that American writers, not only Melville and Faulkner, but, of course, Cooper, Hawthorne, Stowe, Twain and others were not so much interested in depicting the anguish of the rejected Ishmael as they were in showing the guilt of the reluctantly inheriting Isaac. In British fiction and especially in the novels of Dickens, as I was later on to see,[24] this relationship is not between individuals of different races but of different economic classes. In America a white Isaac feels uneasy with the thought that the plantation he has inherited should really have gone to his black brother Ishmael; in Dickens, from as early as *Oliver Twist*, a gentleman feels guilty or should feel guilty with the thought that he is living on a patrimony to which he has no legitimate right so long as others of his species are impoverished. Nicholas Nickleby and Smike are very much like an interracial pair out of American literature.

From very early in his career, from at least as early as *Martin Chuzzlewit*, Dickens tended to combine the luck of his Harlequin figures, the romantic lovers, with feelings of guilt. Walter Gay, who plays this role in *Dombey and Son*, was originally intended to be corrupted by the business morality of the novel's world and the Dick Whittington—sell-your-best-friend-and-rise-in-the-world—dreams of his friends. David Copperfield, the hero of the novel which bears his name, is so troubled by vague and undefinable guilt feelings—about his friend's seduction of little Em'ly, about the early death the wife he had grown tired of, about his dealings with the servant class from which he sprung, about his own rise in the world—that psychological critics have recently been having a field day with him, converting what used to be regarded in Chestertonian days as the blandest of Dickens' characters into one of the most complex. Arthur Clennam, the middle-aged, dreary, romantic lover of *Little Dorrit*, who instead of marrying his sweetheart allowed himself to be shipped off to China, returns with a crippling sense of unworthiness and with a guilty suspicion that the capital on which he lives must have been stolen from someone else. And since Arthur can't find anyone with a legitimate claim on his money and cannot put his finger on any crime he has actually committed, he manages both to impoverish himself and to find himself guilty by investing his own and his partner's funds in a fraudulent financial scheme which goes bankrupt. He fairly rejoices at having done something worthy of being put into prison for.

Pip, the romantic hero of the novel which follows *A Tale of Two Cities*, is similarly successful in getting rid of the shame he has been made to feel in his youth[25] by parlaying it into real guilt, guilt at having snobbishly rejected the people who are dearest to him, and especially at not having rejected the destructive metaphor current in the novel which divides humanity into genteel predators—hounds or spiders—and impoverished victims—varmints or insects—instead of acknowledging everyone, as Joe Gargery does, as a fellow creature. Pip is, of course, both the luckiest and the guiltiest of the romantic heroes, lucky enough to get a fortune merely by wishing for it, and so guilty that Dickens could not make up his mind in the first draft of the novel to let him marry the heroine.

On the other hand, Charles Darnay does most emphatically get the girl, although, as we have seen, she is virtually the only character in *A Tale of Two Cities*, including himself, who can stand him. Charles's marriage, in fact, occurs in the sixteenth of the thirty-one serial parts of the novel, that is to say, the very center, always the place of highest significance in a Dickens story. "Charles Darnay's way," we are told by the author, is the one way "the world of man has invariably gone . . . the way of the love of a woman."[26] He is so lucky that even the immense power of his sense of guilt and unworthiness has no ultimate force against him.

Nevertheless, we ought not to underestimate the depth of that sense of guilt, and we should, I think, give due attention to the question of how far it is justified in relation to the principal action and historical event of *A Tale of Two Cities*: the French Revolution; that is to say, how much of Charles Darnay's guilt is not only an expression of the condition of man after the Fall and of undeniable psychological trauma, but is caused and perhaps justified by Charles's failures as social man.

To begin with, he has not fulfilled the first charge of his life, to sell his mother's jewels and give the money to the sister of the raped peasant girl, Madame Defarge, as it turns out. In fact, we are not told that Charles so much as made an attempt at carrying out this obligation, although it is possible that this is what he was trying to do on those mysterious trips between England and France between 1775 and 1780. This is special pleading in Charles's behalf, for there is no evidence, but I can think of no other explanation for the secrecy of these journeys, a secrecy which, at his English trial for treason, Charles maintains at very serious expense to his case and danger to his life. He told Lucie he "was travelling under an assumed name" because he "was travelling on a business of a delicate and difficult nature, which might get people into trouble."[27] He could not have been divesting himself of his estate, for he had not come into that yet, and it is difficult to imagine who, besides himself and anti-aristocratic agents helping in the search for the wronged girl, might be in any danger. Still it is curious that *Dickens* maintains the secrecy, and curious also that Darney, usually so apt to feel guilty, does not torture himself about this failure to carry out his mother's first command.

On the other hand, Darnay is distraught at his powerlessness to, as he says, "execute the last request of my dear mother's lips, and obey the last look of my dear mother's eyes, which implored me to have mercy and to redress."[28] The powerlessness comes, presumably, from Charles's situation of having been passed over in the inheritance—his wicked uncle rules instead of him—but when he does succeed to the estate, just hours after making this speech, he is still unable to peform effectively:

> he had acted imperfectly. He knew very well, that in his love for Lucie, his renunciation of his social place, though by no means new to his mind, had been hurried and incomplete. He knew that he ought to have systematically worked it out and supervised it, and that he had meant to do it, and that it had never been done. . . . he had watched the times for a time of action . . . until the time had gone by.[29]

But even this confession of failure by Charles misses the point. Presumably his mother's lips and eyes had not implored him to renounce his power, but rather to use it for the sake of the poor.

Nevertheless, the sense of guilt and shame called up by this train of thought impels Charles's return to France for the sake of saving his servant and using his influence to moderate the revolution. Dickens writes "His latent uneasiness had been, that bad aims were being worked out in his own unhappy land by bad instruments, and that he, who could not fail to know that he was better than they, was not there, trying to do something to stay the bloodshed, and assert the claims of mercy and humanity."[30] All very fine, but painful though it is to contradict T. A. Jackson, perhaps the one critic who has something positive to say about Charles, I am not sure Dickens wants us entirely to admire the "large-hearted generosity"[31] of his hero when he sends him back to France, drawn to the loadstone rock. In the first place, he is still not acting to redress as his mother had commanded but only to plead mercy for the members and the agents of his own class. As his assumed name suggests, and it has to be significant in a novel filled with Carlyle's clothing symbols[32] and with symbolic names, Charles Darnay is, at best, a mender, and has no place as part of a revolution. He wants reform; the Defarges, true revolutionaries, want continued abuses to infuriate the people.

In the second place, Charles's impulsive action is strongly reminiscent of the ineffective or unsustained windmill charges on social institutions made by previous romantic heroes in Dickens' novels. He dashes into the French Revolution as Arthur Clennam of *Little Dorrit* took on the Circumlocution Office or as Richard Carstone of *Bleak House* smashed his head against the Court of Chancery. The action is naively vain, as Dickens suggests when he tells us of Darnay that the "glorious vision of doing good, which is so often the sanguine mirage of so many good minds, arose before him, and he even saw himself in the illusion with some influence to guide this raging Revolution."[33] And there is also the possibility of an unworthy subconscious motivation for his action. Since it developed from a sense of shame and guilt, Charles's purpose, like that of Clennam, may be to punish himself. Having failed to redress the wrong as his mother had charged him to do, he may be embracing the opportunity for the violent atonement she had predicted as the alternative. In any event, these are the ways Charles's brief career as a social activist seems destined to turn out—vain and self-destructive.

But before we go too far in joining the chorus which condemns Charles Darnay, it is well to remember that Dickens could never bring himself to believe in the Carlylean hero and that by this time in his career he was highly skeptical of the effectuality of social action of any sort. Dickens may not be criticizing Charles Darnay's qualities as a Revolutionary hero; he is more likely undermining the very concept of romantic heroism by doubting both its motives and its possibilities for success. Charles is at least as powerless in Revolutionary France as he was in bourgeois England, but in the long run he is no less effectual than the other would-be Revolutionary heroes whose fate Carton predicts in the final chapter.

The hero of Bulwer-Lytton's French Revolutionary novel, *Zanoni* (1842), which has long been recognized as one of the sources of *A Tale of Two Cities*,[34] is, unlike Darnay, a figure of immense, almost god-like power in his proper sphere. Nevertheless Zanoni accomplishes nothing to his purpose when he mixes "for the first time . . . among the broils and strategies of man."[35] Zanoni does not altogether fail—he brings about no less an event than the fall of Robespierre—but the purpose for which he acted, which was to save his beloved from the guillotine by hastening the end of the Terror, is absolutely frustrated when Robespierre, foreseeing the end of *his* power, simply advances the date of the execution one day.

> Vain seer [admonishes the author] who wouldst make thyself the instrument of the Eternal, the very danger that now best the tyrant but expedited the doom of his victims. Tomorrow, eighty heads, and her whose pillow has been thy heart.[36]

If the romantic hero cannot find revolutionary identity by acting with romantic, Schilleresque heroism, it is still possible, even in the turmoil of the Revolution, for him to maintain his identity as a lover. Zanoni plays Sydney Carton's part, dying on the guillotine not only for the sake of, but actually in the place of his beloved. And for him it is a significant sacrifice, for having discovered the secret of eternal youth, Zanoni is several hundred years old in 1793 and will live forever if he can only avoid accidents like decapitation.

Similarly, Charles Darnay is rendered physically powerless by the Revolution he had come to France to direct, and he is transformed into a helpless and sleeping infant by the growing strength of Sydney Carton. Nevertheless, he keeps a firm hold on his role as Harlequin. I suggested earlier that the action of the sixteenth number, the wedding of Charles and Lucie, pointed to marriage as the novel's central meaning. Other places one looks for meaning in a Dickens novel are the earliest and latest points of the story. Lawrence Frank notes that "the novel, literally and figuratively originates in a rape,"[37] and while this is true of work as we have it, in Dickens' earliest manuscript, the younger Evremonde twin did not rape the peasant girl; he seduced her by pretending to marry her.[38] So the story was intended also to begin with a marriage, albeit a false one. I think *A Tale of Two Cities* ends with a marriage, as well, the marriage of Carton and the little seamstress, whose innocence and occupation identify her as a substitute for Lucie of the golden thread. The three weddings indicate a progress: we begin with a false and secret marriage; move then to the real but strangely private nuptials of Charles and Lucie; and conclude with a wedding which is both symbolic and highly public. This wedding on the scaffold validates Carton and his great sacrifice. He is dying for Darnay and for Darnay's marriage to Lucie. It is perhaps of equal significance that in an unrendered scene of the novel which presumably took place at La Force Prison, Charles Darnay courted Sydney Carton's bride for him. When the girl approaches Sydney and asks if she can hold his hand in the cart, she still mistakes him for his double, whom both he and the reader have neglected to thank, and those identity, revolutionary and otherwise, is as Harlequin lover.

NOTES

1. "The Absent Clown in *Great Expectations*," pp. 115–133.
2. Michael Booth in *Victorian Spectacular Theatre 1850–1910* (London: Routledge & Kegan Paul, 1981), provides an excellent account of how the Pantomime I am referring to was changing even as Dickens was writing:

    It is no coincidence that the opening lengthened, the fairy element strengthened, and the harlequinade shortened as the interest in fairy culture grew and intensified in the 1830s and 1840s. . . . [The transformation scene still] concluded the opening but no longer introduced the harlequinade, which still remained in truncated form—two to four scenes only—but had no connection with the opening. The opening became all-inclusive, embracing the grotesque, the topical, the ideal, the satirical, low comedy, and fairyland fantasy in the same entertainment as well as panoramas, minstrel and music-hall songs and dances, ballets, performing animals, jugglers, magicians, and specialty acts of all kinds. Toward the end of the century the harlequinade had virtually disappeared in the West End, and a late Victorian pantomime there was almost entirely concerned with the scenic grandeurs, low comedy, and fairyland narrative of the opening. (p. 75)

3. "Charles Dickens" in *Dickens, Dali and Others* (New York: Reynal Hitchcock, 1947), p. 41.

4. T. A. Jackson argues that the same line began with Alfred Jingle and Dick Swiveller. *Charles Dickens: The Progress of a Radical* (New York: International Publishers, 1938), p. 187.

5. Booth testifies to the importance Clown had achieved in the Pantomime when he writes that "The harlequinade . . . was devised by the Clown in consultation with the machinists of the trick-work and the ballet master, sometimes the Harlequin, who supervised the dances" (p. 75).

6. "Nation and Generation in *A Tale of Two Cities,*" *PMLA*, 93 (1978), 450.

7. *A Tale of Two Cities* (Harmondsworth: Penguin, 1970), Book the Second, Chapter 24, p. 269.

8. Book the Second, Chapter 4, p. 116.

9. Book the Third, Chapter 10, p. 361.

10. "*A Tale of Two Cities,*" *Saturday Review*, 17 Dec. 1859, 741.

11. "Dickens' *A Tale of Two Cities*: The Poetics of Impasse," *American Imago*, XXXVI (1979), 231.

12. "Dickens's Attitudes in *A Tale of Two Cities,*" in *Dickens Centennial Essays*, Ada Nisbet and Blake Nevius, eds. (Berkeley: University of California Press, 1971), p. 177.

13. "A Tale of Two Cities," *Life and Letters and The London Mercury*, LXII (1949), 196.

14. "The Demons of History in Dickens' *Tale,*" *Novel: A Forum of Fiction*, II (1969), 138.

15. P. 259.

16. Book the Second, Chapter 10, p. 163.

17. *Dickens: The Dreamer's Stance* (Ithaca: Cornell University Press, 1965), p. 198.

18. Book the Third, Chapter 10, p. 360.

19. "The Pantomime of Life," *Bentley's Miscellany*, I, (1837), 295.

20. *Nicholas Nickleby* (Harmondsworth: Penguin, 1978), Chapter 44, p. 658.

21. In *Under the Management of Mr. Charles Dickens*, Robert Louis Brannan, ed. (Ithaca: Cornell University Press, 1966), p. 130.

22. Book the Second, Chapter 5, p. 118.

23. *Jahrbuch fuer Amerikastudien*, XIV (1969), 107–115.

24. See *The Metaphysical Novel in England and America: Dickens, Bulwer, Hawthorne, Melville* (Berkeley: University of California Press, 1978), pp. 112–113.

25. See Robert Newsom, "The Hero's Shame," *Dickens Studies Annual: Essays on Victorian Fiction*, 11, Michael Timko, Fred Kaplan, and Edward Guiliano, eds. (New York: AMS Press, 1983), pp. 1–24.

26. Book the Second, Chapter 10, p. 160.

27. Book the Second, Chapter 3, p. 102.

28. Book the Second, Chapter 9, p. 154.

29. Book the Second, Chapter 24, p. 271.

30. *Ibid*, p. 272.

31. *Charles Dickens: Portrait of a Radical*, p. 185.

32. See Michael Timko, "Splendid Impressions and Picturesque Means: Dickens, Carlyle, and the French Revolution." published in the present volume, pp. 177–195.

33. Book the Second, Chapter 24, p. 272.

34. Jack Lindsay, *A Tale of Two Cities*, p. 197.

35. Knebworth edition (London: George Routledge & Sons, n.d.) Book Seventh, Chapter X, p. 368.

36. Book Seventh, Chapter XII, p. 376.

37. "Dickens' *A Tale of Two Cities*: The Poetics of Impasse," p. 217.

38. See David Tucker, "Dickens at Work on the MS of *A Tale of Two Cities*," *Études Anglais*, XXXII (1979), 453–454.

Writing the Revolution

Murray Baumgarten

Lives are saved by bits of paper on which a few words have been written in *A Tale of Two Cities* and they are also doomed by them. Letters of safe passage make it possible for Lucie and her father, Jarvis Lorry and Pross to leave France at the end of the novel; but no passport is available for Charles Darnay in his own name and he must use his double's. Madame Defarge's knitting is a deadly form of writing. Gaspard writes on the walls in wine what he will later inscribe in blood. Despite the intentions of their authors, these written messages are ambiguous, just as the inscriptions of servitude Monseigneur inflicts upon his peasants and servants do not lead to desired effects. Meanings change. Sense turns into non-sense. This world is characterized by contradiction from which writing is not excluded. Writing saves here but it also attaints and is tainted.[1]

The inherent difficulties of writing come to a focus in the narrative of Doctor Manette's imprisonment. Serving as the testimony that condemns Evremonde-Darnay, the tale—despite Doctor Manette's later change of heart and acceptance of Darnay into his family—fulfills its original purpose. Recounting the events that brought Manette to his living death in the Bastille, his narrative justifies the absolute judgment, beyond question or qualification, with which it ends. "I, Alexandre Manette, unhappy prisoner, do this last night of the year 1767, in my unbearable agony, denounce" the Evremondes "and their descendants, to the last of their race"—"to the times when all these things shall be answered for. I denounce them to Heaven and to earth"[2] (III, 10, 361). Like Madame Defarge's knitting, Doctor Manette's writing is a pledge to be redeemed by the future.

The condition of the inexorable purpose that encompasses this tale is that it be inscribed—that is, written—in this instance on paper and thus made objective. Only such reification will remove it from the changeable subjectivity governing human life. A statement of value, Manette's account

161

like Madame Defarge's knitting (and in another mood Monseigneur's privileges) is a desperate vow that attempts to remove words and deeds from their contingent situation and render them unconditional.

Like money, this writing of Doctor Manette's and Madame Defarge's is a promise of future payment. (By contrast the *ancien régime* functions on the gold standard). Like money in the era of the rise of capitalism, this writing is the promissory note and coin of moral judgment, to be redeemed at the trial and physical execution of all the Evremondes.

When the revolution calls this note in for payment its signator, the author of the testimony, regrets the uses to which his writing has been put, but does not disavow the intention that led him to his writing. Even its intended victim sympathizes with the conditions and feelings that led his father-in-law to frame his tale and oath, and as he is being led away Charles explicitly tells him not to blame himself or feel remorse at the destruction his writing has wrought. Unable to deal with the unbearable contradictions in which he is caught and which he has helped to articulate, Manette breaks down, reverting to the living death of the beginning of the novel.

Unlike the reader of this scene, Manette does not acknowledge that even written words, like the social order of France to which they are connected, are not unchanging and immortal. Neither Ozymandias' statue nor beaten gold stand outside of time that changes everything into its opposite, nothing, as we know from the Second Law of Thermodynamics, and makes of sense non-sense. We know that all symbols, be they written or hieroglyphic, as well as the phrases they construct (even repeated and rephrased as Madame Defarge's are in her knitting to ensure the doom of the enemies of the people) cannot help but be ambiguous, despite the fixed intentions of their writers: even dollars signed by Ivy Baker Priest change their value. Madame Defarge finds her death in seeking to call the knitted symbols of her writing in for payment. The Marquis is killed because he believes in the eternal authority of the coin of his privilege. Sydney Carton offers himself as ransom for Manette's promissory note. Reunited with Lucie and Charles, who has been miraculously recalled to life, Manette escapes from the consequences of his writing. All the resources of the plot are needed to help Jarvis Lorry, astute banker and man of business, manage to rescue him a second time.

An account of great power, Manette's testimony has the shape of gothic fiction, functioning as a novel in miniature. As such it provides a model of mis-reading, in which writing is taken absolutely, and becomes an imprisoning code. Set in the novel as the mechanism that brings on the final entanglement of Darnay's personal and public life, of his English and French destinies, it forces us to confront the meaning of writing in this novel.

The moral judgment proclaimed by Manette's written testimony is absolute because of its condition as writing. There is no oral context which would shade its meaning, no human presence to recover the conditions and contingencies that led to its production. We remember that Charles Darnay, the person it condemns, has earned his living in England as a teacher of French—of reading and writing. When his double, Sydney Carton mounts the scaffold, his final vision is an unwritten piece of autobiographical writing, voiced beyond any imprisoning code and opening into the prophetic realm where writing is absolute and true.

> One of the most remarkable sufferers by the same axe—a woman—had asked at the foot of the same scaffold, not long before, to be allowed to write down the thoughts that were inspiring her. If he had given an utterance to his, and they were prophetic, they would have been these:

And Carton's vision takes us through the written word to the theatrical spectacle of his self-imagined, self-redeeming execution, concluding with the almost written flourish of his epitaph.[3] In this doubling and redoubling of the theme of writing we cannot help but be reminded of the presence of the author of the book in which these characters and their writing figure. Dickens made his living as a writer and producer of the written word and here surely reflects upon—perhaps more than half-consiously—the conditions and meanings of his profession and his livelihood. In *A Tale of Two Cities* Dickens encounters—along with his readers and so many of his characters—the revolutionary meanings of writing the revolution.

Is there any logic, we ask, to this "Thing called *La Revolution*, which, like an Angel of Death, hangs over France, noyading, fusillading, fighting, gun-boring, tanning human skins?" Carlyle's phrasing, with which Dickens was familiar, like ours is retrospective and concerned with texts and evidence, in short, with writing. "*La Revolution* is but so many Alphabetic Letters," Carlyle says, " a thing nowhere to be laid hands on, to be clapt under lock and key: where is it? what is it?" Perhaps, we respond, it is like scrip printed by a private institution, in an economy off the gold standard but not yet governed by a central banking system. Or is it a new kind of writing not yet accepted by the many? A form of value inchoate and inarticulate? It is all of these and as well the impulse underlying the forms of social organization. In Carlyle's powerful phrasing,

It is the Madness that dwells in the hearts of men. In this man it is, and in that man; as a rage or as a terror, it is in all men. Invisible, impalpable; and yet no black Azrael, with wings spread over half a continent, with sword sweeping from sea to sea, could be a truer Reality.[4]

The sources of this reality we find articulated in the work of a "sixty-year-old smiling public man" who himself helped to make revolution, cultural, political, and social—in Yeats, who recalls its meanings to life in some of his greatest poems. We encounter its power of confusion in the charismatic world of "The Second Coming"

> Things fall apart; the centre cannot hold;
> Mere anarchy is loosed upon the world,
> The blood-dimmed tide is loosed, and everywhere
> The ceremony of innocence is drowned.[5]

These lines evoke not only Yeats's personal experience of historical upheaval but as well the events, mood, and much of the feeling not only of Carlyle's history but also of Dickens' novel of revolution and terror. The nightmare of rebellion begins, Yeats wryly notes in an earlier poem, when sexual energy powers revolutionary will, and individuals take on mythic roles. Playing Helen of Troy, Maud Gonne like Madame Defarge, teaches "to ignorant men most violent ways,"—inciting them as a woman, half-myth, half-dream, until with courage equal to desire, they "hurled the little streets upon the great" ("No Second Troy," p. 89). Here Yeats captures the insurrectionary tenor of the revolutionary century before our own totalitarian one, reminding us that what we hear in Dickens' novel as in Carlyle's great history is the effort to fathom the meanings of a world gone topsy-turvy, and Humpty Dumpty fallen.

Enter Liberty, Equality, and Fraternity, who make democracy a theme of life and art, and endow writing with a political edge. That is what Manette the writer, counts on—an emergent social order that will be governed, as Yeats said in setting for himself a literary program, by the "emotion of multitude." Here, too, Yeats defines the parameters of the inquiry because his enterprise as a writer depends upon its decoding. His phrase helps us to realize how Dickens' novel becomes a form open to the demands of his age. Large enough to encompass democracy and to examine the comedy of its triumph, it is also forceful enough to create the revolutionary emotion of multitude. The novel becomes for Dickens a loose and baggy monster that serves the purposes of the democratic revolution of his era in allowing him to mimic its tumult, dramatize its historical conflicts, and invent the theatre of its personal struggles.

Dickens' interest in the French Revolution was focused by his friendship with Carlyle. *A Tale of Two Cities* echoes much in Carlyle's great history. Not only is Dickens influenced by Carlyle, as Goldberg points out, but the differences between *A Tale of Two Cities* and *The French Revolution* depend upon the priority of the latter. The result is not that the two are in effect the same work; rather Carlyle's historical writing as we shall see makes possible the somewhat different mode of the novel.[6] It is worth noting that in the 1830s as he worked on his history, Carlyle found the revolution fascinating and personally compelling. He confided to Froude, his friend and biographer, that his spirtual health depended upon plumbing its meanings. Carlyle wrote as well to bring the presence of the Revolution to a troubled England and warn it of impending danger. In 1859, when Dickens wrote and published *A Tale of Two Cities*, twenty-two years after the publication of *The French Revolution*, personal and public concerns again came together, as they had for Carlyle.

Remember that 1859—miraculous year—saw among others the publication of Karl Marx's *Critique of Political Economy*, John Stuart Mill's *On Liberty*, Charles Darwin's *Origin of Species*, Samuel Smiles's *Self-Help*, and George Eliot's *Adam Bede*, not to forget Wilkie Collins's *Woman in White*, Edward Fitzgerald's *The Rubaiyat of Omar Khayyam*, and the first four parts of Tennyson's *Idylls of the King*. Along with Dickens these writers explored what Asa Briggs calls a "turning point in the late Victorian revolt against authority"—the crisis in the relations between older and younger generations.[7] Thereby they wrote out the meanings of the revolution which, begun in the last decades of the eighteenth century, yet governed the shape of their lives and art. Brandishing victorious and murderous democracy over their heads, it led them to sort out the contradictory logic of its revolutionary presence.

In *A Tale of Two Cities* revolution leads inevitably to "Republic one and indivisible." Following inexorably upon Liberty come Equality and Fraternity. And then Dickens undermines the slogan—"or Death" (III, 2, 287), the narrator adds, collapsing the years of shifting conflict and sporadic uprising into the Terror. If the political content of the novel is complicated by the sardonic addition of death to the revolutionary motto it is further vexed, in this novel of parallels and doubles, by the parallel sarcasm with which the narrator comments on the responses of French aristocrats and "native British orthodoxy." They "talk of this terrible Revolution as if it were the one only harvest ever known under the skies that had not been sown—as if nothing had ever been done, or omitted to be done, that had led to it" (II, 24, 267).

As the narrative records this belief, it at the same time dissociates the narrator by means of an ironic distancing from the view that the revolution is senseless. Whatever revolution is, no reader of Dickens will call it nonsense. Rather, this novel charts the meaning and sense animating the sea of emotion and action, confusion, fury, and hatred that is the Revolution. Like Carlyle's remarkable history, *A Tale of Two Cities* depends upon the organic imagery of horticulture to frame one of its central themes. The last chapter of the novel roots the awful terror of the Revolution in this context and projects it forward as a warning:

> Along the Paris streets, the death-carts rumble, hollow and harsh. Six tumbrils carry the day's wine to La Guillotine. All the devouring and insatiate Monsters imagined since imagination could record itself, are fused in the one realization, Guillotine. And yet there is not in France, with its rich variety of soil and climate, a blade, a leaf, a root, a sprig, a peppercorn, which will grow to maturity under conditions more certain than those that have produced this horror. Crush humanity out of shape once more, under similar hammers, and it will twist itself into the same tortured forms. Sow the same seed of rapacious license and oppression over again, and it will surely yield the same fruit according to its kind. (II, 15, 399)

This brief chapter as well brings the book to its conclusion with Carton's meditation on the happy harvest made possible by his act of self-sacrifice.

Writing the revolution, Dickens is neither conservative nor radical, but politically multifarious, as the prose of his novel—simultaneously distancing and bringing closer the actions it recounts—sweeps us with him into the shifting historical process. Suspended in the novel's dreamlike ambience, narrator and reader find themselves sympathizing with the revolutionary actors at the same time that they are revolted by their excesses.

Insisting on the organic analogy, neither Carlyle nor Dickens provides us with adequate historical explanations for the Revolution, though they do thereby remind us of the systematic and dynamic qualities of social existence. Novelist and historian share a common rhetoric and a misperception of the crisis that overtook the *ancien régime*. Hunger did not topple it. Prosperity and the revolution of rising expectations brought forward a new class—paper-using notaries and lawyers, merchants dealing in Wemmick's celebrated portable property—to lead the peasantry and emergent proletariat against an uncertain aristocracy. Of this social process, remarked upon by John Stuart Mill and Karl Marx, Dickens and Carlyle remain ignorant. For them France is going downhill, promulgating constitutions and printing paper-money. Certificates of promised sense, like the assignats of the French Revolution, for historian and novelist they turn out to be without value. Intended sense becomes nonsense. The vaguely Christian interests of Dickens and Carlyle as well as their concern to use the revolution in France as a moral touchstone for impending English social convulsion moved both to devise a style that engaged the reader while distancing him into an examination of his own country's situation.

Basing his work on that of his friend, Dickens tells us in the Preface to the First Edition that he yet "hopes to add something to the popular and picturesque means of understanding that terrible time, though no one can hope to add anything to the philosophy of Mr. Carlyle's wonderful book." Dickens' uncharacteristic modesty masks the anxiety of influence and directs us toward an evaluation of the differences between them. Carlyle, the historian, makes it possible for Dickens, the novelist, to represent the revolution in a different form and way. Unlike Carlyle, who brings that time to life by a process of visualization, commentary, and evocation that depends upon our seeing everything through the eyes of the historian who is examining the evidence and questioning the available texts, Dickens engages us through the dreamlike contradictions, split characters, and omniscient narrator—who keeps disappearing into his own apothegms —in the process of decoding the logic of revolution. Carlyle's footnotes remind us of the ontological status of the actions and events he discusses while Dickens implicates us in their unfolding fictional life by means of the gesture of writing repeated throughout the novel.

Carlyle's achievement is the breaking of neoclassic narrative. That accomplishment leads him from the linear order of narrative to a lyric method of portraying the simultaneity of action. Remaining nevertheless just within the bounds of historical writing Carlyle dramatizes a strategy for reading the evidence of the past. Like Michelet he verges on fictional writing, and his hypotactic style refuses to close the meanings of a given event or action into cause and effect. Still, Carlyle does seek the deep structure that determines surface events, locating it in beliefs and moral opinions. In his famous review, John Stuart Mill praised Carlyle's work as a poem and the truest of histories. It brings the conditions, actions, and events which helped bring on the Revolution to life for the reader. By comparison, however, with Dickens' work, Carlyle's remains within the parameters of history. What we are reading is a pointing toward the thing itself, not as in Dickens its evocation as a magic theatrical realm in which we participate as actors as well as spectators.

Carlyle's hero worship is based on the hope of putting Humpty Dumpty together again. He seeks to persuade all the king's horses and all the king's men to their work, thinking perhaps thereby he might recall traditional order to life once more. By contrast Dickens is a democrat who is comfortable with the dissipation of character into role. His narrator is everywhere and nowhere, by contrast with Carlyle's who has a fixed place from which to assay his world. In Dickens' novel the narrator orchestrates the different voices, playing all the parts. The differences between Carlyle's treatment and Dickens' are instructive. Consider how the Carmagnole figures in the two works.

In Carlyle's account we see the origins of this revolutionary dance. It is a ritual that replaces the unthinking Catholicism of the French with another spectacle. Carlyle quotes newspaper reports and eyewitness accounts (including that of Mercier, which Dickens used), in rendering the event:

> In such equipage did these profaners advance toward the Convention. They enter there, in an immense train, ranged in two rows; all masked like mummers in fantastic sacerdotal vestments; bearing on hand-barrows their heaped plunder,—ciboriums, suns, candelabras, plates of gold and silver.

The narrator functions as a journalist, recording the progress of the event. "Not untouched with liquor," they

> crave . . . permission to dance the Carmagnole also on the spot: whereto an exhilarated Convention cannot but accede. Nay "several Members" continues the exaggerative Mercier . . . "quitting their curule chairs, took the hand of girls flaunting in Priest's vestures, and danced the Carmagnole along with them." Such old-Hallowtide have they, in this year once named of Grace 1793 (III, Book V, Chapter 4, 226–227).

Having rendered the scene the narrator of this history reflects upon its meaning:

> Out of which strange fall of Formulas, tumbling there in confused welter, betrampled by the Patriotic dance, is it not passing strange to see a *new* Formula arise? For the human tongue is not adequate to speak what "triviality run distracted" there is in human nature.

Sharing the prejudices of his readers, this narrator cannot take the revolutionary ecstasies of the French seriously. To defend himself against them he reverts to his prejudices:

> Black Mumbo-Jumbo of the woods, and most Indian Wau-waus, one can understand: but this of Procureur *Anaxagoras*, whilom John-Peter, Chaumette? We will say only: Man is a born idol-worshipper, *sight*-worshipper, so sensuous-imaginative is he; and also partakes much of the nature of the ape.

Carlyle's sarcasm colors his account, and while it does not keep him from mentioning the orgiastic details, it does ensure their categorization as animalistic.

Always quick to seize on religious values, Carlyle explores the ways in which the new ritual is an unconscious parody of the old:

> For the same day, while this brave Carmagnole-dance has hardly jigged itself out, there arrive Procureur Chaumette and Municipals and Departmentals, and with them the strangest freightage: a New Religion! Demoiselle Candeille, of the Opera; a woman fair to look upon, when well rouged; she, borne on palanquin shoulderhigh; with red woolen nightcap; in azure mantle; garlanded with oak; holding in her hand the Pike of the Jupiter—*Peuple*, sails in: heralded by white young women girt in tricolor.

The piling up of details renders the scene grotesque. The narrator quickly draws the appropriate moral: "Let the world consider it! This, O National Convention wonder of the universe, is our New Divinity: *Goddess of Reason*, worthy, and alone worthy of revering. Her henceforth we adore."

Despite the ironic tone, the description is faithful to the ideological context. The changing situation is caught in terms of the emotions and beliefs that underlie it:

> And now, after due pause and flourishes of oratory, the Convention, gathering its limbs, does get under way in the required procession towards Notre-Dame;—Reason, again in her litter, sitting in the van of them, borne, as one judges, by men in the Roman costume; escorted by wind-music, red nightcaps, and the madness of the world.

Enthroned,

> Reason sat in azure mantle aloft, in a serene manner. . . . "And out of doors . . . were mad multitudes dancing round the bonfire of Chapel-balustrades, of Priests' and Canons' stalls; and the dancers,—I exaggerate nothing,—the dancers nigh bare of breeches, neck and breast naked, stockings down, went whirling and spinning, like those Dust-vortexes, forerunners of Tempest and Destruction." . . . Other mysteries, seemingly of a Cabiric or even Paphian character, we leave under the Veil, which appropriately stretches itself "along the pillars of the aisles,"—not to be lifted aside by the hand of History. (III, Book V, Chapter 4, 228–229)

Carlyle upholds the dignity of Clio as he renders her orgiastic undoing. The scene is powerfully described, miming the rush of events in a revolutionary time, expressing the entanglement of politics, religion, and sexuality. Piling up phrases in series, the narrator rushes us from event to event, leaving little time for meditation or even feeling. What we feel and think of all this he is sure to tell us, for the narrative voice is the locus of judgment in this work.

By contrast Dickens' use of the Carmagnole is restrained. Where Carlyle used it as an occasion for an implicit lesson, Dickens makes it an ironic occasion of rejoicing for Darnay that in its very excess prepares us for the ensuing disaster of his arrest and conviction. Having been vindicated, the mob embraces Darnay:

> They put him into a great chair they had among them . . . over which they had thrown a red flag . . . not even the Doctor's entreaties could prevent his being carried to his home on men's shoulders, with a confused sea of red caps heaving about him, and casting up to sight from the stormy deep such wrecks of faces, that he more than once misdoubted his mind being in confusion, and that he was in the tumbril on his way to the Guillotine.

The crowd winds its way forward "in wild dreamlike procession." Bringing Darnay to his wife in triumph

> a few of the people fell to dancing. Instantly, all the rest fell to dancing, and the court-yard overflowed with the Carmagnole. Then, they elevated into the vacant chair a young woman from the crowd to be carried as the Goddess of Liberty, and then swelling and overflowing out into the adjacent streets, and along the river's bank, and over the bridge, the Carmagnole absorbed them every one and whirled them away. (III, 6, 314–315)

This narrator, impersonator of all the roles of his world, forces us to take all the events seriously. None of them can be dismissed with a cry of nonsense; unlike Carlyle the novel's narrator does not seek to provide a desperate demonstration of their ultimate unreality.

Echoing Carlyle's account, Dickens compresses it, shaping it to the needs of his fiction. He can do this because Carlyle mediates between him and the historical material. At the same time Dickens has a broader sympathy that allows him to take on the point of view of the participants. Even the terrible aspect of the Carmagnole moves us:

> There could not be fewer than five hundred people, and they were dancing like five thousand demons. There was no other music than their own singing. They danced to the popular Revolution song, keeping a ferocious time that was like a gnashing of teeth in unison. Men and women danced together, women danced together, men danced together, as hazard had brought them together.

They are the multitude caught up in emotion, the moving feeling of their revolutionary frenzy which expresses the camaraderie, the sharing that joins the individual to the mythic life. Instead of Carlyle's noun-heavy prose that heaps adverbial and prepositional clauses upon each other, Dickens' Carmagnole is all movement, all active verbs:

> They advanced, retreated, struck at one another's hands, clutched at one another's heads, spun round alone, caught one another and spun round in pairs, until many of them dropped. While those were down, the rest linked hand in hand, and all spun round together: then the ring broke, and in separate rings of two and four they turned and turned until they all stopped at once, began again, struck, clutched, and tore, and then reversed the spin, and all spun round another way.

What is the meaning we wonder of all this movement? "Suddenly they stopped again, paused, struck out the time afresh, formed into lines the width of the public way, and, with their heads low down and their hands high up, swooped screaming off." In their midst, Lucie stands as a point of reference to set off their barbarism:

> No fight could have been half so terrible as this dance. It was so emphatically a fallen sport—a something, once innocent, delivered over to all devilry—a healthy pastime changed into a means of angering the blood, bewildering the senses, and steeling the heart. Such grace as was visible in it, made it the uglier, showing how warped and perverted all things good by nature were become. The maidenly bosom bared to this, the pretty almost-child's head thus distracted, the delicate foot mincing in this slough of blood and dirt, were types of the disjointed time. (III, 5, 307–308)

As a dance turns into an ecstatic orgy, we witness a world convulsed by polar extremes. In an instant, sense becomes nonsense with no ground between. Dickens has devised a form of writing in which contradiction is central. In this world things are simultaneously real and fantastic, distant and close at the same moment, past and future at once.

In Carlyle's work the narrator stands at the crossing point of opposites, and we share his struggle to force them into sensible shape. The fragments of his world are solid and his standpoint is clear, though the meanings and values of his enterprise as historian and prophet are clouded. By contrast the narrator of *A Tale of Two Cities* disappears into the rendered object, character, or scene. Here where everything must be accounted for, nothing is outside the dream. Narrator and reader experience the disembodied anxiety of the dreamer's stance.

In the dreamer's world events and actions may appear senseless yet are always meaningful. In dreaming, the effort to ascertain the logic of contradictions is fraught with danger. Dream-telling, as Taylor Stoehr points out, is the narrative form that provides access to the dream-work.[8] The contradictions in the dream are also the opposites tugging at the dream-telling narrator. Here writing is the central gesture of decoding and encod-ing—the trope of narration enacted as the narrative of dream-telling. For Carlyle writing may be difficult but its meaning is always positive, while for Dickens it is a code that imprisons as well as expresses. As Jarvis Lorry tells Lucie when he meets her at Dover, "I carry about me, not a scrap of writing openly referring to it. This is a secret service altogether. My credentials, entries, and memoranda, are all comprehended in the one line, 'Recalled to Life;' which may mean anything" (I, 4, 58). Writing is a code connected in some way to the social order. Revolution is an effort to undo existing sense and make of existing social relationships non-sense. But in this novel all social experience might as in a dream or revolution be undone: sense teeters on the edge.

Consider how Jarvis Lorry uses the word nonsense, one of his favorite expletives. It serves him as a way of denying to Charles that he is going to France for reasons not of business but of "gallantry and youthfulness,"—those motives that at the end of the same chapter will take Darnay himself on his fateful journey (II, 24, 267). In Jarvis Lorry's tone we hear the op-posite meaning of the sense of his words. His tone depends upon a flexible comprehension of the difference between business and non-business, the role of messenger and that of actor, the distinction between order and disorder—something outside the grasp of characters like Stryver, who brands Darnay's actions in renouncing his claims as an Evremonde as "the most pestilent and blasphemous code of devilry that ever was known" (II, 24, 269).

The marriage plot of *A Tale of Two Cities* engages these issues. When the Defarges discuss what revolutionary revenge on the Evremondes im-plies, the husband comments: "'I hope, for her sake, Destiny will keep her husband out of France.'" Defarge pleads with his wife to recognize the senselessness of condemning Darnay and Solomon/Barsad in the same breath:

> "But it is very strange—now, at least, is it not very strange"—said Defarge,
> rather pleading with his wife to induce her to admit it, "that, after all our
> sympathy for Monsieur her father, and herself, her husband's name should
> be proscribed under your hand at this moment, by the side of that infernal
> dog's who has just left us?"

Madame Defarge brushes aside his plea with a comment that reaffirms her willingness to plunge into logical contradiction for the cause of re-venge: "'Stranger things than that will happen when it does come,' answered madame. 'I have them both here, of a certainty; and they are both here for their merits; that is enough'" (II, 16, 215).

Madame Defarge lives for the onset of the charismatic world of revenge—for the second coming of revolution in which the order of the past will be replaced by the disorder of the present. When Charles marries Lucie and is accepted by Doctor Manette into their family, the three create civilization out of the sources of hate. The cost of accepting his persecutor's descendant as his son-in-law is also a purchase for Doctor Manette of the right to experience, confront, and thus release himself from the traumatic past. He does not imprison the events of his history in a secret code, to be read out as judgment of revenge and knitted fate, as does Madame Defarge: he implicitly repudiates then the meaning of the written account that later, despite his wishes, will condemn Darnay. Unlike Manette's, Madame Defarge's is the world of the Capulets and Montagues, not that of Juliet and Romeo. For sublime Defarge the revolution will never be over, whereas for beautiful Lucie the bosom of her family can replace the riving search for revenge. In the ordered world glimpsed by Carton at the moment of his apotheosis, there is a difference between sense and nonsense, whereas in the charismatic state the two meet as the juncture of contradiction.

The dramatic situation and the narrator's ability to play all the roles lead to a confusion of sense and nonsense on the part of the actors of the drama. Stryver himself uses these words to explain away the meaning of what he has done in imagining he might ask for Lucie Manette in marriage. "Having supposed that there was sense where there is no sense," he assures Jarvis Lorry, "I am well out of my mistake" (II, 12, 178). Stryver's error is to deny the motive that had brought him to his earlier choice. He strives always to define himself on the side of apparent sense—that is, with the winners. Mistakes are something Stryver does not allow himself, for they would hurt his ability to shoulder his way into society and up the ladder of success. His refusal to acknowledge the existence of change and misperception range Stryver with the French aristocrats who cannot see the humanity of those they oppress. Observing Stryver's reversals as he makes himself into a hypocrite, we understand that we are in a world in which instead of the realistic distinction between sense and nonsense, "the strange law of contradiction . . . obtains" (III, 4, 302). It is of course what the novel has offered us from its beginning sentence. Sense and nonsense are the unending moebius strip of this body politic as contradiction is its literary mode.

What is literature nowadays, Carlyle proclaims in his letters and his published work, but a newspaper. What he objects to, Dickens, the journalist, embraces. The characterization of Sloppy in *Our Mutual Friend* will also serve for Dickens: "He do the Police in different voices" (III, 43). One of the most "fundamental aspects of comic style" Bakhtin reminds us, is this "varied *play with the boundaries of speech types. . . ."* The "comic novel makes available a form for appropriating and organizing heteroglossia that is both externally very vivid and at the same time historically profound."[9]

Like Carlyle, Yeats too will ultimately turn to classical models for his work, whereas Dickens, availing himself of the democratic cultural forms of his time, will evoke his world as spectacle and carnival rather than epic. Joyce follows his lead, imbedding the traditional forms in *Ulysses*, while writing it as Bloomsday—one day in the newspaper life of his city and his culture. It is important to note that for Joyce as for Dickens the columns of the newspaper fold over: we are not in linear but in urban time, where mythic encounters may occur at any street corner. Dickens' representation of the conditions of modern life was echoed by Marinetti in his Futurist Manifesto, when he called for the writing of "the multi-colored polyphonic tides of revolution in the modern capitals."[10] Dickens begins a process in *A Tale of Two Cities* that Joyce will carry further.

Following through the analogy with the history of music, I call this method polyphony. (Carlyle, by contrast, tends to be monophonic and rely on the succession of events.) Dickens' scenes and situations do not function spatially, as Stoehr using Joseph Frank's analogy suggests, but musically. It is worth remembering that Bakhtin's analysis, which is based on the novel's links with rhetoric, focuses on the "hybrid discourse" of the "more complex artistic forms for the organization of contradiction . . . that orchestrate their themes by means of languages—" a method characteristic of "profound models of novelistic prose."[11] The materials Dickens works with are arranged in groups like chords—what counts is not the development of a single melody, as in monophony, but the ordering and progression of the whole. Carlyle's great history has the appearance of a polyphonic work; close reading, nevertheless, reveals the ways in which each thread of the narrative is developed as a separate melodic line in counterpoint with the others. By contrast, Dickens emphasizes his intention when he notes that *All the Year Round*, which *A Tale of Two Cities* initiated, is not a magazine he edited but as he comments on the title page "Conducted." In *A Tale of Two Cities*, in contrast with Carlyle's work, different sections recall each other; characters reflect each other—"split" apart they echo their double's movement. Each situation has a characteristic key signature which modulates into those that follow, as it grows from those that come before. In one trial we hear all the others, culminating in the final deferred execution of Carton, that to carry the musical analogy forward resolves the previously diminished sevenths into the cadence of his self-sacrifice.

Like Beethoven, Dickens can dispense with monophony because the chordal structures and dynamic possibilities available to him are powerful enough to resolve even the most difficult of his disharmonies. (How different for Carlyle who believes no forms exist any longer that can contain the violent energies of the tool-using barbarians of the nineteenth century.) The wild cacophony of the Terror, like the strange sounds of the Chorus in Beethoven's Ninth, leads to resolutions for Dickens that do not shatter their enclosing form. The reality of urban life and its journalistic chronicle for Dickens is unquestioned. It is the condition of his culture and his tale that hurtles us between its two greatest avatars, London and Paris. Even as they change, their norm as the idea of civilization persists. They authorize for Dickens the minting of the coin of his prose—an economy of the imagination no longer available to those who come after.

NOTES

1. See Gilles Deleuze, *Logique Du Sens* (Paris: Les editions de Minuit, 1969), especially the first ten series.
2. Charles Dickens, *A Tale of Two Cities* (Harmondsworth: Penguin, 1970), III, 10, 361. Subsequent citations from this novel will be to this Penguin edition and will be noted in the text.
3. I owe this insight to Linda Paulson.
4. Thomas Carlyle, *The French Revolution*, Centenary Edition (London: Chapman & Hall, 1896), Volume III, Book 6, Chapter 1, p. 248. Subsequent citations to *The French Revolution* will be from this edition and will be noted in the text.
5. William Butler Yeats, *The Collected Poems of W. B. Yeats* (New York: Macmillan, 1970), pp. 184–185. Subsequent citations from Yeats will be from this edition and will be noted in the text.
6. See Michael Goldberg's *Carlyle and Dickens* (Athens: University of Georgia Press, 1972), especially Chapter Seven, pp. 101 and 128.
7. Asa Briggs, *Victorian People* (Chicago: University of Chicago Press, 1970), p. 298, quoted by Albert D. Hutter, "Nation and Generation in *A Tale of Two Cities*," *PMLA*, 93 (1978), 448.
8. Taylor Stoehr, *Dickens: The Dreamer's Stance*, (Ithaca: Cornell University Press, 1965), especially Chapters Three and Four.
9. M. M. Bakhtin, "Discourse in the Novel," in *The Dialogic Imagination*, edited by Michael Holquist, translated by Caryl Emerson and Michael Hol-

quist (Austin: University of Texas Press, 1981), pp. 308 and 301. For a penetrating comment on Bakhtin, see the review by Hayden White in *Partisan Review*, Fall, 1982.

10. "Manifesto of Futurism," in *Marinetti: Selected Writings*, edited by R. W.
Flint and translated by R. W. Flint and A. A. Coppotelli (New York: Farrar,
Straus & Giroux, 1972), p. 42

11. M. M. Bakhtin, "Discourse in the Novel," *The Dialogical Imagination*,
op.cit., p. 275.

Splendid Impressions and Picturesque Means: Dickens, Carlyle, and the French Revolution

Michael Timko

Very few readers are unaware that Dickens was greatly influenced in his writing of *A Tale of Two Cities* by Thomas Carlyle, the play *The Frozen Deep* (an apt description, by the way, for one first coming to Carlyle's prose), and his own concerns and neuroses at the time of his writing the novel, especially his mixed feelings over his own unhappy marriage and the beginning of his affair with Ellen Ternan. While much has already been written about the first of this trinity, the imposing presence of Thomas Carlyle, whose shadow fell on most of the nineteenth-century writers we now classify as Victorian, additional comments on Carlyle's direct influence on Dickens' historical novel might profitably be made. Michael Goldberg has written of Carlyle's influence on Dickens and others coming not so much from "specific doctrines," but rather from "the general quality of his response" to mid-nineteenth-century life. George Ford emphasizes Carlyle's "insistence [on] social criticism" and points outs Carlyle's urging Dickens to attack "the 'vast block-headism' of Victorian society." George Woodcock is insistent on the presence of Carlyle in *A Tale of Two Cities*:

> The decision to choose revolutionary France as his setting was un-doubtedly the fulfilment of an intent which Dickens had long harboured. Almost twenty years before, in 1840, he had first met Thomas Carlyle, and had fallen immediately under the spell of that powerful writer and bizarre personality. The reading of Carlyle's *Chartism* and *The French Revolution* had already influenced Dickens in writing *Barnaby Rudge* (1840–41), and now it was the apocalyptic Carlylean vision of insurgent Paris that Dickens allowed to shape the setting and influence the tone of the novel he planned.

He had read *The French Revolution* repeatedly since its appearance in 1839, and he found no book that was to be of greater use to him.[1]

It is interesting that Woodcock does not mention specifically *Sartor Resartus*, written in the comparative isolation of Craigenputtock in 1830–1831 and published in *Fraser's* (1833–1834). I deliberately stress the place and time for it was at Craigenputtock that many of those Carlylean ideas by which Dickens was influenced in the writing of a *Tale* were fully developed and expounded. Ian Campbell, in his introduction to the Everyman *Selected Essays*, wisely stresses the importance of the years spent at Craigenputtock, particularly his "enlarging and intensifying" vision. "The Carlyle who appeared in Chelsea was quite well known . . . for these essays; many of the ideas of 1834 were to be characteristic of his work throughout his writing career, and so these essays form a major guide to Carlyle's thought and writing."[2]

One specific concern of Carlyle that obviously fascinated Dickens and attracted him to the older writer was a concern that dominates both Carlyle's work and Dickens' novels: a deep interest in people, in living, thinking, feeling human beings. Perhaps this is really the key to the close relationship between the two Victorian writers; they were both deeply interested in human nature, in what makes up this "feeblest of bipeds." As Carlyle puts it in *Sartor*:

> "With men of a speculative turn," writes Teufelsdrockh, "there come seasons, meditative, sweet, yet awful hours, when in wonder and fear you ask yourself that unanswerable question: Who am *I*; the thing that can say 'I' . . . ? Who am I; what is this ME? A Voice, a Motion, an Appearance; — some embodied, visualised Idea in the Eternal Mind? *Cogito, ergo sum*. Alas, poor Cogitator, this takes us but a little way. Sure enough, I am; but lately was not: but Whence? How? Whereto? . . . The secret of Man's Being is still like the Sphinx's secret: a riddle that he cannot rede; and for ignorance of which he suffers death, the worst death, a spiritual. . . ."[3]

Campbell concludes by making two points that have much meaning for the reader of the *Tale*. He emphasizes Carlyle's "insistent dismissal of too-facile searches for a 'philosophy of history,'" in place of "a recognition of history as a 'real Prophetic Manuscript, [which] can be fully interpreted by no man'." He then reminds us of Carlyle's deep concern for and with people: "While the whole shape of history may be hidden, vignettes of the lives and characters of individuals are always available, and this biographical interest colors all Carlyle's historical writings" (vi–vi).

These two interwoven Carlylean ideas about history, so strong in the essays and in *Sartor*, figure strongly in Dickens' best-known "historical" novel: history as prophecy and history as vignettes of the lives and characters of individuals. The first can be seen in Dickens' attempts to adapt in his own way the faith in the historical process that Carlyle had demonstrated so clearly in *The French Revolution*, that faith that K. J. Fielding sees as reflecting Carlyle's belief that "the historical process was ultimately for good."[4] While agreeing with Carlyle, Dickens goes still further and does much more to show the basis for that faith — i.e., the specific religious and philosophical grounds on which his (Dickens') ideas rest. I have written elsewhere of Tennyson's and Arnold's attempts to soften the harshness of Carlyle's religious ideas, those which Fielding characterizes in *The French Revolution* as Carlyle's emphasis on the Old rather than, as in Dickens, the New Testament. Tennyson called Carlyle "at once the most reverent and most irreverent" person he had ever known, and Arnold at one time called Carlyle a "moral desperado." In spite of what seems a positive thrust in Carlyle's writings, and it is evident in *The French Revolution*, there remains always a negative aspect that ultimately undercuts the optimistic claims he makes for some apocalyptic event that would bring forth a new birth and a new day. Dickens was aware of this facet of Carlyle's philosophic thought, and he attempted in his novel to mitigate the harsh Carlylean message, particularly that which called for Destiny (or Nature as Carlyle often referred to it) to wreak vengeance on those feeblest of bipeds who had lost their way.

In his Introduction to *The French Revolution* Traill praises Carlyle as an historian, but even he has to admit that "his habit of the preacher and the moralist was too strong for his instinct of the historian." He elaborates:

> He is too ready to lay all the sins and sufferings of the Revolution at that particular door at which he wishes to knock, too anxious to bring home its guilt and misery to those particular sinners whom he conceived it to be his main mission to indict. He cannot bring himself to assign their due weight to those already predetermined causes which are not directly traceable to individual wrongdoing. (I, xiii–xiv)

Traill is, of course, absolutely right; in reading *The French Revolution* one finds Carlylean themes and ideas applicable not only to the revolution but to the Carlylean universe, all of which impressed Dickens enough to use them in the *Tale*. We find such familiar themes as the need for heroes, the lack of authority and discipline, the call for loyalty and duty, and, above all, the lament over the age's lack of faith. In Chapter II, for instance, right at the very start of his account, Carlyle speaks of the importance of "Symbols" or man's "Realised Ideals," and then he goes on to ask his readers:

> consider only these two: his Church, or spiritual Guidance, his Kingship, or temporal one. The Church: what a word was there; richer than Golconda and the treasures of the world! In the heart of the remotest mountains rises the little Kirk; . . . Strong was he that had a Church . . . : he stood thereby, though "in the centre of Immensities, in the conflux of Eternities," yet manlike towards God and man; the vague shoreless Universe had become for him a firm city, and dwelling which he knew. Such virtue was in Belief; in these words, well spoken: I believe. . . . Neither was that an inconsiderable moment when wild armed men first raised their Strongest aloft . . . and, with clanging armour and heart, said solemnly: Be thou our Acknowledged Strongest. (I, 8–9)

To make sure that the reader knows exactly his point, Carlyle then applies these ideas specifically to the situation in France:

> But of those decadent ages in which no Ideal either grows or blossoms? When Belief and Loyalty have passed away, and only the cant and false echo of them remains; and all Solemnity has become Pageantry; and the Creed of persons in authority has become one of two things: an Imbecility or a Macchiavelism? . . . In such a decadent age . . . had our poor ˌLouis been born. (I, 10–11)

To Carlyle, then, the French revolution was by no means an event to be applauded; on the contrary, it was an event to be deplored. His study of the revolution stands up more readily as a document containing many of his favorite ideas, those which had appealed to Dickens. It is, in fact, not a history at all but, as Traill has called it, a Carlylean drama, with all the characteristics that the genre carries. Traill calls Carlyle a "splendid Impressionist," and the *Revolution* can, in fact, be read as a series of Carlylean impressions buttressed by Carlylean ideas. Dickens, no doubt, read it this way, and his novel can be seen as his own special interpretation of the Carlylean doctrines.

"It has been one of my hopes," Dickens wrote in the Preface to the novel, "to add something to the popular and picturesque means of understanding that terrible time, though no one can hope to add anything to the philosophy of Mr Carlyle's wonderful book." The fact is, however, that Dickens did, indeed, attempt to add to or at least change the focus of Carlyle's pessimistic view. In treating the subject of revolution and violence, Dickens carefully avoids coming to the same conclusions that

Carlyle did, and his doing so helps to explain some of those portions of the novel that seem to many readers to be especially sentimental or, as some have put it, "Victorian." In contrast to Carlyle's Old Testament pronouncements on the need for absolute authority, on the sad consequences of not obeying a stern Lawgiver, Dickens chose to emphasize the positive aspects, those Fielding calls the New Testament elements: the themes of forgiveness, friendship, and, finally, the concepts of love and self-sacrifice. Fielding cites the novelist's use of Christian symbols and the ending as being "borrowed for a purpose not purely Christian and to express not the resurrection of Christ nor certainly of the individual, but to communicate a sense of the mystery and wonder of life.... The emphasis... is on the mystery of love and sacrifice; but of human love and sacrifice" (204). All of these elements, whether human or divine, might be put under the "prophetic" rubric, especially in terms of their contribution to the ultimate meaning of life itself. What Dickens succeeds in doing in his novel, then, is giving concrete representation to the positive in the Carlylean message, particularly in the way that it might be seen in human affairs.

Human love and sacrifice are, of course, evident in much of the novel, and critics have always noted these, although often neglecting Dickens' "debt" to Carlyle. Fielding himself dwells on the Dickensian concern to show the power of love over fear and hate. Carton lays down his life for Lucie; Miss Pross triumphs over Madame Defarge; Lucie's love restores her father. "Love," in these terms stands for "all the forces of life, lasting power and goodness" (204–205). Woodcock stresses Dickens' emphasis on "moral resurgence" and "resurrection": "If all men were as willing to make sacrifices for their fellows as Sidney Carton; if there were more kindnesses like Mr Lorry's, or more like Pross's, or more loyalty in a tight corner like Jerry Cruncher's; then... the world would be a far better place" (22). One hears echoes of *Hard Times* and all of Carlyle's writings, although Woodcock insists they are inherited from *The Frozen Deep*.

Whether one acknowledges Dickens' debt to Carlyle or to the play, the fact remains that Dickens takes Carlyle's "ironical" faith in regeneration and gives it a positive meaning in human terms. The significance of this turn lies in the way that Dickens links revolution and regeneration to the two "realised ideals" spoken of in Carlyle: the nation and the church. Dickens, as did so many of the writers of his age, linked the welfare of the nation with that of the state of the family in that nation, and in *A Tale of Two Cities* we see clearly the close connection between the two, most significantly in those qualities associated with close family relationships:

loyalty, devotion, discipline, fidelity, cooperation, and, of course, courage and love. Albert Hutter has touched on this subject in his essay on "Nation and Generation in *A Tale of Two Cities*"; I would like to approach the large subject he examined from still another direction, one that helps shed light on the way Dickens transformed and developed some of Carlyle's notions.[5] Rather than just father-son relations, I should like to stress the way that Dickens, assuming that his readers would immediately recognize the importance of the "symbol" of the family, constantly evokes the importance of family life, with all of its many and varied ramifications, in the novel.

The subject is a delicate one, for it immediately reminds modern readers of scenes from minor (often wretched) Victorian plays, dramas, and poems that bring to the surface feelings associated with sentimentality and insincere emotion. Perhaps the portrait that immediately comes to mind is that in Tennyson's "The Two Voices," when at the end of that poem the speaker on the Sabbath morn looks out the window and sees the people going to church, among them a stereotypical Victorian family:

> One walked between his wife and child,
> With measured footfall firm and mild,
> And now and then he gravely smiled.
>
> The prudent partner of his blood
> Leaned on him, faithful, gentle, good,
> Wearing the rose of womanhood.
>
> And in their double love secure,
> The little maiden walked demure,
> Pacing with downward eyelids pure.
>
> These three made unity so sweet,
> My frozen heart began to beat,
> Remembering its ancient heat.
>
> I blest them, and they wandered on;
> I spoke but answer came there none;
> The dull and bitter voice was gone.

Much ink has been spilt over this family portrait, but the fact remains that the Victorians saw much in it, including the idea that domestic tranquility meant, indeed, national peace and tranquility. Much of the novel's emotional appeal, Dickens thought, would come from his readers' immediate response to this picture of domestic bliss; they would recognize in it those moral and ethical qualities nurtured in family life that would assure the survival of nation and of mankind itself. Hutter cites Sydney Carton's rediscovering his father in Lorry, and he quotes Carton's reverie: "Long ago, when he had been famous among his earliest competitors as a youth of great promise, he had followed his father to the grave. His mother had died, years before" (451). Hutter goes on to quote the words that had been read at his father's grave, "I am the resurrection and the life," words that contribute so much to the ultimate meaning of the novel itself; however, I think that notice should be given to the brief sentence concerning Carton's mother, who had died "years before." Dickens wants to be certain that we see the connection between Carton's life and his mother's death: Could not his earlier years as "guilty scoundrel" be attributed to the loss of his mother, whose death had broken that circle of domestic bliss so necessary to one's well-being? (Dickens, of course, was having his own domestic problems at this time.) One remembers, too, that Lucie had to do without her father a very long time. Indeed, what of Lucie's mother? We would like to know more of her. In the light of this aspect of the novel, Woodcock's comments on Lucie become slightly ironic: "Lucie . . . projects that yearning which appeared as regularly in Dickens's novels as it did in his life, towards the pristine femininity of vivacious young girls. She does not develop or change as the story progresses, even though she becomes a wife and several times a mother" (23). One might quarrel with Woodcock's speculations, especially as one perceives the way that Dickens weaves together Lucie's thoughts about her own family and home and then of the new family and home with Darnay and their children. "If," Lucie tells her father when they meet for the first time, "when I hint to you of a Home [note that Carlylean need for emphasis by capitalization] there is before us, where I will be true to you with all my duty and with all my faithful service, I bring back the remembrance of a Home long desolate, while your poor heart pined away, weep for it, weep for it!" She then tells him that she will take him back to England, away from "our native France so wicked to you," and concludes:

> "And if, when I shall tell you of my name, and of my father who is living, and of my mother who is dead, you learn that I have to kneel to my honoured father, and implore his pardon for having never for his sake striven all day and lain awake and wept all night, because the love of my poor mother hid his torture from me, weep for it, weep for it!"   (76–78)

Strong stuff, to be sure, but wholly understandable in the context of Carlyle and Dickens, especially with the heavy emphasis on loyalty, discipline, duty, fidelity, devotion, those "realised ideals" of family and national life. France comes off rather badly, but it deserves to when viewed in the light of these qualities.

The same context is useful in judging Dickens' purpose in describing Lucie as young wife and mother:

> Her little Lucie lay on her bosom. Then . . . there was the tread of tiny feet and the sound of her prattling words. Let greater echoes resound as they would, the young mother at the cradle side could always hear those coming. They came, and the shady house was sunny with a child's laugh, and the Divine friend of children, to whom in her trouble she had confided hers, seemed to take her child in His arms, as He took the child of old, and made it a sacred joy to her.

Lucie's "happy influence" binds all in the family together: "Her husband's step was strong and prosperous . . .; her father's firm and equal." Of course, Pross and Lorry are included, and even Carton "would sit among them through the evening." Carton, one remembers, "was the first stranger to whom little Lucie held out her chubby arms"; and the "little boy" had murmured, almost at the last, "Poor Carton! Kiss him for me!"(239–241). Strong stuff again, perhaps, but entirely in keeping with the often misunderstood ending, especially for fully grasping the important role of Carton, the one member of the "family" who holds a sanctuary in all their hearts.

To consider tone and theme in the light of both the Carlylean historical ideals and the family as reflection of nation also helps put into perspective two other threads of the novel: the Defarge and the Cruncher families and their contribution to the total impact of the novel, especially the thematic implications. It is important to keep in mind that the Defarges have no children, a fact that becomes especially significant when one finally learns Madame Defarge's "secret":

> I smite this bosom with these two hands as I smite it now, and I tell him, "Defarge, I was brought up among the fishermen of the sea-shore and that peasant family so injured by the two Evrémonde brothers, . . . is my family. Defarge, that sister of the mortally wounded boy upon the ground was my sister, that husband was my sister's husband, that unborn child was their child, that brother was my brother, that father was my father, those dead are my dead."

The alternation of past and present is revealing. It is no wonder that she can proclaim, "Then tell Wind and Fire (again the Carlylean note) where to stop . . . but don't tell me" (370). As the family, so the nation.

What of the Cruncher family? It is not exactly the picture of domestic bliss; certainly it stands in stark contrast to both the Defarges and the Darnays. However, in spite of the apparent conflict in this family, and Hutter has effectively demonstrated the sexuality and violence that mark

this union (454), there remains not only the "comic" tone associated
with it, but also the thematic emphasis based on the belief of the close
connection between family and nation. In contrast to the Evrémondes
and the Defarges, the Crunchers are the picture of bliss and tranquility.
"Look at your boy: he *is* you'rn, aint't he? He's as thin as a lath. Do you
call yourself a mother, and not know that a mother's first duty is to blow
her boy out?" Jerry is forever telling his wife do her duty: "You was to
honour and obey; why the devil don't you?" " 'I try to be a good wife,
Jerry,' the poor woman protested, with tears" (192). That she is, indeed,
a good wife becomes apparent, for it is Jerry himself who acknowledges
that she has been right all along. " 'First,' said Mr Cruncher, who was all
in a tremble, and who spoke with an ashy and solemn visage, 'them poor
things well out o' this, never no more will I do it, never no more!' . . .
Second: them poor things well out o' this, and never no more will I inter-
fere with Mrs Cruncher's flopping, never no more.' " Interestingly
enough, Miss Pross agrees: " ' 'Whatever housekeeping arrangements that
may be,' said Miss Pross, striving to dry her eyes and composing herself,
'I have no doubt it is best that Mrs Cruncher should have it entirely
under her superintendence' " (392–393). One assumes, too, although
Dickens uncharacteristically fails to include the Crunchers in his final
prophecy, that the Crunchers will, as well as all the others, lead "peaceful, useful, prosperous and happy lives" lives in "that England which
[Carton] will see no more" (404). To make too much of the Cruncher
family subplot is not my object, but it does serve as a most effective
parodic counterpoint to the main one; and the Cruncher family contains
its share of devotion, loyalty, affection, courage, and love.

The attempt by Dickens to "add something to the popular and picturesque means of understanding that terrible time" is more obvious, and
perhaps more successful, in the use he makes of Carlyle's concept of
clothing, a "specific doctrine," in Goldberg's terms, associated with the
Sage of Chelsea's transcendentalism, or, as Dickens calls it, his "philosophy." The progression from history as prophecy to history as the study
of and concern with the lives and characters of individuals is a natural
one; for implicit in Dickens' interest in Carlyle's writings is the latter's
concern with human beings, whether considered as individuals, family
members, representatives of a country, or as children of God. All are
human beings, and to Dickens, as well as to Carlyle, they remain a subject of perennial interest. No matter what one says of the novels in terms
of theme, plot, or meaning, the fact remains that Dickens asks the same
question that Carlyle is always asking: What is man? Consider, for instance, these two quotations from *Sartor Resartus*, from which I have

quoted earlier, the work Woodcock fails to mention in conjunction with *A Tale of Two Cities*:

> With men of speculative turn . . . there come sweet, yet awful hours, when in wonder and fear you ask yourself that unanswerable question: Who am I? . . . What is this ME? . . . The answer lies around, written in all colours and motions, uttered in all tones of jubilee and wail, in thousand-figured, thousand-voiced, harmonious Nature: but where is the cunning eye and ear to whom the God-written Apocalypse will yield articulate meaning?   (I, 41)

* * * * *

> The secret of Man's Being is still like the Sphinx's secret: a riddle that he cannot rede; and for ignorance of which he suffers death, the worst death, a spiritual. . . . Nevertheless there is something great in the moment when a man first strips himself of adventitious wrappages; and sees indeed that he is naked, and, as Swift has it, "a forked straddling animal with bandy legs"; yet also a Spirit, and unutterable Mystery of Mysteries.   (I. 42, 45)

Michael Goldberg has warned us that to ignore Carlyle's links with romanticism is to miss "Carlyle's most vital sources of inspiration as well as the nature of his influence on Dickens" (21). One result of this influence was Dickens' awareness of the mystical or transcendental nature of humanity itself. "If Voltaire's rationalism disabled him from penetrating deeply behind the external appearance, to Carlyle's Novalis, that 'ideal of all Idealists'," matter was but "the veil and mysterious Garment of the Unseen" (26). In Dickens' words this view translated into "the wonders all of us have . . . hidden in our breasts, only needing circumstances to evoke them" (Fielding, 203). John Kucich, in his recent study of Dickens' employment of excess and restraint, characterizes this Carlylean strain in Dickens in these words: "The atmosphere of repression in the good characters' world . . . echoes the narrator's complaint, in the beginning of the novel, against the isolation of the individual within the narrow limits of personal identity." He then quotes from Chapter Three of the novel: "A wonderful fact to reflect upon, that every human creature is constituted to be that profound secret and mystery to every other."[7] I would add a few more lines to make clearer the Dickensian debt to Carlyle:

> My friend is dead, my neighbour is dead, my love, the darling of my soul is dead; it is the inexorable consolation and perpetuation of the secret that was always in that individuality, and which I shall carry in mine to my life's end. In any of the burial-places of the city through which I pass, is there a sleeper more inscrutable than its busy inhabitants are, in their innermost personality, to me, or than I am to them?

Dickens proceeds then to use almost the very words that Carlyle himself uses at various times in his writings:

> As to this, his natural and not to be alienated inheritance, the messenger on horseback had exactly the same possessions as the King, the first Minister of State, or the richest merchant in London. So with the three passangers shut up in the narrow compass of one lumbering old mail-coach; they were mysteries to one another, as complete as if each had been in his own coach and six, or his own coach and sixty, with the breadth of a county between him and the next.   (44–45)

Man, then, is the mystery of mysteries; human beings are distinguishable from one another only by "adventitious wrappages"; where, asks Carlyle, is the cunning eye and ear to yield meaning? Dickens attempts, in the *Tale*, to provide that cunning eye and ear, and the success with which he accomplishes that task accounts in part for the popularity of this "flawed" novel. His procedure yields results precisely because it differs from Carlyle's. The latter keeps emphasizing the need to look beneath the clothing, but he remains abstract; the former simply explores the concept and demonstrates it so dramatically that it becomes meaningful for us. Dickens, in short, took an abstract, philosophic, transcendental idea and gave it form. He clothed the Carlylean concept.

It is worthwhile at this point, perhaps, to insist that Carlyle did, in fact, at times made good, even brilliant, use of his own abstract notion. There are some striking instances of his effective employment of it. Is it a coincidence, for instance, that Mirabeau, after being expelled from Noblesse, "stalks forth into the Third Estate," opens a cloth-shop in Marseilles, and "for moments became a furnishing tailor"? "Even the fable that he did so," writes Carlyle, "is to us always among the pleasant memorabilities of this era" (I, 124–125). Carlyle's description of the first meeting of the Deputies is equally telling:

> The King..., gorgeous as Solomon in all his glory, runs his eye over that majestic Hall; many-plumed...; bright-tinted as rainbow.... We remark only that, as his Majesty, on finishing the speech, put on his plumed hat, and the Noblesse... imitated him, our Tiers-État Deputies did mostly, not without a shade of fierceness, in like manner clap-on, and even crush-on their slouched hats; and stand there awaiting the issue. Thick buzz... between majority and minority...(Hats off, Hats on)! To which his Majesty puts end, by taking *off* his own royal hat again.   (I, 149–150)

One other brief quotation will illustrate the modernity of Carlyle's message as well as his artistry. Carlyle has just been describing the Terror and has just finished telling about the Tannery at Meudon, the Tannery of

Human Skins. Then he comments: "History looking back over Cannibalism, through *Purchas's Pilgrims* and all early and late Records, will perhaps find no terrestrial Cannibalism of a sort, on the whole, detestable. It is a manufactured, soft-feeling, quietly elegant sort; a sort *perfide!*" (III, 247).

In his own interpretation of Carlyle's clothes philosophy, Dickens was intent on trying to tie together all of the various threads of the story, which ultimately culminates in the scenes with Darnay-Carton and Carton's death and "resurrection." Dickens wants, as does Teufelsdröckh, to "expound the moral, political, even religious Influences of Clothes." More specifically, he seems intent on obeying Teufelsdröckh's dictum: "Let any Cause-and-Effect Philosopher explain, not why I wear such and such a Garment, obey such and such a Law; but even why *I* am *here*, to wear and obey anything!" This aim explains why Dickens, although he does point out the dandyism of the king and the aristocracy in order to show their inability to govern or lead, goes even further in his use of the clothing metaphor, that most important symbol of man's moral, philosophical, and spiritual thought. In *A Tale of Two Cities* he demonstrates his belief that the Sage of Chelsea, while essentially correct in his view of man, that "mystery of mysteries," ultimately fails to communicate his "philosophy" because he is not positive enough in his approach. For Dickens, Carlyle remains too easily persuaded of man's faults and weaknesses, too pessimistic about his moral, political, religious nature.

Dickens may have had in mind, for instance, Carlyle's terribly pessimistic view of the world and of man in Book Five of the third volume of his work, "Terror the Order of the Day." In this, and other sections of his study, Carlyle continually talks of soul and spirit, but, like Swift, whom he admired, he keeps harping on the "natural" side of human nature, the bestial, cannibalistic side, the side prone to force and violence. Behind *The French Revolution* lies this view, the result of which causes Carlyle to mention prominently such violent aspects as the tannery of human skins, the stabbing of Charlotte Corday, the voice of the Vengeance supporting every savage notion of Madame Defarge, and countless other incidents that show human beings in their most vile acts. Carlyle's comments reveal what seems to Dickens his complete disappointment in, if not disgust with, man. One can judge Dickens' reaction to the conclusion of the chapter Carlyle calls "Flame-Picture," in which he describes the "Consummation of Sansculottism": "Alas, then, is man's civilisation only a wrappage, through which the savage nature of him can still burst, infernal as ever? Nature still makes him: and has an Infernal in her as well as a

Celestial" (III, 247). In an earlier chapter in this same section, the chapter entitled "Destruction," Carlyle again underscores the cruelty of man: "Cruel is the panther of the woods, the she-bear bereaved of her whelps: but there is in man a hatred crueler than that. . . . What a torrent of Revolution! . . . But indeed men are all rabid; as the Time is" (III, 222). Carlyle's conclusion to his study is clearly pessimistic and unremittingly bleak:

> The World is black ashes; — which, ah, when will they grow green? The Images all run into Corinthian brass; all Dwellings of men destroyed; the very mountains peeled and riven, the valleys black and dead: it is an empty World! Woe to them that shall be born then! (III, 323)

Rather than the infernal in man, Dickens wants to emphasize the celestial; rather than cruelty and killing, Dickens would rather bring out the essential nobility and goodness of man, the nobility that comes from his ability to cooperate with and indeed love other humans and further even be willing to sacrifice his life if necessary. All this is not to deny Dickens' recognition of the violent and cannibalistic and savage in man; he does enough in the novel to demonstrate his awareness of these traits in man. One thinks immediately, for example, of Chapter 12, "Darkness," in the Third Book of the novel, in which Madame Defarge is putting forth her case against all those connected with the Evrémondes. "'Well, well,' reasoned Defarge, 'but one must stop somewhere. After all, the question is still where?'" Madame Defarge replies: "At extermination." Dickens may have been thinking of Carlyle's tannery of human skins.

Dickens is much more disposed to base his "study" of the French Revolution on another of Carlyle's texts, more accurately another one of Teufelsdröckh's saying:

> Matter exists only spiritually, and to represent some Idea, and *body* it forth. Hence Clothes, as despicable as we think them, are so unspeakably significant. . . . Nay, if you consider it, what is Man himself, and his whole terrestrial Life, but an Emblem; a Clothing of visible Garment for that divine ME of his, cast hither, like a light-particle, down from Heaven? (I, 57)

Carlyle himself seemed, to Dickens, at times to confuse matter and spirit, garment and emblem, and he (Dickens) wanted to be sure that the reader of the *Tale* did not make that same mistake. I have already shown Dickens' concern with this point in his first two paragraphs of Chapter 3 of Book the First, "The Night Shadows," in which he presents the Carlylean emphasis on man as a "mystery," a "profound secret." In the chapter just before this one, however, he had already indicated his own important distinction between garment and spirit, the need to distinguish the "wrappage" from the Idea. As the three passengers are plodding up the hill by the side of the mail, each "wrapped to the check-bones and over the ears," Dickens observes: "Not one of the three could have said, from anything he saw, what either of the two was like; and each was hidden under almost as many wrappers from the eyes of the mind, as from the eyes of the body, of his two companions" (38). Dickens makes the same point in Chapter 4, "The Preparation":

> The Concord bed-chamber being always assigned to a passenger by the mail, and passengers by the mail being always heavily wrapped up from head to foot, the room had the odd interest for the establishment of the Royal George, that although but one kind of man was seen to go into it, all kinds and varieties of men came out of it.   (49)

There is no doubt, then, that Dickens is deeply concerned with the Carlylean idea of "wrappings" and their contents; however, with the novelist, the meaning becomes specifically tied in with having the visible garment become but an emblem of the divine element. More specifically, through his emphases on the themes of resurrection and renunciation, Dickens illustrates that, unlike Carlyle, he believes, and wants his readers to believe, that the Celestial rather than the Infernal ultimately triumphs in man.

This Dickensian emphasis is really what accounts for the various doublings of the characters, the play between light and dark, death and resurrection, evil and good. Dickens is always on the positive side; Carlyle usually on the darker one. Carlyle would agree with the lines from Auden that Woodcock quotes: "Those to whom evil is done / Do evil in return"; however, in spite of Woodcock's assertion that Dickens would agree with these lines, I do not think that there is any evidence for it in the novel itself. Dickens seems to be saying, on the contrary, that those to whom evil is done at times turn the other cheek. He seems also to be insisting that, unlike those arithmetical Mills that calculate moral and spiritual aspects on strictly quantitative, logical terms, some human beings do, in fact, return good for evil, and sometimes even find their greatest satisfaction and fulfillment through sacrifice for others. For these same reasons one would also have to disagree with Woodcock's conclusions concerning Carton. Carton is by no means Darnay's darkness; on the contrary, if anything he is Darnay's spiritual "divine Me." Carton's death, rather than a useless gesture, is an heroic one; rather than being one who has "already died in spirit," Carton is a Carlylean hero who knows the true meaning of salvation. His sacrificial death is, in fact, a resurrection, a "coming back to life" (24–25).

An examination of the Carton-Darnay relationship reveals evidence for these claims. To suggest that Carton is "dedicated to debauchery" and has "died in spirit" is to ignore completely both the Carlylean and prophetic strains in his portrait. If one rather sees Carton as an heroic figure awaiting those necessary circumstances to bring out his true nature, his celestial one, then all the pieces begin to fit. There are a number of aspects concerning the Carlylean hero often forgotten by those who condemn Carlyle for his so-called faith in tyrants. The Carlylean hero is strong, but not tyranical. He is, as Carlyle often stressed, one who can come in any form and is molded by the particular and peculiar circumstances of his time. He is also a seer, one who can "solve" the secret of the universe. Here are Carlyle's words:

> Hero, Prophet, Poet—many different names, in different times and places, do we give Great Men; according to varieties we note in them, according to the sphere in which they have displayed themselves! . . . The Hero can be Poet, Prophet, King, Priest or what you will, according to the kind of world he finds himself born into. I confess, I have no notion of a truly great man that could not be *all* sorts of men. . . . The great heart, the clear deep-seeing eye: there it lies.   (V, 78–79)

Carton, we remember, is the first to put forward the strategy that frees Darnay — that is, the remarkable resemblance between the two. Lorry, on the stand earlier, could only say that all the passengers were "wrapped up" and positive identification was impossible. It is crucial, too, to take notice of the actual words that Dickens uses to describe the rest of the trial. "Mr. Stryver fitted the prisoner's case on the jury, like a compact suit of clothes." Barsad, not so incidentally, is compared to Judas at this point. The Attorney-General then turns "the whole suit of clothes Mr. Stryver had fitted on the jury, inside out." Finally, "came my Lord himself, turning the suit of clothes, now inside out, now outside in, but on the whole decidedly trimming and shaping them into grave-clothes for the prisoner." Then, once more, while the jury is considering, it is Carton who sees what is happening to Lucie (104–107). Perhaps this is rather slim evidence to support a Carlylean hero, but it does fit Carlyle's criteria. It is essential to keep in mind, too, that as John Clubbe has said, for Carlyle "some men approximate the [heroic] ideal more than others. . . . Any individual who controls the chaos swirling around him, however temporarily, is a hero for Carlyle.''[8] In *A Tale of Two Cities*, Carton, as depicted by Dickens, fulfills that function.

Of his "spiritual" role, his role as the individual character Dickens uses to portray the "divine Me," even more can be said. Hutter calls the rescue implausible; Woodcock calls the ending "a sop to the reading public." Both of these statements ignore, I think, the context in which Dickens would have us see Carton's actions taking place, that which Fielding stresses when he speaks of the importance of the words that Carton keeps saying over and over, the words said at Carton's father's graveside: "not simply as a seemingly pious ending, but as a vital expression of the Christian ethic, which all along has been contrasted with the savagery of the Revolution" (165). Dickens has Carton himself suggest the importance of the divine Me inside the wrappage, for in the crucial scene in which Lucie rejects his offer, he tells her: "Within myself, I shall always be, towards you, what I am not, though outwardly I shall be what you have heretofore seen me" (182). This scene occurs almost right at the center of the novel, long before all is resolved.

It is on the impact and effect of the final scenes, however, especially the tone and spirit of these, that one bases one's final assessment of the novel, especially its moral and aesthetic totality. One cannot simply ignore the death of Carton; what he says and does is what Dickens wants us to remember, both of his character and of the meaning of the novel itself. For these reasons the rescue scene becomes a crucial one. Darnay, awaiting death, is in the position Carton will shortly be—that is, with death imminent he must "compose his thoughts" and try to comfort those he leaves behind. He is Everyman, and like him, unlike Carton, his concern is with his worldly goods. The final words concerning Darnay by the author have to do with his writing to Lorry, to whom he explains "his worldly affairs"; Dickens makes much of this: "He never thought of Carton. His mind was so full of the others, that he never once thought of him" (377). No wonder, then, when Carton does appear, "a light of a smile on his features," Carton exclaims: "Of all the people upon earth, you least expected to see me?" (379). In fact, significantly, Darnay thinks first that Carton is "an apparition of his own imagining" (379). The rest of the scene is nothing less than an enactment of the Carlylean clothes philosophy as Dickens perceived it and wanted his readers to understand it. The two exchange clothes, but the "celestial" spirit of Carton provides the force and guidance. "With a wonderful quickness, and with a strength both of will and action, that appeared quite supernatural, he forced all these changes upon him" (380).

What follows both echoes Carlylean language and demonstrates Carton as saviour and "resurrection man," this time in the full sense of the words spoken over his father's grave. Clothes now become fully emblematic and take on Carlylean meaning; they are indeed "wrappings," but wrappings in Teufelsdröckh's sense: "Let any Cause-and-Effect Philosopher explain, not why I wear such and such a garment, over such and such a law; but even why *I* am *here*, to wear and obey anything!" The Spy, as Carton hands over to him the limp Darnay, fails to grasp the true meaning of Carton's words or actions. "Don't fear me. I will be true to the death," says Carton, and the Spy's answer is that of a cause-and-effect philosopher rather than a Carlylean tailor: "You must be, Mr Carton, if the tale of fifty-two is to be right. Being made right by you in that dress, I shall have no fear" (382). Irony can go no further. Indeed, one almost wishes that Dickens, in his apparent eagerness to utilize the Carlylean clothes philosophy, had not made the young woman a seamstress; it is a touch that comes dangerously close to flirting, as he so often does, with sentimentality rather than sentiment.

Carton's death and resurrection, then, demonstrate the interest of Dickens, influenced by Carlyle, in history as prophecy and as human action rather than an indulgence in sentimentality. Character and theme are of a piece. To point out the parallels between Carton and Christ is easy enough to do, and to deplore these if one is so inclined; however, the thrust of the passages dealing with Carton's final moments seem directed not so much at presenting a "Christian message" as conveying Dickens' sense of the human potential, particularly in the development of the celestial that is part of the Carlylean Invisible Me. In spite of the "Infernal" part of their nature, most human beings, Dickens insists, are more like Carton; they contain a great capacity for love, the quality of which is demonstrated by his sincere (a favorite Carlylean word) love and concern for others. This point is an important one, for it answers the charge that Carton is either selfish, concerned only with carrying on his own name, or that he is doing it only for Lucie, his lost love. Witness his concern for the seamstress, whose hand he keeps in his until the very last moment. Witness his prophecy, which includes many more than Lucie in its sweep; for he perceives not only Lucie but the entire family around her leading, and the adjectives are significant in terms of what they entail for the nation as well as the individuals themselves, "peaceful, useful, prosperous and happy" lives. The contrast of the "beautiful city and a brilliant people" that Carton prophesies with Carlyle's world of black ashes is symptomatic of their chief difference. In direct opposition to Carlyle's painstaking and carefully detailed description of the Terror and the consummation of sansculottism, Dickens insists on depicting not the wages of sin and violence but the mystery that lies in man's willingness to give all, even his life, for love of his fellow man.

The final prophetic words of Carton, spoken while he has what Dickens describes as a sublime and prophetic look, reveal how Dickens was able ultimately to absorb the Sage's clothes philosophy into his own view of human nature. Dickens is careful, however, to emphasize that in spite of their being "else so wide apart and differing," they have "come together on the dark highway, (words which remind one of the three post travellers at the beginning of the novel) to repair home together" (402). Carton's prophecy, then, is Dickens' attempt to respond to Carlyle's plea for someone to "expound the moral, political, even religious influences of Clothes." In doing so, he was intent on both softening the Sage's harsh judgment of human nature and mitigating his bleak, pessimistic view of the world itself. Carton points to something far, far better than the black, ashy, empty world Carlyle portrays at the end of *The French Revolution*; he sees one where people meet eye to eye, voice to voice, hand to hand, heart to heart, spirit to spirit, all children of the Universal Mother. Perhaps Dickens was even more prophetic than he realized. If Traill is accurate in his characterization of Carlyle as a "splendid Impressionist," whose materials "seem little else than the mere massed colours on a painter's palette"; then Dickens, perhaps, deserves to be called the sublime realist, whose depiction of events and people in *A Tale of Two Cities* gives form and shape to those dazzling colors and breathes life and meaning into what might have remained for many either overpowering but ultimately confusing dabs of paint or simply meaningless blobs.

NOTES

1. Michael Goldberg, *Carlyle and Dickens* (Athens: University of Georgia Press, 1972) pp. 3–4; George Ford, *Dickens and His Readers* (New York: Norton, 1965), p. 91; George Woodcock, ed., Charles Dickens, *A Tale of Two Cities* (Harmondsworth: Penguin Books), p. 12. All references to *A Tale of Two Cities* are to the Penguin edition.

2. Thomas Carlyle, *Selected Essays* (Everyman Edition), ed. Ian Campbell, p. v.

3. *Sartor Resartus*, *Works*, I, 41–42. All references to Carlyle's works are to the volume and page of the Centenary Edition, ed. H. D. Traill, 30 vols. (London: Chapman and Hall, 1896–1899). The one exception to this is that I cite the specific volumes of *The French Revolution*—i.e., I, II, or III, rather than the volume numbers in which they appeared in the *Works*, II–IV.

4. K. J. Fielding, *Charles Dickens: A Critical Introduction* (London, 1958; 2nd ed. revised and enlarged, 1965), p. 199.

5. Albert D. Hutter, "Nation and Generation in *A Tale of Two Cities*," *PMLA*, 93 (1978), 448–462.

6. See my " 'The Central Wish': Human Passion and Cosmic Love in Tennyson's Idyls," *Victorian Poetry*, 16 (1978), 1–15.

7. John Kucich, *Excess and Restraint in the Novels of Charles Dickens* (Athens: University of Georgia Press, 1981), p. 175.

8. John Clubbe, "Epic Heroes in *The French Revolution*," in *Thomas Carlyle 1981*: Papers Given at the International Thomas Carlyle Centenary Symposium, ed. Horst W. Drescher (Frankfurt: Peter Lang, 1983), p. 183.

The Rhetoric of Soliloquy in *The French Revolution* and *A Tale of Two Cities*

Carol Hanbery MacKay

> Men's words are a poor exponent of their thought; nay
> their thought itself is a poor exponent of the inward un-
> named Mystery, wherefrom both thought and action
> have their birth. No man can explain himself, can get
> himself explained; men see not one another, but distorted
> phantasms which they call one another; which they hate
> and go to battle with: for all battle is well said to be
> *misunderstanding.*[1]

> A wonderful fact to reflect upon, that every human crea-
> ture is constituted to be that profound secret and mystery
> to every other.[2]

Both Carlyle and Dickens are acutely conscious of the mystery of the
human mind. Yet despite their protestations about that mystery, they attempt to cross its boundaries—to assail and comprehend the separation
through language and imagery. In *The French Revolution* (1837) Carlyle
is trying to make contact with the ghosts of the past, while in *A Tale of
Two Cities* (1859) Dickens is trying to transcend the boundaries that separate individual consciousnesses. Both employ two contrasting modes of
rhetoric—the rhetoric of isolation and the rhetoric of transcendence—to
express the separation of human minds and the effort to bridge that separation. Paradoxically, the usual forum is the soliloquy—or especially in
Carlyle's case, the far-ranging voice of the author in cosmic monologue.[3]
And for both authors, the catalyst that causes the rhetoric of isolation to
give way to the rhetoric of transcendence is violence, whether factually
reported or imagistically conceived.

We know that Carlyle and Dickens are acutely, sometimes even painfully, aware of the separation of human minds not just because they expound upon this theme but because they demonstrate it in their portrayal of historical personages and fictional characters. Robespierre can serve to epitomize this unknowable separation for Carlyle. Calling upon him as a "hapless Chimera" and assigning him the epithet of "seagreen ghost," Carlyle emphasizes the difficulty of knowing his thoughts, much less recreating him (*FR*, 3.6.6.274–275), but it is Robespierre's role as victim in fulfilling the prophecy of "the Revolution, like Saturn, . . . devouring its own children" (*FR*, 3.4.8.201) that ultimately confirms such separation and tragic misunderstanding. And Sydney Carton is, of course, Dickens' prime example of the isolated mind. Alone, unloved, castigated and self-castigating, Carton too is misunderstood. Yet it is precisely because Carton is so eloquent and expressive in soliloquy that we come to see the power of language to transcend the boundaries of human consciousness—even though those boundaries form barriers in the world that he physically inhabits.

Despite the fact that Carlyle declares that "no man can get himself explained" and that men are but "distorted phantasms" to one another, he tries to contact these ghosts of the past by evoking their physicality through violent rhetoric. Let us examine a typical evocation:

> On, then, all Frenchmen, that have hearts in your bodies! Roar with all your throats, of cartilage and metal, ye Sons of Liberty; stir spasmodically whatsoever of utmost faculty is in you, soul, body, or spirit; for it is the hour! Smite, thou Louis Tournay, cartwright of the Marais, old-soldier of the Regiment Dauphiné; smite at that Outer Drawbridge chain, though the fiery hail whistles round thee! Never, over nave or felloe, did thy axe strike such a stroke. Down with it, man; down with it to Orcus: let the whole accursed Edifice sink thither, and Tyranny be swallowed up for ever! Mounted, some say, on the roof of the guard-room, some "on bayonets stuck into joints of the wall," Louis Tournay smites, brave Aubin Bonnemère (also an old soldier) seconding him: the chain yields, breaks; the huge Drawbridge slams down, thundering (*avec fracas*). Glorious: and yet, alas, it is still but the outworks. The Eight grim Towers, with their Invalide musketry, their paving-stones and cannon-mouths, still soar aloft intact;—Ditch yawning impassable, stone-faced; the inner Drawbridge with its *back* towards us: the Bastille is still to take! (*FR*, 1.5.6.190–191)

This passage initiates the typical Carlylean rhetorical pattern: it begins with an apostrophe, a direct address, as if to suggest that Carlyle is trying to break down ego and time boundaries. Then he invests his subject with physical detail, using violent imagery and his own disjointed Germanic rhetoric, as if to goad himself and us as much as the Frenchmen he seems to be inciting.[4] What follows is the kind of rhetoric that extends and magnifies—in this case, it pulls back to widen the scope and draw spatial parallels by multiplying the towers that remain to be taken.

Here we witness Carlyle employing incidents and characters as symbols: the people storming the prison represent his very effort to establish connections, to transcend barriers. (Interestingly enough, he underscores his skill by appearing to deny it: "To describe this Siege of the Bastille [thought to be one of the most important in History] perhaps transcends the talent of mortals"—*FR*, 1.5.6.191.) Like Carlyle, Dickens too employs symbolism to describe the taking of the Bastille: heads, façades, mazes, the prison itself all point to isolation, while the surrounding ocean of the people of St. Antoine becomes an image of violent transcendence[5]:

> The sea of black and threatening waters, and of destructive upheaving of wave against wave, whose depths were yet unfathomed and whose forces were yet unknown. The remorseless sea of turbulently swaying shapes, voices of vengeance, and faces hardened in the furnaces of suffering until the touch of pity could make no mark on them. (*TTC*, 2.21.249)

By surrounding a symbol of isolation—the governor of the prison—the crowd highlights him as a representative of boundaries and separation. But it is Madame Defarge, "immovable" next to him and seeming to parallel him, who is the linking, transitional figure. It is her act of violence—the decapitation of the governor—that paradoxically unifies him with the group, now an "ocean of faces" in Dickens' rhetoric of transcendence.

From these two examples, we can begin to characterize the contrasting modes of rhetoric employed by both Carlyle and Dickens. The rhetoric of isolation usually involves a lone central figure, façades, solid boundaries, stillness, an absence of emotion, a sense of ineluctability that could only be disrupted by violence. In contrast, the rhetoric of transcendence employs multiple figures, parallels, reification, movement, emotion, foreshadowing that crosses boundaries of time and consciousness. This latter category encompasses the imagery of the abyss in man as well as his organic vision, which Albert J. LaValley traces back to Carlyle's "Characteristics" (1831) and *Sartor Resartus* (1833–1834).[6] As for the transitional rhetoric—the rhetoric of violence—it seems to gain momentum for Carlyle as *The French Revolution* proceeds; by the third volume, the historical violence that he reports is paralleled by his rhetoric until, in LaValley's terms, his response to the violence causes the work to become "riddled with ambivalent feelings, ambiguities, and contradictions."[7]

Dickens, on the other hand, succeeds in uniting the two opposing forms of rhetoric in Carton's last soliloquy: Carton is at once the lone emotionless figure and the prophet who sees beyond time and space.

But Carlyle is still trying to achieve a similar balance between isolation and transcendence. By apostrophizing a solitary historical figure, he is in a sense isolating him in order to enter his consciousness, albeit speculatively. Even the reader can be evoked in this fashion, as witness the concluding paragraph of *The French Revolution*:

> And so here, O Reader, has the time come for us two to part. To some was our journeying together; not without offence; but it is done. To me thou wert as a beloved shade, the disembodied or not yet embodied spirit of a Brother. To thee I was but as a Voice. Yet was our relation a kind of sacred one; doubt not that! For whatsoever once sacred things become hollow jargons, yet while the Voice of Man speaks with Man, hast thou not there the living fountain out of which all sacrednesses sprang, and will yet spring? Man, by the nature of him, is definable as "an incarnated Word." Ill stands it with me if I have spoken falsely: thine also it was to hear truly. Farewell.
> (*FR*, 3.7.8.323)

Ultimately, Carlyle sees language as a linker of minds, as allowing the writer and reader to move together from the past to the future. The apostrophe is the key here: it permits Carlyle to address the reader as he elsewhere addresses individual historical personages, whom he reconstitutes as if they were both living creatures and his own creations. Typical of the soliloquist, Carlyle as apostrophizer is trying to energize himself by reifying a terminus of communication—someone to whom he can direct his rhetoric, someone whom he can persuade to his way of thinking. Yet despite this effort to link writer and reader, to unify them, the act of unification can at best be only temporary.

"Bursting forth" is in fact Carlyle's acknowledged creative process, a process that involves a leap from self-negation to self-creation.[8] This is the movement of mind we can witness in many soliloquists, who goad themselves with self-doubt and self-castigation into resolution and the promise of action. Sydney Carton's first soliloquy, a mere "muttering" and not a "bursting forth," may seem fixed in self-negation and the rhetoric of isolation, but it nonetheless prefigures his final act and the rhetoric of transcendence:

> "Do you particularly like the man [Charles Darnay]?" he muttered, at his own image; "why should you particularly like a man who resembles you? There is nothing in you to like; you know that. Ah, confound you! What a change you have made in yourself! A good reason for taking to a man, that

he shows you what you have fallen away from, and what you might have been! Change places with him, and would you have been looked at by those blue eyes as he was, and commiserated by that agitated face as he was? Come on, and have it out in plain words! You hate the fellow!''

(TTC, 2.5.117)

Despite his self-loathing and isolation, Carton's raising of the theme of "what might have been" leads him to the notion of changing places with Darnay, which foreshadows his life-exchange and a transcendent achieving of his "what might have been" in Lucie's eyes.[9] The images of doubling and alternative pasts thus serve as the touches of transcendence that will later "burst forth." Even the ambiguity of "You hate the fellow" points to this transcendence: not only does Carton hate Darnay as a rival and a reminder of what he might have been, but he also hates himself—with the kind of self-negation that will eventually become energized into self-creation. That that process is well under way is apparent in Carton's second soliloquy, when he carefully plots out his plan to indeed change places with Darnay. "Let me think it out!" he says to himself, insuring that his resolution will lead to inviolate action (TTC, 3.12.367).[10]

For both Carlyle and Dickens, the challenge is to reify their "characters"—whether they be once-living historical figures or their own creations. Carlyle in particular seems preoccupied with the tension between solidity and abstraction, brought to the fore by the rhetoric of isolation and the rhetoric of transcendence. Not only does he employ such recurrent motifs as chimeras and ghosts, but he repeatedly tries to cloak ideas in solid form. This effort receives impetus from his typical practice of apostrophizing.[11] Note, for instance, one of his evocations to Hope:

> With these signs of the times, is it not surprising that the dominant feeling all over France was still continually Hope? O blessed Hope, sole boon of man: whereby, on his strait prison-walls, are painted beautiful far-stretching landscapes; and into the night of very Death is shed holiest dawn! Thou art to all an indefeasible possession in this God's-world; to the wise a sacred Constantine's-banner, written on the eternal skies; under which they *shall* conquer, for the battle itself is victory: to the foolish some secular *mirage*, or shadow of still waters, painted on the parched Earth; whereby at least their dusty pilgrimage, if devious, becomes cheerfuler, becomes possible.

(FR, 2.1.6.34)

Yet it is not Hope or even any of the many personages Carlyle tries to evoke by means of direct address who come alive as much as he does through the rhetoric of his narration.[12] Whereas Dickens can manipulate his plot structures and create character from scratch, Carlyle as historian has factual limitations to contend with. Nonetheless, by overlaying his history with rhetorical extremes and shifts, Carlyle depicts his own mind at work—a titanic force in the psychodrama of separate minds struggling to contact and understand one another.

As for Dickens' efforts to reify his characters, John Forster acknowledges *A Tale of Two Cities* as a "deliberate and planned departure" from his usual practice:

> To rely less upon character than upon incident, and to resolve that his actors should be expressed by the story more than they should express themselves by dialogue, was for him a hazardous, and can hardly be called an entirely successful[,] experiment.[13]

Certainly the events of the revolution seem to overshadow Dickens' characters, who are themselves less developed and more one-dimensional than we find in most of his other novels. But like Carlyle, Dickens is here implicitly working with the mystery of the human mind, and it is often the attempt to cross boundaries of consciousness, rather than an explication of them, that counts. In this sense, then, Dickens' own narrative strategy parallels Carlyle's, though on a less sustained scale. On the other hand, Dickens operates from the more solid vantage point of the creator of character. That he chooses to modulate his exploration of the minds of these characters by taking a speculative tone and by primarily limiting himself to Carton's movement of mind as a soliloquist only makes more impressive his final transcendence.

Whereas Carlyle's speculation requires self-goading marked by apostrophe and fustian, Dickens' speculation assumes a quieter, more ruminative manner. A speculative tone or conditional mode informs the speech of not only the narrator of *A Tale of Two Cities* but many of its characters as well. Such a mode softens the blow of sudden news, whether it be joyous or devastating, and it serves the solitary soliloquist who bewails the alternative past of "what might have been." In particular, it is Carton's mode in his own direct discourse as a soliloquist, and it supplies the refrain in his dictation to Darnay, "If it had been otherwise . . ." (*TTC*, 3.13.381), itself recalling how Lucie would have reclaimed him "if anything could" (2.13.180) and ultimately reminding her of their conversation to that effect in the world beyond the novel.[14] So it is perhaps only fitting that Dickens approach Carton's soliloquies speculatively. Even his apparently repeated cry in the darkness outside the Darnay household, "God bless her for her sweet compassion!" (2.20.239), comes from a ghostly, conditional center of consciousness. At the same time, however, it bridges Carton's separation from Lucie and parallels and prefigures the introduction to his final soliloquy. Dickens introduces Carton's last words by announcing, "If he had given an utterance to his, and they were prophetic, they would have been these" (3.15.404). This manner creates a paradoxical effect, for the words are at once unspoken and yet transcendently true.[15] In effect, then, these last words gain the power of a cosmic monologue in their mode and scope, and Dickens underscores their transcendence by including in the indicative, "and they were prophetic."

At this point, we might well ask how the rhetorical styles of Carlyle and Dickens serve their subject matter in *The French Revolution* and *A Tale of Two Cities*. If their overt subject matter is the revolution but their covert theme is that the mystery of the human mind can be assailed, then their two contrasting modes of rhetoric create a provocative tension. Furthermore, the violent yet transcendent image of the mob as a single sea provides a significant link between the rhetoric of isolation and the rhetoric of transcendence: it underscores the ineluctability of violent upheaval for both society and the self, given the implications of self-interest and isolation. So if Carlyle's final vision remains in turmoil at the end of *The French Revolution*, that does not deny the coherence of his own mind in evaluating the contending forces—his perspective, if not the revolution, resolves itself in the rhetoric.[16]

Writing after the fact of the revolution (and in Dickens' case, constructing his own fiction), both authors can be said to know the future. Thus they can aesthetically prefigure and control the "prophecies" that seem central to their works. With Carlyle, this prophetic element contributes to a sense of *The French Revolution* as epic, an impression augmented by his use of mythological allusions and Homeric apostrophes.[17] Even more so, of course, the prophetic tone fits with Carlyle's self-image as a prophet for his own age, a solitary voice speaking to the multitude but not always heard and frequently unheeded. With Dickens, the prophetic element operates through parallels and doubling, and it centers on Sydney Carton.[18] Carton himself is constantly moving back and forth across time—planning the future by drawing on the past. His "might have been" theme takes precedence for him, cancelling out a possible physical happiness in this world, but it provides the opening for his final act of self-sacrifice and self-transcendence that insures him eternal peace. It is perhaps this attitude toward time and his ability to move freely across its boundaries that allow him to joyfully prophesy a world without his presence yet one that he informs through Lucie's son, whom he confidently predicts will bear his name.[19]

Finally, let us examine Carton's cosmic monologue as a forum for uniting the rhetoric of isolation and the rhetoric of transcendence. His situation and "sublime" demeanor emphasize him as the isolated figure, while his ranking of individual oppressors who will perish employs the rhetoric of isolation. But the violence of "this retributive instrument" ushers in a series of transcendent parallelisms. Each of the four long paragraphs preceding the final two lines begins with "I see," and all of the sentences begin with that same prophetic "I see." Parallelism invests the imagery, too: he looks ahead to an image of Lucie and Charles lying side by side in their grave. Then Carton apparently reverses the usual rhetorical movement, concentrating next on the isolated image of Lucie's son:

> "I see that child who lay upon her bosom and who bore my name, a man winning his way up in that path of life which once was mine. I see him winning it so well, that my name is made illustrious there by the light of his. I see the blots I threw upon it, faded away. I see him, foremost of just judges and honoured men, bringing a boy of my name, with a forehead that I know and golden hair, to this place—then fair to look upon, with not a trace of this day's disfigurement—and I hear him tell the child my story, with a tender and a faltering voice."   (3.15.404)

The image of this boy growing into manhood and fulfilling the promise of what Carton might have been embodies both contrasting forms of rhetoric, however. The young Sydney Darnay succeeds as an individual but as an individual who is part of society, and he recovers the name of his namesake. The doubling redoubles with the birth of yet another Sydney, who comes to this transfigured place of terror to hear anew the tale of Sydney Carton. The tale now begins its transcendent cycle.

NOTES

1. Thomas Carlyle, *The French Revolution*, Vol. 3, Bk. 3, Ch. 2, p. 121, in *The Works of Thomas Carlyle*, ed. H. D. Traill (London: Chapman & Hall, 1896). Future citations to this Centenary Edition will appear in parentheses in the text.

2. Charles Dickens, *A Tale of Two Cities*, ed. and intro. George Woodcock (Harmondsworth: Penguin, 1970), Bk. 1, Ch. 3, p. 4. Future citations to this edition will appear in parentheses in the text.

3. "Cosmic monologue" is a concept that encompasses the range of voices between John Milton's God in *Paradise Lost* and James Joyce's Anna Livia Plurabelle in *Finnegans Wake*. It seems particularly apt for characterizing Carlyle's brand of rhetoric—one that tries to conjoin omniscience with human limitations, to impress a truth on an audience whom the soliloquist himself must prod into consciousness.

4. In *Carlyle and His Era* (Santa Cruz, Calif.: Dean E. McHenry Library, 1975), pp. 18–19, Murray Baumgarten argues the interrelation between Carlyle's violent language and his method of perception. Technique and perception thus reflect each other as well as Carlyle's subject—the modern world in the process of self-energizing.

5. For an accounting of the ocean as metaphor for the mob in both works, see Michael Goldberg, *Carlyle and Dickens* (Athens: University of Georgia Press, 1972), pp. 120–121.

6. See *Carlyle and the Idea of the Modern: Studies in Carlyle's Prophetic Literature and its Relation to Blake, Nietzsche, Marx, and Others* (New Haven: Yale University Press, 1968), pp. 127–129.

7. *Ibid.*, p. 159.

8. See his letters to John Sterling and Ralph Waldo Emerson, as discussed by Louise Mervin Young in her section, "The Process of Historical Composition," in *Thomas Carlyle and the Art of History* (Philadelphia: University of Pennsylvania Press, 1939), pp. 140–147.

9. The theme of "what might have been" exists for Carlyle in the figure of the Comte de Mirabeau, whose death in 1791 ended the last hope for moderation. John P. Farrell sums up the impact of Mirabeau's death as "the major tragedy of *The French Revolution.*" See *Revolution as Tragedy: The Dilemma of the Moderate from Scott to Arnold* (Ithaca: Cornell University Press, 1980), pp. 223–226.

10. For a similar yet more extended soliloquy elsewhere in Dickens (1864–1865), see John Harmon's attempt to "think it out" at the turning point of *Our Mutual Friend*, ed. and intro. Stephen Gill (Harmondsworth: Penguin, 1971), Bk. 2, Ch. 13, pp. 421–430. Another example of the "living-dead," Harmon is plotting the possible consequences of an exchange of identities, but his choices conflate the extremes of physical death and cosmic transcendence. As J. Hillis Miller concludes in *Charles Dickens: The World of His Novels* (Cambridge, Mass.: Harvard University Press, 1958), p. 248, "it is only in *Our Mutual Friend* that [Dickens] is able to put the two motions of resurrection, descent into death and return, together in a single person."

11. G. L. Brook, in fact, treats Dickens' use of the apostrophe as largely reflecting Carlyle's influence. See *The Language of Dickens* (London: Andre Deutsche, 1970), pp. 16–17 and 48–49. Carlyle, of course, employs the apostrophe freely throughout *The French Revolution*, but Dickens limits his use of it in *A Tale of Two Cities*, consolidating it to serve the Carlylean practices of personification and mythopoeia. See especially his addresses to La Guillotine (*TTC*, 3.5.304) and to Vengeance (3.15.401).

12. Thus, despite his prodigious feat of consulting and directly quoting hundreds of memoirs, Carlyle remains his own subject matter. By Charles Frederick Harrold's enumeration, almost a third of the work "contain[s] no historical material whatever, but express[es] Carlyle's reactions to events or ideas of the Revolution." See "Carlyle's General Method in *The French Revolution,*" *PMLA*, 43 (1928), 1150, n. 1. In this important respect, then, *The French Revolution* is an extension of *Sartor Resartus*, whose narrator (the Editor) may be

considered the story's protagonist. See Georg B. Tennyson's line of argument in *Sartor Called Resartus: The Genesis, Structure, and Style of Thomas Carlyle's First Major Work* (Princeton: Princeton University Press, 1965), pp. 174–176.

13. *The Life of Charles Dickens*, ed. A. J. Hoppé, rev. ed. (London: Dent, 1969), II, 232. This statement of intention paraphrases a letter to Forster, 25 August 1859, when *A Tale of Two Cities* was still in serial production.

14. For a melodramatic inturning into its own world that strains our credulity, see Tom Taylor's dramatic adaptation (London: Thomas Hailes Lacy, [n.d.]). The final scene depicts Lucie and Charles watching the tumbrils roll by; when Carton spots the couple, he smiles and waves; the play then concludes with a tableau of Lucie and Charles in prayer (p. 56). Dickens did have a hand in this adaptation, however. In a letter of 20 January 1860, he sent a pastiche of Carton's final soliloquy to Villiers, who was playing the lead in Paris. Incorporated into Taylor's published play, this version juxtaposes the well-known final words with "Farewell Lucie, farewell life!" and is relegated to the jail scene (p. 52). Dickens' manuscript is reproduced in *Yale University Library Gazette*, 37 (Oct. 1962), illus. opposite p. 89.

15. Granting Carton "some visionary power," Richard J. Dunn nevertheless emphasizes that "the substance of that vision remains hypothetical and incommunicable." See "Far, Far Better Things: Dickens' Later Endings," *Dickens Studies Annual*, 7, ed. Robert B. Partlow, Jr. (Carbondale: Southern Illinois University Press, 1978), p. 231. I, however, argue that Dickens is exploiting the visionary's tension between direct awareness of the universal and the difficulty of communicating that insight. Not only does Dickens' rhetoric undercut any sense of the final speech as hypothetical and incommunicable, but he builds the soliloquy on a familiar (albeit intuitive) model: as we assume that any consciousness has the power to review a lifetime in a single moment, so we who read this novel overhear such a recital extended into the future. Carlyle, too, acknowledges the mysterious hold of the "Unnameable" and the "Infinite" in Madame Roland's request "to write the strange thoughts that were rising in her" (*FR*, 3.5.2.211; cited in *TTC*, 3.15.404).

16. See, for example, his effort to define "this thing called *La Révolution*" (*FR*, 3.6.1.248–249).

17. John Stuart Mill's review of *The French Revolution* accords it epic stature in its own right: "This is not so much a history as an epic poem." See *London and Westminster Review*, 27 (July 1837), 17.

18. In *A Tale of Two Cities*, parallels and doubling also manifest themselves in twins who are rivals. For a study of how the double plot and divided characters express generational and class conflicts, see Albert D. Hutter, "Nation and Generation in *A Tale of Two Cities*," *PMLA*, 93 (1978), 448–462.

19. Despite all the attention to this last soliloquy as prophecy, its final words recall the past as much as they speak to the future: "It is a far, far better thing I do than I have ever done; it is a far, far better rest that I go to than I have ever known." Yet the rhetorical emphasis of "far, far"—for both the present and

the future—shows Carton resolutely moving beyond the past. And the future has already arrived for him—"it is a far, far better rest"—signaling that he has indeed attained his cosmic grasp.

Prophetic Closure
and Disclosing Narrative:
The French Revolution
and *A Tale of Two Cities*

Chris R. Vanden Bossche

Just how seriously can one take the promise of resurrection at the end of *A Tale of Two Cities*, and how optimistic can one be about the restoration of order at the conclusion of *The French Revolution*? Readings of these works seem to turn on these questions, and the answers are, not surprisingly, diverse.[1] I want to discuss what makes endings in general troubling to us, our desire not only to find that the characters in a story live happily every after, but to be made happy ourselves by the way the story ends. While I will be making some distinctions between the works of Dickens and Carlyle in this paper, my focus will be on a common exploration of this doubled desire as manifested by the curious voicing of the prophetic observations with which *The French Revolution* and *A Tale of Two Cities* conclude.

The problematics of Victorian narrative endings do not necessarily reflect authorial failure or cultural weakness, but a shift in the conception of narrative and narrative ending itself. It has now become commonplace to claim that modern literature is not mimetic, that it refers to itself rather than to a world that no longer exists as a stable reality. To put it another way, the world is (always) already organized by codes; as Diogenes Teufelsdrockh would say, it is clothed and textured; indeed, he might well say it is textualized. The author who desires to represent the real no longer does so by attempting to faithfully mirror the flux of history, but by deviating from the codes that structure it. Artistic narratives tell us about these codes by deviating from them; they disclose rather than attempt to

209

achieve the closure of providing a full account of the world.[2] More specifically, these two works by Carlyle and Dickens do not tell us about the French Revolution; they use that event analogically to tell us about their (or our) own time. Yet, because they recognize the desire for closure as a deeply seated human, and cultural, need, these works do not entirely deny it, but become instead a commentary on how these desires pull us in opposite directions.

In the mimetic model of narrative, closure occurs when the main character crosses a boundary from the imitable and narratable world into inimitable and non-narratable transcendence (for example, the marriage idyll): one can end the narrative because the time it represents literally ends and the meaning of the character's life is fully given.[3] Since the disappearance of transcendental reality erases this boundary, causing the narrative that attempts to imitate human life to become potentially endless, Victorian novelists often problematize their conclusions by providing a double for the character who has moved into the transcendental idyll of marriage, a double whose life could be narrated endlessly without closure—like Becky Sharp in relationship to Amelia at the ending of *Vanity Fair*. The potential endlessness of this second narrative forces writers to find a means of closure that does not depend on reference to an imitated object, but on the relationship of the ending to the symbolic construct of the work itself. At first glance, *The French Revolution* and *A Tale of Two Cities* would seem to reach closure by providing *both* halves of the doubled pair with a transcendental conclusion: the marriage of Darnay and the analogous "arrangement," a sort of shotgun wedding, that ends the French Revolution are supplemented by Carton's resurrection and the rebirth of sansculottism, but the latter events are foretold in ambiguously voiced prophetic speeches that put this traditional Christian moment of closure into question.

Both works cast the conventional narrative ending, which sketches in the future, in the form of a prophecy. They point towards the problematic nature of prophecy which presumes that all time is already complete and therefore closed so that one can see a fixed future. Prophecy, as Mikhail Bakhtin has argued, is inscribed within a completed history in which the prophet writes the inspired divine logos or interprets signs that are unambiguously complete; for it, the future is just as finished as the past.[4] Carlyle and Dickens revise the prophetic by creating prophecies that do not correspond to the past and future projected by the narratives that they close. Carlyle emphasizes this by ending with a prophecy that refers to the past just narrated rather than the future beyond it, a prophecy of the revolution itself. Even though it is given, as the Carlylean narrator says, *"ex-post facto,"* it proclaims the success of the revolution in terms that do not correspond to his depiction of it, not too surprising since the prophet is the quack and con-artist, Count Cagliostro.[5] Furthermore, with it, Carlyle ends his history, so carefully constructed from "facts," with a fiction that he had written himself in his previous work, "The Diamond Necklace."

The famous conclusion of *A Tale of Two Cities* would seem at first to be problematic only because it is excessively sentimental, but it is useful to contrast this sentimental conclusion with that of *The Frozen Deep*. There, Wardour, the Carton figure, after a long struggle to overcome his desire to kill his rival Aldersley, gives his life to save him, but *A Tale of Two Cities* reverses the order: in the closing chapters, we see Carton's bravery, and it is only in the final prophetic speech that one can see the underlying rivalry. That is, Dickens introduces unsettling ambiguity rather than closure in Carton's final speech. The image of self-sacrifice created by this speech puts the authenticity of that very self-sacrifice into question by envisioning a future that nearly effaces Darnay (only portraying his death) and foretelling a line of sons named for Carton. Like Cagliostro's prophecy, Carton's vision of a peaceful Paris is problematic in the light of the reader's knowledge of its tumultuous history and further revolutions in 1830 and 1848. Furthermore, as with Cagliostro's prophecy, the voicing itself is problematic; though the Dickensian narrator cites the speech in direct quotation, he cites only what Carton would have written *"if"* he had given utterance to his thoughts and *"if"* they had been prophetic (3, 15, 404).[6] Is he telling us what he knows in Carton's words, or is he telling us what Carton *would* have thought; is this the reality or only Carton's fantasy? In so far as he assumes this passage as his own, the Dickensian narrator would seem to absolve Carton's prophecy from its self-aggrandizing tendency and to make the pathetic conclusion authentic. Yet, instead of assuming completely omniscient authority for Carton's apotheosis as he might have done, he allows us to see the desire hidden behind it.[7]

While these closing speeches express the desire for resolution, they end up unsettling it, deferring closure. I would like to stress, however, that uncertainty about the transcendental conclusion does not simply manifest an uncertainty about transcendental reality since this would only be a continuation of the mimetic impulse; it manifests instead a newly evolving understanding of the relationship between narrative and world, that narrative constitutes the world, which causes the artist to revise the relationship between the narrative and its ending. Thus while Frank Kermode aptly argues that the modern tendency to experience apocalypse as imminent throughout time rather than coming at the end of closed time finds its correlative in the discovery of meaning at every moment in the narrative rather than in its telos, it would be just as correct to argue that the modern understanding of narrative reconstitutes our sense of time and human endings.[8] Put another way, instead of the desire to defer closure creating an extended digression or "peripeteia" that forms the body of a narrative and the desire for closure bringing about the ending, the modern view is that these desires are registered simultaneously, closure and its deferment occurring at every point in the narrative. Instead of substituting new narrative units along a sequence moving toward a final closing event, narrative sequences substitutions that keep repeating previous narrative units and thus threaten never to reach an end—the paradigmatic as powerful as, if not dominating, the syntagmatic.

Carlyle and Dickens build their narratives from units of similarity that emphasize the symbolic significance of events rather than the continuity of time outside the narrative.[9] Many of the events recorded in Carlyle's history, like "The Feast of Pikes" and "The Night of Spurs," are treated with disproportionate amplitude when considered in terms of political causes and effects, but are central to his vision of the symbolic structure of the revolution. His characteristic sentence construction is representative of his narrative construction: a series of parallel clauses, related to one another thematically, not temporally (this is reinforced by the persistent use of the present tense which tends to imply the contemporaneity of events):

> Blood flows; the aliment of new madness. The wounded are carried into houses of the Rue Cerisaie; the dying leave their last mandate not to yield till the accursed Stronghold fall.   (*The French Revolution*, 1, 5, 6, 192–193)

Chapters and even books follow the same syntax, as, for example, when he creates a "Flame-Picture" from a discontinuous series of anecdotes. Similarly, Dickens' use of the rhetorical device of anaphora, as Taylor Stoehr has noted, extends itself to the way he constructs his narrative, building it from "echoes," doublings, and repetitions.[10] The movement between the chapters "Monseigneur in Town" and "Monseigneur in the Country" does not advance the plot; as their titles, and as parallel scenes by a fountain, indicate, it provides comparisons that build a symbolic picture of the French aristocracy. The proliferation of doublings produces the same effect, beginning with the title cities. The narrative does not portray a circular journey of temporal continuity, as a journey from the home of London to the dangers of Paris and back home again might have done, but disconnected jumps between two locations that are made to become reflections of one another. Dickens' defense of the concealment of Manette's letter until near the end of the novel is based upon notions of narrative suspense, but the choice also emphasized the symbolic importance of Manette's narrative. Rather than placing it at the beginning of the novel where the events belong chronologically or syntagmatically, he embeds Manette's story within the trial that leads to Darnay's equally unjust incarceration (and which follows upon the September massacres that echo the violence of the Evremonde brothers). It becomes a doubled contrast to the first trial of Darnay in which justice prevails and Manette is able to free his son-in-law.[11] In both works, the inevitability with which events do move forward is not the inevitability of cause and effect, but of the code that structures culture and society; events are what Carlyle calls the "public efflorescence" of a "secret essence" (*The French Revolution*, 3, 3, 1, 117).

These writers seek to show the way the world is coded rather than to give the illusion that their narrative is a window upon unmediated reality. The narrative moves neither according to the events to which it refers, the French Revolution, nor to an imagined series of events similar to that one, but by a series of symbolic transfers that refer to a cultural code. In doing so, it discloses the code that remains hidden as the deep structure of events like the Revolution and that constantly emerges in the lives of the protagonists of *The French Revolution* and *A Tale of Two Cities*. More concretely stated, the subtext of the law produces the scenes of trial and imprisonment which occupy a central position in these works. The very pattern of narration that defers closure by showing that events keep repeating themselves rather than finishing history is a pattern of failure to escape enclosure. But the desire to escape enclosure is complimented by the equally strong desire to achieve closure.

Instead of discovering an end to conflict that would enable closure, however, these works point to the problem embedded within the very desire for closure. Each of the three volumes of *The French Revolution* concludes with a failure to find a set of laws adequate to the beliefs of the French people (1, 6, 1, 215): the failure of monarchy (indicated in the penultimate book as the fall of the Bastille and as the end of feudal law); the constitution "burst in pieces" which is described as a building that is meant to replace the Bastille; and the final "arrangement" based on greed, not the needs of the people. *A Tale of Two Cities*, also written in three parts, records a series of movements in and out of the hands of the law; Dr. Manette's release from prison; Darnay's decision to return to France, described as entry into prison; and the exchange through which Carton enters and Darnay leaves prison. The final part, by combining the movements of the previous two does not make them cancel each other out, but indicates the inevitable interrelatedness of the two movements: you cannot get out without going back in.

While both works seem to have a surface story about the search for proper government, the underlying story is about the desire to escape the order of the law. The revolution is the process, Carlyle says, through which "anarchy breaks prison" but, in fact, the destruction of the Bastille, as both authors make clear, does not destroy the law and its prisons: instead the Terror becomes "the order of the day" and the whole state a prison. The prison embodies the law just as the courtroom is the scene of its enactment. The importance of both in Dickens' works cannot be understated, but they are equally important in Carlyle's history where the trial of Danton, like the trials of Darnay, demonstrates that justice is always illusory and the courtroom always perverts it. Both of these trial scenes portray the failure of eloquence and emphasize that the verdict has been decided in advance. The proliferation of prisons in Dickens is almost too well known to need comment; I would only note that unjust and unfair trials are nearly as common, the court of Chancery being, of course, the central metaphor of *Bleak House*. Already in *Pickwick* Dickens combines the unfair trial with imprisonment, and one can see the darkening of Dickens' vision in the contrast between that comedy and the hopelessness of *A Tale*.

The law does not inhibit anarchic violence, it perpetrates it, and these writers reject revolution at least in part because they despair for its success. Those who attempt to free themselves from the law tend to end up back in its prison; the desire for absolute freedom as a desire to escape imprisonment forever is a desire for closure that becomes enclosure.[12] The doubled desire for closure and its deferment manifests itself as three types of authorial figures in these works: those who strive to destroy the law in order to live only in the real, but end up being imprisoned by this desire, the Defarges, Jacques, and the Jacobins; those who would make the law entirely adequate to the real, also seeking closure but this time at the level of the law, Darnay and the Girondins; and those who do not attempt to abolish the law, but to transgress and disclose it, Carton and Cagliostro as avatars of the Dickensian and Carlylean narrators.

The Girondins believe they have written a constitution that will bring an end to the revolution (*The French Revolution*, 2, 5, 1, 297), but it, like the feudal chateaus, goes up in flames; Darnay, who hopes to urge the French people to stop their violence, ends up, like Manette and the Girondins, imprisoned. While the Jacobins and Defarges seem to want the opposite, the absolute destruction of the law of the aristocracy, their desire also takes the form of closure; Madame Defarge's knitting, creating a text of judgments passed on the aristocracy, demonstrates that this desire is linked to the law rather than to rebellion.[13] The figure of Doctor Manette dramatizes how these opposed figures express the same desire for closure when in Darnay's two French trials he takes exactly opposite sides: first, he works to free Darnay without in the least satisfying the Defarges' demand for justice, and then, in his letter read at the second trial, condemns the Evremonde brothers "and their descendents, to the last of their race" (3, 10, 361).

The desire to transgress the law rather than completely escape it, combines the desires for closure and its deferment; this brings us back to the speakers of the enigmatic prophecies, Cagliostro and Carton. Superficially, Cagliostro's prophecy only expresses the desire for the closure of apocalypse, yet this wish for the complete annihilation of imposture is spoken by an imposter. The underlying ambivalence makes itself felt in the narrator's response to the prophecy: " . . . has it not been fulfilled, is it not fulfilling?" (3, 7, 8, 323). This expresses perfectly the doubled desire for closure and its absence, projecting us out of the completed past into the incomplete present (in the move from the past tense to the present). The last volume of the history demonstrates that, indeed, the Directory does not complete the revolution, but only defers its conclusion to a future date, that sansculottism has only gone "underground." The volume begins with "September" and ends with "Vendemiaire"—almost the same month, but slightly later and so more autumnal than autumn—two names for the same season of ripeness with no final harvest; for the people still lack food and cry once again for "bread, not speeches" as they had five years previously (3, 7, 4, 303). Human order is never commensurable with human need; "Mammonism," not a higher order, replaces feudalism (3, 7, 7, 314). Even though the Carlylean narrator clearly desires the orderly "arrangement" that follows the Terror, he also argues that any attempt to use "cullotisms," laws or formulas, is to use "old cloth . . . and cannot endure" (3, 7, 6, 311). The end of the Terror brings neither naked sansculottism nor proper attire, but dandyism, the carmagnole replaced by Cabarus balls at which women wear their sheer empire gowns over "flesh-coloured drawers" (3, 7, 5, 291–295 *et al.*).

Carlyle's fear of violence may also be his fear of the law, and the lack of closure corresponds, after all, to the historical events. Similarly, the fact that, as Johnson and others argue, the love plot and the revolution plot of

A Tale do not fit one another does not indicate failure[14]; the triumphal
swell of Carton's vision, with its odd echoes of the ironical opening chapter, does not so much conceal the problem as help bring out the impossibility of bringing about the desired resolution. Carton, as Dickens' stand-
in, both seeks to find closure within the cultural code and to transgress
it.[15] Carton, like Dickens, omnisciently foresees his story's conclusion (3,
11, 364); compares himself to an eddy, echoing the narrator's water imagery (3, 9, 344; 3, 12, 373); authors a final letter to Lucie that he makes
Darnay write for him just as Dickens makes his characters speak (3, 13,
381); and, finally, frees Darnay through a substitution of likenesses
analogous to the writer's device of metaphorical substitution. Furthermore, only Carton, among the major characters, is English (Lorry, Pross,
Stryver, and Cruncher all are minor characters with comic functions), his
very Englishness presenting us with the image of a Dickens figure who
enters the drama to straighten everything out. Indeed, Carton becomes
the dramatic master of the last part of the novel, literally "plotting" its
happy ending: the literal safety of the Darnay/Manette family as well as
the imagined end of the Terror and return of the family to a Paris reborn
as the heavenly city that follows Carlyle's apocalypse. But, as we have
seen, this is only the surface text of his prophecy; it also continues the
desire of the terrorists to eliminate the Evremondes for it nearly effaces
Darnay. The desire for order once again turns violent and patriarchal.[16]

Yet, Carton, like Cagliostro, remains a shady character, a trickster. He
achieves his ending through a transgression of the law; while others work
through the law, Carton, as a lawyer, sees that salvation lies in attacking
the law, not individuals (Barsad, another transgressor also can move in
and out of prison at will). But he does not escape the law, and his trick
does not resolve the conflict between justice and love. How could one
meet the demands of Madame Defarge's anger—her anger at the family
who violated and killed her sister is truly sympathetic—and the demands
of Lucie Manette for her husband? Darnay is himself a doubled figure as
his two names indicate: he is the innocent son of his mother D'Aulnais
and the guilty son of his father Evremonde; Carton's action does not resolve this conflict for he cannot save the "Evremonde" pointed out by
Barsad from being guillotined. The name—Evremonde—is the same;
only the body—Carton's—has been changed to protect the innocent—
Darnay.[17]

At the same time, Carton exposes the law and becomes a figure for
Dickens the disclosing narrator. Carton imagines Lucie's son, named
after him, as the teller of his story, another authorial figure who, like

Dickens (Lucie's son would have to be born after 1793 and would not be too much older than Dickens), tells a tale of two cities that would also have the ambiguity of being a tale of two fathers. Rather than happily ending, this narrator literally sends us back to hear the story again. But here, we find the escape of transgression achieved not by Carton or Cagliostro, but by the act of narration, even as something apart from the narrator, which escapes their controlling presence. The indeterminant provenance of these speeches, the way they tend to float free from any anchoring voice, prevents them from being closed and conventional prophecies. Carton and Cagliostro are not so much men as masks, yet one cannot pin this mask upon the narrator either. The only privilege afforded these speeches is the conventional privilege of being placed at the end of the narrative, but at the end of narratives that have dramatized endpoints as those points at which closure is deferred; instead of the ending giving meaning to the body of the narrative, the middle undoes the meaning of the ending.

My emphasis on repetitive patternings as against syntagmatic and realist narrative may sound similar to Northrop Frye's notion that the meaning of narrative lies in its ability to reveal basic human archetypes and that, because mythic narratives show these most plainly, they are the most meaningful.[18] But, as I hope to have shown, this is only half of the function of narrative for these writers; the other half might be represented by the opposing attitude toward myth held by Roland Barthes. For Barthes, the function of literature is to deviate from the constraining myths of culture. While Frye sees the myths as representing archetypal reality, for Barthes they are a historical and cultural language. I tend to side with Barthes, but I think he too tends to miss the important point that we still very much want our myths to correspond to our needs and our realities.[19] So Carlyle and Dickens want to create new myths for their culture but see that they can do so only be deviating from enslaving ones.

We must ask why Dickens and Carlyle were not more radical, but it is not enough to blame their conservatism, if it is that, on political pusillanimity or capitalist co-optation; the answer lies in the way they are caught between their conflicting desires. Not as providers of solutions but as those who understand what makes it so difficult to find solutions, did they become such compelling writers. When Carlyle compares his book to the French Revolution itself, he refers not only to the desire for freedom but the wish for a higher law. We have here a wish for the spirit not the letter of the law, but this wish is expressed in an era in which the existence of the spirit is much in doubt.

The doubled authorial desire results in an enormous production of writing: both Carlyle and Dickens write so they can achieve rest, then travel to a place to find this rest only to find themselves restless until they can start writing again. Both fond of long walks, their walking seems to be a continuation of writing rather than a respite from it, for it too never has a goal. They find rest only in work so they can never stop working, Carlyle writing that he must "work to keep his heart at rest."[20] Since work is freedom, Carlyle finds the freeing of slaves and the elimination of mandatory labor in prisons absurd, merely knitting one's chains into festoons.[21] Only in the actual play of his style do we find freedom even as he denies the validity of art. Dickens, who also shows the relationship between imprisonment and work in the figure of Doctor Manette making shoes, seems to find greater joy in art's transgressive qualities, in turning the prison into a playground.

NOTES

1. Since almost everyone who discusses *A Tale* sees the ending as crucial, I will note only three extremely divergent positions, those of Albert Hutter, who finds in the resurrection theme a resolution of Oedipal conflict, Robert Alter who sees the ending as successfully asserting pessimism, and George Woodcock, who affirms the resurrection theme while dismissing the final speech as a "sop" to Dickens' reading public. See Albert D. Hutter, "Nation and Generation in *A Tale of Two Cities*," *PMLA*, 93 (1978), 456; Robert Alter, *Novel*, 2 (1969), 141–142; and George Woodcock, Introduction, *A Tale of Two Cities*, p. 24. Albert LaValley finds the ending of *The French Revolution* a problematic affirmation of Napoleonic repression while H. M. Leicester argues that Carlyle self-consciously undercuts this notion. See Albert La Valley, *Carlyle and the Idea of the Modern* (New Haven: Yale University Press, 1968), pp. 161–164 and 182, and "The Dialectic of Romantic Historiography: Prospect and Retrospect in *The French Revolution*," *Victorian Studies*, XV (1971), 16–17. All references to *The French Revolution* are to the Centenary Edition, ed. H. D. Traill (London: Chapman & Hall, 1899).

2. I use the term "closure" in the broad sense that indicates the attempt to discern full and complete meaning in a sign, to close it, as well as in the more restricted sense of the completion of meaning at the end of a narrative. See Roland Barthes, "From Work to Text," in *Image-Music-Text*, trans. Stephen Heath (New York: Hill and Wang, 1977), pp. 155–164.

3. This formulation is a synthesis of several theoretical formulations on the nature of narrative. The notion of boundary is drawn from Jurij Lotman, *The Structure of the Artistic Text*, trans. Ronald Vroon (Ann Arbor: Michigan Slavic Contributions, 1977). He argues that the basic events that form the plotted text (a narrative) are events that result from crossing a boundary between plotless ideology and plotted revolution (pp. 232–239); endings, therefore,

would involve a movement back into the plotless. Some American theoreticians describe this as a movement between the narratable and the non-narratable. See Peter Brooks, "Repetition, Repression and Return: *Great Expectations* and the Study of Plot," *New Literary History*, 11 (1980), 523, and David A. Miller, *Narrative and Its Discontents: Problems of Closure in the Traditional Novel* (Princeton: Princeton University Press, 1981), pp. ix–xi.

4. M. M. Bakhtin, "Epic and the Novel: Toward a Methodology for the Study of the Novel," in *The Dialogic Imagination: Four Essays*, trans. Caryl Emerson and Michael Holquist, ed. Michael Holquist (Austin: University of Texas Press, 1981), p. 31.

5. For Carlyle's own accounts of this figure, see "Count Cagliostro" and "The Diamond Necklace" in *Critical and Miscellaneous Essays*, vols. 3 and 4.

6. Dickens evokes the episode (recorded in Carlyle's history) in which Mme. Roland expresses the wish to write down her thoughts as she approaches the scaffold. It is notable that the final episode reverses gender roles by having Carton soothe a young woman whereas Roland had soothed a young man (part of a general tendency to reverse gender, see below).

7. Garrett Stewart's argument that the second clause of the narrator's introduction of Carton's speech only seems to be parallel to the first, but permits one to read it as non-conditional (i.e. "If he had given utterance to his, and they were prophetic,"), does not alter the force of my argument that Dickens makes the status of this prophecy ambiguous although he was certainly in the position to avoid this. It comes down to a trick of syntax, not unlike the trick that Carton employs to get Darnay out of jail and himself into heaven. See "The Secret Life of Death in Dickens," *Dickens Studies Annual: Essays on Victorian Fiction*, 11, Michael Timko, Fred Kaplan, and Edward Guiliano, eds. (New York: AMS Press, 1983), pp. 177–207. Richard Dunn has also noted the ambiguity of this passage, and a general tendency in the later novels to make the final vision of the future ambiguous, most notably in the "visionary" conclusion of *David Copperfield*. See "Far, Far Better Things: Dickens' Later Endings," *Dickens Studies Annual*, 7, ed. Robert B. Partlow, Jr. (Carbondale: Southern Illinois University Press, 1978), pp. 230–231.

8. Frank Kermode, *The Sense of an Ending* (Oxford: Oxford University Press, 1967), p. 101.

9. This is the quality in Carlyle that George Levine describes as anti-narrative because it frustrates the syntagmatic thrust of traditional narrative, but it is at the same time a misleading term because his works are, after all, narratives. This essay is very much indebted, however, to his excellent analyses of style and form in Carlyle. See *The Boundaries of Fiction* (Princeton: Princeton University Press, 1966), pp. 45–51. For a view that opposes mine, by arguing that Dickens is different from Carlyle in this regard, see Robert L. Caserio, *Plot, Story and the Novel: from Dickens and Poe to the Modern Period* (Princeton: Princeton University Press, 1979).

10. Thus while I agree with Taylor Stoehr that anaphora is a general principle of composition in Dickens, I disagree about how it works and about its significance. Part of the disagreement that will not be evident from my remarks here

stems from Stoehr's assertion that the effect is to efface the narrator whereas I find that this patently rhetorical device draws attention not only to the narrator but to the narrative, that, contrary to what Stoehr finds, its effect alienates one from the thereness of objects. See *Dickens: The Dreamer's Stance* (Ithaca: Cornell University Press, 1965), pp. 14–19.

11. Dickens' defense is in a letter to Wilkie Collins. Significantly, he had also disagreed with Collins's proleptic revelation of the ending of *The Frozen Deep. The Letters of Charles Dickens and Wilkie Collins*, ed. Laurence Hutton (New York: Harper, 1892), pp. 95–96 and 59.

12. While I am endebted to a number of post-structuralist theoreticians of narrative, I dissent from their critique of the closure of "traditional" narrative in so far as it posits this as a reality and not a critical distinction. That is, Barthes's attempt, for example, to draw a definite line between "work" and "text" or "readerly" and "writerly" involves his own distinction in closure. Similarly, Hayden White seems implicitly to argue for an "annals" form of history because it does not require the closure needed to "moralize" events, thus moralizing his own distinction. Finally, as pertinent to the theme of these works, one finds notions of "permanent revolution" that are similarly paradoxical since revolution is opposed to permanence. Derrida uses this phrase several times to characterize Blanchot's *La Folie du jour*. See Roland Barthes, *S/Z*, trans. Richard Howard (New York: Hill and Wang, 1974); Hayden White, "The Value of Narrativity," in *On Narrative*, ed. W. J. T. Mitchell (Chicago: University of Chicago Press, 1981), pp. 1–23; and Jacques Derrida, "The Law of Genre," in *On Narrative*, pp. 51–77.

13. My view of the law is quite similar to that of the imprisoning past as characterized by Elliot Gilbert's essay in this volume; I would argue, in fact, that the past takes the form of the legal code.

14. Edgar Johnson, *Charles Dickens: His Tragedy and Triumph*, 2 vols. (New York: Simon and Schuster, 1952), p. 981.

15. The identification between Dickens and Carton is felt by most readers and is further supported by Dickens' comments in the preface to the novel, and his choice of the parallel role of Wardour in *The Frozen Deep*. But there is some ambiguity since it is Charles Darnay who carries Dickens' initials (repeated in Carton/Darnay), and who gets to live on with Lucie. Similarly, there is a close relationship between Cagliostro and Carlyle for which see my "The Speech of God-devils: Masonry and Freemasonry in Carlyle's Early Works," in *Scottish Studies: Thomas Carlyle 1981*, ed. Horst W. Drescher (Bern and Frankfort: Lang, 1983), pp. 71–87. I would note also that Cagliostro dies in the year in which sansculottism dies, and that the theme of rebirth suggests that Carlyle, born in 1795, is himself its reincarnated spirit.

16. One aspect of this question that I have not pursued is the way in which Carton interposes a male line (mentioning his father and imagining a yet unborn son and grandson) for a female line that goes from Darnay's mother to Lucie to her daughter. One will also recall that Lucie's son died.

17. This might be more completely stated in the following terms: The name (sign = signifier: *Evremonde* + signified: aristocrat) is the same, only the body (referent: *Carton's* body) has been changed to protect the innocent (sign = referent: *Darnay*).

18. Frye consistently criticizes the "realism" of the novel for "displacing" the mythic patterns of romance. See *The Anatomy of Criticism: Four Essays* (Princeton: Princeton University Press, *1957*), pp. 131–140, and *The Secular Scripture: A Study of the Structure of Romance* (Cambridge, Mass.: Harvard University Press, 1976), chapter 2. Frye sees these mythic structures as "archetypal" or universal while my argument proceeds from the Lacanian position that the unconscious itself is structured like a language, and thus a cultural code.

19. *Mythologies* (Paris: Seuil, 1957), pp. 215–268.

20. Journal cited in James Anthony Froude, *Thomas Carlyle, A History of His Life in London: 1834–1881* (London: Longmans, Green & Co., 1884), I, 171. His journals often record a desire for rest from his work (see I, 46, 55, 135, 318), as well as the equation of writing with wandering (I, 38, 215).

21. *Sartor Resartus*, 1, 7, 199. See also "Model Prisons" in *Latter-Day Pamphlets*, and "The Nigger-Question" on the subject of slavery (*Critical and Miscellaneous Essays*, 4, 359).

Carlyle, Dickens, and
the Revolution of 1848

Michael Goldberg

Critical discussion of Carlyle and Dickens on the subject of revolution has tended to concentrate on the revolution of 1789. This is hardly surprising given *A Tale of Two Cities* and Carlyle's *History*, yet such a focus has inevitably overshadowed and obscured the importance of the other revolution, the series of political explosions in the name of popular democracy which unsettled Europe in 1848 and whose impact on both writers is of considerable interest. For one thing, the social upheavals of mid-century occurred at a time of decisive change in both their working lives, and not only stimulated that change but contributed to its direction.

Dickens, busy with the last numbers of *Dombey and Son* when the revolution broke out in France, stood at a turning point in his life and art. It is now an established orthodoxy to observe that at this time Dickens had come to regard Victorian society in a radically fresh way. The nature of the change in his outlook is best described by Bernard Shaw in his seminal 1912 preface to *Hard Times*. What began in *Dombey* and culminated in *Hard Times*, he suggests, was comparable to a religious conversion which led Dickens to a conviction of social sin. In *Bleak House* the book that immediately preceded *Hard Times*, Dickens was "still denouncing evils and ridiculing absurdities that were mere symptoms of the anarchy that followed the industrial revolution. . . . He had not dug down to the bed rock of the imposture. . . . He saw nothing but individual delinquencies, local plaguespots, negligent authorities." But in *Hard Times* all this had changed. In that novel Dickens joins Karl Marx, Carlyle, Ruskin, and Morris "rising up against civilisation itself as against a disease." This broadly based perception was expressed in such books as Carlyle's *Latter-Day Pamphlets*, *Hard Times*, and later on in the Socialist movement which convinced even those dubious about socialism, "that the condition of the civilised world is deplorable, and that the remedy is far beyond the means of individual right-eousness."[1] It is in *Dombey and Son*, written in part under the shadow of European revolution, that Dickens first expressed what Kathleen Tillotson calls "a pervasive uneasiness about contemporary society which takes the place of an intermittent concern with specific social wrongs."[2] In short, Dickens had come to view social evil as a malignant organism for which the only logical cure might be the radical surgery of revolution.

The revolution and the urgent stream of such visitors to Cheyne Row as Louis Blanc, Mazzini, Gavan Duffy, and Leigh Hunt drew Carlyle closer to contemporary politics than ever before. His immediate interests found their way into manuscript and print. In his first excursion into the field of political journalism, he wrote a series of articles on Ireland, which he felt constrained to revisit in 1849, and he was busy with the rough drafts of what were to become *Latter-Day Pamphlets*. As his major production of the period, the *Pamphlets* were largely a response to the European uprisings and, as in the case of *Hard Times*, represent a turning point in Carlyle's ca-reer and reputation—a change which brought imputations, not always well founded, of a dramatic alteration in his political thinking. Froude and For-ster, the two latter-day Boswells, remind us that both Carlyle and Dickens were extremely restless during this time, and as we now easily recognize they were about to move in new directions.

All of which is not to argue that the revolution of 1848 was the immedi-ate or exclusive source of these shifts in their thinking and writing; but it formed the indispensable backdrop against which such changes occurred and should be measured.

We should remember that for both Carlyle and Dickens the first French revolution was something of an historical exercise. It was an event frozen in time, something they read about and about which they had the leisure to theorize, whereas the revolution of 1848 they saw in actual progress, shifting and changing direction almost daily. For Carlyle, the historian of revolutions, it was particularly strange to find himself in the unique posi-tion of contemporary witness to the revolts sweeping Europe, agitating Ireland and threatening to engulf England.

The first European rumblings occurred in January 1848 when rebellion broke out in Sicily, where the Sicilians succeeded in imposing a constitu-tion on their king, as did the people of Piedmont. In Milan, where patriots manned the barricade, Marshall Radetzky encircled the fortifications around the city, and popular upheavals drove Metternich from Vienna. There were revolts in Germany and Poland, and revolution spread quickly to Paris which once again became the "city of insurrections." The Guizot government fell, and a disguised Louis Philippe fled to England much to the scornful glee of Carlyle and the consternation of Dickens. As if by "sympathetic subterranean" influence, all Europe "exploded, boundless, uncontrollable," and the year 1848 was, in Carlyle's view, "one of the most singular, disastrous, amazing, and, on the whole, humiliating years the European world every saw. Not since the irruption of the Northern Barbarians has there been the like."[3] Kings everywhere precipitously vacated their thrones as the populace took government into their own hands. The order of the day was anarchy; "how happy," observed Carlyle, "if it be anarchy *plus* a street-constable!"[4] This in general, as Carlyle described it in 1850, was "the history, from Baltic to Mediterranean, in Italy, France, Prussia, Austria, from end to end of Europe, in those March days of 1848."[5]

Though concerned about some implications of the European revolutions, Carlyle's initial reaction to the news from Paris was one of "almost sacred joy," as he wrote in the *Examiner* of March 4, 1848. The overthrow of the French monarch, "flung out; he and his entire pack, with a kind of exquisite ignominy,"[6] was cause for celebration. "It is long years," he wrote to Emerson four days later on February 28, "since I have felt any such deep-seated pious satisfaction at a public event."[7]

Dickens greeted the new republic with comparable enthusiasm, a sign if not of influence at least of compatability of sentiment. "Mon Ami," he wrote to Forster on February 29, 1848, "I find that I am so much in love with the Republic that I must renounce my language and write solely in the language of the French Republic,"[8] which he temporarily did, signing himself Citoyen Charles Dickens. Carlyle's response was predictably more analytical. He wrote an unsigned article on French politics for the *Examiner* on March 4. Another, meant to follow it on March 11, was suppressed by the editor John Forster "lest Carlyle's candour might damage the circulation of the paper."[9] This suppressed article is not included in the appendix of Richard Herne Shepherd's 1881 *Memoirs of the Life and Writings of Thomas Carlyle*, among the six articles which he noted "are all we have been able to trace" of "Carlyle's fugitive political contributions to journalism."[10] Nor is it to be found in the 1892 reprinting of Carlyle's articles in Percy Newberry's *Rescued Essays*. The article, entitled "Prospects of the French Republic," is, however, in the Forster collection at the Victoria and Albert Museum. In it Carlyle makes a contrast between the first and the second French republics and in so doing implicitly a comparison of the Romantic and Victorian responses to revolution. The two great advantages of the newly emerged republic are that it is secure from outside attack: "all nations in the presence of their own inevitable democracy know well that this Republic is not a thing to be lightly or suddenly attacked''; and also ''no Frenchman now expects a millennium close in the rear of it, which in regard to the old Republic all Frenchmen did.'' The new republic is ''not required to be miraculous, but only to be a practicable one. Enthusiastic hope is not there to issue in fierce disappointment.'' In short, the high millennial hopes bestowed by the Romantic era on the first French republic, only to be cruelly betrayed during the reign of terror, had given way in Victorian times to more realistic expectations. Carlyle, of course, feared that like all modern republics the French one was likely to prove to be only a ''government of Talkers,'' that is, ''a government that does not govern but merely produces parliamentary eloquence.'' Still the Republic was France's noblest feat, and ''the world's chief heroism for two hundred years.'' The new provisional government had started well, and as what was to follow was ''hidden in black clouds,'' Carlyle wrote, we can only say ''may it be wise'' and ''from the heart of all good citizens of all countries bid it good speed.'' That was early in March, when Carlyle saw the third French revolution as a stage in the completion of the first, part of a revolutionary process whose accomplishment was essential, ''for rest is not in the world till then.''[11]

However, by the end of the March and the beginning of April, Carlyle was no longer so sanguine about the political prospects in France. In a letter to Thomas Erskine on March 24, he found in ''this immense explosion of democracy'' cause for both celebration and despair, and he predicted long years of ''weltering confusion'' before ''anything can be *settled* again.'' Hardly since the ''invasion of the wild Teutons and wreck of the old Roman Empire has there been so strange a Europe, all turned topsy turvy.''[12] By April, the ''future for all countries'' filled him ''with a kind of horror.''[13]

In March, Carlyle told Emerson, who was then visiting England, that he had known ''European revolution was inevitable,'' but he had ''expected the old state of things to last out his time.'' In the light of recent European events he revised his estimate to give ''our institutions, as they are called, aristocracy, church, etc., five years. . . .''[14]

Carlyle's prediction was soon disproved by events, for the European revolutions spent their energy without accomplishing their long-term aims. It is true that before the threat of popular revolution the European monarchs had fled ''like a gang of coiners'' surprised by the police, but within two years of the uprising in France, Louis Napoleon ruled the Second Empire with the support of the Catholic church, and French bayonets reinforced the position of Pope Pius IX, who in 1846 had donned the Papal tiara as a ''reforming Pope.'' Largely because their conception of it was strongly colored by previous historical experience, the 1848 revolution had seemed to many observers the "great decisive struggle." Even after the setbacks of 1849, according to Engels, "vulgar democracy expected a renewed outbreak from day to day." He and Marx, however, believed that the "first chapter of the revolutionary period was closed and that the next phase could only begin with a new world crisis." As Marx put it, parodying the ritual formula for monarchist succession, "*The Revolution is dead!—Long live the revolution!*"[15]

In his own separate way Carlyle had arrived at a similar conclusion. By 1850, he saw that some "remounting,—very temporary remounting,—of the old machine, under new colours and altered forms," would soon ensue in most countries:

> Kings will be admitted back under . . . "Constitutions," with national Parliaments, or the like fashionable adjuncts; and everywhere the old daily life will try to begin again. But there is now no hope that such arrangements can be permanent; that they can be other than poor temporary makeshifts, which, if they try to fancy and make themselves permanent, will be displaced by new explosions, recurring more speedily than last time.[16]

New "street-barricades, and new anarchies, still more scandalous if still less sanguinary, must return and again return, till governing persons everywhere know and admit" that "universal *Democracy*" had "declared itself as an inevitable fact"[17] The hastily restored European order could not endure, and did not deserve to, and its restoration meant only that the need for change had been postponed. In England, too, Carlyle predicted "sore times" ahead and judged that the "trade of governor will not long be possible as poor Lord John [Russell] and the like of him are used to manage it."[18] For although England would resist the introduction of democracy "in the form of street-barricades and insurrectionary pikes," the "tramp of its million feet is on all streets and thoroughfares, the sound of its bewildered thousandfold voice is in all writings and speakings, in all thinkings and modes and activities of men."[19]

It seemed for a time as if revolution on the European model might enter England through the back door of Ireland or spontaneously erupt in the ranks of the Chartist movement which reached its peak in April 1848. The legitimate outrages which had moved Carlyle to write his essay on *Chartism* in 1839 had not been redressed, and now almost a decade later some 200,000 chartist petitioners were expected to demonstrate in London. In *Chartism* Carlyle had also condemned English misrule of Ireland and in the "hungry forties" conditions were even worse after the successive failure of the potato crops which brought Irish refugees streaming into English industrial towns in the north.

The Irish giant "despair" was to be seen everywhere "blue-visaged, thatched in rags, a blue child on each arm; hunger-driven, wide-mouthed, seeking whom he may devour."[20] Carlyle did not join in the popular outcry against the Irish nomads nor even against the landlords supposedly responsible for pauperizing them. England, through long neglect and misrule, deserved the army of Irish beggars now laying waste to its towns. But he did see that the Irish pauper parading his "rags and hunger, and sin and misery" was an "irrepressible missionary" to "our own people . . . heralding to us also a doom like his own."[21] For this destitute Irish army was bound to transform not only the political institutions of England but the structure of society itself.

Ireland seemed a great social laboratory where the social ills of England existed in magnified form, and where, particularly, organic government had broken down. In the summer of 1849, Carlyle decided to visit the "huge suppuration" that was Ireland to study conditions for himself. It was immediately apparent that revolutionary forces were gathering. John Mitchel, whom Carlyle had met in 1846, had come to believe that a peasants' revolt was imminent, and having left both the *Nation* and the Young Ireland Party, was readying the country for a rebellion openly advocated in his new journal *The United Irishman*. The *Nation*, too, though not radical enough for Mitchel, also appealed to Irishmen to throw off the English yoke. One such appeal by the lady who was to become the mother of Oscar Wilde, called for a bold, decisive move against the English garrison "and the land is ours."[22] These revolutionary aspirations began to be taken seriously in England when, after the fall in February 1848 of the French government, Irishmen danced round bonfires in the certain hope that Ireland's turn to be free had now come. The Government of Westminster judged the moment had arrived to suppress the public preaching of sedition and dispatched additional troops to Ireland while arming itself with the provisions of the Treason Felony Act. Carlyle considered these moves unsympathetically, for while he approved the putting down of rebellion, without strong constructive measures to accompany it, he regarded such a policy as bankrupt. When Parliament resumed after the Easter recess of 1848, Carlyle launched a stinging attack on Lord John Russell's "remedial measures" for Ireland. Russell, he told readers of the *Spectator* on May 13, had earned the applause of all sane men for suppressing "pike-rioting" and by indicating to the Irish that their wrongs were not to be redressed by "street-barricades just at present." But the urgent question arose "by what means, then, *are* Irish wrongs to be redressed?"[23]

The Government's measures made for "prohibition of Repeal treason" but they offered no cure of "the disease which produces" it.[24] Nor did the government suggest "how the Irish population is to begin . . . to live on just terms with one another and with us,—or, alas, even how it is to continue living at all." An existence based on the treacherous potato was, after the blight and the famine which followed it, no longer possible. Did the Whig administration not also realize, he asked despairingly, that some form of "real government" for Ireland was indispensable? Did it know that the French king had fled Paris and that Europe had risen behind him to declare that it was done with "sham government"? All these facts indicated that "a *new* and very ominous era, for Ireland and for us, has arrived."[25] It is obvious that Carlyle saw the situation in Ireland in terms of the revolutions in Europe. He also saw that Irish discontent had its counterpart in the Chartist movement, which had been neither remedied nor extinguished by the demonstration of April 10. With both Chartism and Ireland in mind he asked,

> does our chief governor calculate that England, with such a Chartism under deck, and such a fireship of an Ireland indissolubly chained to her, beaten on continually by an anarchic Europe and its all-permeating influences . . . can keep the waters . . . by her old constitutional methods?"[26]

The *Pamphlets* deal with many topics, but their unifying core is democracy, the "grand, alarming, imminent, and indisputable Reality" of the time. If the long-range future for democracy had seemed assured since the first French Revolution of 1789, its immediate advent was now certain after the collapse of the third.

Carlyle's objections to democracy are not particularly palatable to modern tastes, and they were bitterly opposed by many of his contemporaries, but they have not always been clearly understood. Partly because of the effect of such misunderstanding on his reputation in general, and on the neglected *Pamphlets* in particular, the grounds for his hostility to early democracy deserve wary inspection.

Carlyle's feeling about the immense explosion of democracy was more complicated than one of simple rejection. Indeed he was as much depressed by the failure of the 1848 French revolution as he was by some of the implications that would have attended its success. To the extent that revolutionary democracy had shown up imposture and corruption he applauded it as a necessary first step towards future regeneration. Thus the expulsion of sham governors had pleased him far more than their restoration in 1849. The revolutions had contained an inchoate stirring against the very shams Carlyle had hated all his life; they had proved that a longing for justice and veracity still existed on the part of the governed, and they served notice that such charlatans as Louis Philippe could found no "habitation upon lies."[27] But, on the other hand, that the world "in its protest against False Government" should find no remedy save that "of rushing into No Government or anarchy"[28] struck him as ludicrous. He favored extirpating false government as had happened in France, but he sought a different end result from those who merely wanted access to the rights and privileges seemingly guaranteed by a democratic constitution. Here, as elsewhere, a characteristic mixture of radical and reactionary strains converge in Carlyle's thinking, leaving him opposed both to the vestiges of the ancient regimes and to the new utopianism with which many hoped to replace them.

Carlyle believed in order, but it is clear that he did not wish to prop up the existing political order. He accepted even more willingly than many of his contemporaries the inevitability and the desirability of change, and in the aftermath of the revolutionary failures of 1848 he perceived that the need for change was more urgent than ever. "There must be a new world, if there is to be any world at all. . . . These days of universal death must be days of universal newbirth, if the ruin is not to be total and final."[29] The alternatives were not "Stay where we are, or change?"[30] but how change was to be brought about and whether in Britain the transition to the new era could be made "pacifically."

He was at odds, however, with the prevailing belief that "once modelled into suffrages, furnished with ballot-boxes and suchlike,"[31] the transition to democracy would be at once achieved. He was more inclined to ask with Burke, "Is it because liberty in the abstract may be classed amongst the blessings of mankind, that I am seriously to felicitate a madman, who has escaped from the protecting restraint and wholesome darkness of his cell, on his restoration to the enjoyment of light and liberty?"[32] To use his own metaphor, if the old house of Europe had partially broken down and the "front wall of your wretched old crazy dwelling" had fallen prostrate into the street, was it sane for the whole household to burst forth celebrating the "new joys of light and ventilation. . . ."[33]

This summary by no means exhausts the complexity of Carlyle's response to European democracy, but it offers an impression of its broad contours. To conclude with a general comment—the 1848 revolutions helped to stir the social thinking of both writers in ways that were profound and productive. The revolution broke Dickens' faith in the adequacy of reform and alerted him to the ongoing process of revolutionary change and the constant possibility of the fire next time. In the mid-fifties, for instance, he recognized that the "sullen, smouldering discontent" in England was "like the general mind of France before the breaking out of the first Revolution," and that any accident might touch off "a conflagration as never has been beheld since."[34] For Carlyle, the revolution led to his most penetrating thinking about democracy, and his strictures against what he saw as its dangers and distortions led to his increasing isolation as a moral teacher and to the lowering of his reputation towards the end of the century.

Despite protests against Carlyle's views in *Latter-Day Pamphlets* there were critics who saw the value of his struggle to comprehend the major political and social changes occuring in the mid-century. Emerson, for one, said of the *Pamphlets*: "it is a pretty good minority of one; enunciating with brilliant malice what shall be the universal opinion of the next edition of mankind. And the sanity was so manifest, that I felt the over-gods had cleared their skirts also to this generation, in not leaving themselves without witness."[35]

NOTES

1. Reprinted in *The Dickens Critics*, George Ford and Lauriat Lane, Jr., eds. (Ithaca: Cornell University Press, 1961), pp. 126, 127, 128.

2. *Novels of the Eighteen-Forties* (Oxford: Oxford University Press, 1961), p. 157.

3. "The Present Time," in *Latter-Day Pamplets* (London: Chapman & Hall, 1898), p. 5.

4. *Ibid.*, p. 6.

5. *Ibid.*

6. James Anthony Froude, *Thomas Carlyle: A History of His Life in London 1834–1881*, 2 vols. (London: Longmans & Co., 1884), I, 429.

7. *Correspondence of Carlyle and Emerson*, ed., C. E. Norton (London: Chatto & Windus, 1883), II, 163.

8. *Life of Charles Dickens* (Boston: James Osgood, 1875), p. 404.

9. D. A. Wilson, *Carlyle at His Zenith* (London: Kegan Paul, Trench, Trubner & Co., Ltd., 1927), p. 22.

10. (London, 1881), II, 21.

11. *The Examiner*, March 4, 1848, p. 145.

12. Froude, I, 430–431.

13. *Ibid.*, I 435.

14. *Letters of Matthew Arnold*, ed., George Russell (London, 1895), I, 8.

15. *Class Struggles in France 1848–1850* (New York: International Publishers, 1964), p. 59.

16. "The Present Time," p. 8.

17. *Ibid.*, pp. 8–9.

18. Froude, I, 438.

19. "The Present Time," p. 9.

20. "Downing Street," in *Latter-Day Pamphlets*, p. 94

21. *Spectator*, May 13, 1848, p. 463.

22. July 29, 1848.

23. P. 463.

24. *Ibid.*

25. P. 464.

26. *Ibid.*

27. Froude, I, 430.

28. *Ibid.*

29. "The Present Time," p. 2.

30. "The New Downing Street," in *Latter-Day Pamphlets*, p. 157.

31. "The Present Time," p. 14.

32. Edmund Burke, *Reflections on the Revolution in France* (Harmondsworth: Penguin, 1970), p. 90.

33. "The Present Time," p. 10.

34. Edgar Johnson, *Charles Dickens: His Tragedy and Triumph,* 2 vols. (New York: Simon and Schuster, 1952), II, 841.

35. *The Correspondence of Emerson and Carlyle*, ed., Joseph Slater (New York: Columbia University Press, 1964), pp. 497–498.

Carlyle and Dickens:
Heroes and Hero-Worshippers

Branwen Bailey Pratt

> Dillettantism, hypothesis, speculation, a kind of amateur
> search for Truth, toying and coquetting with Truth; this
> is the sorest sin. The root of all other imaginable sins.
> THOMAS CARLYLE, *On Heroes, Hero-Worship
> and the Heroic in History*, II, 73.

Scholars have long since established evidence of Carlyle's influence on Dickens—linguistic echoes, thematic similarities, outright borrowings. More problematic but equally significant are the reasons for that influence—the conscious and unconscious motives that impel one writer to use another's work as a source, to regard another as an inspiration or literary ancestor, as a focus for emulation or rebellion. Such questions justify themselves by the contribution they make to literary studies, even in the face of Carlyle's stated abhorrence of the "amateur-search for Truth," a statement which, if the word "amateur" is understood in its literal sense, is one possible definition of literary criticism. Such a search finds in the subtext of the two men's works and letters, as well as on the surface, substantial bases for speculation about the nature of their relationship and the ways each functioned in the other's mental and literary life. While Dickens acknowledged *The French Revolution* as his historical source for *A Tale of Two Cities*, he seems to have been unaware of the effects Carlyle's prescriptive attitudes toward heroism had on the novel's plot, on its characters, and perhaps on himself as its author and as a man.

"Whether I shall turn out to be the hero of my own life, or whether that station will be held by anybody else, these pages must show" (Charles Dickens, *David Copperfield* [London: Oxford University Press, 1970], I, 1). So writes the novelist David Copperfield, whose inner life and external experience alike frequently parallel those of the novelist Charles Dickens.

> The Hero as Man of Letters. . . [rules] from his grave after death, whole na-
> tions and generations. . . . [He is not] extant in the world to amuse idleness,
> and have a few coins and aplauses thrown him. . .He. . .is the soul of all.
> What he teaches, the whole world will do. . . . [He] is sent hither specifically
> that he may discern for himself, and make manifest to us. . . [the] Divine
> Idea.   (HHW, V, 154, 155, 156).

So writes the essayist and historian Thomas Carlyle in his own person (although in the rhetorical style he shares with his approximate alter ego
Diogenes Teufelsdrockh).

Each author expresses his perceptions of the psychic functions the hero
performs for the individual and for the race, the reasons "We all. . . love,
venerate and bow down submissive before Great Men" (HHW, I, 15).
Even as the idea of heroism prompts one man to question the outcome of
his life, the writer-Hero's interpretations of the Divine Idea determine the
conduct of present and future generations. Psychoanalytic theory is more
specific: hero worship is a narcissistic choice of object that increases self-
esteem and so restores the ego to wholeness. Whoever possesses an excellence which the ego lacks for the attainment of its ideal beocmes loved, or
in the case of the hero, idealized. By acting out the fantasies of omnip-
lence which the ego lacks for the attainment of its ideal becomes loved, or
as an outlet for the grandiose ambitions ordinary people can conceive, but
cannot fulfill. Identification with the leader's greatness helps his followers
to manage feelings of inadequacy: without risk or responsibility, they can
participate vicariously in his nobility and his achievements. The hero-
leader derives corresponding psychic benefits: the veneration of his wor-
shippers assures him of his worthiness, their dependency reinforces his
sense of power, their homage assures him of his place in posterity.[1]

Positively, certainly, didactically, Carlyle describes in his lectures *On
Heroes, Hero-Worship, and the Heroic in History* (delivered 1840, published 1841) the contributions Great Men of the past have made to mankind's welfare. Even more positively, certainly, didactically, he prescribes
the messianic role the writer as hero must fulfill in the present. Dickens,
who acquired the nickname "Boz" from his younger brother's mispro-
nunciation of "Moses," would have had to become a reincarnation of
that leader to equal the achievements Carlyle envisions. To the contrary,
the writer-protagonist of his most overtly autobiographical novel, *David
Copperfield*, questions his heroic capabilities in tentative, hesitant, ultimately passive language that expresses a self-doubt as intense as Carlyle's
self-assurance.

In 1840, when the two men first met, their stations in life were very different. Carlyle was forty-five, an acknowledged pundit firmly established

in the public's regard—the Sage of Chelsea; Dickens, twenty-eight, a newly famous comic novelist, the Inimitable Boz. That same public had recently seen him rise like a rocket, but was not yet certain whether or not he would come down like the stick. Both men saw human existence as—in a Carlylean phrase—"the infinite conjugation of the verb 'to do'"; even in the context of the energetic type Victorians called "The Doer," they distinguished themselves as Over-Doers. Agreed about the inequities and inanities rampant in nineteenth-century Britain, they worked together to better the world—to organize writers in the struggle for international copyright law, to defend Mazzini's integrity, to raise funds for Samuel Johnson's improverished god-daughter, to found the London Library. Always, though, what they wrote and what was written about them create the impression that Carlyle—who at age thirty-seven had confided to his mother that John Stuart Mill was his "partial disciple"—saw himself as a Great Man and Dickens as a small one.[2] Referring to Carlyle, Dickens most often uses the words "noble" and "manly"; referring to Dickens, Carlyle most often uses "little" and "small," which in his vocabulary are distinctly pejorative. Dickens apparently deferred to this judgment while at the same time trying continually to alter it. His letters as well as his novels suggest that he was unconsciously seeking from the older man not friendship, but some kind of imprimatur, some endorsement of himself by an authority he regarded as unimpeachable.

After their first meeting, Carlyle described "Pickwick" to his wife as

a fine little fellow...a small compact figure, very small, and dressed a la d'Orsay rather than well...a quiet, shrewd-looking little fellow, who seems to guess pretty well what he is and what others are.[3]

On that occasion, the "little fellow" had demonstrated the shrewdness of his judgment by treating Carlyle with admiring solicitude bordering on adulation, an attitude he largely maintained throughout their thirty-year acquaintance. John Forster (who once in all seriousness addressed Carlyle as "My Prophet") records that Carlyle was a hero to Dickens, and hero and hero-worshipper they continued.[4] Carlyle's condescending references to Dickens's small stature—presumably the outward and visible sign of a lack of significance in the grand scheme of things—likewise persisted.

In so extremely serious a universe as the one Carlyle inhabited, and in such parlous times, Boz's novels, like Scott's and Thackeray's, failed to sound the "divine awakening voice" which would rouse "the Heroic in all Men" (CME, IV, 55). Dickens instead sought

his heroes in the region of blackguardism and the gutters, where heroic magnanimities and benevolence...were never found; and delineate[d]

them . . . by ell-deep mimicry instead of penetration to the real root of them
and their affairs; which indeed is much farther down![5]

Carlyle's enjoyment of Dickens' humor gradually modified his early
contempt for *Pickwick* as "lowest trash," *Copperfield* as "the innocent
waterest of twaddle," and *Great Expectations* as "that Pip nonsense";
the writing of novels nevertheless remained in his eyes too trivial, compared with the writing of historical biography, to be considered "a noble
employment under this Sun; or . . . in fact, any employment at all, different from what we see at Astley's Ampitheatre."[6] His appreciation of *A
Tale of Two Cities* was relayed off-handedly through Forster: "When
you go to Dickens, our best regards. *A Tale of Two Cities* is wonderful!"[7]
Even in the letter praising Dickens for possessing "in the inner man of
him a tone of real Music . . . which makes him in my estimate one of a
thousand," he was softening his refusal to join the novelist's intimate circle at a celebratory dinner.[8] Little Boz, in his dandiacal yellow waistcoats,
could never remotely approach the heroic stature of Shakespeare, the
"melodious Priest of . . . the 'Universal Church' of the Future and of all
times," whose history plays gave Britain its national epic (HHW, II, 111).
From the beginning to the end of their friendship, Carlyle maintained that
Dickens' talent best suited him for the less than respectable profession of
actor, an opinion he first advanced in a letter to his wife:

I had to go yesterday to Dicken's [sic] Reading . . . to the complete overset-
ting of my evening habitudes, and spiritual composure. Dickens does it
capitally (such as it is); *acts* better than any Macready in the world; a whole
tragic-comic-farcic *theatre* visible and performing under one *hat*; and keeping us laughing (in a sorry way, some of us thought) the whole night.[9]

The well-known characterization of Dickens as Schnüspel (the name
itself a diminutive) in *Past and Present* similarly decries the extraordinary
success of the American tour:

O if all Yankee-land follow a small good "Schnüspel the distinguished
Novelist" with blazing torches, dinner-invitations, universal hep-hep-
hurrah, feeling that he, though small, *is* something; how might all Angle-
land once follow a hero-martyr and great true Son of Heaven!
                                                    (P & P, II, III, 70)

Even given Carlyle's habit of ironically mocking himself and others, this
passage carries a distinct nuance of envy: Schnüspel in his smallness, the
writer feels, neither deserves nor puts to its best use the idolatry he
receives. Jane Carlyle's remarks are wittier, but no less contemptuous:
"Dickens writes 'for the greatest happiness of the greatest number' (of

Cockneys).''[10] Writing to Forster after Dickens' death, Carlyle describes him as ''of rare and great worth as a brother man . . . a most cordial, sincere, clear-sighted, quietly decisive, just and loving man.''[11] All that, however, was faint praise from one who required of a writer that he be a Heroic Preacher of the Divine Idea.

A direct personal experience of God would tend to give one a certain everlasting confidence; so it apparently affected Carlyle. Describing Mahomet's response to divine revelation, he clearly identifies with the hero as prophet:

> That Mahomet's whole soul, set in flame with this grand Truth vouchsafed him, should feel as if it were important, and the *only* important thing, was very natural. That Providence had unspeakably honoured *him* by revealing it, saving him from death and darkness; that he therefore was bound to make known the same to all creatures; this is what was meant by ''Mahomet is the Prophet of God.''   (HHW, II, 57)

The ambiguous anaphoric use of the pronoun ''it'' allows the inference that the prophet's soul felt that *it*, no less than holy Truth, was ''the only important thing''—a kind of dual reading that emerges from much of Carlyle's work.

Destined by his father for the ministry, Carlyle chose instead to receive—or invent—his own revelation. He fulfilled paternal expectations by preaching his way to heroism through writing. At a time when many of those most ardently seeking truth in the intellectual-religious maze of Victorian England were unable to find it, he knew it. His idiosyncratic semisecular theism replaced the Christian creed with his personal belief in repentance and regeneration; religious obligations with his doctrines of work, productivity, duty, and renunciation; and the exemplary lives of the saints with his accounts of his chosen heroes. He preached that hero worship was in itself ennobling: ''No nobler feeling than this of admiration for one higher than himself dwells in the breast of man'' (HHW, I, 11). Beginning with his study of Goethe, whom he regards as hero, savior, and literary father, Carlyle's writing repeatedly expresses veneration for great men and implicitly asserts his position as their spiritual son. Hero worship—''the feeling 'I am small, the beloved one is great','' psychoanalytic theory points out, ''is . . . an unconscious reminiscence of a time when this was literally true.''[12] The worshipper's feelings toward the hero derive from his reverence for the father of childhood, the larger-than-life representative of the world outside the home and the absolute authority within it. Carlyle's claims of hereditary greatness suggest that his seemingly absolute belief in the rightness of his own perceptions was rooted in a sense that he had the approval of an ultimate authority—the most admirable and righteous of men, his father, and beyond him, God.[13]

Carlyle idealized his father, a stone mason, as a builder and creator who

> believed that man was created to work, not to speculate, or feel, or dream . . . [he was] a man of perhaps *the* largest natural endowment it has been my lot to converse with . . . he worked unweariedly and perhaps performed (with the tools he had) more than any other man I ever knew.
>
> (Rem, I, 7)

The writer qualifies this intended encomium perhaps more than he realizes by repeating "perhaps" and adding the parenthetical "with the tools he had." Whether his doubts involve his father's excellence or his own ability to match it is indecipherable; unquestionably, the doubts exist.

James Carlyle named his first son after his father, Thomas, of whom that namesake later wrote that he was "a fiery man; irascible, indomitable: of the toughness and springiness of steel."[14] As the boy grew, his father recognized his unusual gifts and, at some financial sacrifice, sent him to school and then to university. Carlyle followed the paternal example of devout productivity, moving from idolization of the father to identification with him, always with some sense of the father's ultimate superiority. Acting out the family myth he had created, he emulated his grandfather's fiery nature and what he perceived as his father's heroic creativity until he became, almost, his own ego ideal. In his accounts of Goethe and Frederick the Great, in *Heroes and Hero Worship*, in frequent peripheral remarks throughout his work, as he praises his heroes for their militant earnestness and grandiose sense of mission, he is confirming aspects of his own identity. What he says about Great Men describes his ideal image of himself as much as it does the leaders he adjures the reader to worship and venerate. Knowing that his actual father believed him worthy to pursue the highest of callings, the preaching of the Gospel, he naturally assumed that his heavenly Father had selected him to receive, and to communicate, divine revelation. He presented himself to the world as priest, judge, prophet, and hero, and the world accepted him as all four.

Charles Dickens was not so fortunate. The grandfather for whom he was named turned out to be an embezzler. Unaware of his singular abilities, his father regarded him in childhood as a source of entertainment and in adulthood as a source of financial support. Genial, well-meaning, hopelessly improvident, John Dickens neither served his son as an ego ideal nor forwarded his interests, as Dickens' abandoned attempt at autobiography attests:

> I know my father to be as kindhearted and generous a man as ever lived. . . . He was proud of me, in his way, and had a great admiration of the comic singing. But, in the ease of his temper and the straitness of his means, he appeared to have utterly lost . . . the idea of educating me at all, and to have utterly put from him the notion that I had any claim on him in that regard whatever. [15]

The writer remembers his father most vividly as the kindly man who stood him up on the table at family gatherings, applauding his childish renditions of popular comic ballads. It is Chesterton who best understands the effect the elder Dickens' attitude toward the young boy had on the mature author:

> His father found it more amusing to be an audience than to be an instructor; and instead of giving the child intellectual pleasure, called upon him, almost before he was out of petticoats, to provide it. . . . [B]ehind all . . . his gigantic tours and his ten thousand editions, the crowded lectures and the crashing bass, the thing we really see is the flushed face of a little boy singing music-hall songs to a circle of aunts and uncles. [16]

Being able to make an audience laugh—or cry—was something Dickens had been able to take for granted since childhood; it was the world's opinion of his moral stature that remained a question in his mind. His efforts to make Forster into a father confessor had failed when he found himself unable to complete the autobiographical fragment; his letters and novels attest to his continuing unconscious attempt to make Carlyle into a father confirmer. What he needed was not affirmation of his abilities as a comic entertainer, but validation of himself as the kind of man the idealized father figure most valued: a devout follower of the Right and the Good, a serious and effective reformer—a Hero-Writer whose works would transform the world.

Like John Dickens, Carlyle applauded the novelist for his histrionic and comic gifts. (Also like John Dickens, he habitually took idiosyncratic liberties with language, a trait Dickens notes several times in his letters.) Carlyle, however, considered himself a teacher and Dickens (along with much of the rest of England) his pupil. When he responded to the novelist's request for information about the French Revolution by sending him two cartloads of books, he was acting to some extent in the spirit of mockery; the recipient, however, thanked him humbly:

I cannot tell you how . . . specially interesting and valuable any help is to me
that comes from you. . . . If I should come to a knot in my planing, I shall
come back to you to get over it.[17]

One need not be a Lacanian to observe that human relationships have
their mirroring function, that we conceive of and recognize our selves in
part as we see those selves reflected in the eyes of others. Dickens loved actual mirrors, and hung five in the tiny chalet where he worked. He once
wrote jokingly that he had decided to dedicate himself to the contemplation of virtue, and had bought a looking-glass for the purpose.[18] He was
always looking into one mirror or another—friends, audiences, protégés,
various young women, readers, correspondents. Each showed him a
slightly different view of himself, as a group of letters about the completion of *Hard Times*, all written within two days, demonstrates. To Wills
and Forster he writes that he is "stunned with work"; to Wilkie Collins,
that he is "bobbing up, corkwise, from the sea of *Hard Times*," ready for
"five days of amiable dissipation and unbounded license in Paris," and
will be "glad to have so vicious an associate." Writing to Carlyle, he
earnestly requests permission to dedicate the book to him: "It contains
what I do devoutly hope will shake some people in a terrible mistake of
these days. . . . I know it contains nothing you do not think with me, for no
man knows your books better than I."[19] And he concludes with the
postscript "I wouldn't flourish to you if it were not in the nature of me."
To the man he called in another letter "Carlyle, who knows everything,"
he apologizes for the flourish he characteristically added to his signature—a minute, self-aggrandizing celebration of identity, an instance of
phallic exhibitionism on a very small scale.[20] In this relationship he is
neither the Inimitable comic novelist Boz nor the insouciant boulevardier
who was Collins's companion. Rather, he is a filially submissive young
man (of forty-two) proffering for his venerable superior's approval a
book he has produced in accordance with that superior's views. Nine
years later, inviting Carlyle to hear him read the trial from *Pickwick*, he is
still pointing out both the reforming function of his work and its—and
his—debt to Carlyle as moral guide: "You would find [in it] a healthy suggestion of an abuse or two that sets people thinking in the right direction. . . . I am always reading you faithfully and trying to go your way."[21]

Much has been made of the anxiety writers suffer because of the influence previous generations exert over them: the author, Harold Bloom
asserts, must "kill" his literary fathers in order to free himself to create
his own work.[22] But the reverse is also true: a literary ancestor can be in-

corporated into the self and into the work, where he serves as a source of strength and enrichment—what recent psychoanalytic theory terms a good internalized object.[23] Dickens' Carlylean postures, his many direct and indirect borrowings, testify not to the anxiety of influence but to his need for the security of emulation. Carlyle represented the morally admirable father-mentor he had always lacked: to be reflected favorably in the infallible mirror of his opinion would be undeniable confirmation as the ideal self, the virtuous son in whom the ideal father was well pleased. In 1859, when he was writing *A Tale of Two Cities*, Dickens badly needed this confirmation. He had recently "put away" his wife at the cost of public scandal and private guilt and, less publicly, taken the young actress Ellen Ternan as his mistress; he had left his publishers after a bitter quarrel. His growing sons seemed unmotivated and his ability to guide them inadequate; his friends were beginning to die, and his own health to fail.

The childless Carlyle was a father figure to his age. His self-image included the omniscience, if not the omnipotence, of the perfect father of childhood, and his consequent dogmatism soothed the doubts that plagued his contemporaries. For many Victorians, Carlyle offered the wonderful irresponsibility of absolute reliance on a leader, the freedom from decision-making and moral ambiguity they had previously found in God. Carlyle was as willing to accept worship as his adherents were to make him an idol. Yet the near-obsessive quality of his concern with heroism and its lack, sincerity and hypocrisy, authenticity and fakery, suggests that he was less successful at convincing himself of his heroic nature than he was at impressing it upon others.[24] Further, his oeuvre demonstrates a nearly equal fascination with imposture and "Quackery": "In all of us [the] charlatan element exists," he admits in the midst of his observations on Napoleon (HHW, VI, 241). His long essay on Cagliostro, "the king of Quacks" who claimed divine authority as renovator of the universe, reveals a somewhat uncomfortable identification with the false prophet who deceives a gullible world in need of a messiah. Defending Mahomet against nineteenth-century charges of being an "Imposter" and "a Theatricality," he quotes Novalis's assertion of the self's need for validation: "'It is certain,' says Novalis, 'my Conviction gains infinitely, the moment another soul will believe in it'" (HHW, II, 43, 58). Despite his best efforts to make his life a continuation of his father's, despite acceptance as the preeminent spiritual leader of his time, within himself he was, apparently, never certain that his claims to heroism were entirely genuine.

His attempts at conviction gained infinitely, however, from his quasi-paternal relationships with such men as Leigh Hunt and John Ruskin. He acted as nurturing father to both, writing them affectionate letters of advice and trying to direct Ruskin (who, after his own father's death, addressed him as "Papa") away from frivolous aesthetic questions toward serious social concerns. He regarded these fellow writers not as colleagues or rivals, but as lesser men, symbolic children who needed the guidance he, with his superior endowment, could give them. As his authoritative interest in their lives and careers strengthened their self-confidence, their infinite admiration and unquestioning belief countered the unconscious self-distrust that underlies his conflicting preoccupations with heroes and charlatans.

Despite the younger man's obvious wish for it, Carlyle was unable to give Dickens his patriarchal support. Like his strong interest in Quackery, his marked, continuing need to belittle the most prominent novelist of his time betrays uncertainty about his own stature: criticizing another writer for "smallness" and lack of heroic seriousness allowed him to project doubts about his own greatness and heroism away from himself. Denigrating Dickens served also to reassure the older man that the younger was less of a threat to his preeminence than he seemed. Neither Ruskin nor Hunt challenged Carlyle's position as either writer or reformer; Dickens challenged both, as Trollope's caricatures of the equally influential "Dr. Pessimist Anticant" and "Mr. Popular Sentiment" in *The Warden* attest.

Boz's reputation equalled, if it did not surpass, Carlyle's. His followers, including as they did the uneducated masses, were more numerous. His power over his fellow men, though different in quality, was greater in quantity. Further, he was something Carlyle, the preacher of productivity, was not—the father of that Victorian ideal, a large family. Perhaps most alienating of all, where Carlyle was admired, Dickens was loved. To extend affection and approval to a man who so nearly outdid him in so many ways would have required a generosity and self-confidence greater than Carlyle could command. He defended himself against unconscious feelings of inadequacy by looking down on Dickens; Dickens did the same by looking up to him.

A Tale of Two Cities is one manifestation of Dickens' wish for acceptance as Carlyle's disciple. The same need for communication that made serial publication and public readings necessities for the novelist made his imagined readers extraordinarily present in his mind as he wrote: he planned *The Old Curiosity Shop* as consolation to those who had lost loved ones to death, *Martin Chuzzlewit* as admonition to those tempted by self-interest. In true Carlylean apostolic fashion, he designed *A Tale of*

Two Cities as a warning to his countrymen that the horrors of revolution in France would repeat themselves in Britain if the rich and powerful continued to ignore the sufferings of the poor and powerless. He may or may not have been aware that the presentation copies he sent Carlyle were as often passed on to relatives as read by the great man; however, since *A Tale of Two Cities* so directly derived from *The French Revolution*, he could assume that what he wrote in *this* book would receive Carlyle's close attention, and he himself—potentially—Carlyle's approval.

Certainly the book's serious moralistic-historical tone demonstrates the priestly and prophetic mission of the writer as hero more directly than does any other Dickens novel. It is also the least comic of his works: Miss Pross and the Crunchers are figures from a morality play first, humorous Dickensian types second. And embedded within the theme of conflict between fathers and sons is a portrait of the artist himself as ne'er-do-well turned hero.

Sydney Carton is Dickens' familiar dandiacal, semi-Byronic, perversely attractive, slightly Bohemian, somewhat wicked aristocrat. Descended from Lord Frederick Verisopht, the fop who dies nobly in *Nicholas Nickleby*, he numbers among his brothers the comically reformed Dick Swiveller of *The Old Curiosity Shop*, the tragically drowned James Steerforth of *David Copperfield*, James Harthouse, near-seducer of Louisa Bounderby in *Hard Times*, and Eugene Wrayburn, the almost-villain, later half-hero of *Our Mutual Friend*. All these young men share the two major Dickensian sins—the mortal one of sexual desire and the venial one of social irresponsibility. All are redeemed through either reform and regeneration in this world, or death and presumed rebirth into a better one hereafter. And all are partial confessions by the author. Only Carton, however, dies heroically in Carlylean terms as Dickens understood them.

Carton first appears in the courtroom, wig askew, gown torn (one of the book's many oblique references to the Clothes Philosophy), looking "slovenly if not debauched," his manner "so careless as to be almost insolent"—the embodiment of Carlyle's Gospel of Dilettantism and Insolent Do-Nothingness. (Charles Dickens, *A Tale of Two Cities* [London: Oxford Univ. Press, 1972], I, III, 72). His first action, however, counters the negative impression the narrator's description of him has created: he alone notices that Lucie is faint and about to fall, and summons help. Consistently, we hear about Carton's laziness, profligacy, and wickedness, but see him doing only good deeds—as if the narrator, or the author, were of two minds about the character. Carton talks foolishly and sometimes drunkenly; in action he is always godly, righteous, and sober. He characterizes himself as a frequenter of low haunts and low companions, a "dissolute dog who has never done any good and never will," then conceives and carries out the plan that brings about Darnay's rescue. Our sympathy for him is solicited in an emotional passage that begins with the desert imagery Dickens' letters so often use to describe his own life:

> Waste forces within him, and a desert all around . . . [he] saw for a moment, lying in the wilderness before him, a mirage of honourable ambition, self-denial and perseverance. In the fair city of this vision, there were airy galleries from which the loves and graces looked upon him, gardens in which the fruits of life hung ripening, waters of Hope that sparkled in his sight . . . [a] man of good abilities and good emotions, incapable of their directed exercise, incapable of his own help and his own happiness, sensible to the blight on him, and resigning himself to let it eat him away.
>
> (TTC, II, V, 85)

As frequently happens in Dickens, an innocent, beautiful, moralistic young woman preaches the sinner into a state of sanctity. Lucie Manette, in a linguistic foreshadowing of Carton's last words from the scaffold, urges him "The best part [of your life] might still be; I am sure that you might be much, much worthier of yourself," (TTC, II, XIII, 143). With her as confessor and absolver, Carton's better nature revives and he repents the life he has led in the Victorian underworld. His last interview with the banker, Mr. Lorry, is his reconciliation with the world of the fathers—the world that recognizes earnest, hard-working Charles Darnay as its son. No longer careless, Carton comforts the weeping old man:

> "I could not see my father weep, and sit by, careless. And I could not respect your sorrow more, if you were my father." . . . There was a true feeling and respect in his tone . . . that Mr. Lorry, who had never seen the better side of him, was wholly unprepared for.   (TTC, III, IX, 293)

Wearing not his creator's yellow waistcoat but the white riding coat and top boots of the dandy, Carton resumes his "vagabond and restless habits" and prowls the streets all night, as Dickens often did. Walking by the river, he sees "an eddy that turned and turned, purposeless, until the stream absorbed it, and carried it on to the sea—'Like me!'" (TTC, III, IX, 299). A prodigal son, he has found his place in the world through the Christ-like sacrifice of his life for Darnay, the virtuous son who has lived his life in submission to authority. This is Dickens' special pleading, his claim to heroism as asserted in the prescription Carlyle quotes from his hero, Goethe:

Well did the Wisest of our time write: "It is only with Renunciation . . . that Life, properly speaking, can be said to begin" . . . there is in man a HIGHER than Love of Happiness: he can do without Happiness, and instead thereof find Blessedness! . . . Love not Pleasure: love God: this is the EVERLASTING YEA.   (SR, II, IX, 153)

The dissolute young man who loves pleasure is an autobiographical study of one side of Dickens' personality, as surely as is David Copperfield of another. Through renunciation and repentance (for Carlyle "of all acts the most divine"), Sydney Carton/Dickens simultaneously saves and becomes his better self, Charles Darnay/Dickens (HHW, II, 47).[26]

But his sacrifice does not transform the world, only the lives of the few he loves. As always, Dickens feels most intensely not about the greatest happiness of the greatest number or the regeneration of the world after the Revolution's evils have expiated themselves, but about the happiness of individuals. *A Tale of Two Cities* impressed Carlyle as "wonderful," but neither the novel nor its author met his standards for the heroic.

NOTES

1. Sigmund Freud analyzes the functions the great man performs in the mental life of the race in "Moses and Monotheism," *The Standard Edition of the Complete Psychological Works of Sigmund Freud* (London: Hogarth Press, 1939), XXIII, Essay III, part 2. For an illuminating discussion of the Victorians' need for and worship of heroes, see Walter Houghton, *The Victorian Frame of Mind* (New Haven: Yale University Press, 1956), Chapter 12.

2. Ian Campbell, "Carlyle's Religion: The Scottish Background," in John Clubbe, ed., *Carlyle and His Contemporaries* (Durham, N.C.: Duke University Press, 1976), p. 3.

3. John Clubbe, ed., *Froude's Life of Carlyle* (Columbus: Ohio State University Press, 1979), p. 388.

4. Edgar Johnson, *Charles Dickens: His Tragedy and Triumph*, 2 vols. (New York: Simon and Schuster, 1952), II, 645; John Forster, *The Life of Charles Dickens* (Boston: Estes and Lauriat, 1872), III, 480 and index.

5. Alexander Carlyle, ed., *New Letters of Thomas Carlyle* (London: John Lane, 1904), II, 282.

6. Clubbe, *Froude*, 367; Charles Richard Sanders, *Carlyle's Friendships and Other Studies* (Durham, N.C.: Duke University Press, 1977), 246; Forster, III, 335; Sanders, 243.

7. Carlyle, *New Letters*, II, 205.

8. Kathleen Tillotson, ed., *The Letters of Charles Dickens* (Oxford: Clarendon Press, 1974), IV, 147n.

9. Clubbe, *Froude*, p. 574.

10. Madeline House, Graham Storey, Kathleen Tillotson, eds., *The Letters of Charles Dickens* (Oxford: Clarendon Press, 1974), III, 609n.

11. Forster, III, 475.

12. Otto Fenichel, *The Psychoanalytic Theory of Neurosis* (New York: Norton, 1945), p. 336.

13. In the final sentence of the *Reminiscence* describing his father, Carlyle's syntax merges the Heavenly Father with the earthly one, as Chris R. Vanden Bossche points out in "The Speech of God-Devils: Masonry and Freemasonry in Carlyle's Early Works," in *Scottish Studies: Thomas Carlyle 1981*, ed. Horst W. Drescher (Bern and Frankfort, 1983), pp. 71–87.

14. Clubbe, *Froude*, p. 89.

15. Forster, I, 18.

16. G. K. Chesterton, *Charles Dickens: A Critical Study* (New York: Dodd, Mead, 1906), p. 21.

17. Walter Dexter, ed., *The Letters of Charles Dickens*, Nonesuch Edition (London: Hogarth Press, 1938), III, 97.

18. Clarendon *Letters*, IV, 21.

19. Johnson, II, 799; Dexter, *Letters*, II, 567.

20. Dexter, *Letters*, II, 335.

21. Dexter, *Letters*, III, 348.

22. Harold Bloom, *The Anxiety of Influence* (New York: Oxford University Press, 1973).

23. For a thorough explanation of object relations theory see W. R. D. Fairbairn, *Psychoanalytic Studies of the Personality* (London: Routledge and Kegan Paul, 1976), Chapter 4.

24. For the notion that Carlyle was uneasy about his own heroism and for the reference to his essay on Cagliostro, I am indebted to Chris R. Vanden Bossche.

25. Johnson, II, 911.

26. Outside the scope of this essay, but worth pointing out, are the interesting connections between the plot of Wilkie Collins's play *The Frozen Deep*, the central situation of *A Tale of Two Cities*, and the authorial fantasy of rescuing the beloved woman perceptible in Dickens' description of Carton's last hours.

"To Awake From History": Carlyle, Thackeray, and *A Tale of Two Cities*

Elliot L. Gilbert

I

England also had its French Revolution, a revolution history has rather unexcitedly labeled "The First Reform Bill." Like most English versions of continental movements, this English "French Revolution" was rather belated, did not take place, in fact, until nearly half a century after its Gallic counterpart. Also like most English versions of continental movements, it was comparatively subdued. To be sure, this revolution too was preceded by acts of violence—by riots, machine-breaking, rick-burning, tax strikes, and other demonstrations—but these stopped well short of the wholesale insurrectionary destructiveness of the 1789 rebellion across the channel. Indeed, the First Reform Bill, as its name implies, was a constitutional revolution, one that even included a typically English comic opera plot twist that would have done credit to the Gilbert and Sullivan of *Iolanthe* or *The Gondoliers* and that, in addition, gives a wry new meaning to the phrase "a tale of two cities." For where the people of Paris, with characteristic rationalism and directness, undertook to destroy the power of their aristocrats by bloodily reducing their number, the government in London succeeded in curtailing the power of the House of Lords, which had voted against the Reform Bill, by threatening to create so many new lords favorable to the bill that the legislation would be sure to pass. And in fact, such an important political, economic, and social watershed was this revolutionary act of Parliament that historians have come to date the Victorian Period not from 1837, the year Victoria ascended the throne, but rather from 1832, the year of the passage of the First Reform Bill.

Despite their differences, these French and English revolutions had several striking similarities. First, they were both efforts to shift the balance of political power in their countries, to take authority away from those who exercised it by virtue of hereditary right and to give it instead to those who had earned it more or less through their own achievements. For decades during the late eighteenth and early nineteenth centuries, the real economic power of the state had come more and more to be controlled by entrepreneurial capitalists, by self-made "captains of industry," to use Carlyle's famous phrase, while the political power of the state remained in the hands of men whose only claim to it was that they had been fortunate in their genealogies, that, like their fathers and grandfathers before them, they were inheritors of land. Eventually, however, the gulf between real and traditional power in these nations grew so great that it could no longer be denied or minimized, and at that point a correction of the imbalance occurred, in France through regicide and the Terror, in England by a widening of the franchise.

A second similarity between the French and English revolutions, one growing out of the first but moving dramatically beyond it, was that both the 1789 rebellion and the 1832 legislation constituted massive and deliberate attacks on history. I am speaking more than metaphorically here, for the French Revolution in particular had as one of its most conscious intentions a literal rejection of the past, a denial of the right of history to influence the present. Regicide is, of course, an obvious assault on genealogy, on the authority of the past, but just as significant were new laws restricting the right to make wills and abolishing the distinction between legitimate and natural children, and revolutionary calendar reforms establishing, among other things, the autumn equinox of 1792 as the beginning of a new chronology. For its part, the First Reform Bill, though more moderate in its methods and more figurative than literal in its language, was quite as vigorous as the French Revolution in its assault on the power of history, in its rejection of the idea that the forms and records of the past should be allowed to control the energies of the present.

Ironically, this attack on history was taking place at a time when history had just begun to come into its own as an intellectual and academic discipline, as a truly rigorous inquiry into the past demanding, in Frederic Harrison's words, "belief in contemporary documents, exact testing of authorities, scrupulous verification of citations, minute attention to chronology, geography, paleography, and inscriptions."[1] In his book *History and Historians of the Nineteenth Century*, G. P. Gooch calls the period a renaissance of historical science. Gooch argues that prior to this time true historical research had been impossible, in part for technical reasons—limited access to documents, for instance, and restrictions on the freedom to announce results—but more importantly because of what he describes as a "lack of the critical faculty in dealing with the value and testimony of authorities."[2] Plainly, it was the growth of such a critical faculty among historians, the development of a scientific skepticism in dealing with historical materials that finally made possible rigorous researches into the past and produced, in turn, the nineteenth-century renaissance of historical writing of which Gooch speaks.

But curiously, it was just this very success of scientific history at recovering the past that encouraged resistance to it. For one thing, what soon became clear was that, seen in too much detail and known too well, the past can grow burdensome and intimidating, revealing—to use a metaphor from Tennyson's poem "The Epic," written about this very issue—all the models that now cannot be *re*modeled. John Stuart Mill's fear, expressed in his *Autobiography*, that all the best combinations of musical notes "must already have been discovered" was one contemporary example of this anxiety. Another was George Eliot's statement in *Middlemarch* that "a new Theresa will hardly have the opportunity of reforming a conventual life . . . the medium in which [her] ardent deeds took shape is for ever gone." Such a conclusion follows unavoidably from the idea that history, just by existing, leaves its readers with a deep sense of their own belatedness and impotence, with what Walter Jackson Bate calls an "accumulating anxiety" surrounding the question "what is there left to do?"[3] "The world is weary of the past, / Oh, might it die or rest at last," writes Shelley in *Hellas*, expressing a desire for oblivion, a longing for the end of history that constitutes the ultimate anxiety of influence.

Not coincidentally, Shelley appears as a character in *Nightmare Abbey*, a conversation novel published 1818 by Thomas Love Peacock, in which the poet, participating in a debate on the subject of history, is shown repeating the sentiments he expressed in *Hellas*, as well as in his more-often quoted "Ozymandias." To "wander among the venerable remains" of the past, says the Shelley character,

> is much the same as if a lover should dig up the buried form of his mistress, and gaze upon relics which are any thing but herself.

To study history, he continues, is to steep oneself in corruption, to

> meet at every step the more melancholy ruins of human nature—a degenerate race of stupid and shrivelled slaves, grovelling in the lowest depths of servility and superstition.

A very different view of the past is expressed by a second participant in the debate. For this speaker, the study of history reveals a lost golden age, one with which the present compares very poorly. "*We* see a hundred men hanged," he declares,

> where [our ancestors] saw one. We see five hundred transported where they saw one. We see five thousand in the workhouses where they saw one. . . . We see children perishing in manufactories where they saw them flourishing in the fields. We see prisons where they saw castles. We see masters where they saw representatives. In short, they saw true men where we see false knaves.

What is notable about this exchange is that, while the two opinions expressed are diametrically opposed, they are both powerful attacks on history. The Shelley character, for instance, arguing that the past is degenerate and corrupting, sees it as an enervating burden to the present which the present ought properly to ignore.[4] For his part, the second speaker, in challenging the Shelleyan position by celebrating the glories of the past, inevitably shows how these glories denigrate the present, trivialize it and hold it up to contempt. Thus he too argues, at least by implication, that the past must be rejected if the present is to fulfill itself and be judged on its own terms. Certainly, for both of Peacock's debaters, the appropriate motto would be Stephen Daedalus's well-known assertion in *Ulysses* that "history . . . is a nightmare from which I am trying to awake," the word "nightmare" in the passage perhaps representing Joyce's tribute to the earlier novel.

But what does it mean to speak of awaking from the nightmare of history? How does one go about rejecting the past, especially a past that the new historical science has so scrupulously researched and exhaustively reported? Interestingly, such rejection was made possible for the nineteenth century by the very skepticism about documents and authorities that had been instrumental in promoting the new history. For such skepticism was not, of course, the private possession of historians. Rather, it was a characteristic intellectual attitude of the period, a habit of questioning traditional values, of rejecting abstract and absolute standards, which not only took such political forms as the French Revolution and the First Reform Bill but also encouraged a general philosophical and cultural relativism, a romantic substitution of subjective, personal experience for objective reality. Trying to explain a similar but later version of this relativism, Hermann Bondi speaks of how, in order to understand Einstein, "we must be prepared for universal public time to break up into a multitude of private times."[5] It was just such a break up of consensus about objective truth, just such a loss of faith in a universal public reality, that provided the metaphysical underpinnings for the nineteenth-century attack on history.

Specifically, this loss of faith took the form of a rejection of history as a trustworthy objective account of past events, as, in Northrop Frye's words, "a primary verbal imitation of action [which] makes particular statements [and] is judged by truth of correspondence."[6] It was especially the idea of judging history "by truth of correspondence," of trusting the historical record to bear a one-to-one relationship to some absolute reality, that began to be questioned during this period. But deprived of the authority of such correspondence, the historical record became just another literary text, one that reflected much more accurately the personal preoccupations of its writer than any nominal subject matter. Such a view has long since become commonplace in modern studies of the theory of history. Hayden White, for example, in a recent examination of what he calls "the historical imagination of nineteenth-century Europe," writes of the need

> to view [nineteenth-century] historical consciousness as a specifically Western prejudice by which the presumed superiority of modern, industrial society can be retroactively substantiated.[7]

The presence in this passage of such terms as "prejudice," "presumed superiority," and "retroactively substantiated" makes it plain that for scholars like White—as already for such a late eighteenth–early nineteenth-century philologist as F. A. Wolf, who astonished Europe by declaring Homer to be a fictional construct—history exists much more surely as the projection of the mind of the historian than as an objective record of the past.

We have ourselves seen a striking example of the manipulative and retroactive nature of the historical imagination. I have spoken several times thus far of what, already in the nineteenth century, historians had come to call the First Reform Bill. But it must be obvious that this could not have been the name by which this bill was originally known, since it was not until some thirty-five years later that there was a Second Reform Bill. For historians, then, to call the 1832 measure the First Reform Bill, even for the sake of making a retroactive comment about its relationship to the later event, is to misrepresent the experience of those who actually framed, debated, and voted on what for them was a unique piece of legislation. (Similarly, for history to call the 1914–1918 war "World War I" is to falsify the real experience of participants who after all thought of the conflict as "the war to end all wars.") Even more manipulative is the dating of the Victorian Period from a time five years prior to the accession of

Victoria. Nothing could more clearly reveal the extent to which history, for all its aspirations to objective, scientific truth, in fact approaches to the condition of imaginative literature.

It was such a perception that helped make possible the nineteenth-century attack on history, an attack that was, like the French Revolution and the First Reform Bill, in both of which that attack was embodied, a radical assault on authority, on the authority of texts, of genealogies, of patrilineal culture; an assault, ultimately, on all efforts of the past to subvert the sovereignty and independence of the present. Certainly, this was one of the grand themes of Victorian literature. Writers of all kinds dealt with it, with the exciting potential for a new freedom and personal fulfillment that the overthrow of authority can make possible, but also with the danger of self-absorption, isolation, and silence which the absence of authority inevitably creates. And of the many books that treated this complex subject in the nineteenth century, none did so more richly or more powerfully than Charles Dickens' *A Tale of Two Cities*.

II

It has taken me a long while to get to Dickens' novel, but I must ask the reader to continue to be indulgent and let me postpone discussion of that book for still a few pages more. We know that as a writer, and especially as an editor, Dickens was always keenly aware of current literary interests and in particular liked to rise to the challenge of other writers' achievements. And since it is my view that the definitive statement about the nineteenth-century historical consciousness that Dickens makes in *A Tale of Two Cities* is offered in part as a response to works on this theme by other authors, it is essential that I begin by considering some of these earlier efforts.

No contemporary writer was more deeply admired or respected by Dickens than the man who, when he was applied to for help in researching *A Tale of Two Cities*, sent his younger colleague (as Edgar Johnson tells us) "two cartloads of books."[8] Thomas Carlyle, as celebrated author of *The French Revolution*, was, of course, the right man for Dickens to consult about his forthcoming novel on that subject. But it was, more importantly, Thomas Carlyle as major innovator in the field of nineteenth-century history for whom—and, so to speak, *against* whom—Dickens understood he would be writing his own book about the historical imagination.

Perhaps Carlyle's most innovative idea as an historian, one he shared with Augustin Thierry in France, was his sense of the contemporaneity of the past, his conviction that, in G. P. Gooch's words, "the past was not dead and that its actors were men of like passions with ourselves."[9] Certainly, some of the most memorable moments in Carlyle's works are those in which the writer seeks to promote this passionate anachronistic vision, to wheedle the readers of _Past and Present_, for example, into the realization that Coeur-de-Lion was not "a vapour Fantasm . . . not a theatrical popinjay with greaves and steel cap on it, but a man living upon victuals," that King Lackland "did live and look in one way or the other, and a whole world was living and looking along with him," and that "the good Joceline" talks with us out of the pages of his book "with such clear familiarity, like a next-dooor neighbour . . . and looks on us so clear and cheery [that] in his neighbourly soft-smiling eyes we see so well our _own_ shadow." Carlyle, who had, in _Sartor Resartus_, called time "your grand anti-magician and universal wonder-hider," here rejects chronology as the key to an understanding of humanity and its experience; rejects, that is (as I have written elsewhere[10]) the view that human history consists of a series of events linked by a superficial causality and that the way to preserve and communicate that history is to present those events as far as possible in the order in which they actually occurred and to look with disdain upon all but logical explanations of the connections between them. Carlyle insisted that in the hands of Dryasdust, his archetypal scientific scholar, such a theory of human experience could produce nothing but the most trivial historical accounts, compendiums of "tombstone information," as he puts it in his essay of Boswell's _Life of Johnson_, arranged with scrupulous unimaginativeness in strictly chronological order.

The principle of anachronism operates on every level of Carlyle's work—the grammatical as well as the conceptual—and may be seen in action in even the briefest paragraphs, chosen nearly at random. The following passage from _The French Revolution_, for example, makes the point well. "Great in a private station," Carlyle writes,

> Necker looks on from the distance; abiding his time. "Eighty-thousand copies" of his new Book, which he calls _Administration de Finances_, will be sold in a few days. He is gone; but shall return, and that more than once, borne by a whole shouting Nation. Singular Controller-General of the Finances; once Clerk in Thelusson's Bank!

At first glance, the passage seems to be steeped in time: past, present, future, and abiding. But as we read, we notice how skillfully Carlyle has managed to subvert the idea of chronology by arranging the elements out of their natural order, alluding first to an event which is yet to occur, next retreating to the present, then returning to the future—first to the near future and then to futures beyond that—and ending quite gratuitously in the past. One result of this anachronistic manipulation of material is that the character Necker appears to us not as people conventionally do in stories that aim for suspense through plot development—passing in stages through the various scenes of their lives from beginning to end—but as a figure wholly achieved at once, immediate, his past, present, and future all existing in an eternal present, a present he dramatically shares with the reader. It is appropriate that a passage like this should have been written about the French Revolution, whose intention also was, as we have noted, the defeat of time.

When we read Carlyle today, we cannot help but respond favorably to the liveliness of his approach to history, cannot fail to sympathize with his efforts to make us feel that we ourselves are the immediate contemporaries of the figures he writes about. Part of what we feel is the authentic spirit of the late eighteenth and early nineteenth centuries with their earnest efforts to substitute the personal and the domestic ("Coeur-de-Lion . . . a man living on victuals") for the public and the institutional. Yet there is some danger in the invitation Carlyle issues to readers to obliterate distinctions between past and present, some danger in encouraging people to think that all historical personages are just like themselves and all historical values just like their own. "The least blessed fact one knows of," Carlyle writes about the Terror in *The French Revolution*, "on which necessitous mortals have ever based themselves, seems to be the primitive one of Cannibalism: that *I* can devour *Thee*."

The cannibalistic ingestion of the past by the present that Carlyle recommends, the presumptuous subsuming of everything in the universe under the single category of the self, is a form of the solipsism that always threatens the Romantic imagination and that certainly led to the bloody denouement of the 1789 rebellion. Carlyle was himself aware of this threat, and he mocked his own excessiveness even in some of the most extreme of his later essays. In "Occasional Discourse on the Nigger Question," for example, he presents his ideas in the form of a public lecture, including audience responses in the text as asides. "Some emotion in the audience," one of these asides informs us, "which the Chairman suppressed." "Increased emotion," says another, "again suppressed by the Chairman." "The President, in a resolved voice, with a look of official rigour . . . enjoined 'Silence, Silence!' The meeting again sat motionless."[11] This suppression of alternate views from the audience, this insistence by the speaker that audience members conform entirely to his own opinions, finally the successful silencing of the audience are all inevitable consequences of the reductivist

Carlylean theory of history. And with the silencing of the audience, with its disappearance as an entity independent of the mind of the speaker, the speaker too is silenced, no longer having anyone to address; he is confined as a solitary prisoner to his "own dream of a world," as Walter Pater has put it, ringed round by "that thick wall of personality through which no real voice has ever pierced on its way to [him], or from [him] to that which [he] can only conjecture to be without."[12]

III

Carlyle wrote a strange kind of quasi-fictional history, as if he were trying to show, with the *form* of his work as well as with is content, his contempt for Dryasdust historians and their tombstone chronologies. William Makepeace Thackeray wrote true novels, of course, though in books like *Catherine*, *Barry Lyndon*, *Henry Esmond*, *The Virginians*, and *Denis Duval* he tried to give the impression of writing history. And his two sets of lectures, *The Four Georges* and *The English Humorists*, are indeed historical studies, based in part on the overflow of his research for *Esmond*. Nevertheless, Thackeray was always very much of two minds about the historical enterprise, sometimes attacking it, sometimes examining the painful consequences of attacking it, but always subtly subverting it by the very use of the novel form. For the genre of the novel was from its beginnings a kind of literary "First Reform Bill," substituting for the "universal public time" of the theatre a "multitude of private times" in individual easy chairs; freeing middle-class readers from the aristocratic subject matter and hierarchical values of tragedy and offering them instead congenial accounts of entrepreneurial heroes and their bourgeois, ahistorical domesticity.

It is probably reasonable to speak of *Vanity Fair* as one of Thackeray's historical novels, though the story is set at a time less than forty years prior to its date of composition. If it *is* an historical novel, however, it is one in which formal history has very notably been left out—or at least pushed far into the background. For example, while the book is set at the time of the Battle of Waterloo, and while most of the major characters are at one point close enough to the battlefield to hear the sound of cannon, Thackeray offers no descriptions of fighting and indeed very ostentatiously concentrates on domestic matters in Brussels during the whole of the famous struggle. Again, though the activities and influence of Napoleon are major elements in the story, Napoleon himself never appears on the scene as a character. The object of this strategy, it seems clear, is to permit Thackeray to make a statement about the comparative importance of the public vs. the private, the official vs. the personal, the historical vs. the domestic spheres, with the author plainly proposing a reversal of the traditional priorities.

There is another way in which history is attacked in *Vanity Fair*. The Napoleon who figures so prominently, if so silently, in the book embodies one of the most striking rejections of history that history records. As a product of the anti-historical French Revolution, Napoleon is an apocalyptic hero who comes to power without the authorization of patrilineal descent and who, like the revolution itself, represents not a continuation and fulfillment of history but a decisive break with it. Self-authorizing and self-confident, he scorns the assistance of genealogy and draws his strength instead almost entirely from interior resources, as his celebrated gesture of snatching the crown from the hands of the Pope and placing it on his own head at his coronation dramatically proclaims. With such a gesture of independence from history, Napoleon came to symbolize, both for those who revered him and those who hated him, the deepest and most authentic spirit of the early nineteenth century, and it is in this symbolic role that he broods over the pages of Thackeray's best-known novel.

The fictional character in the book most closely identified with the Napoleonic model is, of course, Becky Sharp. Thackeray showed considerable insight in choosing a woman for this role, for it was women, perennially unauthorized, unsponsored, unenfranchised by patrilineal culture, who had the most to gain from the nineteenth-century experiment in anti-history. The French Revolution was, after all, in a very important sense a feminist revolution. In particular, the Revolutionary law making natural children the equals of legitimate offspring had the effect of taking from men their familiar right to direct and subdue female sexuality. What followed was a *Carmagnole* of sexual "misrule" in which traditional attitudes toward gender were dramatically reexamined. Mary Wollstonecraft for example, whose *Vindication of the Rights of Woman* was published in the first year of the newly proclaimed French Republic, elsewhere describes the violent part women—often "with the appearance of furies"[13]— played in the overthrow of the old regime, descriptions from which, perhaps, Dickens derived his Madame Defarge and the other *Eumenides* of the guillotine. Certainly, many nineteenth-century observers perceived the French Revolution as uniting an attack on history with a strong assertion of female independence.

Becky Sharp is Thackeray's embodiment of that attack and that assertion. Born of disreputable, foreign parents, penniless, and a woman, Becky, like Napoleon, is determined to make her mark in a world which everywhere asserts that it has no significant place for her. And relying upon her own courage and will, she overcomes her historical disabilities and achieves a considerable worldly success, holding her own against— and sometimes even triumphing over—a moribund aristocracy represented by the crudities of Sir Pitt Crawley and the corruption of Lord Steyne. It is true that, had Thackeray gone no further than this in *Vanity Fair*, he would have produced just another conventional mid-nineteenth-century tale about the victory of a deserving woman of the people over a wicked nobleman. But, mocking these conventions himself in his Preface, the novelist soon makes it clear that his more serious purpose in the story is to examine the dangers, both to society and to the individual, of such a victory.

Among the most notable of those dangers is the fact that as traditions are weakened and absolutes subverted in the new anti-historical dispensation, human beings tend to grow isolated from one another, to be silenced by the disappearance of shared standards, of a common vocabulary of values; that as more and more people are free to achieve success, success becomes more and more difficult to define. "I think I could be a good woman if I had five thousand a year," Becky declares famously, anxious to find the words for measuring her ambition and reduced to what she perceives is the only language left. In the end, the exile that is Napoleon's fate becomes hers as well for presuming, like him, to be the sole arbiter of her own life. The final page of the novel is filled with images of separation and silence. Becky is last seen confined, speechless, to the booth of a fair. Her long-absent husband, Rawdon Crawley, himself silenced by his exile to the aptly named Coventry Island, is dead. Her son will not speak to her, nor will Amelia and Dobbin. But Amelia cannot speak to Dobbin either about what most troubles her. "Come children," Thackeray writes in the book's last paragraph, concluding with a phrase that suggests both isolation and silence, "let us *shut up* the box and the puppets, for our play is played out" [italics mine].

The mention of puppets here does suggest a possible cure for the moral vertigo, the metaphysical nausea that so often afflicts readers of *Vanity Fair*. For where there are puppets, there must be a puppet master, and while in the world of the novel the undermining of all objective judgment may have left the characters no firm moral ground on which to stand, surely the puppet master must be standing on some such ground outside the novel for the benefit of the reader. The puppet master is, of course, Thackeray, who introduces himself in this capacity in his remarks "Before the Curtain" at the beginning of the book. And because Thackeray is always addressing us directly in the story, interpreting events and behavior, telling us what to think, we may conclude that in him at least we have an independent and unironic source of truth, truth that a Napoleonic subjectivity has otherwise banished from the universe.

But a minor event occurs near the end of the novel that shatters all our confidence in the narrator as an objective guide, in the puppet master as an absolute point of reference. For in the scenes set in the small German state of Pumpernickel, the narrator himself makes an appearance as one of the characters. This is surely the most destabilizing moment in *Vanity Fair*. At one end of a set of puppet strings is the narrator, skillfully manipulating a figure at the other end who is also the narrator. One could hardly desire a more brilliant metaphor for the self-reflexiveness and vertiginousness of a world seeking to survive in the absence of any universally accepted authority.

IV

Dickens' attitude toward such vertiginousness in Thackeray's work may be inferred from his complaint about the latter's habit of "feigning a want of earnestness."[14] It was not so much any levity in the presentation of the moral problem that Dickens objected to. Rather, it was Thackeray's failure to offer some positive resolution of the problem, indeed, his bleak contentment that the problem should not be solved, that provoked Dickens' disapproval. Carlyle, on the other hand, troubled Dickens precisely because of the Draconian solutions he proposed to contemporary social, economic, and political problems. For though Dickens often agreed with his older colleague's diagnoses of society's ills, he entirely rejected "Carlyle's [solipsistic] doctrine of leaders divinely born to command and a populace endowed only with the right to obey,"[15] seeing in such a doctrine a symptom of, rather than a cure for, those ills. Thus, when Dickens set out to write *A Tale of Two Cities* (his own examination of the anti-historical impulse in the nineteenth century), it was with his usual determination to move beyond these and all other literary rivals both in his presentation of the issues and in the resolution he would propose.

Dickens begins at once to lay out those issues in *A Tale of Two Cities* with the brilliant rhetorical flourish of the opening paragraph. In a famous series of antitheses—"It was the best of times, it was the worst of times" and so on—antitheses that immediately invoke the thesis of the title, he at first seems to be trying to identify some very specific moment in history in the approved manner of the new historical science. But after he has assembled an extraordinary number of details which must infallibly, we suppose, distinguish the particular moment in question from all other, similar moments, he suddenly surprises us by announcing that these details fit the "present period" just as well as they do the previous century. In this dramatic and unexpected telescoping of two historical periods into one, Dickens adapts Carlylean anachronism to his own study of the confluence of past and present, past and present being just two more of the many contrasting but interdependent "cities" about which his tale is to be written.

The thematic statement of the opening paragraph is supported in the rest of the book by a number of images and metaphors all tending to promote the mythic and cyclical over the historical and linear. The many foreshadowings in the story, for example, help perform this function: the broken wine cask, the echoing footsteps, perhaps most memorably the evocation of the trees, already growing in the forest, that will soon be cut down and fashioned into the guillotine. In these foreshadowings, past, present, and future rush together to subvert the sovereign power of chronology, just as the revolution itself seeks to subvert the sovereign power of genealogy. The word "Evrémonde" serves a similar anti-historical purpose in the novel. Ostensibly identifying a specific genealogical line, the name, a multilingual, two-cities pun on "everyman" or "all-the-world," and with family affiliations encompassing the full range of human behavior from the villainous to the near saintly, comes in the end to designate the whole human race.

The most ubiquitous, perhaps, of the anti-historical metaphors in the novel is that of resurrection. The first page of the book contains the phrase "recalled to life," the last page the words "I am the Resurrection and the Life," and between these two poles of the story are literally dozens of second births, from the grotesque comedy of Jerry Cruncher's body snatching, through the poignancy of the aging Jarvis Lorry traveling in a circle "nearer and nearer to the beginning," to the resonant scenes of Doctor Manette resurrected from the tomb of his prison cell, Evrémonde from the doom of his family name, Carton from the death of his soul. But resurrection, celebrating a cyclical view of existence, necessarily rejects the vision of life as a linear progress through time, in one direction only and without possibility of return, a vision that is the unavoidable first assumption of historical science. Thus, *A Tale of Two Cities* would seem to be irrevocably committed to the widespread nineteenth-century attack on history I have been examining here, and therefore to the subsequent disillusionment with that attack I have already noted in the work of Carlyle and Thackeray.

Such disillusionment does indeed appear to begin midway in the novel with a shift in Dickens' attitude toward the revolution. Revolution implies, after all, etymologically as well as politically, a turning, a cyclical movement of renewal. Thus anyone who promotes an anti-historical view of life would seem to be obligated to support a revolution that itself constitutes an attack on history. Yet readers of *A Tale of Two Cities* cannot help but notice how Dickens' initial sympathy for the revolutionary figures in his book begins to wane as the story proceeds. There is, of course, one obvious practical explanation for this change of heart. We naturally sympathize more intensely with people when they are oppressed than when they themselves become oppressors, and it is just such a metamorphosis that occurs in the revolutionary group as the novel develops. But there is another, more important, issue involved here, a deeper problem that Dickens confronts in his consideration of these events and that moves him in the direction of a quite original analysis of them. For where Carlyle, Thackeray, and others concentrate on the way in which the rejection of the dead hand of history can lead to an equally destructive solipsism, Dickens sees the failure of the French Revolution as deriving not from its overthrow of history but from its capitulation to it.

Interestingly, the character in the novel who most fully embodies that capitulation to history is Madame Defarge, the figure in the story who is also most likely to be misunderstood. As a worker, and particularly as a woman, Thérèse Defarge would seem to have more to gain than anyone else from a successful assault on patrilineal culture and the historical record that supports it. And from Dickens' description of her unfailing attendance at the grim ceremonies of the guillotine, she does indeed appear to be one of those implacable bacchantes and enemies of patriarchal history of whom Mary Wollstonecraft writes. But in fact there is no more ferociously dedicated historian in *A Tale of Two Cities* than Madame Defarge. True, the medium of the historical record she compiles is the traditionally female one of knitting, but in no sense does that activity perform the domestic function of, say, Lucie Manette's sewing. For though Madame Defarge writes her history with matriarchal needles and yarn, she is as obsessed with genealogy as the most unreconstructed patriarchal aristocrat, wholly committed, like that aristocrat, to judging her fellow human beings not by their abilities or by their actions (in the anti-historical spirit of, for instance, the First Reform Bill) but entirely by their birth. It is on this principle that she persists in hunting down the innocent Charles Darnay and his even more innocent wife and child. But her obsession with the authority of the historical record is carried to even greater lengths. Called upon to select between the living testimony of Doctor Manette and the obsolete account of his earlier, vengeful autobiography, she chooses—and forces the whole of the Revolution to choose with her—the past over the present, the historical over the personal, the moribund written word over the living man. Not by chance is her second-in-command called "The Vengeance," a fact that for Dickens deeply compromises the revolutionary ideal since desire for revenge constitutes the ultimate surrender to history, an absolute forfeiture of *liberté*.

Because Madame Defarge is so powerful and representative a figure, it seems clear early in the book that for both dramatic and ideological reasons she will eventually have to participate in some decisive, summary action. But the reader is not likely to foresee that such action will take the form of a fateful physical encounter with the bizarre Miss Pross, although from the start Miss Pross is described as almost masculine in appearance and strength as if to establish, in one more foreshadowing, the plausibility of her final victory. The struggle in which that victory occurs symbolizes many of the major conflicts of the novel, in particular those that alienate the two cities of the title from one another: nationality, language, temperament, philosophy. Miss Pross, a typical English grotesque, portrayed as unmarried, alienated from her brother, and curiously androgynous, as if to emphasize that her connections with others are not—and can never be—genealogical, embodies in her relationships all that is ahistoric, domestic, and personal. Significantly, it is in the house in which she serves that Doctor Manette moves out of the dead past into the living present. Madame Defarge, on the other hand, represents—whatever her personal grievance—all that is abstract, public, and *im*personal, and it is under her influence that Doctor Manette is driven back into the prison of his own history. In the light of the terms we have established for discussing these polarities, the fates of the two women seem entirely appropriate. Madame Defarge, devoting herself obsessively to the record of the dead past, herself dies in an unyielding pursuit of her historical imperative. Miss Pross, on the other hand, anti-historical and private, must withdraw behind a wall of silence through which, to quote Pater again, "no voice will ever pierce on its way to her." The fact that nothing but the most exaggerated Victorian notion of crime and punishment would require Miss Pross to suffer deafness for her part in Madame Defarge's death makes her fall into silence particularly significant, a sign that Dickens, operating within the framework of the nineteenth-century debate about history, perceived this fate to be philosophically unavoidable.

But if this is so, then we are approaching a crisis. For we have now come to a moment only half-a-dozen pages from the end of the novel, and Dickens still has not advanced appreciably beyond the point reached by

Carlyle and Thackeray in their own examinations of what I have been
calling the anti-historical nineteenth-century impulse. That is, the options presented by all three writers are virtually the same. On the one
hand, an association with history and historical science leads, we are told,
to belatedness, decay, and the death of the heart. Carlyle's Dryasdust,
Thackeray's Lord Steyne, Dickens' French aristocrats and their strange
confederate Madame Defarge all make this clear. On the other hand, a
withdrawal from history into the private and solipsistic condemns one to
isolation and silence, a fact we learn from the narrator of "Occasional
Discourse," from Napoleon and Becky Sharp; most of all from the early
Sydney Carton, a self-reflexive looker-in-mirrors and an especially egre-
gious case of the English disease of "doing as one pleases." And apparently there is no way out of either of these metaphysical prisons, for every
effort to escape from one cell only leads to the Monte Cristo-like frustration of tunneling into the other.

It is in the celebrated final chapter of *A Tale of Two Cities* that Dickens
finally advances, as he had hoped he would, beyond the historical speculations of his literary colleagues to point a way out of this impasse; although the scene in the Place de Guillotine that chapter describes seems,
at first, merely to recapitulate the old dilemma. In the background are all
the familiar emblems of a mechanical and enervating historical science.
The tumbrils move heavily toward the square, bearing their burdens of old
histories, past injustices, like the cartloads of books Carlyle mockingly
sent to Dickens. The steady counting out of the prisoners' numbers mim-
ics the dull chronologies of Dryasdust. And it is history as a machine of
death that is symbolized by the brisk, mindless working of the guillotine.

In the foreground, set against this vast, impersonal public display, is the
preternaturally private relationship of Sydney Carton and the young
seamstress (who sews, we may presume, rather than knits). Entirely silent
about his own fate out of concern for the girl's, Carton advises her to see
and think of nothing around her, to ignore, as it were, past and future and
live only in the immediate present, advice in which we may recognize a curiously transfigured version of the irresponsible behavior that had earlier
blighted his own career. But here that anti-historical behavior leads to intimacy not isolation, and Carton's silence is the silence not of one who
withdraws himself from the world but rather of one who withholds
himself for the sake of another, is mute in order to permit another to
speak, a familiar Dickensian resolution. Again, there is a foreshadowing
of this resolution in Carton's earlier activities as a brief writer whose
name never appears on his work. That namelessness also returns in a new

form at the end of the story. For Carton, choosing to die under the name of another, decisively repudiates the absurd mechanics of genealogical connection. While the seamstress, who is herself nameless and who, we learn, cannot write, demonstrates the insignificance of formal history in the face of an even momentary living bond.

As much of an enemy as Dickens was of the mechanical and formal, however, it was never any part of his desire to repudiate genealogy and history in themselves any more than he wished to promote revolutionary anarchy. Indeed, as a writer he had the greatest possible stake in preserving the authority of texts, the immediacy and vitality of the written record, and in *A Tale of Two Cities* in particular he undertook to span what to others seemed the unbridgeable gulf between history and life, to make these two cities one. The whole book is artfully structured to achieve this goal, though Dickens' point only becomes fully clear on the last page where Sydney Carton, about to mount the scaffold, pauses to prophesy about events that are to follow his death. It is true that in part this prophecy merely serves the conventional novelistic ends of the author, providing him with an unobtrusive way of informing his readers about the future careers of the characters they have become interested in. But throughout Carton's visionary internal monologue an additional note is sounded. "I see," the prophetic speaker intones, alluding here to Charles and Lucie,

> that I hold a sanctuary in their hearts, and in the hearts of descendents, generations hence . . . I see that child who lay upon her bosom and bore my name, a man winning his way up that path of life which once was mine. I see him winning it so well that my name is made illustrious there by the light of his. . . . I see him . . . bringing a boy of my name . . . to this place . . . *and I hear him tell the child my story*, with a tender and faltering voice. [italics mine]

What is so striking about this passage is how full of genealogy and history it is. In his last moments, Carton returns obsessively to thoughts of "descendents," of "generations," of those who will one day bear his name; in particular, he is preoccupied with the image of a child yet unborn who, growing into a man, will become the historian of his present sacrifice. These, however, it is clear, are genealogy and history with a difference, not baleful voices from the past with dread authority to impose upon and enervate the present, but rather, in Dickens' powerful proleptic vision, a vitalizing genealogy and history of the future.

The whole of *A Tale of Two Cities* shares in this prolepsis. Whatever present moment we may have arrived at in the story, for instance, the book's rich texture of foreshadowings operates to urge us toward moments still to come. Footsteps advancing on the future haunt the novel, paradoxically "echoing" sounds that have not yet been made; and these foreshadowings, taken together, themselves constitute a meta-foreshadowing of the Carton prophecy. Even death is forced out of the service of the past, for, described from the start as a "farmer" with furrow-plowing tumbrils, as a sower, death can, despite its worst intentions, only prepare the ground for new life. And, of course, Dickens gains considerable support for the validity of his foresight from the fact that the speculative future about which he has his hero prophesy is already the confirmed past and present of his readers.

The Carton/Dickens ideal of a history of the future that will rescue the nineteenth century from the history of the past is more than just figurative, however. The chief adverse power of the past is, we have seen, its ability to dash the hopes of the present and blight the future. Just to be able to *imagine* a vital future, then (the novel suggests), is already in a very practical way to have defeated the worst that the past can do. Dickens clearly derived this resolution at least in part from his own ebullient nature, from his own resistance to belatedness. Reading Carlyle and Thackeray, he did not think of how their work diminished his opportunities. Rather, he saw in their accomplishments a challenge to fresh accomplishments of his own. And from his response to their challenge came a book that, in the face of profound nineteenth-century disillusionment about the uses of the past, argues for a kind of history that is not a nightmare. In Dickens' celebratory conclusion to *A Tale of Two Cities*, Sydney Carton awakes both out of the history of his dead past and into the history of a living future.

NOTES

1. "The History Schools," *The Meaning of History* (New York and London: Macmillan, 1908, orig. 1893), p. 121.

2. (New York: Longmans, 1913), p. 11.

3. *The Burden of the Past and the English Poet* (Cambridge, Mass.: Belknap Press, 1970), p. 3. This paragraph contains material from my essay "The Female King: Tennyson's Arthurian Apocalypse," *PMLA*, 98 (1983), 863–878.

4. In an essay called "The Use of History" in *The Meaning of History*, Frederic Harrison makes a strong statement of this position. "What is this unseen power," he writes,

> that seems to undo the best human efforts, as if it were some overbearing weight against which no man can long struggle? What is this ever-acting force which seems to revive the dead, to restore what we destroy, to renew forgotten watchwords, exploded fallacies, discred-

ited doctrines, and condemned institutions; against which enthusiasm, intellect, truth, high purpose, and self-devotion seem to beat
themselves to death in vain? It is the Past.   (pp. 17–18)

5. *Relativity and Common Sense: A New Approach to Einstein* (New York: Dover Publications, 1980), p. 65.

6. *The Great Code: The Bible and Literature* (New York: Harcourt Brace Jovanovich, 1982), p. 65.

7. *Metahistory: The Historical Imagination in Nineteenth-Century Europe* (Baltimore: The Johns Hopkins University Press, 1973), p. 3.

8. *Charles Dickens: His Tragedy and Triumph*, 2 vols. (New York: Simon and Schuster, 1952), II, 948.

9. Gooch, p. 169.

10. This and the following paragraph are extracted from my article "'A Wondrous Contiguity': Anachronism in Carlyle's Prophecy and Art," *PMLA*, 87 (1972), 432–442.

11. An only slightly more benign version of this appears in the last paragraph of *The French Revolution* where Carlyle writes: "Ill stands it with me if I have spoken falsely: thine also it was to hear truly."

12. "Conclusion," *Studies in the History of the Renaissance* (London: Macmillan, 1873), p. 209.

13. *An Historical and Moral View of the Origin and Progress of the French Revolution and the Effect it had Produced in Europe*, Book V, chapter 2, reprinted in *A Wollstonecraft Anthology*, ed. Janet M. Todd (Bloomington: Indiana University Press, 1977), p. 133. It is notable that the founding of women's revolutionary clubs in France reached a peak in 1793, the first year of the Terror. Just as significantly, when the Terror had run its course and efforts were being made to restore civil order, these women's societies were systematically suppressed and many of their leaders executed.

14. Charles Dickens, *Cornhill Magazine*, IX (1863), 130.

15. Johnson, I, 315.

Plotting and Scheming: The Design of Design in *Our Mutual Friend*

Robert Kiely

Before coming to Dickens, I want to recall a few well-known passages in *Pride and Prejudice* in which the word "design" is used. In Chapter 1, Mrs. Bennet tries to interest Mr. Bennet in their new neighbor, Mr. Bingley, who is rich, young and unmarried:

> "What a fine thing for our girls!" [she says].
> "How so? How can it affect them?"
> "My dear Mr. Bennet," replied his wife, "how can you be so tiresome! You must know that I'm thinking of his marrying one of them."
> "Is that his design in settling here?"
> "Design! Nonsense, how can you talk so!"[1]

In Chapter 6, Elizabeth Bennet and her friend Charlotte Lucas discuss the budding romance between Bingley and Elizabeth's sister Jane. Charlotte thinks that Jane should "make the most of every half-hour in which she can command his attention."

> "Your plan is a good one," replied Elizabeth, "where nothing is in question but the desire of being well married; and if I were determined to get a rich husband, or any husband, I dare say I should adopt it. But these are not Jane's feelings; she is not acting by design." (19)

Finally, in Chapter 19, the Rev. Mr. Collins, in one of the most ludicrous marriage proposals in literature, interrupts his flow of false passion:

> "Before I am run away with by my feelings on this subject, perhaps it will be advisable for me to state my reasons for marrying—and moreover for coming into Hertfordshire with the design of selecting a wife, as I certainly did." (101)

It is surprising to find a writer so controlled, so justifiably famous for the perfection of "design" in her own narratives, using the word this frequently in its negative sense. Mrs. Bennet is a silly meddler in other people's lives; Charlotte is a cynic about love; Mr. Collins a pompous, clumsy, egocentric fool. Outside of the realm of art, to be a "designing person," to have a "scheme" or "plot" would almost invariably seem to be morally suspect. In this bad sense, "design" means oversimplification, manipulation and concealment. Insofar as it emanates from a single and narrow source (especially a Mrs. Bennet or a Mr. Collins) a design is an attempt to curtail the full range and complexity of things, to control the lives of others and to hide its own purpose.

Jane Austen obviously does not admire aimless, impetuous characters who act at random, and yet there is a strong sense of confidence in natural order and in the steadiness of her own designing hand that allows her most thoughtful and intelligent characters a considerable degree of artlessness. Emma Woodhouse tries unsuccessfully to shape her own world while the more admirable Elizabeth Bennet responds with spirit and intelligence to situations she did not create.

Near the end of Chapter 6, Book II of *Our Mutual Friend*, an exchange occurs between Mortimer Lightwood and Eugene Wrayburn in which the attitude toward design, if not the literal meaning of the word, is quite different. Mortimer is questioning his friend's intentions with regard to Lizzie Hexam:

> "Eugene, do you design to capture and desert this girl?"
> "My dear fellow, no."
> "Do you design to marry her?"
> "My dear fellow, no."
> "Do you design to pursue her?"
> "My dear fellow, I don't design anything. I have no design whatever. I am incapable of designs. If I conceived a design, I should speedily abandon it, exhausted by the operation."[2]   (348)

Unlike that of Jane Austen, Dickens' reputation has not depended significantly on his mastery of design. Though few contemporary critics would agree with Henry James that an English pudding is a fair simile for the shape and structure of the Victorian novel, it nonetheless remains true that Dickens' genius is more often associated with characterization, humor, the creation of eccentric voices and symbolic atmospheres, than with the composition of coherent wholes. At first glance, it would seem that Jane Austen, working from her peculiar strength as a shaper of sustained forms, prefers characters who leave the designing to her. Whereas,

Dickens, if the exchange between Mortimer and Eugene has a meaning *for* the novel as well as *in* it, feeling less sure of his abilities as a maker of overall schemes, transfers some of the burden and the anxiety to his characters.

Before reaching this or any other conclusion, it is necessary to examine not simply certain characteristics of the design of *Our Mutual Friend*, but the treatment of design as one of the many subjects of the book. One need not be straining hard for signs of creeping modernism in Dickens to note his lifelong preoccupation with the tendency of the human imagination to project its schemes on the world. In *Our Mutual Friend* this preoccupation reaches an intensity and self-consciousness unmatched in his other books. In calling the Victorian novel *naif*, James argued that it had "no consciousness of itself behind it."[3] It seems to me in precisely this respect that James was wrong about a number of novels of the period, but perhaps none more than *Our Mutual Friend*. If we take self-consciousness about the nature of the imaginative composition to be one of the indicators of modernism, or at least of aesthetic sophistication, *Our Mutual Friend* makes a particularly illuminating case study.

It will be helpful to have Dickens' or Mortimer Lightwood's definition of the word "design" before proceeding. Mortimer elaborates by asking Wrayburn three questions: "What is to come of it? What are you doing? Where are you going?" (II. 6. 348).

Mortimer's questions might well be the queries of an editor to an author only half way through a manuscript. But whether applied to writing or sexual pursuit, they raise the same issues. Design, as Mortimer uses the word, implies a goal or conclusion; as an imagined configuration, it presupposes a completion, a closing of the lines. It is conceived of in temporal terms and one of its primary functions is to link the present with the future. It demands that present action be thought of in sequential and directional terms. It asks not only what the end will be but what route will be followed in reaching that end. Mortimer's questions also press heavily on the responsibility of authorship. As individuals act and speak, patterns begin forming, whether or not they are aware of them. And though the accumulation of these patterns is not fully within the control of an isolated individual, there is sufficient possibility of control and predictability to make authorial awareness imperative. Finally, questions demand answers. The responsibility of the author is not merely to continue doing what he is doing, that is, proceeding blindly with an unacknowledged design, but to describe his own motions, literally to *articulate*, join together seemingly random steps until a pattern emerges that can be seen and judged. While Krook's rag and bone shop in *Bleak House* is a bizarre image of Chancery and the law, the Shop of Venus, *articulator* of bones, is a grotesque substitute for the writer's study, where articulation—the joining of parts and putting things into words—is the order of business.

As in much of Dickens' fiction, the reader finds not only a complexity of the linear plot, but a dense layering of fictional design, based on a third person authorial narrative. What is most striking and perhaps modern about *Our Mutual Friend* is the number and richness of the fictional designs that emanate not from the authorial voice but from various characters and the degree to which these secondary fictions intrude upon, overlap, and frequently undermine the authority of the primary design. In this respect, Dickens looks ahead more to Nabokov than to Conrad because he appears to be calling into question the possibility of disentangling truth from even the most outrageous fictions. (But I am anticipating my argument.)

Most of the secondary fictions to which we are introduced in *Our Mutual Friend seem*, on first sight, do have in common one noteworthy trait: an obvious and absurd falsehood, e.g., Lady Tippins's "grisly fiction" about being pursued by handsome lovers; the Podsnaps and Veneerings pretending to be old friends; Silas Wegg's imagining inhabitants of the house on the corner; the Lammles duping each other about nonexistent inheritances. These are all occasions in which the reader recognizes at once the discrepancy between the facts of the primary narrative and the claims of the secondary fictions. Some of these are cases of deliberate lying for social or financial gain, or appear to be signs of vain and not entirely honorable characters. In other words, the reader feels clear both about distinct levels of fiction and fact and the moral basis for keeping them separate.

But the reader also discovers that *Our Mutual Friend* is a book crowded with authors of secondary designs, and that all of these authors are by no means disreputable. Lizzie Hexam sees pictures in the fire, recalling the past and foretelling the future of her brother as a prize-winning scholar and successful young school master; Jenny Wren treats her father like a delinquent child until she herself can hardly remember whether she is his mother or daughter; she also describes the fragrance of invisible flowers and the beauty of invisible children dressed in white who come to visit her; the dying child Johnny is presented with a toy replica of Noah's ark to absorb his attention in his last hours; and the good-natured Noddy Boffin behaves like a miser in order to bring out the true nature of Bella Wilfer.

As in the earlier examples, there are instances of deliberate lying as well as self-deception in these fictions. Unlike the earlier cases, however, the motivation is benevolent or, where there is no conscious motivation, the effect of these secondary designs is beneficial. They give comfort, console, or encourage; they appeal to the best in human nature, that which is hopeful, gentle, unselfish. Furthermore, Dickens makes it more difficult for the reader to label them as purely false. It is as obvious, except in the case of Noddy Boffin, that the inventions do not participate in the same level of factual reality as that set forth on the primary narrative design. But they each have their own claim to validity. Lizzie's pictures in the fire, after all, are images of memory and hope; Jenny Wren does act like her father's guardian; the invisible children she sees and the consoling animals of Noah's ark suggest a supernatural reality which Dickens is unwilling to dismiss; and Noddy Boffin's temporary attack of greed suggests a natural and believable temptation for a man of modest means who suddenly inherits great wealth. In short, for a variety of reasons, the reader finds it impossible to arrive at uniform judgments about the truth or falsehood of these fictions.

Not only vicious and deceitful characters have designing minds. Good and bad alike are storytellers. Nearly everyone in this novel, including a few about whom we are not required to make a moral judgment, is an author. Indeed, one of the most important as an expression of Dickens' theoretical and self-conscious musings on fictional design, precisely because he has no importance in the plot, is Lightwood's clerk a "dismal boy, whose appropriate name was Blight." When Noddy Boffin, Lightwood's only client, arrives in the solicitor's exceedingly dim and inactive office, Blight acts out the part of a busy clerk in a practice brimming over with clients:

> "Would you take a seat in Mr. Lightwood's room, sir, while I look over our Appointment Book?" Young Blight made a great show of fetching from his desk a long thin manuscript volume with a brown paper cover, and running his finger down the day's appointments, murmuring, "Mr. Aggs, Mr. Bags, Mr. Caggs, Mr. Daggs, Mr. Faggs, Mr. Gaggs, Mr. Boffin. Yes, sir, quite right. You are a little before your time, sir. Mr. Lightwood will be in directly."
>
> "I'm not in a hurry," said Mr. Boffin.
>
> "Thank you, sir. I'll take the opportunity, if you please, of entering your name in our Callers' Book for the day." Young Blight made another great show of changing the volume, taking up a pen, sucking it, dipping it, and running over previous entries before he wrote. As, "Mr. Alley, Mr. Balley, Mr. Calley, Mr. Dalley, Mr. Falley, Mr. Galley, Mr. Halley, Mr. Lalley, Mr. Malley. And Mr. Boffin."
>
> "Strict system here; eh, my lad?" said Mr. Boffin, as he was booked.
>
> "Yes sir," returned the boy. "I couldn't get on without it."
>
> By which he probably meant that his mind would have been shattered to

pieces without this fiction of an occupation. Wearing in his solitary confine-
ment no fetters that he could polish, and being provided with no drinking-
cup that he could carve, he had fallen on the device of ringing alphabetical
changes into the two volumes in question, or of entering vast numbers of
persons out of the Directory as transacting business with Mr. Lightwood. It
was the more necessary for his spirits, because, being of a sensitive temperament, he was apt to consider it personally disgraceful to himself that his
master had no clients.   (I. 8.131)

This long and amusing digression on fiction all but forces a paradigmatic reading since neither the character nor the situation have more than
a passing significance within the linear plot. Like many of the inventive
characters in the book, the dismal boy is keeping up appearances. But
more is involved than pride and social convention. When the narrator interprets his ''I couldn't get on without it,'' as meaning ''that his mind
would have been shattered to pieces without this fiction of an
occupation,'' everyone connected with the novel—author and reader—as
well as every character in it, is implicated. The statement is lifted out of
time and place and tossed in all directions. For an instant, the backdrop of
Fleet Street and the Temple is removed like so much cardboard and a
wider more barren vista is revealed. We are for a moment in a world Samuel Beckett might have created in which a character who has been urged to
try on a pair of boots for no particular reason says, ''We always find
something to give us the impression we exist?''[4] The immediate motiva-
tions for ''putting our own construction on things'' are, as Dickens
shows, morally and psychologically diverse, but behind them all is the
universally shared dread of no story at all. If individuals do not provide
their own version of things, they risk being left out of the design altogether or being the pawns in other people's plots.

In turning our attention to one of the two major designs in the novel,
the story of John Harmon, we see at once that, though his plight can be
described in a number of ways, he is, on several levels, the victim of other
people's plots. First of all, Mortimer Lightwood in a tone of deliberate
mock-melodrama recounts the story of the Harmon family, the rich and
mean father, ''the venerable parent''; how he turned his wife out of the
house and later did the same to his daughter upon learning ''that she was
secretly engaged to that popular character whom the novelists and ver-
sifiers call Another'' (I. 2. 56). Continuing in his tone of arch satire, Mortimer introduces John Harmon as ''the man from Somewhere'' and explains how his inheritance is made ''conditional on his marrying a girl
who at the date of the will was a child of four or five years old and who is
now a marriageable young woman.'' Thus, John Harmon, whom the

reader has not yet met, is presented twice bound, first, by a self-parodying narration that casts doubts on its own seriousness and validity, and second, by a parent who tries to direct his life from beyond the grave.

When the reader learns that Harmon has been the victim of robbery and attempted murder, it seems to be the physical and violent working out of a fate that has already been enacted verbally by Mortimer and legally by the "venerable parent." Dickens, with immense skill, makes the reader want to hear Harmon's story from Harmon. And it is important to see that this is not simply a matter of giving him his due or setting the record straight. Something much more important is at stake. To exist only as a character in someone else's plot is, certainly in Harmon's case, perhaps in every case, to suffer some form of abuse and violence. Assuming authorship appears to be imperative for survival.

Even the assumption of the pseudonyms Julius Handford and John Rokesmith, though they give Harmon a measure of control over his own destiny, do not completely extricate him from a scheme not of his own devising. Harmon-Handford-Rokesmith goes about observing others, but his most urgent need is to find himself. When he returns to Limehouse Hole in order to retrace the steps of his would-be murderer, he repeatedly comes full circle to the question of his own identity:

> He tried a new direction, but made nothing of it; walls, dark doorways, flights of stairs and rooms, were too abundant. And, like most people so puzzled, he again and again described a circle, and found himself at the point from which he had begun. "This is like what I have read in narratives of escape from prison," said he, "where the little track of the fugitives in the night always seems to take the shape of the great round world, on which they wander; as if it were a secret law."
>
> Here he ceased to be the oakum-headed, oakum-whiskered man on whom Miss Pleasant Riderhood had looked, and, allowing for his being still wrapped in a nautical overcoat, became as like that same lost wanted Mr. Julius Handford, as never man was like another in this world. In the breast of the coat he stowed the bristling hair and whisker, in a moment, as the favouring wind went with him down a solitary place that it had swept clear of passengers. Yet in that same moment he was the Secretary also, Mr. Boffin's Secretary. For John Rokesmith, too, was as like that same lost wanted Mr. Julius Handford as never man was like another in this world.
>
> "I have no clue to the scene of my death," said he. "Not that it matters now."   (II. 13. 421–422)

Dickens goes out of his way in this passage to generalize Harmon's experience and to link it with literary narrative. His search for the "scene of the crime" and for his "murderer's" identity is a story that goes in circles, a narrative of no escape. Of greater importance than the identity of the "murderer" is that of the victim. Yet he can make no progress, it appears, by following the leads of others. He must assume authorship and tell his own version of the crime. A major impediment to his doing so, of course, is that Harmon regards himself, not as the author of his own life, but as others have imagined him, which most recently, is as a dead man. The repetition of "never man was like another in this world" forces the words out of their colloquial connotation into suggesting that Harmon may indeed be like no one else in the world because he cannot locate a true identity behind the externally and self-imposed masks. When he passes a churchyard, he observes that he "no more holds a place among the living than these dead do," not a promising beginning of a character sketch nor of an assumption of authorial responsibility.

Yet when Harmon does begin to take hold, it is not through action but articulation that he does so. It is in perfect keeping with the novel's preoccupation with narrative design that he comes to terms with himself and what he calls the "real side" of his situation by narrating his own story to himself. His determination to do so is a deliberate, painful choice, and it is introduced not merely as another rendition of a familiar plot, but as an event, a crisis and an encounter in which the *act* of narrating is as significant as the information carried by the narrative:

> "[The situation]...has a real side, so difficult that, though I think of it every day, I never thoroughly think it out. Now, let me determine to think it out as I walk home. I know I evade it, as many men—perhaps most men—do evade thinking their way through their greatest perplexity. I will try to pin myself to mine. Don't evade it, John Harmon; don't evade it; think it out!
>
> "When I came back to England, attracted to the country with which I had none but most miserable associations, by the accounts of my fine inheritance that found me abroad, I came back, shrinking from my father's money, shrinking from my father's memory, mistrustful of being forced on a mercenary wife, mistrustful of my father's intention in thrusting that marriage on me, mistrustful that I was already growing avaricious, mistrustful that I was slackening in gratitude to the two dear noble honest friends who had made the only sunlight of my childish life or that of my heartbroken sister. I came back timid, divided in my mind, afraid of myself and everybody here, knowing of nothing but wretchedness that my father's wealth had ever brought about. Now, stop, and so far think it out, John Harmon. Is that so? That is exactly so."   (II. 13. 422–423)

These first paragraphs of Harmon's narration have much that distinguishes them from earlier renditions of his story. Unlike Harmon's own earlier fragmented efforts to come to terms with himself, this is a carefully controlled, elegantly balanced set piece with obvious literary overtones, including an opening phrase which is a grown-up version of "once-upon-a-time." Unlike Lightwood's melodramatic parody, Harmon's narrative is earnest in tone, filled with his need to get things right. Furthermore, it is told in part as a response to other narratives, "the accounts of my fine inheritance," which seem not only to bind his future but to define his character. We learn for the first time *from him* that he is not simply a good man caught in a nasty trap, but rather an uncertain one who fears that he may be the inheritor of his father's avaricious disposition as well as his fortune. The issue of paternal legacy and the predestined design of the son's life contained in it broadens to the point where it embraces genetic as well as financial and legal consequences. The risk of John Harmon's narrating his own story increases with his and the reader's recognition of the fundamental importance of his doing so. He cannot find himself without assuming authorship of his own life and yet he fears that in trying, he may trace a design that reveals him as a mirror image of the dreaded "venerable parent."

When Harmon forces himself to recall and put into words the terrifying moment in which he was sucked under water and nearly drowned, he tries to describe the physical sensations, but, more importantly, he attempts to give expression to the interior or psychological experience of being suddenly brought so close to death. The conventional literary treatment of such moments usually includes fleeting memories of life and loved ones. But in this case, Dickens, the master inventor of names, has his narrator struggle to describe what it feels like to lose one's name, to feel it slipping away and, at the same time, to be aware of an identity that exists apart from name. It is as though he experiences the loss of one "I" and the recovery of another more fundamental one.

> "This is still correct? Still correct, with the exception that I cannot possibly express it to myself without using the word I. But it was not I. There was no such thing as I, within my knowledge.
>
> "It was only after a downward slide through something like a tube, and then a great noise and a sparkling and a crackling as of fires, that the consciousness came upon me, 'This is John Harmon drowning! John Harmon, struggle for your life. John Harmon, call on Heaven and save yourself!' I think I cried it out aloud in a great agony, and then a heavy horrid unintelligible something vanished, and it was I who was struggling there alone in the water.
>
> "I was very weak and faint, frightfully oppressed with drowsiness, and driving fast with the tide. Looking over the black water, I saw the lights racing past me on the two banks of the river, as if they were eager to be gone and leave me dying in the dark. The tide was running down, but I knew nothing of up or down then. When guiding myself safely with Heaven's

> assistance before the fierce set of the water, I at last caught at a boat
> moored, one of a tier of boats at a causeway, I was sucked under her, and
> came up, only just alive, on the other side.''   (II. 13. 426)

In this extraordinary passage, Harmon is actually able to narrate his own experience of a kind of death in which the most dramatic moment is the shift from calling upon himself in the third person, using the name he has been given by his father, to using the simple first person in recalling his struggle for survival. It is also crucial to see that whereas John Harmon, as usual, is a passive victim of someone else's plot, the self stripped down to ''I'' actively and literally takes hold of his life, ''guiding myself safely. . . I at last caught at a boat moored.'' In casting off or losing his name and the negative legacy it implies, Harmon discovers a self that has apparently always been there but which he has not known. All that he and the reader know about this self is that it possesses a hitherto unrealized energy and a powerful will to survive. It sounds very much like what Jung calls the preconscious base of the psyche:

> On this complicated base, the ego arises. Throughout life the ego is sus-
> tained by this base. When the base does not function, stasis ensues and then
> death. Its life and its reality are of vital importance. Compared to it, even
> the external world is secondary, for what does the world matter if the en-
> dogenous impulse to grasp it and manipulate it is lacking? In the long run,
> no conscious will can ever replace the life instinct.[5]

Jung's contrasting of the life instinct and the conscious will casts an interesting light on Harmon's fearful and depressed consciousness of his inheritance (a will in both the legal and psychological sense cast like a net over his life) and the nameless ''I'' that has an existence apart from it. But even more pertinent to our discussion is Jung's use of the words ''grasp'' and ''manipulate'' as the natural, indeed, necessary corollaries of the life instinct. Like ''designing,'' ''plotting'' and ''scheming,'' the words ''grasping'' and ''manipulating'' have suffered from a bad reputation which, according to Jung, and I am arguing according to Dickens also, they do not entirely deserve. For not only does John Harmon or the ''I'' that is left of him physically grasp at life, but he proceeds to manipulate it as does any author faced with a confusing assortment of material and other people's rendering of it.

If, as Dickens appears to be suggesting, some form of inventive manipulation or design is necessary for survival, then the moral issue is not whether or not to create your own plot, but what the nature and especially the consequences of the plot may be. It is obvious that John Harmon takes advantage of his supposed drowning to spy on the Boffins and especially Bella Wilfer in order to find out what kind of wife she would make. It can also be said that as an author, Harmon seems to rely more on observation of his characters than on outright manipulation. Yet, of course, by pretending to be a man of no family or fortune, he forces people to react to him according to information controlled and indeed invented by himself. However, it must not be forgotten that Harmon's motive is not merely to test others but to watch them in order to find himself. Though his life instinct has saved him, his ego, or perhaps to use terms more appropriate to Dickens, his moral and social self, is still in serious need of reconstruction. Thus, as the mirror held up by his father filled him with anxiety and self-contempt, that held up by the Boffins and ultimately Bella provide him not only with a sense of trust and love for them, but, just as important, with hope for himself.

Near the end of the book, when the old schemes and plots are unravelling and new ones about to begin, Harmon makes a speech that seems exaggerated and formal, but is nontheless an important statement of the convergence of moral and psychological aims of his scheme: "I owe everything I possess, solely to the disinterestedness, uprightness, tenderness, goodness (there are no words to satisfy me) of Mr. and Mrs. Boffin." Had Harmon been scheming in order to get his fortune back, this speech would be pure cynicism. But if we have read the story as *he* narrates it, we have seen that his real anxiety was about despair not poverty. Though with the help of the Boffins he repossesses his fortune—and in Dickens that is never to be sniffed at—what is of much greater significance according to *his* design is that, seeing generosity as within human reach, he has taken possession of a new and better self.

The second major plot in *Our Mutual Friend*, that which involves Eugene Wrayburn and Lizzie Hexam, though it is not an exact parallel with the story of John Harmon, does provide some striking comparisons with regard to the subject of authorship and design. Wrayburn too is the son of a domineering parent, though his is still alive. He refers to him ironically as M. R. F., "my respected father." He is also the inheritor of a paternal legacy which includes class, profession, and income, as well as a sense of superiority and an attitude toward work, that is, that he should not have to do any. Like Harmon, Wrayburn is not able to rid himself of his legacy until his life is brought to a crisis, but unlike Harmon, he seems unaware for much longer that he can be caught in the designs of others. He thinks himself above the fray, outside the petty machinations of other mortals. Even when he begins to fall in love with Lizzie Hexam, he refuses to give

his feelings a name or place them in a narration for which he takes authorial responsibility. As has been shown, when his friend Mortimer asks him
what his design is with respect to Lizzie, he answers that he has none.

When Bradley Headstone casts him in the role of rival, Wrayburn
scoffs at him and at the idea that he could allow himself to become sufficiently interested in another human being, especially of Lizzie's class, to
merit such a label. However, when Wrayburn notices that Headstone and
Lizzie's brother are following him around London in the hope that he will
lead them to Lizzie, he plays a cruel cat-and-mouse game with them. In
tracing a meaningless design through the streets of the city, he behaves
like a contemptuous and cynical author baiting a gullible reader while
refusing to deliver a message. Dickens encourages the literary analogy
through Wrayburn's response to Mortimer's charge that his behavior is
reckless:

> "You charm me, Mortimer, with your reading of my weaknesses. (By-
> the-bye, that very word, Reading, in its crucial use, always charms me. An
> actress's Reading of a chamber-maid, a dancer's Reading of a hornpipe, a
> singer's Reading of a song, a marine-painter's Reading of the sea, the kettle-
> drum's Reading of an instrumental passage, are phrases ever youthful and
> delightful.) I was mentioning your perception of my weaknesses. I own to
> the weakness of objecting to occupy a ludicrous position, and therefore, I
> transfer the position to the scouts."   (II. 10. 605).

Certainly, one common model of the author-reader relationship allows
the author so much superiority of insight and knowledge as to make the
reader feel lost and ludicrous. The inequality of this relationship, indeed
the sadism of the author, is compounded if, in fact, the author possesses
no special information, has no superior skill except in the creation of
meaningless designs, and has no objective beyond his own pleasure in
humiliating the reader. The result is like Joyce or Nabokov run wild,
everybody's worst suspicions about modernist obscurantism, and, it has a
special poignancy for the academic critic searching, like Bradley Headstone, around every corner for another clue:

> "...I goad the schoolmaster to madness. I make the schoolmaster so
> ridiculous, that I see him chafe and fret at every pore when we cross one
> another. The amiable occupation has been the solace of my life,... I have
> derived inexpressible comfort from it. I do it thus: I stroll after dark, stroll a
> little way, look in at a window and furtively look out for the schoolmaster.
> Sooner or later, I perceive the schoolmaster on the watch; sometimes accom-
> panied by his hopeful pupil; oftener pupil-less. Having made sure of his
> watching me, I tempt him on, all over London. One night I go east, another
> night north, in a few nights I go all round the compass. Sometimes, I walk;

sometimes, I proceed in cabs, draining the pocket of the schoolmaster, who then follows in cabs. I study and get up abstruse No Thoroughfares in the course of the day. With Venetian mystery I seek those No Thoroughfares at night, glide into them by means of dark courts, tempt the schoolmaster to follow, turn suddenly, and catch him before he can retreat. Then we face one another, and I pass him as unaware of his existence, and he undergoes grinding torments. Night after night his disappointment is acute, but hope springs eternal in the scholastic breast, and he follows me again to-morrow. Thus I enjoy the pleasures of the chase, and derive great benefit from the healthful exercise."

"This is an extraordinary story," observed Lightwood, who had heard it out with serious attention. "I don't like it." (III. 10. 605–606)

Dickens, who loved mysteries and composing complicated schemes, cannot have dissociated himself entirely from this portrait of the artist. But there is a major difference since Dickens' designs, however intricate, usually do lead somewhere. And Eugene Wrayburn, whether he intends it or not, is led somewhere with them.

Wrayburn's passion for Lizzie brings him to the point where he begins to see himself as others—especially Lizzie—see him. And to the realization that if he is to change those views, he must begin to counter them with designs of his own composing that are more than ingenious circles intended to mislead the pursuer and allow himself the apparent luxury of having no character. When he finds Lizzie in her country hiding place and tries with unaccustomed sincerity to appeal to her feelings, he cannot at first tell his own story but only challenge hers: "Don't be hard in your construction of me," he begs. And later he asks if she could have felt differently toward him if they had not been separated by class, the exchange is significant:

"How can I tell you what I should have done, if you had not been what you are?" [she asks.]
"If I had not been what *you make me out to be*," he struck in, skillfully changing the form of words, "would you still have hated me?"
(IV. 6. 762; italics mine).

Dickens reminds us that Wrayburn's cleverness, his skill with words does not fail him in a rare moment of earnest feeling. On the contrary, he tries, for the first time in the novel, to use his skill in order to probe real feelings and, as important, to raise the possibility of changing himself by challenging the legacy which he had ignorantly assumed to be the unalterable scheme of his life.

But incipient authors need help. It is fundamental to Dickens' moral as well as to his aesthetic vision that the creative act, though it begins with individual energy and instinct, can be brought to fulfillment only through some form of reciprocity or, to use the guiding term of the novel, mutuality. For Dickens, novel writing is initiating one side of a dialogue. His imaginative awareness of audience, of the reader not just enjoying but somehow entering in through the open doors of his sentences and situations, is one of the great qualities of his genius. John Harmon needs Bella and the Boffins not simply to trust and love him but to give him a voice and a character.

Lizzie Hexam's rescue of the battered Wrayburn, with its baptismal overtones, is also, in narrational terms, a last effort at rescuing a character out of the amorphous assemblage of upper-class clichés that he has been using as an excuse for identity. If John Harmon has been the "man from somewhere," a shadowy figure without clear definition much the same can be said about Eugene Wrayburn whose true self has been lost in a haze of indifference and boredom. In the description of Harmon's near-drowning, the most dramatic shift was from his name to the first person pronoun. In Wrayburn's case, the grammatical shift is even more startling. The dapper young barrister of good name becomes a body, an "it":

> Once, she let the body evade her, not being sure of her grasp. Twice, and she had seized it by its bloody hair.
>
> It was insensible, if not virtually dead; it was mutilated and streaked the water all about it with dark red streaks. As it could not help itself, it was impossible for her to get it on board. She bent over the stern to secure it with the line, and then the river and its shores rang to the terrible cry she uttered.
>
> But, as if possessed by supernatural spirit and strength she lashed it safe, resumed her seat, and rowed in, desperately, for the nearest shallow water where she might run the boat aground. Desperately, but not wildly, for she knew that if she lost distinctness of intention, all was lost and gone.
>
> (IV. 6. 768–760)

As the despairing Harmon had been reduced to an "I" clinging to its life, the arrogant Wrayburn is reduced through the vulnerability of his body to a state of equality with all mortals. At the point of death, the barrier between him and Lizzie is removed. She "grasps" his body, maneuvers the boat, and literally calls him back to life with her cry of recognition which, because unspecified, invites the reader to join the rescue and supply a name. The transformation from "it" to "Eugene" feels like a collaborative effort in which the reader is allowed imaginatively to share in Wrayburn's rehabilitation. Finally, it is both ironical and decisive that in rescuing this unmotivated man of no design, Lizzie "knew that if she lost distinctness of intention, all was lost and gone." She, at least, has a clear design, for "distinctness of intention" is a definition that Lightwood,

Dickens, and presumably even Austen would accept, and she pursues it with the skill she has learned as her father's apprentice.

The moral and aesthetic assumptions informing this highly charged scene play an important part in this book of multiple fictions. Artfulness, the skillful construction and energetic pursuit of a design, may be put to good or bad use, but without it, "all is lost and gone." Lizzie's work may be arduous, but her motive is simple: she wants to save Eugene. Against great odds, the sheer weight of his body, the fact that he may already be dead, etc., she projects or imagines a life worth saving and capable of being saved and, acts, like all authors, not simply in response to the given facts, but as one who "grasps" and "manipulates" them for her own purpose. That her purpose is a generous one is not insignificant, since it is generosity that adds power to skill, that enables her to act out and accomplish what her mind pictures.

When Eugene, recalled to life by Lizzie, begins slowly to regain consciousness, he demonstrates in the few broken phrases that he can utter, a new will to take hold of life by making choices with schematic consequences. He does not want his assailant to be pursued; he wishes to shield Lizzie from scandal and harm; and, finally, he proposes marriage both as a sign of his love and as a way of rescuing Lizzie from poverty after what he presumes will be his imminent death. When he is up and about and almost fully restored to health, he forms another plan and, interestingly, tries it out on his friend Mortimer by sketching a false narrative about emigrating to the colonies with his bride. When Mortimer reluctantly agrees that it might be a reasonable plan, Wrayburn vigorously contradicts him and declares his intention to stand by his wife in the face of Society's inevitable objections and to join his old friend and partner in real work. His own comment on the idea brings to mind once again the necessity for design or in Lizzie's terms, "distinctness of intention." "In turning to at last," he says, "we turn to in earnest."

Surely, if one common trait of modernist fiction is a display of self-consciousness about the nature and function of narration, *Our Mutual Friend* amply qualifies as a forerunner of the type. And although all the vicious forms of deception—Weggery and Podsnappery—are held up to ridicule because of their selfish and destructive intent, the possession of a "designing" imagination is not in itself condemned. On the contrary, the need to author one's own designs is associated with the most universal and fundamental human instinct, the urge to live. We invent to survive. But, and here again Dickens anticipates a number of modern writers, the best kind of authorship involves cooperation; it is a process of declaration and interpretation, invitation and response, an implied dialogue, a mutual faith in meaning.

Finally, the most radical and perhaps most modern characteristic of *Our Mutual Friend* has to do with the extent to which the novel and its author refuse to allow the reader to make simple discriminations between fiction and truth. The Beckett-like glimpses of a meaningless universe are arresting even though they are momentary and do not prevail. Dickens may not have had Austen's confidence in natural order, but he did believe judgments could be made between good and bad, workable and unworkable designs, according to their relative harmony with large psychological and moral truths. But the task is not always simple or the method obvious.

Often accused of exaggeration and distortion, occasionally anxious as in the preface to *Bleak House*, to give factual support to some of his more outlandish episodes, Dickens asserts and defends the honor and truthfulness of his profession with particular conviction in *Our Mutual Friend*. One of the biggest liars in the book, Rogue Riderhood, insists on getting small details straight. When he tries to persuade Lightwood that his nickname has no meaning, Lightwood dismisses the point: "Never mind that." "'Scuse *me*, Lawyer Lightwood, it's part of the truth, and as such I do mind it, and I must mind it and I will mind it."

By contrast, Venus, the articulator of bones, seems an author after Dickens own heart. He deals in illusions, gives animation to that which seems inert, but, most importantly, he strings together odd pieces in order to make a whole of them. Though he has a low opinion of himself, seeing himself in what he calls a "bony light," he cheers himself up with the knowledge that what he does contributes to understanding the science of life. "I am proud of my calling after all," he says. And it is, after all, this quaint and ingenious artificer, one who makes dead things seem to come alive, who holds the key to one of the central mysteries of the novel. He possesses a truth as well as a good heart and the skill of an artist. It is in the telling of the story of his partial acquiesence in Wegg's plot that he reveals all three to Boffin and the reader. In short, the narrative contains truths that its parts cannot sustain.

As Venus prepares to thread together his words, it is impossible not to hear the voice of Dickens inviting the reader ever deeper into complicity with his own designing ways: "And now, sir," said Venus, "having prepared your mind in the rough, I will articulate the details."

Our pulse quickens. Our attention revives. No one, we say to ourselves, can begin a story like Dickens (or his surrogates). It calls out something very deep in us. The invitation to listen is like a summons to life.

NOTES

1. Jane Austen, *Pride and Prejudice* (New York: Holt, Rinehart, and Winston, 1964), p. 2.

2. Charles Dickens, *Our Mutual Friend* (Harmondsworth: Penguin, 1977. All references are to this edition.

3. Henry James, "The Art of Fiction," in *Partial Portraits* (Westport, Connecticut: Greenwood Press, 1970), p. 376.

4. Samuel Beckett, *Waiting for Godot* (New York: Grove Press Inc., 1954), p. 45.

5. C. G. Jung, *Memories, Dreams, Reflections* (London: Collins and Routledge and Kegan Paul, 1963), p. 381.

Growing Up in Fiction and in Fact: Protagonist and Reader in Thackeray's *Pendennis*

Michael Lund

Although Thackeray's *Pendennis* (1848–1850) had begun its appearance in serial form six months earlier, Dickens' *David Copperfield* (1849–1850) figures as the first English Bildungsroman in Jerome Buckley's standard study of the genre, *Season of Youth: The Bildungsroman from Dickens to Golding*. *Pendennis* clearly contains many of the elements in Buckley's definition of the genre: "childhood" (in sketches); the "conflict of generations" (Arthur's resistance to the direction of his mother, Helen Pendennis, and his uncle, Major Pendennis); "provinciality" (the world of Dr. Portman, the Vicar of Fairoaks, and Mr. Smirke, his curate); the "larger society" (London's literary and social worlds); "self-education" (Arthur's literary apprenticeship); "alienation" (Pen as cynical critic of society); "ordeal by love" (his romances with the Fotheringay, Blanche Amory, and Laura Pendennis); and the "search for a vocation and a working philosophy" (the fundamental plot of the novel).[1] Buckley skips over Thackeray's novel, nonetheless, because of a serious weakness he sees in its central character; Arthur Pendennis, Buckley claims, develops very little, "[i]nsofar as he 'develops' at all during a prolonged and protected adolescence. . . ."[2]

Recent developments in literary theory, however, are changing such fundamental concepts as "form" by which we have traditionally classified works of art and identifying new elements by which fiction creates and develops character. Susan R. Suleiman in the "Introduction" to a new anthology, *The Reader and the Text: Essays on Audience and Interpretation*, identifies "a preoccupation with audience and interpretation" as "central to contemporary American and Continental theory and criticism."[3] Suleiman sees this preoccupation as a "movement away from the formalist and New Critical emphasis on the autonomy of 'the text itself' toward a recognition (or a re-recognition) of the relevance of context, whether the latter be defined in terms of historical, cultural, ideological, or psychoanalytic categories."[4] Thus, the "form" in "the text itself" might be understood in relationship to its "context," that is, the "audience" which perceives it.

The social and literary contexts in which Thackeray's second major novel appeared have been discussed in considerable detail in the classic work of Gordon Ray and in more recent studies by John Sutherland, Edgar Harden, and Robert Colby.[5] *Pendennis* appeared at a time when the aftershocks of turbulence in Europe (the Revolution of 1848), continued religious debate inspired by such events as the Oxford Movement and new discoveries in science, rapidly altering literary standards in an expanding reading public, and the unsettling effects of relentless middleclass growth created an atmosphere of constant social and intellectual change. Thackeray as author is able to link his fictional events to this mood of the times by structuring the novel around contrasts between country (the old, stable life) and city (a new and changing society), between the traditional sacred philosophies (of Helen and Laura) and the modern worldly visions (of Blanche and Emily). That is, Thackeray surrounds the lives of his novel's characters with the furniture of the real Victorian world. Even under the pressure of monthly deadlines, Thackeray produced a sustained, detailed portrait, with commentary, of the full context of his nineteenth-century world.

While this cultural background has already been closely studied in many respects, the temporal framework which governs the reader's assimilation of Thackeray's text reveals additional ways in which the novelist utilized the literary resources of his era, particularly the serial format. The time involved in reading any work of fiction can be a tool used by the novelist to establish or extend features of his work. Thackeray's use of the reader's time, especially the months of serialization, suggests a consummate Victorian author realizing to the full the "form" of the Bildungsroman, a major genre of his century.

The "audience" which read *Pendennis* in twenty-four monthly numbers from November, 1849, to December, 1850, was encouraged by the artist to add its own sense of passing time to the world of the novel. To define the "form" of this Bildungsroman, then, within new and evolving critical systems, one must not only describe the protagonist's evolution in the text (as Buckley does); one must also attempt to measure the reader's development outside the text, as I shall try to do here.[6] In the new critical climate, as characters grow up in fiction, readers grow up in fact. Before considering in detail some of the ways in which Thackeray's reader grows up, I want to review first some more traditional ground concerning the ways in which his characters develop.

I

   The central figure of the Bildungsroman, Thackeray's protagonist, exists like all of his fictional creations within a comfortable Victorian view of character: he matures, but he does not change dramatically. As the author puts it in perhaps the most frequently cited passage of *Pendennis*,

> We alter very little. When we talk of this man or that woman being no longer the same person whom we remember in youth, and remark (of course to deplore) changes in our friends, we don't, perhaps, calculate that circumstance only brings out the latent defect or quality, and does not create it. The selfish languour and indifference of to-day's possession is the consequence of the selfish ardour of yesterday's pursuit: the scorn and weariness which cries *vanitas vanitatum* is but the lassitude of the sick appetite palled with pleasure: the insolence of the successful *parvenu* is only the necessary continuance of the career of the needy struggler: our mental changes are like our grey hairs or our wrinkles—but the fulfilment of the plan of mortal growth and decay: that which is snow-white now was glossy black once; that which is sluggish obesity to-day was boisterous rosy health a few years back; that calm weariness, benevolent, resigned, and disappointed, was ambition, fierce and violent, but a few years since, and has only settled into submissive repose after many a battle and defeat.[7]

Thus, "it was the same Pendennis" (II, 210) first introduced in Number 12 of this history who appears before the reader here in Number 19. That the "development of the mind of a worldly and selfish, but not ungenerous or unkind or truth-avoiding man" (II, 236) is gradual, steady, and undramatic does not mean that Thackeray has failed to show the development he intended.

   This fundamental philosophy of character also inspires a favorite point of view in Thackeray's fiction, the panoramic vision of history where one travels easily from present to past or future. Because characters "alter very little," their natures are not greatly dependent on time; the narrator can see the same identity at both ends of a decades-long continuum. In the following typical instance of time-telescoping vision in *Pendennis*, for example, the hero attends a "Dinner in the Row" during his emergence as a professional writer in London and is ignored by a prominent poetess:

Indeed, Miss Bunion having considered Mr. Pendennis for a minute, who gave himself rather grand airs, and who was attired in an extremely fashionable style, with his very best chains, shirt studs, and cambric fronts, was set down, and not without reason, as a prig by the poetess; who thought it was much better to attend to her dinner than to take any notice of him. She told him as much in after days with her usual candour. "I took you for one of the little Mayfair dandies," she said to Pen. "You looked as solemn as a little undertaker; and as I disliked, beyond measure, the odious creature who was on the other side of me, I thought it was best to eat my dinner and hold my tongue."

"And you did both very well, my dear Miss Bunion," Pen said with a laugh.

"Well, so I do, but I intend to talk to you the next time a great deal: for you are neither so solemn, nor so stupid, nor so pert as you look."

"Ah, Miss Bunion, how I pine for that 'next time' to come," Pen said with an air of comic gallantry:—But we must return to the day, and the dinner at Paternoster Row.   (I, 342)

The Pen of the future in this passage is, of course, much "changed" from pompous young self (not unfairly described as a "Mayfair dandy"); but Miss Bunion is also correct in asserting that much of the change is in how he "looks" to her (and how he will look that "next time"). Arthur has risen in the eyes of the fashionable world, and Miss Bunion is simply accepting that revaluation. Narrative leaps in time like the one in this passage are made in a world where people hold consistent if developing natures, changing as much in the ways they are perceived by others as in their private selves.

Thackeray's characteristic point of view and his belief in essentially stable character combine with a reluctance to depend exclusively on conventional concepts of plot in fiction to achieve the primary context within which the protagonist develops. Buckley points out that the typical Bildungsroman hero undertakes a journey full of trials, "by parents, by money, by the city," that resemble tests faced by "the knights of old romances";[8] these trials constitute the plot of the Bildungsroman. Pen's evolution from naive provincial youth to successful London author— highlighted by his changing relationships to parental figures (Helen and the Major), his loves (Emily Costigan, Blanche Amory, Laura), and his rivals (Foker, Pynsent, Warrington)—follows this pattern. But in Thackeray's case, it is not only this conventional plot which promotes the development of Pen's character but also the social conventions which create his identity as he moves through them. Thackeray says in a "Preface" to the completed novel that "the 'exciting' plan" of a typical adventure story "was laid aside" (II, vi) in the actual composition because he knew

his narrative gifts did not lie in describing action.⁹ Thackeray's particular
skill is the ability to chronicle the social poses and perceptions which
define people. The first sentences of the novel set the pattern for his unique
presentation of character development:

> One fine morning in the full London season, Major Arthur Pendennis came
> over from his lodgings, according to his custom, to breakfast at a certain
> Club in Pall Mall, of which he was a chief ornament. As he was one of the
> finest judges of wine in England, and a man of active, dominating, and in-
> quiring spirit, he had been very properly chosen to be a member of the Com-
> mittee of this Club, and indeed was almost the manager of the institution;
> and the stewards and waiters bowed before him as reverentially as to a Duke
> or a Field-Marshal.
>
>   At a quarter past ten the Major invariably made his appearance in the best
> blacked boots in all London, with a checked morning cravat that never was
> rumpled until dinner time, a buff waistcoat which bore the crown of his sov-
> ereign on the buttons, and linen so spotless that Mr. Brummel himself asked
> the name of his laundress, and would probably have employed her had not
> misfortunes compelled that great man to fly the country. Pendennis's coat,
> his white gloves, his whiskers, his very cane, were perfect of their kind as
> specimens of the costume of a military man *en retraite*. At a distance, or see-
> ing his back merely, you would have taken him to be not more than thirty
> years old: it was only by a nearer inspection that you saw the factitious na-
> ture of his rich brown hair, and that there were a few crow's-feet round
> about the somewhat faded eyes of his handsome mottled face.   (I, 1–2)

As the point of view of the passage shifts, providing "a nearer
inspection," we become more aware of the Major's real identity beneath
his artful appearance: he declines from a celebrated figure of London
society—youthful, regal, military—to an old man in disguise—alone,
balding, rumpled, retreating, perhaps even, like Brummel, shadowed by a
hint of disgrace. When, near the end of the novel, we see the Major's
"shaking hands, the wrinkled and quivering face, the old eyes weeping
and winking" (II, 320) as his schemes for Pen have failed, it will be not
only a series of dramatic events which have produced this character, but
also the multiple points of view which have allowed us to see Pen's uncle
fully in the end.

Similarly, the central character of Thackeray's Bildungsroman, "who
does not claim to be a hero, but only a man and a brother" (II, 372), will
not develop as dramatically as, say, David Copperfield, whose journey
through life begins at an earlier point and is filled with many more exciting events which shape his character. In her fine article on Thackeray and
time, Jean Sudrann accurately states that Pen's development in the novel
is limited. In the end, she argues, "Arthur Pendennis simply drifts into

domestic bliss.''[10] However, as Sudrann goes on to say, Thackeray still makes "the reader himself experience the movement of time within the frame of the novel" by repeatedly turning to "the image of passing time"[11] in the narrative. His shifting perspective, presenting all the novel's characters in different lights and consistently remarking on the passage of time, insists that we recognize the characters' inevitable aging. Thackeray's narrative, however, insists that time passes not only in the protagonist's world but in the reader's world as well. It is to this process of the reader's growing up that I now wish to turn.

II

By a number of methods, Thackeray's narrative in *Pendennis* throws his reader back into the time frame of the real world, creating a second context within which Pen as protagonist develops. The real time involved in reading this novel, in its original serial form, was more than two years, a fact of the nineteenth-century literary experience seldom considered in measuring the impact of Victorian fiction. In twenty-six months, the serial reader can be said to have changed significantly. W. J. Harvey, one of the few critics to have considered the long novel as a special kind of fiction, has suggested that works which involve an extended reading time present unusual problems for literary analysis: "a massive novel enforces a prolonged and probably interrupted reading. To this extent the reader is himself much less a fixity and much more a variable. . . . [T]he writer *may* be able to manipulate and control to some extent this prolonged interaction of life and art."[12] After the famous passage about time, change, and character from *Pendennis* which I cited earlier, Thackeray continues with an authorial intrusion which does "manipulate [the] interaction of life and art," drawing attention to the reader's existence in his own frame of reference:

> Lucky he who can bear his failure so generously, and give up his broken sword to Fate the Conqueror with a manly and humble heart! Are you not awestricken, you, friendly reader, who, taking the page up for a moment's light reading, lay it down, perchance, for a greater reflection,—to think how you, who have consummated your success or your disaster, may be holding marked station, or a hopeless and nameless place, in the crowds who have passed through how many struggles of defeat, success, crime, remorse, to yourself only known!—who may have loved and grown cold, wept and laughed again, how often!—to think how you are the same, *You*, whom in childhood you remember, before the voyage of life began?   (II, 211–212)

Both by the content of his commentary, and by the way it breaks into the narrative flow of Pen's story, Thackeray's direct address to the reader recalls him from the fictional world to the real world, making the reader recognize that time has passed in his own frame of reference even if it has seemed to pass rather uneventfully in Pendennis's world. Laying down this book he has been reading for 500 pages (and for Thackeray's original audience, twenty-two months), the reader is made to confront the fact that he himself has grown older as he read.

In addition to such passages of authorial intrusion, another narrative technique in Thackeray, the extended flashback, also emphasizes the reader's time scheme and his existence in that frame. For instance, we begin this novel with Major Pendennis breakfasting at his Pall Mall Club, "according to his custom" (I, 1), where he receives the urgent letter from Helen Pendennis which announces Pen's plan to marry Emily Costigan. Number 2 concludes with "the writing of those two letters which were laid on Major Pendennis's breakfast table, in London, at the commencement of Prince Arthur's most veracious history" (I, 64). This return to the reader's starting place reminds him of the time he has spent reading to fill in the background behind the writing of the two letters. Some sixty-three pages of text have interposed—narration of Pen's ancestry, early childhood, and acquaintance with the provincial acting troupe—and sixty days of events in the nineteenth-century serial reader's life. The Pen who awaits the Major has changed not in Thackeray's text but in the contexts of the reader's expanded knowledge and experience.

Thackeray's narrative method, which consistently refers to two time schemes, is also illustrated in the structure of Chapter 8, entitled "IN WHICH PEN IS KEPT WAITING AT THE DOOR, WHILE THE READER IS INFORMED WHO LITTLE LAURA IS."[13] Pen awaits the interview with his uncle, which had been forecast in the letter Helen Pendennis wrote and the Major received in the first two numbers of the novel. Pen is called to the meeting by Laura: "'Lead on, Laura,' Pen said, with a half fierce, half comic air—'lead on, and say I wait upon my uncle.' But he was laughing in order to hide a great anxiety: and was screwing his courage inwardly to face the ordeal which he knew was now before him" (I, 66–67).

With Pen stopped at this moment of anxious anticipation, the narrator recounts a number of earlier happenings: histories of Laura's parentage, her father's relationship with Helen Pendennis, her early childhood at Fairoaks, and the Major's own love life. The narrator concludes his digression some ten pages after Pen was "kept waiting" at the door: "Thus it was that Laura Bell became Mrs. Pendennis's daughter" (I, 76). When Pen is allowed to enter the room on the doorstep of which he was forced to pause, the reader's understanding of the situation has been developed considerably. The flashback moves the reader forward through time, while the protagonist is frozen in time. In a sense, Pen's character has been "developed" in the narrative, but not simply by the method of chronicling events as they occur. Pen's forward movement within the novel's time scheme resumes only at the end of this narrative interlude, as the Major effectively begins undermining his sentimental romance with the Fotheringay. The next eight chapters chronicle the coming apart of the engagement, of Arthur's growth as Bildungsroman hero who learns (from the Major, from Bows, from Emily herself) more about the nature of his world and how to live intelligently in it.

In Thackeray's *Pendennis*, then, two kinds of time exist within which we mark the protagonist's growth: the time which measures the occurrence of events in the fictional world of the characters; and reading time, which measures the occurrence of events in the reader's world as he turns pages of the novel. While the first is, as in all Bildungsromans, an important context for the protagonist's growing older, the second—reading time—is also significant, revealing Thackeray's particular skill at utilizing all aspects of his serial format. A passage in the novel's second installment reveals how the time which clocks events occurring in Thackeray's fictional world is often relatively unimportant. At this moment in the novel Pen is being called by the universal experience of youthful romantic love:

> Was Pen frightened at the summons? Not he. He did not know what was coming: it was all wild pleasure and delight as yet. And as, when three years previously, and on entering the fifth form at the Cistercians, his father had made him a present of a gold watch which the boy took from under his pillow and examined on the instant of waking: for ever rubbing and polishing it up in private and retiring into corners to listen to its ticking: so the young man exulted over his new delight; felt in his waistcoat pocket to see that it was safe; wound it up at nights, and at the very first moment of waking hugged it and looked at it.—By the way, that first watch of Pen's was a showy ill-manufactured piece; it never went well from the beginning, and was always getting out of order. And after putting it aside into a drawer and forgetting it for some time, he swapped it finally away for a more useful time-keeper.   (I, 39)

The gold watch does not serve to mark the time of fictional events for the reader; the different periods of Pen's life (when he got the watch, when it went bad, when he traded it, and when he fell in love) are instead blended together into one moment of reading. A later passage on clocks and time again suggests that the exact times of events in this fictional world are not terribly significant:

> [Pendennis] did not come home [from Oxbridge] at Easter; but when he arrived for the long vacation, he brought more smart clothes; . . . And he had

a new French watch and gold chain, in place of the big old chronometer, with its bunch of jingling seals, which had hung from the fob of John Pendennis, and by the second-hand of which the defunct doctor had felt many a patient's pulse in his time. It was but a few months back Pen had longed for this watch, which he thought the most splendid and august time-piece in the world; and just before he went to college, Helen had taken it out of her trinket-box (where it had remained unwound since the death of her husband) and given it to Pen with a solemn and appropriate little speech respecting his father's virtues and the proper use of time. This portly and valuable chronometer Pen now pronounced to be out of date, and, indeed, made some comparisons between it and a warming-pan, which Laura thought disrespectful, and he left the watch in a drawer, in the company of soiled primrose gloves, cravats which had gone out of favour, and of that other school watch which has once before been mentioned in this history.

(I, 172)

The many times referred to here—the years of Pen's father's medical practice, of his death, of Pen's early schooling, of his leaving for college, of the present—are so mixed in the complex sentence and paragraph construction that the reader recalls the earlier, similar passage about watches as much as he distinguishes the time scheme of fictional events. That is, clocks in *Pendennis* signal the passage of time in the reader's world as much as they mark events in Pen's life. In this passage, we remember not only the various stages of the protagonist's development but also the stages of our own reading experience. We see Pen moving from his years at Grey Friars to his adventures at Oxbridge in the traditional growth of a Bildungsroman hero; but we also are urged by this passage, which echoes the passage read 140 pages (or four months) earlier, to recognize our own forward movement in time as it is accentuated by our on-going reading of the novel.

Thus, Thackeray uses two temporal frames of references—time in the novel, and time outside the novel—to increase the sense of Pen's development as Bildungsroman hero. When movement in one kind of time seems to stop in the fiction, action occurs in the other time scheme, so that, relativistically, there is always a sense of change and growth in the literary experience. If no clock is ticking to mark the passing of time in Pen's life, there is often a clock ticking in the reader's own time; and the reader, not always aware of the difference, registers a sense of time's passing and of a character's developing.

This narrative method, emphasizing the reader's movement through the pages of the novel as well as Pen's movement within the fictional world, is used extensively by an author who believes in the essential stability of character through time and in storytelling by flashback and other jumps in time.[14] While the reader observes, the hero advances through time and experience; then the hero may be stopped at a particular moment of time while the reader advances through his reading experience. In order to encourage the reader's awareness of process in the fictional world, Thackeray even goes beyond these narrative techniques which draw attention to the passing of reading time. Specifically, he uses the reader's existence outside the reading moment—that is, the time beween installments when the reader is not actually reading.

III

Thackeray nearly always concludes his serial installments of *Pendennis* with the hero at some crucial moment in his history. In the thirty days before the next issue resumes the story, the reader, impressed by the final dramatic image of the number, extends Pen's fictional life in his own real time.[15] As Thackeray himself insists, "the poetical figures live in our memory just as much as the real personages" (II, 104). At the end of Number 2, for instance, Dr. Portman bursts out in amazement that surely Pen does not plan to marry the Fotheringay, inspiring a typical dramatic conclusion for the part:

> Pen put on his most princely air. "What else, Dr. Portman," he said, "do you suppose would be my desire?"
> Utterly foiled in his attack, and knocked down by this sudden lunge of Pen's, the Doctor could only gasp out, "Mrs. Pendennis, ma'am, send for the Major."
> "Send for the Major? with all my heart," said Arthur Prince of Pendennis and Grand Duke of Fairoaks, with a most superb wave of the hand. And the colloquy terminated by the writing of those two letters which were laid on Major Pendennis's breakfast-table, in London, at the commencement of Prince Arthur's most veracious history.   (I, 64)

Arthur maintains this majestic pose for the original-parts reader much longer than he does for the modern single-volume reader. The major begins the erosion of Pen's sentimental, grand gesture immediately in the next chapter: "Our acquaintance, Major Arthur Pendennis, arrived in due time at Fairoaks . . ." (I, 65). While the modern reader contemplates Pen's bold statement for only a second, the Victorian serial reader witnesses Pen's heroics for a precise length of (real) time—from December, 1848, to January, 1849. The process of Pen's development as Bildungsroman hero is significantly expanded and deepened in Thackeray's original format.

This tactic of making Pen's final appearance in a number one of his sentimental, pompous, or egotistical moments dominates the installment structure of *Pendennis*, figuring in sixteen of the twenty-two parts (excluding the final double number).[16] Pen is seen rejecting the unexciting company of Dr. Portman (end of Number 1); bravely awaiting the outcome of Costigan's interview with the Major (Number 3); eagerly departing for Oxbridge (Number 5); romantically inspired by Blanche Amory (Number 7); dining ostentatiously in London (Number 9); envisioning himself as a new literary star (Number 10); appearing as aloof, cynical, worldly lover (Numbers 12, 19, 20, 21); proudly aware of his first success as a novelist (Number 13); taking the stance of profound philosopher (Number 14); playing the role of noble patron of the lower classes, particularly Fanny Bolton (Number 15); looking self-consciously repentant (Number 17); and rising to nobility as squire of Fairoaks (Number 18). After each of these appearances at or near the conclusion of a monthly installment, the reader takes over the imaging of Pendennis, the young protagonist with the exaggerated sense of himself doomed for yet another fall. That fall, or the undermining of the hero's pompous stance, starts again with the resumption of text, in the next issue of serial publication. In the meantime, Thackeray has used the real time of the reader's existence to lengthen the process of the protagonist's growth.

Certain aspects of Pendennis's life are specifically given additional existence in the reader's world as he waits between numbers. When Pen's mother discovers Fanny Bolton attending her sick son in his London chambers (at the end of Number 16), for instance, the reader is given thirty days to speculate about the nature and extent of the young protagonist's mistakes. Of course, his actions are hardly as lamentable as Helen believes (or the reader might have suspected), but Thackeray's use of the serial format intensifies his character's life and our reactions to it. Thackeray allows his protagonist to fall considerably in the world's eyes during that month-long delay in the resolution of the plot, and then Pen turns out to be innocent enough to still serve as a novel's hero. It is almost as if Pendennis receives all the benefits of guilt (in the intensity of the reader's reaction) but then ends up innocent of all charges.[17] Pen's recovery, both from sickness and from infatuation (in Number 17), is also not as sudden as it might now seem to single-volume readers. "Our duty now is to record a fact concerning Pendennis," explains the narrator,

> which, however shameful and disgraceful, when told regarding the chief personage and Godfather of a novel, must, nevertheless, be made known to the public who reads his veritable memoirs. Having gone to bed ill with fever, and suffering to a certain degree under the passion of love . . . when he

rallied up from his bodily ailment, his mental malady had likewise quitted
him, and he was no more in love with Fanny Bolton than you or I.

(II, 139)

When we recall *Pendennis*'s original format, we realize that Pen has not
been ill for a mere ten pages, but in the reader's mind, for at least thirty
days. Thus, major events in the protagonist's life—infatuation, sickness,
and recovery—are intensified and lengthened by Thackeray's use of the
serial form, by his use of time outside of his fiction as well as time within
his fiction.

Thackeray similarly uses breaks in his serial publication to intensify the
hero's growing attachment to Blanche Amory near the end of the novel,
and to appear to reduce the chances of his marrying Laura, the clear heroine of the story. That is, the final resolution of Pen's fate and the entire
novel are developed in the reader's time as well as in the time of the novel.
At the end of Number 20, Thackeray's narrator seems to insist that marriage to Blanche is all that awaits his jaded hero whose youthful passions,
we are led to believe, are forever behind him:

> Ah! What answer is given to those [tears] in the eyes of a young woman?
> What is the method employed for drying them? What took place? O ring-
> doves and roses, O dews and wildflowers, O waving greenwoods and balmy
> airs of summer! Here were two battered London rakes, taking themselves in
> for a moment, and fancying that they were in love with each other, like
> Phyllis and Corydon!
> When one thinks of country houses and country walks, one wonders that
> any man is left unmarried.   (II, 256; Number 20 ends here)

When Pen later announces to his uncle that he plans to marry Blanche
even though he does not love her and she will have no fortune, the reader
is again urged to conclude that no escape is likely:

> Arthur took his [the Major's] hand, which the old man left to him; it was
> quite passive and clammy. He looked much oldened; and it seemed as if the
> contest and defeat had quite broken him.
> On the next day he kept his bed, and refused to see his nephew.
>   (II, 320; Number 22 ends here)

Since this is the end of the next-to-last installment (the last being a traditional double number, parts 23 and 24), the reader is encouraged by this
memorable final scene to anticipate an inevitable, sad conclusion to the
protagonist's romantic life. Pen's self-sacrificing decision to accept a fate
created by his own mistakes is given additional force in the literary experience; in the reader's time between Numbers 20 and 21 and between Numbers 22 and 23/24, Thackeray's audience expands these images of the pro-

tagonist rejecting his worldly uncle's offer and maturing in his own vision of the world and his place in it. In the space between numbers the reader adds to the development of the protagonist in Thackeray's Bildungsroman.

IV

This extended time of the literary experience provided by the serial format is, of course, shared by other important novelists of the nineteenth century.[18] Critical consideration of character development in the major works of Dickens, George Eliot, Dostoevsky, Flaubert, Tolstoy, James, Howells, Hardy, and others needs to take this temporal context into account whenever the impact of novels on the tradition is to be measured or an author's achievement in a particular genre is to be determined. Because many modern editions of classics like *David Copperfield, Middlemarch, The Brothers Karamazov, Madame Bovary, Anna Karenina, The Portrait of a Lady, The Rise of Silas Lapham, The Major of Casterbridge,* and others do not always include clear identification of installment divisions, too many critical studies ignore this important feature of the works' original reception. How important the simple time of reading a long novel can be is demonstrated again by one unusual feature of Thackeray's *Pendennis.*

In the course of publication, Thackeray became ill and the issue of Number 12 was delayed from October, 1849, to January, 1850. During this three-months' interruption in the original reading of Thackeray's Bildungsroman, the reader expanded elements of the novel even more than usual, and one key feature of all installment literary experience was underscored—the reader's inevitable affection for the characters.[19] Number 11 of *Pendennis* ends with Pen, the literary critic, suffering the first unfavorable review of his poems at the hands of a competitor: Mr. Bludyer, the reviewer,

> had a certain notoriety in his profession, and reputation for savage humor. He smashed and trampled down the poor spring flowers [Pen's poems] with no more mercy than a bull would have on a parterre; and having cut up the volume to his heart's content, went and sold it at a bookstall, and purchased a pint of brandy with the proceeds of the volume.   (I, 352)

This unflattering picture of the literary profession at the conclusion of the number, and others in the same issue, led to an extended debate in the press between John Forster, Thackeray, and others about the integrity of Victorian letters.[20] Part of the reason for the intensity of the debate may have been the extra time Number 11 of *Pendennis* stayed on the public's mind before it was succeeded by Number 12—three times as long as usual. The extra-long time between installments also added to the audience's involvement with the career of Arthur Pendennis, the protagonist of the novel.

Although Thackeray himself was unable in those three months to further the development of the central character in his Bildungsroman, his original reader lived with the novel's protagonist three months longer. When Number 12 of *Pendennis* did appear, it was warmly received by its readers, perhaps more warmly than it merited.[21] One reader's response to the reappearance of the lost fictional family of *Pendennis* is typical of the uncritical reception which Thackeray was allowed after his sickness and suggests the involvement his audience had with his characters:

> There were many thousands of readers who, when it was announced in the public prints, that owing to the serious indisposition of the author, the periodical issue of *Pendennis* was temporarily suspended, took the matter to heart as though some dear friend and cherished companion had been suddenly smitten like a child at play, and carried from the bright, cheerful, outer atmosphere to the darkness and stillness of the sick-chamber. He was lost to us for a while, and we missed him. Many, it is true, had freely exercised the "glorious privilege" of grumbling, and had complained, with critical regularity, once a month, that *Pendennis* was a "falling-off—not equal to *Vanity Fair*"; but they did not like to go without it for all that, and pushed eager questions into every quarter about the chance of its reappearance. And when it reappeared, after a painful interval of some months, grumblers and admirers alike rejoiced.[22]

Despite reservations about the quality of the novel, and even the attractiveness of its hero, this reviewer (and others) warmly, often sentimentally, welcomed back the fictional world which Thackeray had created. This extra-long gap between installments underscores the effects of serial publication: through the long months of reading—of the reader's, author's, and characters' association—critical objectivity decreased and a sense of shared life increased. The rhetorical tone of the review ("smitten like a child at play," "lost to us for a while," "the darkness and stillness of the sick-chamber") suggests the intensity of the serial reader's identification with the world of the fictional characters. The Victorian parts-reader carried the world of the novel into his own, real world, expanding and extending key elements of the author's creation to meet deeply felt personal and societal needs. The continued appearance of *Pendennis*, its hero and his company, reinforced the reader's awareness of his own continued existence, his success or his failure, his growth or decay. In a sense, the serial novel became a clock for the reader, measuring his movement through this world.

V

Thackeray's achievement in *Pendennis*, then, deserves increased recognition. He chronicles his protagonist's evolution from naive provincial youth to sophisticated London literary man and husband, avoiding some aspects of the conventional Bildungsroman formula because of his belief in the stability of character through time. Thackeray, however, takes special advantage of the dominant nineteenth-century genre—the serial novel—to further his protagonist's growth in the twenty-six-month length of his Bildungsroman. By stressing the passing of time in the reader's experience through a variety of narrative techniques, Thackeray keeps his protagonist always in motion in the eyes of his observer. The sense of development or change is consistently a part of the reader's response to the text, even though Pen may not be changing swiftly or dramatically in any one monthly installment. Even between parts, the reader's time is used to expand or extend key elements of the novel. Such interaction of the reader's world with the world of the fiction as the novel is coming out in installments is an aspect of the literary experience of many nineteenth-century masterpieces which needs further study. Although Thackeray, like some of his contemporaries and other novelists later in the century, felt some frustration with the process of serial composition—insisting, for instance, that his next novel, *Henry Esmond* (1852), not appear in parts—his major accomplishments are in that mode: *Vanity Fair* (1847–48) and *The Newcomes* (1853–55). The monthly appearance of a new issue of a nineteenth-century serial novel, by Thackeray, Dickens, Eliot, or another, meant two things to its readers: an extended life for the characters of that world (Rebecca Sharp, Arthur Pendennis, and Ethel Newcome continue to grow up); and an on-going life for the readers (who are growing up also). Thackeray's narrative skills are revealed in his ability to engage the reader's real existence (part of the novel's context) to supplement the fictional existence of his own creation (the novel's text).

NOTES

1. Jerome H. Buckley, *Season of Youth: The Bildungsroman from Dickens to Golding* (Cambridge, Mass.: Harvard University Press, 1974), p. 18.
2. Buckley, p. 29. Recent studies of *Pendennis* touching on the development of character include Robert Bledsoe, "*Pendennis* and the Power of Sentimentality," *PMLA*, 91 (1976), 871–883; Robert A. Colby, *Thackeray's Canvass of Humanity: An Author and his Public* (Columbus: Ohio State University Press, 1979); Ina Ferris, "The Demystification of Laura Pendennis," *Studies*

in the Novel, 13 (Summer, 1981), 122–132; and Thomas L. Jeffers, "Thackeray's *Pendennis*: Son and Gentleman," *Nineteenth-Century Fiction*, 33 (1978), 175–193.

3. *The Reader and the Text: Essays on Audience and Interpretation*, ed. Susan R. Suleiman and Inge Crosman (Princeton: Princeton University Press, 1980), p. 6.

4. *The Reader and the Text*, p. 5.

5. *Thackeray: The Age of Wisdom* (New York: McGraw-Hill Book Company, Inc., 1958); Edgar F. Harden, *The Emergence of Thackeray's Serial Fiction* (Athens: University of Georgia Press, 1979); John Sutherland, *Thackeray at Work* (London: The Athlone Press, 1974); and Colby (cited above). Colby in particular demonstrates how "*Pendennis* is best savored in connection with its original circumstances and milieu" (p. 304).

6. The shifting of "form" from its place within the text to a position in the reader's response to a text is one of Stanley Fish's contributions to the current debate. In summarizing the development of reader-oriented criticism, Jane P. Tompkins, in *Reader-Response Criticism: From Formalism to Post-structuralism*, ed. Jane P. Tompkins (Baltimore: The Johns Hopkins University Press, 1980), p. xxii, explains Fish's contention: "Texts are written by readers, not read, since, the argument now states, the formal features of the text, the authorial intentions they are normally taken to represent, and the reader's interpretive strategies are mutually interdependent."

7. William Makepeace Thackeray, *The History of Pendennis: His Fortunes and Misfortunes, His Friends and His Greatest Enemy* (London: Bradbury & Evans, 1848–1850), II, 210. I am citing here the original parts publication, the pagination of which corresponds to the later two-volume edition. Thus, Number 13 begins with page 1 of Volume II. Subsequent references to *Pendennis* will be made in the text and will include volume and page numbers in parentheses. For a detailed history of *Pendennis*'s publication, see Peter L. Shillingsburg, "Thackeray's *Pendennis* in America," *Papers of the Bibliographical Society of America*, 68 (1973), 325–329.

8. Buckley, p. 22.

9. A preface appeared at the end of the final double number, and in later editions is usually included at the beginning of the novel. For further analyses of Thackeray's narrative technique in this novel, see Edgar F. Harden, "Theatricality in *Pendennis*," *Ariel*, 4 (1973), 74–94; Barbara Hardy, *The Exposure of Luxury: Radical Themes in Thackeray* (Pittsburgh: University of Pittsburgh Press, 1972), pp. 37–45; and Juliet McMaster, *Thackeray: The Major Novels* (Toronto: University of Toronto Press, 1971), pp. 51–86.

10. "'The Philosopher's Property': Thackeray and the Use of Time," *Victorian Studies*, 10 (1967), 365.

11. Sudrann, 369.

12. *Character and the Novel* (Ithaca: Cornell University Press, 1965), p. 110. Harvey underestimates, I think, the effect of serialization on the reception a novel might enjoy, calling it only "a minor point" (p. 111); but his observations about the form have given me considerable direction in this study.

13. Martin Fido, "*The History of Pendennis*: A Reconsideration," *Essays in Criticism*, 14 (1964), 363–379, also discusses the reader's coming to find out who Laura is in the first two numbers of the novel. James Wheatley, *Patterns in Thackeray's Fiction* (Cambridge, Mass.: The M.I.T. Press, 1969), p. 135, has justly praised *Pendennis*'s first two numbers as "a unit as controlled and sustained as anything he ever wrote."

14. Another conspicuous example of this technique occurs in Number 9, where Altamont/Amory confronts his daughter, Betsy/Blanche. Before Amory has the chance to reveal his identity, the sound of disturbance in the nearby ballroom distracts these characters *and* the narrator. Thackeray then backs up the narrative to account for the noise of the confrontation between Pen and Miroblant.

15. I have made the same point, more briefly, in reference to *David Copperfield* in "Clocking the Reader in the Long Victorian Novel," *Victorian Newsletter*, No. 59 (Spring, 1981), 23–24.

16. For other aspects of Thackeray's composition, see Edgar F. Harden, "The Serial Structure of Thackeray's *Pendennis*," *Revue de l'Universite d'Ottawa*, 45 (1974), 167–180. Wheatley, p. 106, has also drawn attention to the process of Pen's growth as a series of falls which lead to wisdom, but fails to link it to the novel's serial structure. In the "Introduction" to the Penguin *Pendennis* (Baltimore: Penguin Books, 1972), J. I. M. Stewart touches briefly on the effects of installment structure when he observes that the narrator's style in the novel is "welcome whenever he drops in on us (*Pen* dropped in, after all, in monthly parts); and we are quickly led, somehow, to acquiesce in the assumption that just this is what, at the moment, we require of a novel" (p. 10). Robert A. Colby, *Fiction with a Purpose* (Bloomington: Indiana University Press, 1967), pp. 138–177, also discusses some of the effects of serialization, including response to many of the novel's illustrations. At one point, he specifically points to things Victorians "could have been reading in between the installments of *Pen*" (p. 148), which would have also affected the ways in which the audience reacted to the protagonist's growth.

17. Jeffers, p. 185, explains this episode within the context of Pen's sexual development.

18. In "Teaching Long Victorian Novels in Parts," *Victorian Newsletter*, No 58 (Fall, 1980), 29–32, I explore how this extended time frame can be copied in the classroom.

19. Peter L. Shillingsburg, "The First Edition of Thackeray's *Pendennis*," *Papers of the Bibliographical Society of America*, 66 (1971), 42, points out that a reason behind the demands for reprints of the early numbers "may have been pressure from readers made impatient by the four-month delay in the publication of volume one as a whole, imposed by Thackeray's illness."

20. Ray, pp. 113–116 and pp. 136–138, summarizes the dispute.

21. Ray, p. 109, notes that "Thackeray's contemporaries found Pen's battle with himself and eventual redemption intensely interesting: to later readers it has seemed increasingly insipid." Although much modern disfavor is a response to Thackeray's treatment of certain issues, complaints like Robert Alan Dono-

van's that "Thackeray's imaginative vision does not confront life as process, as a continuing movement of development and change," in *The Shaping Vision: Imagination in the English Novel from Defoe to Dickens* (Ithaca: Cornell University Press, 1966), p. 199, seem to me to miss much of the original character of the work.

22. David Masson, "The Literary Profession," *Eclectic Magazine*, 21 (November, 1850), 364; reprinted from *North British Review*, 13 (August, 1850). See also *The Literary World* (February 16, 1850), where a reviewer notes that Thackeray's illness "darkened the cheerfulness of club rooms" (p. 151).

Wilkie Collins's Suicides: "Truth As It Is in Nature"

Barbara T. Gates

The violence of murder and accidental death fascinated Victorian novelists as it did the Victorian public. Dickens never tired of reading his own words on the death of Nancy in *Oliver Twist* or of providing dramatic endings for characters like her murderer, Sykes, who swung from his noose suffering "a terrific convulsion of the limbs."[1] Nancy's and Sykes's deaths are far from unique in the writing of Dickens and his contemporaries. Citing *Bleak House* as his example of the "foul" concern with death in the contemporary novel, John Ruskin catalogued all eleven of its deaths or deaths-to-be, noting among them assassination, spontaneous combustion, insanity and "a lively young French-woman left to be hanged."[2] "All of these deaths," he went on, "are grotesquely either violent or miserable, purporting thus to illustrate the modern theology that the appointed destiny of a large average of our population is to die like rats in a drain, either by trap or poison."[3]

Conspicuously missing from Ruskin's list is an overt act of suicide. The subject of self-destruction through self-murder was not widely offered to the middle-class readers of mainstream Victorian novels. Eliot's Hetty lacks the courage for the act. Trollope creates an occasional Melmotte or Lopez, clichés of ruined businessmen. And Dickens has Merdle and a few down-and-out ruined women—in a sense Merdle's female counterparts in cliché, debased through sex, not finance, whose final fall is usually from one of London's bridges. Cruikshank's famous eighth plate from *The Drunkard's Children* titled and pictured such a fall: "The Maniac Father and The convict Brother are Gone.—The poor Girl, Homeless, Friendless, Deserted, Destitute, and Gin Mad, Commits Self Murder." In the plate, a pathetic young woman plunges through the air while two shocked bourgeois figures—a man in top hat and a woman—look on more in horror than in pity. Since novelists like Dickens and Trollope knew their readers well, it would appear that bourgeois novel readers, who so loved Victorian studies in scarlet, wanted the line drawn at self-destruction.

There were, I believe, good reasons for this. Most Victorians feared suicide far more than they did murder. Certainly both acts were subversive, contrary to the Ten Commandments and to Victorian secular notions of self-help and the judicious exercise of will-power, but suicide was more easily internalized than murder. A writer for *Temple Bar* observed of murder and murderers that "there is always something agreeable to us in the misfortunes of our neighbours. It would certainly seem as though a record of their vices is eminently pleasing."[4] Self-murder, on the other hand, could lead to a painful inner search for motives. Murder might also satisfy the Victorian sense of justice, since murderers could be caught and imprisoned or in turn be killed for their crimes—an eye for an eye; suicide however, was an audacious personal challenge to the will of God in which human justice could never really intervene. Thus if murder caused sensation among the Victorians, suicide was a source of anxiety and disgrace. Middle-class families took great pains to disguise suicide, with physicians sometimes cooperating in the concealment.[5] Such collusion occurred not only because suicide was immoral and illegal but also because the insanity plea was the only way of saving the property of a proven suicide from reverting to the Crown. Victorian families of a *felo-de-se*, the legal term for suicide, faced the awful dilemma of choosing the lesser of two evils: hereditary insanity as a future stigma, or poverty as an immediate prospect, at least if the suicide were a breadwinner. These alternatives—little better than Dickens' choice of a slow death in the workhouse or a quick one out of it for the poor—were to be avoided at all costs. Clergy as well as medical men were enlisted in cover-ups, since until the 1880s proven suicides could not be buried in consecrated ground.

Because suicide was taboo as a subject in Victorian England, only a few early and mid-Victorian novelists were willing to make it central to their fiction. Those who did were mainly writers living outside the sphere of cosmopolitan, English mores. In Yorkshire, Emily Brontë based the remote, cosmic and violent world of *Wuthering Heights* in a plot that revolves around the suicides of her first generation of characters.[6] While Sheridan Le Fanu, removed from Victorian England both through his Irish blood and his extraordinary psychological use of the Gothic, wove bizzare suicides into the pages of stories like "Green Tea" and novels like *Checkmate, Uncle Silas, Willing to Die,* and *A Lost Name.* But until suicide law was liberalized in the 1880s and suicide became more widely discussed, there was in Victorian England only one well-known novelist whose work included suicide after suicide: Wilkie Collins.

One might expect the "sensation school" of novelists, with whom Collins is usually grouped, to have invented countless self-murders. Their aims included revealing hidden secrets like incest, bigamy, and murder; they introduced into fiction what Henry James called "those most mysterious of mysteries, the mysteries which are at our own doors."[7] Yet the secrecy and mystery of suicide were not subjects that most sensation novelists wanted to reveal, and Collins's avidly read fellow sensationalists included few suicides among their high toll of violent deaths. Collins however moved ever more deeply into what Ulrich Knoepflmacher calls "the counterworld of Victorian fiction"—a world of amorality and darkness, "opposed to the lawful, ordered Victorian values to which novelist and reader tacitly agreed to subscribe."[8] From *Antonina* in 1850 at the beginning of his career to *Blind Love* in 1890 at its end, Collins painted a whole gallery of self-destructives, ranging from Roman nobles to lonely, isolated wives and mothers, amoral heroines, crazed vivisectionists, and discredited barons. Their violent ends both offer insight into Collins's relationship with his intended audience and elucidate Collins's special talent for portrayal of character.

To the distraction of Dickens and others of Collins's immediate contemporaries and literary friends, Collins never shed a desire to shock the bourgeoisie. In large part drawing upon the same middle-class readership as did Dickens and Trollope, he resented its pretensions far more than did Dickens, who always wished to belong to the class whose follies so often irked and dismayed him. Collins's prefaces and essays characteristically lectured this middle-class public, warning it to set aside narrow-minded notions of what was or was not acceptable in fiction:

> Readers in particular will, I have some reason to suppose, be here and there disturbed, perhaps even offended, by finding that "Armadale" over-steps, in more than one direction, the narrow limits within which they are disposed to restrict the development of modern fiction—if they can. Nothing that I could say to these persons here would help me with them as Time will help me if my work lasts. I am not afraid of my design being permanently misunderstood, provided the execution has done it any sort of justice. Estimated by the clap-trap morality of the present day, this may be a very daring book.

Judged by the Christian morality which is of all time, it is only a book that is daring enough to speak the truth.[9]

Phrases like "clap-trap morality" worried Dickens who, a few years before this preface to *Armadale*, warned his sub-editor for *Household Words* to "look well to Wilkie's article. . . and not to leave anything in it that may be sweeping, and unnecessarily offensive to the middle class. He always has a tendency to overdo that."[10] All the same, the illegal, the immoral, and the shocking continued to fascinate Collins, who thought the middle class needed to think about such things and was not afraid to use fiction to portray life's offenses. He wanted to give "the truth as it is in Nature,"[11] not to exclude the violence, obsession, or despair which he saw as basic to human nature, itself red in tooth and claw. Thus in the preface to *The Law and the Lady* (1875), Collins warned his readers that "characters which may not have appeared, events which may not have taken place, within the limits of our own individual experience, may nevertheless be perfectly natural Characters and perfectly probable Events for all that."[12] Earlier, in his essays in *Household Words* in the late 1850s, he had envied Balzac the free choice of subjects which made him unfit reading for lovers of English novels and had showed interest in reaching and educating an "Unknown Public" of three million English readers who devoured penny-novel journals. And still later, in the preface to *Jezebel's Daughter* (1880), he would complain that "there are certain important social topics which are held to be forbidden to the English novelist. . . by a narrow-minded minority of readers, and. . . the critics who flatter their prejudices."[13]

Certainly one of those topics was suicide, a subject that appealed to Collins both because it was subversive and because it was an ultimate test of character. Collins's novels involving suicides are not formulaic. No suicide in Collins is unmotivated, nor is self-destruction divorced from the painful social conflicts that beset character. By the 1860s when the sensation novel dealing with modern life had come into its own, Collins's characters begin to contemplate suicide as a solution to contemporary moral dilemmas. Like him, they are doubters of both human and divine justice. Magdalen Vanstone (*No Name*, 1862), whose personal struggle to attain legitimacy after finding out that her loving parents, now dead, were never legally married, becomes the focus of such a dilemma. Magdalen is at the center of Collins's plot and of his preface, where the novelist insists that he means her to personify the war between Good and Evil raging within one individual. At the turning point of the novel Magdalen must, however, choose not between good and evil but between two evils:

whether to throw herself into a river or to trick her cousin, Noel Vanstone, into marrying her and through him reclaim her name and rightful inheritance. Suicide seems the nobler way, but Magdalen chooses deceit. Successful in ensnaring the foolish, weak Vanstone, she then approaches her wedding day with total revulsion and redetermines to die, this time by laudanum:

> The bottle was so small, that it lay easily in the palm of her hand. She let it remain there for a little while, and stood looking at it.
> 'DEATH!' she said. 'In this drop of brown drink—DEATH!' As the words passed her lips, an agony of unutterable horror seized on her in an instant. She crossed the room unsteadily with a maddening confusion in her head, with a suffocating anguish at her heart. She caught at the table to support herself. The faint clink of the bottle, as it fell harmlessly from her loosened grasp, and rolled against some porcelain object on the table, struck through her brain like the stroke of a knife. The sound of her own voice, sunk to a whisper—her voice only uttering that one word, DEATH—rushed in her ears like the rushing of a wind. She dragged herself to the bedside, and rested her head against it, sitting on the floor.
> 'Oh, my life!' she thought; 'what is my life worth, that I cling to it like this?'[14]

Broken in resolve, she leaves her life to "chance." Watching a fleet of coasting vessels, she determines to kill herself if an odd number of them passes by her window within a half hour's time. When instead an even number floats by, she feels newly born—Providence, not "chance" is on her side. Magdalen is, however, practical and skeptical enough to keep a little laudanum in reserve—just in case it was not Providence acting after all.

Throughout *No Name*, Collins engages his readers' sympathy for this deluded, divided woman. Magdalen is spirited, bright, resourceful—and she can be very kind. For the foolish wife of Captain Wragge, her partner in entrapping Noel, she feels genuine love and compassion. Finding Mrs. Wragge "the only innocent creature in this guilty house,"[15] she takes her to her heart as well as into her quarters. Moreover, from the beginning Magdalen is herself society's victim, as are many of Collins's heroines, all of whom may have as their proto-type Caroline Graves, the real and once-suicidal "woman in white." To escape the taint of illegitimacy, Magdalen makes a truly illegitimate marriage. Tricked out in disguises, acting one part and then another to fool Noel and become somebody, she loses her original selfhood, even in her own eyes; contemplating suicide, she validates the absurd legal image of herself as nonexistent. But Collins must have felt this dose was too strong for readers to swallow in 1862.

Much as he provided Caroline with his own support from 1854 onwards, he ultimately provides Magdalen with a nurturing, redemptive sister in Norah and an acceptable husband in a minor character named Captain Kirke ("church"), who appears at the novel's contrived conclusion.

Not so fortunate is Lydia Gwilt in Collins's next novel, *Armadale* (1866). More brilliant, more evil, more intriguing than Magdalen, Lydia is beyond human redeeming. Unlike Magdalen, she knows who she is and appears to know what she wants: Allan Armadale's money. She plots to marry the kindly Ozias Midwinter under his concealed real name, Allan Armadale, and eventually to murder Armadale, deny Midwinter, and claim the vast Armadale inheritance. But all goes awry for her: she nearly kills Midwinter in place of Armadale, then saves Midwinter and kills herself. Despite her malicious intentions and evil machinations, our sympathy for Lydia builds early in the second volume of *Armadale* with the introduction of "Miss Gwilt's Diary." Lydia, we find, has terrible pangs of conscience over using Midwinter as a pawn and thinks longingly about what it would have been like to raise his children. She too finds consolation in laudanum—as did Collins in the 1860s, when his health was beginning to fail—but through the drug she finds her usual readiness for any occasion slipping away. Unlike Magdalen's, Lydia Gwilt's meditations on her situation—"without prospects, friends, or hopes of any kind—a lost woman"—are violent:

> "What is the way? I can't see it. I could tear my own hair off my head! I could burn the house down! If there was a train of gunpowder under the whole world, I could light it, and blow the whole world to destruction—I am in such a rage, such a frenzy with myself for not seeing it!
> "Poor dear Midwinter! Yes, '*dear*.' I don't care. I'm lonely and helpless. I want somebody who is gentle and loving to make much of me; I wish I had his head on my bosom again; I have a good mind to go to London and marry him. Am I mad? Yes; all people who are as miserasble as I am are mad. I must go to the window and get some air. Shall I jump out? No; it disfigures one so, and the coroner's inquest lets so many people see it."[16]

Miserable like Magdalen, Lydia is nevertheless not "mad" enough to lose perspective, to leave her fate to chance, or to tear the web of appearances that she has so carefully spun around herself. Once, long before, she had been deceived by a bigamist and might then have been desperate enough to attempt suicide, but Miss Gwilt is a survivor, at least for a time. Her hard-headed intelligence, sense of humor, and ingenuity set to work to allay her pain and win her reader sympathy.

Without doubt, Lydia Gwilt's eventual suicide is intended as atonement. Guilt and atonement are keys to *Armadale*, where Midwinter feels

guilt for his father's murder of Allan Armadale's father and atones by becoming Armadale's protector; and in the end Lydia feels guilt for a whole
lifetime of deceit and crime. She has driven others to death—a poor married music master, for example, who tried to blow out his brains for love
of her. Her name, Gwilt, sums up her final realization. So to Midwinter
she says:

> "Forget me, my darling, in the love of a better woman than I am. I might,
> perhaps, have been that better woman myself, if I had not lived a miserable
> life before you met with me. It matters little now. The one atonement I can
> make for all the wrong I have done you is the atonement of my death. It is
> not hard for me to die, now I know you will live. Even my wickedness has
> one merit—it has not prospered. I have never been a happy woman."[17]

And to God, after poisoning herself with the purple flask intended for
Allan Armadale:

> "Oh, God, forgive me!" she said. "Oh, Christ, bear witness that I have suf-
> fered!"[18]

Magdalen Vanstone and Lydia Gwilt are in many ways typical of the
sensation heroines of the 1860s, sisters to Mary Braddon's Lady Audley.
They are daring outcasts, women whose combination of intelligence and
strong will lends excitement to the novels in which they appear, yet who
are punished according to the severity of their crimes. By the 1870s, however, Collins's novels follow fewer of the melodramatic, crime-and-
punishment patterns expected by readers of sensation novels. "Miss
Gwilt's death quite upset me,"[19] Collins would say, and he would never
give us another suicide like it. As early as the 1860s Collins was disil-
lusioned with the limited world view of the sensationalists. For him fate or
Providence had "lost its effectiveness as the controlling mechanism of an
ordered and predictable universe"[20] after *Armadale*.

Nowhere is this more in evidence than in Collins's next two novels
presenting suicides, *The Law and the Lady* (1875) and *The Fallen Leaves*
(1879). "Providence has its favourites," says Mrs. Farnaby in *The Fallen
Leaves*, and I am not one of them."[21] Even in her means of self-destruction, Mrs. Farnaby is unlucky. Her death by strychnine poisoning becomes grotesquely violent and horrible:

> The fell action of the strychnine wrung every muscle in her with the torture
> of convulsion. Her hands were fast clenched; her head was bent back: her
> body, rigid as a bar of iron, was arched upward from the bed, resting on the
> two extremities of the head and the heels: the staring eyes, the dusky face,
> the twisted lips, the clenched teeth, were frightful to see.[22]

Far more sinned against than sinning, Mrs. Farnaby would not deserve such an ignominious death if one's way of life determined one's death. Cheated by her own husband, who spirited away their tiny baby, she has mourned and sought her daughter for sixteen years. Suicide is a final act of despair over her lack of success in finding the girl.

Collins's delineation of Mrs. Farnaby's character is the strongest element in an otherwise weak novel. She is one of a gallery of characters in the later novels whose tormented deaths actually help bring the novels alive, a haunted woman whom we follow step by step on her journey to suicide. Long before we know of her secret grief over her daughter, her eyes betray her as one who "lives in some . . . hell of her own making, and longs for the release of death; and is so full of bodily life and strength, that she may carry her burden with her to the utmost verge of life."[23] Mrs. Farnaby is also painfully sane, like Lydia Gwilt. Collins's women do not escape easily into madness, as do many sensation heroines, but instead they cope with their suffering. Mrs. Farnaby tries "every means of relief"[24] from her mourning: she writes, learns foreign languages, smokes cigars, learns Euclid, uses a microscope, works at a lathe, and swings Indian clubs and dumb-bells until she is so fatigued that she drops to the floor and finds oblivion in an hour or two of forgetful sleep. Religious consolations, sought at the last minute even by Lydia Gwilt, Mrs. Farnaby renounces as useless to her, just as Collins did. Her tears are under control, but her heart remains broken.

Mrs. Farnaby is ably drawn as a woman full of paradoxes. Collins watches her despair, "still unconsciously deceiving itself under the disguise of hope,"[25] and traces both her conscious and unconscious motivation. Her whole nature is maternal, and her graphic dreams of reunion with her daughter keep her searching on and out into a world beyond the prison of a home where she is locked up with the man who first betrayed her. That world too betrays her, for it is the unfair, unpredictable world of Collins's novels of the 70s, a world that drives its inhabitants to desperation. It finally tricks this physically strong woman—who will not yield to "the unutterable misery that wrung her to the soul"[26]—into believing her daughter forever unattainable. This same ironic world ultimately discovers her Sally to Mrs. Farnaby only on her agonizing deathbed. Yet Mrs. Farnaby's death does not end her story. A suicide letter and coroner's inquest remain to lend still more irony to the world of the novel. In the letter, Mrs. Farnaby, soon to fall victim to the violent convulsions, writhings, and paroxysms of agony caused by strychnine, believes that she goes to her death as one goes to sleep when tired. In the inquest, the inquiry yields a verdict of "Death by Misadventure." The true story of Mrs. Farnaby's life and death remains known only to Collins's protagonist, Amelius, and to Collins's readers. Victorian readers and critics alike were, however, quick to pronounce this painful novel of life lived in *in extremis* as one of Collins's failures. This particular counterworld was more than they could tolerate.

As Collins discovered by the 1870s, the secrecy surrounding suicides made them fitting subjects for the detective novel. Both *The Law and the Lady* and the later *I Say "No"* (1884) are unraveled through the discovery of suicide. In neither book is there a detailed portrait of a self-murderer like Mrs. Farnaby, nor is there suspense as to whether a character like Magdalen Vanstone will take his or her own life. Instead the suicides in this detective fiction have taken place long before the openings of the novels and are discovered only as the action unfolds. But character is still of the utmost concern here. In murder stories the reader wants to find the murderer: who did it? what was his or her motive? In these detective novels of suicide, the question ultimately becomes not who killed the dead person but why he or she should want to die. Motivation is still the key to truth, but all judgments must be based upon historical record or partial knowledge, since the self-murderer has passed from the scene. Suspense is heightened as we search for absolute truth and can only find partial truths. Drama is increased as we ourselves become the detectives.

The Law and the Lady emphasizes all this by offering as its detective/protagonist/first-person narrator a woman who stands most to gain by discovering the story's secret. Valeria Macallan is second wife to a man with a past. He has married Valeria under an assumed name, Eustace Macallan, to cover the fact that he has been tried for allegedly poisoning his first wife, Sara. At the time of Sara's death in Scotland, a jury could return a verdict of "Not Proven," allowing a person like Macallan his freedom, but condemning him to shame. When Valeria eventually learns Macallan's story after her marriage to him, her humiliated husband wants to leave her for her own sake. To keep him she is determined to exonerate him, and so turns detective. What she uncovers is a concealment of suicide that has been so successful that even Macallan himself has been unaware of it. Sara, who had originally tricked him into marriage, had become so distraught over Macallan's indifference to her that she had poisoned herself with arsenic pathetically purchased to clear her complexion and make her more attractive to her husband.

The true "secret" of this very dramatic story is that rejection in love followed by suicide is a verdict more terrible than "Murder Not Proven."

Sara Macallan's self-destruction—and it is that from start to finish—will never be revealed to the world. Valeria uncovers a suicide letter indicating in Sara a misery so deep that life no longer held any interest for her, and a love so obsessive that a mere smile from Macallan might have saved her. Concealment had begun immediately, through an eccentric admirer of Sara's, abetted by a physician, but it is carefully continued by Valeria, the woman who wanted truth at all costs:

> There, on the table before me, lay the triumphant vindication of my hus-
> band's innocence; and, in mercy to him, in mercy to the memory of his dead
> wife, my one hope was that he might never see it! My one desire was to hide
> it from the public view![27]

Valeria is "sickened" and "horrified" by this letter but ultimately feels she must at least offer it to Macallan. She leaves to him the decision to read or not to read:

> "Let me be sure that I know exactly what it is I have to decide," he proceeds.
> "Suppose I insist on reading the letter—?"
>   There I interrupt him. I know it is my duty to restrain myself. But I cannot
> do my duty.
>   "My darling, don't talk of reading the letter! Pray, pray spare
> yourself—."
>   He holds up his hands for silence.
>   "I am not thinking of myself," he says. "I am thinking of my dead wife.
> If I give up the public vindication of my innocence, in my own lifetime—if I
> leave the seal of the letter unbroken—do you say, as Mr. Playmore says,
> that I shall be acting mercifully and tenderly toward the memory of the
> wife?"
>   "Oh, Eustace, there cannot be the shadow of a doubt to it!"
>   "Shall I be making some little atonement to any pain that I may have
> thoughtlessly caused her to suffer in her lifetime?"
>   "Yes! yes!"[28]

Macallan foregoes the reading, and the verdict of "Not Proven" stands, but the Macallans are spared the further taint of a suicide revealed in their past.

By the 1880s, just after the death by a self-inflicted wound to the throat of Collins's old and close friend, the largely unappreciated painter, Edward Mathew Ward, in January of 1879, there are still more significant changes in Collins's fictional presentations of suicides. They are now men, not women, and their deaths are even more violent than Mrs. Farnaby's. Ward himself lay dying for five days. In I Say "No", the second of Collins's detective novels involving a suicide, the *felo-de-se* is described in the manner of a Victorian newspaper account, a graphic, seemingly dispassionate style that fails to blanket the underlying horror:

> The internal jugular vein had been cut through, with such violence, judging by the appearances, that the wound could not have been inflicted, in the act of suicide, by the hand of the deceased person.[29]

The bloody secret of this act of self-violence is kept through a cover-up quite true to life in Victorian England. Concealment here is instigated by a friend of the family, Sir Richard, a "great London surgeon" whose efforts are carefully described:

> "He went with Miss Letitia to the inquest; he won over the coroner and the newspaper men to his will; he kept your aunt's name out of the papers; he took charge of the coffin; he hired the undertaker and his men, strangers from London; he wrote the certificate—who but he! Everybody was cap in hand to the famous man!"[30]

This suicide is discovered only years later. James Brown, the victim, was a man who like Sara Macallan suffered from unrequited love. Again his means of death have been unknown to his beloved, who finds out about her lover from his now-grown daughter and responds with a stock Victorian reaction, along with no little remorse for once having said "no" to poor Brown:

> "Do you suppose I could for a moment anticipate that he would destroy himself, when I wrote my reply? He was a truly religious man. If he had been in his right mind, he would have shrunk from the idea of suicide as from the idea of a crime."[31]

One reason why she deduces that Brown must have been insane at the time of his death is that she knows a deliberate suicide would quite literally be guilty of crime.

So any conventional Victorian would have thought. Collins, as we have seen, thought differently. For him, cruelty was crime. His James Brown's sane despair becomes clear enough as the story unfolds, though he is never seen in so pitiful a light as Sara Macallan. The unrequited love of a male is an unorthodox theme in Victorian novels, where women die like Didos but men, like Trollope's Lopez, more often die for money. In this case Collins stays closer to the confines of orthodoxy. Still, there is daring in Collins's portrayal of Brown and "truth to Nature" in Collins's assessment of the cover-up and choice of the means for Brown's suicide. Victorian statistical tables and court proceedings show a higher incidence of the use of sharp instruments in male suicides and of poisons in female *felo-de-ses.*[32] Collins kept his suicides true to the trends, consulting Jacques Peuchet's six-volume *Mémoires tirés des archives de la police de Paris* (1838), with its actuarial study of suicide, which he held as a significant part of his personal library.[33]

By the time Collins wrote *Heart and Science* in 1883, his sympathy for suicidal characters led him into a serious artistic problem. Here the suicide is a vivisectionist in an avowedly anti-vivisectionist novel. Even more than Lydia Gwilt's death, Dr. Benjulia's self-set conflagration in his laboratory is intended as punishment for evil ways. But Collins seems to have liked Benjulia in the way that Dickens liked Fagin, not because he is a good man but because he is intent on and knowledgeable in his profession and pitiable in his defeat. Benjulia is Faustian, will stop at nothing to ensure his longed-for medical breakthrough. Like Gwilt, he knows what he is doing and seems willing to pay the price:

> "My last experiments on a monkey horrified me. His cries of suffering, his gestures of entreaty, were like the cries and gestures of a child. I would have given the world to put him out of his misery. But I went on. In the glorious cause I went on. My hands turned cold—my heart ached—I thought of a child I sometimes play with—I suffered—I resisted—I went on. All for Knowledge! all for Knowledge!"[34]

This perverse kind of tenacity both alarms and softens reader response to Benjulia. We know he is "horrified" because we have seen his tenderness toward good little Zo, a girl who is his one genuine admirer in this book. Yet in order to proceed with his research, he becomes willing to allow not just animals but young women to face death. Heart consistently loses to science in Benjulia's world until finally the doctor is anticipated in his discovery and violently sets both himself and his animals free from science's grasp. Here again Collins does not leave his character after the suicide but in a kind of coda to his story adds an inquest that further modifies our conception of the now-dead doctor:

> Where were the motives? One intelligent man, who had drifted into the jury, was satisfied with the evidence. He held that the desperate wretch had some reason of his own for first poisoning himself, and then setting fire to the scene of his labours. Having a majority of eleven against him, the wise juryman consented to a merciful verdict of death by misadventure. The hideous remains of what had once been Benjulia, found Christian burial. His brethren of the torture-table attended the funeral in large numbers. Vivisection had been beaten on its own field of discovery. They honoured the martyr who had fallen in their cause.[35]

Somehow Benjulia has been forgiven his cruel vivisection and we, like his colleagues, are expected to see him more as the martyr than the persecutor.

In the end this narrative sympathy extends to all of Collins's suicides, perhaps because Collins felt some affinity with the maimed and strange pariahs who inhabited the borderlands of Victorian society. His suicides become his ultimate outcasts—dead-ended, through with society, hopeless of reconciliation. Not a religious man himself, Wilkie Collins was willing to forgive his characters the worst of all sins: despair. This concern with suicide as an act of hopelessness, rather than atonement as in *Armadale*, along with Collins's increased use of detail about the self-destroyers and his switch from women to men as suicidal characters suggest that the ailing Collins felt more and more empathy with them as his physical health deteriorated. During years of illness, extending from the 1860s through to the 1880s when Collins became a semi-invalid and all but a hermit because of intense attacks of gout and rheumatic pain, he seems to have found truth in suffering, and to have relayed it through the people of his novels. Contemporary descriptions of Collins after the failure in health are startlingly like his own descriptions of characters like Mrs. Farnaby. Rudolf Lehman, who painted Collins's portrait in 1880, saw before him a man whose eyes "had a weird, far-off look about them."[36] We recall Mrs. Farnaby's eyes, reflecting her self-made hell.

In our own century, Alethea Hayter has attributed Collins's sympathy with outcasts to his use of opium, begun the year he was writing *No Name* and continued throughout his life. Hayter finds Collins's sensitivity typical of users, whose insights into deformity are remarkable. To her mind, Collins's continual dosing with opium eventually took a toll on his writing:

> His faculty of observation of external objects began to be deadened; his understanding of normal human beings turned into mechanical characterization; his fascination with abnormal human conditions—deformity, disease, insanity—became more morbid. At its best it was real humanitarian sympathy, but there was often something less admirable about it, a tinge of excitement, of obsession.[37]

In terms of his suicidal characters, I believe this judgment is true, certainly of the books of the 1880s. Benjulia and Brown are far more morbid and mechanical than is Lydia Gwilt, for example; though Collins might simply have found it harder—because closer to home—to portray male *felo-de-ses*. I am, however, inclined to agree with Kenneth Robinson that Collins never really developed the obsessions of an opium addict. Robinson credits Collins's sense of pity to "the morbid expression of some deep psychological maladjustment, the causes and precise nature of which are obscure"[38] both because of Collins's reserve and the dearth of contemporary documents by and about him. Focusing on Collins's suicidal outcasts, I have tried further to suggest that the author's compassion for them in their needs and violent despair stems from his love and sympathy for suicidal friends like Caroline and Ward and ultimately from his own darkening view of the universe. Commitment to "truth as it is in Nature" inspired Collins to show not just the grey within people like Magdalen Vanstone but the blackness of existence for people like Mrs. Farnaby, whose life ends in total eclipse. Mrs. Farnaby is trapped in a Hardyesque universe; no matter how hard she works to extricate herself, that universe conspires to defeat her. Still, none of Collins's characters is suicidal by temperament. The blows life deals them or their misapprehensions of the relative insignificance of their own wills drive them to end their lives.

Collins never allowed these suicidal characters to carry his novels to their conclusions, just as throughout his illnesses he never quit working, fighting pain, or caring. He managed the traditional, mid-Victorian happy ending to books full of wretchedness. Magdalen Vanstone advances the action of *No Name*, but sweet and stoical Norah resolves the plot. Like Carlyle, Tennyson, and so many other Victorian writers, Collins was driven both to reveal suffering and to work through to a positive and not always believable conclusion in his writing. If in addition to his physical afflictions Collins was truly marked by some deep and now indefinable psychological maladjustment, as Robinson believes, he may have found a way to exorcise it through fiction. With his Magdalens and Benjulias he could descend into laudanum, misery, anger, frustration, and alienation; with his Norahs and Zos he could re-emerge from this bleak world of experience and escape to innocence. Even while presenting the grim and violent subject of self-destruction, Collins thus managed to appeal to an audience who, like Arnold, wanted to find a sunrise at the end of dark night.

NOTES

1. London: Oxford University Press, 1949, p. 391.
2. *The Complete Works of John Ruskin*, ed. E. T. Cook and Alexander Wedderburn (London: George Allen, 1908), XXXIV, 272.
3. *Ibid.*

4. "Our Novels. The Sensation School," *Temple Bar*, XXIX (1870), 424.

5. See my "Suicide and the Victorian Physicians," *Journal of the History of the Behavioral Sciences*, 16 (1980), 164–174.

6. See my "Suicide and *Wuthering Heights,*" *VN*, 50 (1976), 15–19.

7. Quoted in Kathleen Tillotson, "The Lighter Reading of the 1860's," an introduction to Wilkie Collins's *The Woman in White* (Boston: Houghton Mifflin, 1969), p. xvi.

8. "The Counterworld of Victorian Fiction and *The Woman in White*," in *The Worlds of Victorian Fiction*, ed. Jerome H. Buckley (Cambridge, Mass.: Harvard University Press, 1975), p. 352.

9. *The Works of Wilkie Collins* (New York: Peter Fenelon Collier, *ca.* 1900), VIII, "Preface."

10. Quoted in Richard Stang, *The Theory of the Novel in England, 1850–1870* (New York: Columbia University Press, 1959), p. 200.

11. Preface to *No Name* (New York: Stein and Day, 1967).

12. *Works*, V, (3).

13. *Works*, XXVII, 5–6.

14. *No Name*, pp. 388–389.

15. *Ibid.*, p. 307.

16. *Works*, VIII, 158.

17. *Ibid.*, p. 599.

18. *Ibid.*, p. 560.

19. Quoted in Kenneth Robinson, *Wilkie Collins: A Biography* (1951; rpt. London: Davis–Poynter, 1974), p. 173.

20. Winifred Hughes, *The Maniac in the Cellar: Sensation Novels of the 1860s* (Princeton: Princeton University Press, 1980), p. 161.

21. *Works*, XXI, 394.

22. *Ibid.*, 406.

23. *Ibid.*, 89.

24. *Ibid.*, 123.

25. *Ibid.*, 134.

26. *Ibid.*, 397.

27. *Works*, V, 535.

28. *Ibid.*, p. 558.

29. *Works*, XXIX, 191.

30. *Ibid.*, p. 390.

31. *Ibid.*, p. 501.

32. See especially Forbes Winslow, *The Anatomy of Suicide* (London: Henry Renshaw, 1840), William Wynn Westcott, *Suicide: Its History, Literature, Jurisprudence, Causation and Prevention. A Social Science Treatise* (London: H. K. Lewis, 1885), and Henry Morselli, *Suicide An Essay in Comparative Moral Statistics* (London: Kegan Paul, 1881).

33. See Nuell Pharr Davis, *The Life of Wilkie Collins* (Urbana: University of Illinois Press, 1956), pp. 168–169.

34. *Works*, XXV, 278.

35. *Ibid.*, p. 533.

36. Quoted in Robinson, p. 269.

37. *Opium and the Romantic Imagination* (Berkeley: University of California Press, 1970), p. 270.

38. Robinson, p. 302.

George Eliot and Objects:
Meaning as Matter in
The Mill on the Floss

John Kucich

It is a commonplace to observe that George Eliot's early novels cherish
a world of objects. It is equally well understood that these objects are
never purely natural, or "noumenal," but that they are always embedded
in human centers of meaning. We have grown comfortable with the notion that Eliot values natural objects only insofar as they serve human
knowledge, motives, and needs; that she considered an intimate relation
between man and matter to be one phase of her moral program. In a representative way, Bernard Paris claims that Eliot, as a realist, may have
had "a spontaneous delight in concrete reality," but only as a "starting
point," since "the sophisticated realist, like the scientist, wants to add to
our knowledge of the nature of things." Eliot's aim was finally to digest
"concrete reality" for man's general improvement:

> like most of the other positivists, she wanted not only to describe, but also to
> relieve the human condition. . . . Only through positive knowledge could
> man adapt himself to reality and reality to his needs. Realism was thus the
> servant of moralism.[1]

Similarly, David Carroll claims that Eliot tries to bring psychological and
physical reality into balance for her protagonists, and that those few objects that remain unmediated by the minds of her characters only become
"meaningless and terrifying."[2] Even Elizabeth Ermarth, in an essay inspired by Merleau-Ponty, writes about the cultural and moral values to be
gained by Eliot's version of phenomenological reduction.[3] For these readers and many others, a general extension of man into the natural world,
with the satisfaction of his fundamental needs the only standard, is an
Eliotic ideal.

We should not assume this principle too quickly, however. Although Eliot certainly did aspire to write "natural history," nevertheless, the conjunction of man and matter in her early novels is never an innocent one. Such conjunction always reveals the impoverished, reductive character of human efforts to appropriate the world, even while seeming to promise an idyllic harmony. In the very first chapter of *The Mill on the Floss*, for example, the narrator surveys rustic objects in what has conventionally been understood as a benign, Wordsworthian discovery of the world's symbolic plenitude: corn, ships, trees, rooftops—all can be said to take their meaning within a human act of imagination and memory; all are composed in relation to the narrator's Wordsworthian desire to unite mind with matter.[4] But what escapes notice in this scene is a more disturbing drama, one that takes its threatening qualities only in retrospect, from the pressure of the novel's later events. Following the lead of the Dutch painters she admired, in this opening Eliot has commercial objects relentlessly interpenetrate natural ones.[5] And given the novel's eventual horror over St. Ogg's commercial single-mindedness, the resulting hybridized landscape can be seen as much more ambiguous and threatening than it is usually thought to be.

> A wide plain, where the broadening Floss hurries on between its green banks to the sea, and the loving tide, rushing to meet it, checks its passage with an impetuous embrace. On this mighty tide the black ships—laden with the fresh-scented fir-planks, with rounded sacks of oil-bearing seed, or with the dark glitter of coal—are borne along to the town of St. Ogg's, which shows its aged, fluted red roofs and the broad gables of its wharves between the low wooded hill and the river brink, tinging the water with a soft purple hue under the transient glance of this February sun. Far away on each side stretch the rich pastures and the patches of dark earth, made ready for the seed of broad-leaved green crops, or touched already with the tint of the tender-bladed autumn-sown corn. There is a remnant still of the last year's golden clusters of bee-hive ricks rising at intervals beyond the hedgerows; and everywhere the hedgerows are studded with trees: the distant ships seem to be lifting their masts and stretching their red-brown sails close among the branches of the spreading ash.[6]

In this description, raw matter is never left at rest; it is always invaded by economic matter. In that sterile and, at best, amoral way (as the novel will later define provincial economy), it is actively stripped of its distance from man. "Black ships" are abruptly superimposed on a natural, watery "embrace" that had sought its own self-enclosed consummation; the wharves and roofs of St. Ogg's show between hill and river bank, "tinging" the water; the earth is "touched again" with corn; the bee hives are seen "rising at intervals" above the hedgerows; and the ships even merge visually with the ash branches. As the passage goes on, after meeting horses that must work to earn their feed, as well as a farmer who must work to earn his dinner, we are introduced to the mill and its house, "as old as the elm and chestnuts that shelter it from the northern blast." The pastoral overtones here pull our sensibilities toward approval, yet our familiarity with the novel's great, brooding theme—Maggie's inability to free herself from a world that is overly pragmatic, and overly "economic" in a number of senses—should make us wary of regarding any loss of natural independence to commercial uses too lightly.

These fusions of commercial with natural objects, which subject the entire landscape to the functional use of man, begin very subtly to suggest George Eliot's fundamental perception about material things: the perception that a world of autonomous objects does not exist, and that such a condition is inherently claustrophobic. The major symbolic objects of *The Mill on the Floss* only magnify such fusions, and such claustrophobia: the mill itself, source of Maggie's longing for origins, is rooted in nature but swamped by its commercial destiny; the boat that bears her away in romantic passion—what Stephen Guest calls "natural law" (VI, 14)—is, ironically, a commercial Dutch vessel that can accommodate the two lovers only with diffculty on the poop; and even the landscape of the Red Deeps, where Maggie meets her lover, Philip Wakem, appeals to her at first because of its irregular surface, which was formed by an abandoned stone quarry—the place is described slightingly by the narrator as "mimic rock and ravine" (V, 1).

Not only are there no purely natural objects in *The Mill on the Floss*, nothing antecedent to a commercialized culture, but Eliot pointedly insures that even those objects presented as symbolic alternatives to St. Ogg's are laced with economic significance. In the largest sense, all the things in this world have been imprisoned by human use, bracketed by their function. The world external to man has disappeared. And while the deceptively nostalgic tone of the opening passage may persuade us that the cohabitation of man and nature is benign, the novel very gradually reveals its ominous aspects.

Despite Eliot's humanism,[7] a novel like *The Mill on the Floss* does not merely acquiesce to man's conception of himself as the measure of all things; in part, and against the grain of its own explicitly humanistic themes, it is appalled by man's universal and irreversible amalgamation with matter. This ambiguity certainly does not undermine Eliot's humanism, but it does make humanism in her novels a much more complicated affair than it seems. For George Eliot's humanism, like that of most Victorian writers, is severely tested by her reaction against the scientific and industrial pragmatism of her age, which helped to make all human designs on the world appear to be rapacious.

What eventually makes the ambiguity in Eliot's fusions of natural and commercial objects visible, in fact, is the novel's sustained attack on the runaway commercialism—and the related cultural narrowness—of English life. After all, *The Mill on the Floss* contains, in the Dodsons, a bitter satire on rural materialism.[8] More broadly, the novel seems to lament the destruction of Maggie's natural energies (she is often called "wild," or compared sympathetically to animals),[9] by the constricting economic and procedural preoccupations of St. Ogg's, a town that has fallen "out of keeping with the earth" (IV, 1) and that has traded "the grandeur of the wild beast" for an "oppressive narrowness." In very explicit ways, Eliot regards the victory of man over matter as a blight. This blight lies not only in man's tendency to misuse or misinterpret things, his fallibility—which is how we usually qualify Eliot's faith in man[10]—but in his very belief in his right to use things at all, to make of matter a human medium. For the Tullivers and for St. Ogg's, at least, the widespread use of nature for human purposes has destroyed its romantic, creative power, and Maggie's hopeless separation from the organic world of her childhood—which has somehow become bound up in the legal and financial status of the mill—underscores the urgency of that loss. The conjunction of natural sites with functional sites haunts the very title of the novel, and Tom and Maggie are destroyed finally not just by nature and the flood but by "wooden machinery" (in a letter to her publisher, Eliot insisted on the adjective[11]). As we shall see, too, Eliot's world of enslaved objects is not just a response to her fears about industrialization or commercialism per se. An interfusion of man and matter is already present in Maggie and Tom's childhood world as a determining cultural condition for their failed emotional relations. In general, despite her widely recognized reverence for the products and worldly concerns of man, Eliot seems to tell us through Maggie that the loss of purely natural objects in nineteenth-century England has diminished human life.

From this point of view, the opening chapter's wistful conjunctions of man and matter ("I remember those large dipping willows . . . I remember the stone bridge . . .")—not to mention Maggie's very affection for the mill itself—seem at first to be oddly skewed. In these pastoral impulses, George Eliot does seem to desire an alternative to the debased, narrowed reality her acculturated nature often represents. But Eliot's remedy for this debasement does not finally entail any kind of redemptive return to natural objects; such a gesture seems impossible in the novels.[12]

On one level, the few instances of her characters' immersion in the material world are incomplete or distorted: Maggie, surrendering thought to the force of the tide and the objects of the river when she runs away from Stephen, is terrified by the idea of an unregulated world;[13] Hetty Sorrel, alone in nature in *Adam Bede*, is abandoned to sin. On another, even though critics often point to Eliot's desire to make human experience "particular"—that is, excessively detailed and localized—as a naturalizing narrative device, there is an insuperable doubleness here. For, as the critical tradition has long recognized, Eliot does rigorously insist on combining her "particularity" with intellectual and moral programs.
Following Ruskin, she emphasizes—more scrupulously, perhaps, than she sometimes seems aware herself—that the world can ultimately have beauty and value only through its human associations. Thus, in a famous letter written in 1866, she claimed to want "to make certain ideas thoroughly incarnate, as if they had revealed themselves first to one in the flesh and not in the spirit."[14] But the real order of generation here, masked by "as if," is important. Furthermore, in the very next sentence, Eliot proves herself to be quite clear about what use the particularizing of her ideas has; she calls it "aesthetic teaching": "I think aesthetic teaching is the highest of all teaching because it deals with life in its highest complexity." Or again, several years later, she refuses "to adopt any formula which does not get itself clothed for me in some human figure and individual experience" mainly because abstract formulas alone do not "help others to see."[15] Statements like these[16] are usually cited to demonstrate Eliot's repugnance to bald appropriations of the world by the human mechanisms of theory. But if they do show her working to make theory accountable to experience, in their didactic strains they also betray an appetite for putting even the specific and seemingly discontinuous details of life in service of a complex human design, both scientific and moral.

If she is to redeem human experience from the narrowness implicit in any appropriation of the natural world, then, Eliot can only do so by discovering a "nonhuman" or material dimension within the life of man itself—not by returning us to nature. In this discovery, which anticipates a great deal of modernist and postmodernist thinking about the relation between man and nature, we may find the tenuous complexity of Eliot's humanism. For Eliot is only able to exalt man by inverting his reduction of nature to functionality. That is to say, Eliot's novels ultimately explore the functionality of things within human experience only in order to naturalize it, to make functionality itself into a kind of material world. Specifically, the novels describe both objects and human lives as intersecting in a plurality of functional relations—in a kind of static structure of human meaning—that through its size and density restores to both orders some of the monumentality of unmolested nature, without ever denying the molested status of man and his appropriated objects. So it is that the novels themselves, whatever intellectual or moral program underlies them, also strike us as somehow monumental—unfixed by whatever purposes to which we put them.

It is easiest to see this process at work in an early novel like *The Mill on the Floss* simply because Eliot had not yet abandoned material objects for that naturalized psychological world of the later works, the world in which Dorothea Brooke learns to conceive the behavior of others "with that distinctness which is no longer reflection but feeling—an idea wrought back to the directness of sense, like the solidity of objects."[17] In *The Mill on the Floss*, it is a single object—the mill itself—that forms the physical center of the novel and also becomes the ground for the various human dramas. In the first chapter, the little girl who stares at the mill wheel, "rapt in its movement" (I, 1), warns us that the novel will be an investigation into the human significance of the mill. But it is also clear even at this point that the mill's importance lies partly in its ability to attain a self-completion free of the human world through its very functionality, transformed now into a seemingly autonomous energy: "the rush of water and the booming of the mill bring a dreamy deafness . . . like a great curtain of sound, shutting one out from the world beyond" (I, 4). Maggie's pleasure in the mill as a child stems from this same self-completion; a man-made machine, the mill can nevertheless become a naturalized world:

> The resolute din, the unresting motion of the great stones giving her a dim delicious awe as at the presence of an uncontrollable force, the meal for ever pouring, pouring, the fine white powder softening all surfaces and making the very spider-nets look like faery lace-work, the sweet pure scent of the meal—all helped Maggie feel that the mill was a world apart from her outside everyday life.

And for the reader, the mill will finally acquire some of the nonhuman materiality Maggie finds in it as a child.

Before we explore how it does, however, it is important to see the various destructive ways in which things become humanized for the characters of the novel. For it is not just through an economic appropriation that objects like the mill are reduced to human uses, though this is, perhaps, the most obvious of man's intrusions on the world. If commercial rapacity were the only human transgression against nature here, the novel would simply have polarized the world of St. Ogg's against Maggie's moral standards. As we will see, however, this familiar polarity is only a tangential one. Rather, man and matter are fused, to the detriment of both, through a general cultural appropriation of the world—both physical and moral—in terms of use. And only by tracing the dangers of this pandemic functionality can we see how functionality itself is ultimately transformed, and exalted as a natural process.

Most importantly, characters use their control of things as a means to master each other, to aggressively assert their own identities. Tom, for example, achieves a self-righteous dominance over Maggie and over Philip Wakem through his competence with "outdoor things" (I,3). As a child, Tom's sense of identity is crucially bound up in things—his "one point of interest" in dressing himself each day lies in transferring "the contents of his everyday pockets to those actually in wear" (I,9)—and this kind of identity never loses its relation to mastery. His superiority over Maggie comes from his knowledge of how to manipulate objects—fishing line, kites, card houses, lozenge boxes—and his early attempt to prove himself over Philip centers—almost disastrously—around a sword. As a young man, too, Tom's masterful relation to things saves him his dignity: he revenges his father's injuries by learning his way around the world's objects, by learning how to be like the fellow his Uncle Deane had praised, the fellow who "can tell you the cubic contents of anything in no time" (III,5).

Tom's aggressive use of things is not at all aberrant in his world. Mr. Tulliver attempts to conquer the world of lawyers by claiming an unimpeachable right to water. Mr. Wakem satisfies his casual vindictiveness against Tulliver through his purchase of the mill. More comically, Uncle Pullet uses his mastery of a music box to prove to the world that his character "was not of that entire nullity which might otherwise have been attributed to it" (I,9). Even a sympathetic character like Bob Jakin takes his revenge against class injuries by getting the best of Mrs. Glegg in a battle over material goods. But most striking in this context, perhaps, because it is most ineffectual, is the way the women in the novel achieve their place in the world only through their control of domestic objects: either by establishing how men are allowed to use them, as when Mrs. Glegg keeps her husband off her clean floor or dispenses his cup of tea only as a pretext for a lecture; or by impressing each other with the value, or lack of it, of things—the debate over the value of Bessy's "chany" and teapot is the most painful example of this combat, Mrs. Pullet's nearly sacerdotal bonnet the most ridiculous. Thus, too, Mr. Tulliver's injuries to his wife are entirely conceived to lie in his losing her personal possessions.

In this context, even Maggie, who is incompetent about the management of Tom's things, tries to restore the balance between herself and
others through a thing, her Fetish. Yet we should note that Maggie's
Fetish, an object of plural significance and use, diverts her aggression
rather than being an instrument of it, and in that way avoids direct use as
a means of human manipulation. And, more crucially, Maggie's refusal
to be treated as a thing by her mother—to have her hair and dress and behavior regulated according to rule—is a rebellion against this aggressive
confusion of mastered objects with mastered identity. After all, even Mr.
Tulliver is afraid Maggie will bring "none the bigger price" (I,2) because
of her cleverness. Maggie's great crisis in the novel is finally provoked by
Tom's attempt to control her as a thing in his battle with the Wakems. Insensitive to her human needs, Tom tries to reduce Maggie to the status of a
possession of the Tulliver family, to conceive her value only as it contributes usefully to the Tullivers' goals, which are related both to economics
and to identity: the recovery of financial independence and respectability.

But the human use of things in the novel is more complex than simply
the conversion of things into instruments of assertion. Characters in the
novel also communicate with each other through objects—in fact, they
communicate more effectively through objects than they are able to without them. The Tullivers demonstrate this principle dramatically through
their use of the Bible: sentiments are only considered trustworthy insofar
as they become a part of the book, through writing in it or swearing upon
it. Occasionally, this kind of reified communication is sympathetically
presented as the only kind of understanding characters are allowed to
achieve, as when Tom offers Maggie plum cake after their first fight. The
reconciliation is never sealed by speech, passing only through the exchange of an object, yet Maggie hungrily prizes this kind of union, and
the narrator refers to it later as a "sacrament of conciliation" (V,5). The
value of Tom's gift of his pocketknife to Bob Jakin is effective in a similar
way, and Wakem's restoration of the mill to the Tullivers succeeds in conveying his good intentions toward his son, if not to the Tullivers themselves. Tom's competence with money, too, comes to embody his emotional ties to his family: "I have a different way of showing my
affection," he tells Maggie (V,5), to which she responds, "Because you
are a man, Tom, and have power, and can do something in the world."

More often, however, bound so closely to the world of objects, these reified exchanges remain frustrated, as is Mrs. Tulliver's vain attempt to
display affection for Tom by intending her valuable things for him as heir-
looms, or Mr. Tulliver's inadequate expression of his worries for Maggie
through the money he loans to his sister. And for the most part, this kind

of communication betrays the hopelessly inadequate nature of a human world devoted to objects as symbols of feeling: the imprisonment of matter in human use is in this sense the imprisonment of human nature itself. Tom, in particular, frequently misunderstands the signifying power of things in communication, reading Maggie's neglect of his rabbits and general carelessness with things as lack of affection, interpreting Bob Jakin's covetous need of his half-penny as betrayal, presuming that his own gift of a new fishing line for Maggie adequately fulfills an emotional exchange. Such inadequacy in communication is made comic when Mrs. Tulliver and Mrs. Pullet find an affinity for each other in their common preference for spots over stripes, or when Mr. Tulliver is won over by Stelling's putting his thumbs through his waistcoat in a recognizable way, or when Mr. Glegg believes that the lives of his garden vegetables display "remarkable coincidences" (I,12) with events in human history. And such inadequacy in communication reaches tragic proportions when Tom assumes that Maggie's feelings for Philip or for Stephen can be understood only in terms of their use value—that is, in relation to the Tulliver's reacquisition of respectability. Even Mrs. Pullet's tears, early in the novel, have become artificial, a sign of luxury, a commodity. The lending of money to relatives at interest is a monstrous instance of this reification of human exchange; but on even the smallest level, Mr. Pullet can think of absolutely nothing to impart to his nieces and nephews but peppermints.

Despite Eliot's discomfort with the fusion of human life with humanized things, however, some of her more lyrical passages on memory share in the conjunction of human life with use-objects. Tom's pocketful of things are not just instruments of domination for him; they are also "relics of the past" (II,1) through which he remembers life at the mill and Maggie when he is away at school. And Maggie's own ties to the past are also accomplished through her associations with objects that form a "home-scene" in and around the mill, that "sweet monotony where everything is known and *loved* because it is known" (I,6). Maggie's grief at being parted from her books, for example, and her fear that "the end of our lives will have nothing in it like the beginning" (III,6), derives from the same general tendency to prize objects as tokens of human meaning that leads her father to litigation and that frustrates her relations to Tom. We must ask ourselves at this point: is there some difference between Maggie's investment of personal meaning and emotion in objects and, say, Tom's? Does such a difference consist only in the content of Maggie's associations with things, or is there a more fundamental difference, a methodological one?

That there is such a fundamental difference in Maggie's approach to the workings of human significance becomes clearer when we consider the other characters' persistent belief that objects always signify in some single human way. Singleness, in fact, is usually taken as the condition of an object's usability. In *The Mill on the Floss*, characters continually overestimate the direct correlation between objects and particular human use, too strictly valuing objects as complete measures of themselves or their intentions. This is apparent in Mrs. Tulliver's grief over the sale of her personal things: her sense of scandal lies in the return to public circulation of things that bear her name, things that had been singled out of the public world as unequivocal representations of her identity. The gap between public, multiple, uncontrolled significance and the private determination of an object's meaning strikes Bessy as an obscenity. Early in the novel, Bessy's literalism about things is even a source of comedy, as when she misunderstands Mr. Tulliver's hyperbole about her finding fault with moles, or when she comprehends Tom's education only through reference to laundry and meals. But Bessy is not alone in her single-mindedness. In general, the Dodson family believes that the things and procedures they have adopted as personal, their "family traditions" (IV,1), take on an extraordinary, totemic value through their very singleness—so much so that things remaining in the public domain come to seem dangerous, polluted. Mrs. Glegg is afraid of draughts in strange houses, and none of the Dodsons will sample anyone else's butter or jam for fear they may have spoiled.

In many related ways, all the characters express their belief in single correspondences between objects and significance: Mr. Tulliver, through his faith in book bindings; Mr. Stelling, in his conviction that, in regard to education, there is "one remedy for all things" (II,1); Mr. Deane, in his contempt for the use value of Tom's knowledge. Mr. Glegg's confidence in the singleness of every object's function extends even to his suspicion of Bob Jakin's generosity with Laceham goods, which cannot be tied to a single, recognizable motive: "I've no opinion o' transactions where folks do things for nothing. It allays looks bad" (V,2). Mr. Tulliver so equates his entire identity with his management of the mill—the singleness of his economically useful role—that loss of the mill literally robs him of consciousness, at first, and then of life.

Over against this tendency to view things as imprisoned in single human meanings and uses, Eliot presents us, partly through Maggie, with the actual plurality of every object's human significance. The customary opposition of literal and metaphorical approaches to reality identified with the Dodsons and Tullivers is not quite accurate: for Maggie, human meaning is not synecdochic, or visionary—it is diffuse. This diffusion is implicit in

Maggie's lyrical reminiscences, as when the narrator refers to the things of childhood as "a language," the "mother tongue of our imagination" (I,5). On the one hand, this comparison only confirms the tendency to appropriation that is pandemic in Maggie's world: that most human of systems, language, is here used to describe how Maggie directly transforms natural objects into signs for human meaning. On the other hand, though, the crucial fact about language, as Maggie tells Tom later, is that a word "may mean several things. Almost every word does" (II,1).[18] Maggie's reading of the dictionary has taught her what she sees again, more vividly, in her encounter with the gypsies: that a single language, or a single system of knowledge—like those of geography and history, which she fails miserably to teach to those alien pupils—does not have a direct, functional relation to the world. And Maggie's version of reality, in contrast to Tom's, is often multiple. Whereas Tom is always convinced of the irrevocable justice of his actions, "Maggie was always wishing she had done something different" (I,6). Her stories about frogs and grasshoppers, which inspire in Lucy a delighted "semi-belief," are annoying to Tom because they playfully violate the singleness of things, which he demonstrates his control over by destroying Maggie's animals. The plurality of Maggie's world, in fact, is what distinguishes her at the end of the novel from other characters and their inflexible demands on her behavior. What Eliot suggests here, especially through her awareness of language's multiplicity—the famous discussion of metaphor as the undermining of human thought ("we can so seldom declare what a thing is, except by saying it is something else" [II,1]) further reinforces this—is that the human uses of things are not as final, fixed, and imprisoning as they appear. Though this does nothing to restore the absolute "thingness" of objects, it does make the human world larger, more textured—less reductive than any conviction of human efficiency would have it.[19]

Maggie's simple notion about the meaning of words as multiple is crucial in at least two ways for the novel's efforts to monumentalize human meaning. First, the notion that words have more than one meaning guarantees that human signs have a materiality apart from their function.[20] Maggie is aware of this as she pores over Tom's Latin text: she skips the rules of syntax to dwell instead on the strangeness of the Latin words themselves, which, freed of direct meaning, take on a naturalized foreignness: "these mysterious sentences snatched from an unknown context,—like strange horns of beasts and leaves of unknown plants, brought from some far-off region, gave boundless scope to her imagination" (II,1). Words, cut off from meaning, denote an entire world of their own. This delight in the Latin words as sensuous images precedes Maggie's knowledge that she could "learn to interpret them." Tom, who is too devoted to the rigidity of correspondences between signs and their signifieds, to an economy of meaning, has no appreciation of this materiality. Language for him never acquires the corporality that it has for Maggie, although even for Tom, the nonlinguistic, human objects he is more familiar with sometimes reveal a similar corporality as signs: he sees that "the pattern of the rug and the grate were 'first ideas' that it was no more possible to criticize than the solidity and extension of matter" (II,1).

Second, an awareness that things may function as signs in more than one way is the beginning of a perception of meaning as a texture of possibilities, or, in the language of modern linguistics, as a semiotic structure. That is to say, by being multiple, the referents of such signs present themselves as a plane of grouped, interrelated meanings that cannot be separated from each other, but cannot be resolved into a final coherence—a logical, rational synthesis—either. The plurality of meaning is both arbitrary and fixed. And as a fixed plane of meanings, the structure of human meaning can be perceived as inefficient and idiosyncratic—not reducible to a diagram, a machine for further use. Structural signification, in this sense, thereby acquires some of the non-instrumental materiality of natural things.

In his essay, "The Eiffel Tower," Roland Barthes points out that the chief feature of the nineteenth-century's discovery of the human prospect—the panorama of an urban, as opposed to a natural landscape—lies in such a perception of human but corporal structure: human objects, when viewed from above, can be grouped and composed by the observer into an arbitrary but harmonious set of relationships, just as natural objects can be, in the very act of turning them into signs for themselves, a map of their own existence that the viewer can "read."[21] Perception of structure thereby creates a tension between our purely functional understanding of human signs and our recognition that through an arbitrary multiplicity they form their own unique wholeness. Barthes defines structure, in this sense, as a "concrete abstraction": structure can be conceived not as a means to analysis but as a nonreducible end in itself, almost a physical composition, a "corpus of intelligent forms."[22]

By presenting us with the multiple significance of human objects, George Eliot provides us with a similar kind of panoramic perspective. And in terms of our perception as readers, this perspective reveals a new kind of material texture: human objects and human life in the novels take on the sprawling dimensions, the coherent but unstable randomness, of the natural.[23] The nonhuman monumentality of Eliot's work lies chiefly in this direction: dangerous tendencies to transform all matter into human functions are redeemed when they are seen to produce a pluralized texture of meanings, a living structure of composed but rationally incompatible fragments, rather than simply a one-to-one correspondence between object and function. As Barthes puts it, perception of the structural qualities of human meaning makes "the exploration of language . . . (correspond) to the exploration of the cosmos."[24] And in both these ways, then—through the materiality of signs and through that of their signifieds—appropriated objects can appear as naturalized, a world more permanent than its functionality at first indicates, an eternal dwelling place for individual men.

This process of corporalizing use-objects emerges most clearly if we look at the mill itself. A nearly invisible, enigmatic presence, sketched briefly at the beginning of the novel and then mostly forgotten by the descriptive energies of the narrator, the mill hovers in the background like a darkened stage on which all events transpire and are framed. We are always aware of the mill as the possible limits of the novel's meaning even though we seldom look at it, and even though, in the third volume, Maggie is displaced from the mill, although still psychically oriented toward it—as her return to the mill at the novel's end suggests. Our suppressed awareness of the mill thus helps magnify it as a material sign: the mill stands for everything and nothing at the same time, representing its own physical centrality in the Tullivers' lives and its ability to gather into itself endless mnemonic associations.

The mill is itself the measure of all meaning for the Tullivers. It is a cosmos. Almost everyone in the family feels the mill's tremendous emotional impact, which surpasses its economic significance: in some way, it mediates between them and their origins; it becomes a "first idea" with all the "solidity and extension of matter." Mr. Tulliver agrees to remain at the mill because it reminds him of several generations of his family. Even Tom, for the most part narrowly obsessive about money, pauses at one point to realize that he has an "old, deep-rooted affection" (V,6) for the mill that stems from his familiarity with it. This meaning of the mill is not analogical; it precedes thought and use, or even specific memories. The mill reminds the Tullivers mainly of itself, its constancy throughout time as a human sign, and, in this sense, of the reassuring, "natural" permanence of human order.

But beyond this fundamental sign-function of the mill—which lies before reference, giving the mill an infinite kind of extension in time and space—we are also made aware that the mill has many specific kinds of significance, which are different for each character, and that these differences even reveal some of the incompatibilities between them. Mr. Tulliver sees the mill first as a symbol of his independence and unassailability—he refuses to pass it on to his son—and then, through its loss, as a sign of his dependence. Tom sees the mill in a slightly more active way, as the proof of his own strivings against the world, what the narrator calls his "ambitious resistance to misfortune" (IV,1). Maggie values the mill in yet another way, as the symbol of an impossible harmony between herself and Tom. For Mrs. Tulliver, on the other hand, the mill is more negative, a liability: "I wasn't fond o' the noise of it . . . and if I'd known as the mills had so much to do with the law, it wouldn't have been me 'ud have been the first Dodson to marry one" (III,7).

As we move outward from the family, the mill acquires even more meanings. For Wakem, it is an indifferent means of proving his righteousness; for Lucy, the mill appears to be the one impediment to Maggie's marrying Philip. Though the mill carries all of these meanings, because of their very plurality it seems to be defined by no one of them singly. Neither does it fuse them all in a kind of symbolic coherence. These purely local uses of the mill as meaning come detached from its more enigmatic presence as a pure sign at the center of the novel, and in their variegated interdependence create a labyrinth of significance. Seeing the mill in this way as a "concrete abstraction" gives a new resonance to Eliot's conception of a "network of relations" in her work, even if that phrase is one she used primarily in an ethical context.[25]

Many other objects in the novel are similarly presented as conjunctions of divergent human meanings. The jam puff that Maggie and Tom quarrel over, for instance, is for Maggie first an object of sacrifice and for Tom an object of competition, then for Maggie a source of reverie and for Tom a symbol of Maggie's greed. Maggie's helplessness in the face of the shifting meanings of the jam puff underscores our privileged position, as observers, to sort out these changing functions, to perceive them as an intelligible texture. Similarly, Tom's pocketknife has a plural significance, being first a gift to Bob, then a symbol of Bob's defiance as well as of his boyish susceptibility to the allure of things. When Bob reminds Tom of the gift many years later, the knife is first a source of shame to Tom, then a sign of his benevolence. Bob's pack full of merchandise also has a tier of significations, which Bob manipulates in his duel of wits with Mrs. Glegg, promoting it alternately as a bargain and as a previously spoken-for collection, and profiting from it in both material and psychological terms.

Tom's education, too—not a thing, certainly, but his initiation into the useful knowledge of things—has a range of meanings. For Mr. Tulliver, it is to be "a bread" (I,2) to Tom, but it is also to be an instrument of gaining dignity before the lawyers, and a means of assuring that Tom will not displace his father. For Mr. Stelling, the education has an entirely different significance, connected to his own empty reverence for classical learning and his attempt to rise in his profession. For Mr. Deane, it is an object of resentment and contempt. And for poor Tom, it signifies only misery: he is left "in a state of blank unimaginativeness concerning the cause and tendency of his sufferings, as if he had been an innocent shrewmouse imprisoned in the split trunk of an ash tree in order to cure lameness in cattle" (II,1). Many of the physical objects in *The Mill on the Floss*—the sheets of music that Stephen uses as a pretext to see Maggie and that Philip uses to sing his love; Maggie's sewing; the note marking the Moss's debts; Philip Wakem's deformed body, which makes him an unusable thing—are charged in this way with divergent meanings.

What is more important, though, is the way that the human order itself, apart from objects, acquires monumentality through this plurality of structure. Eliot's most successful remedy for the loss of natural objects in nineteenth-century English life is to return to human events themselves, through a perception of the structural qualities of human motives, the nonhuman irreducibility of matter. These structural qualities turn time itself into a readable, material pattern.[26] Human events are overdetermined in her novels, and the process of change always leaves traces that stratify it, saving it from being lost to flux. Even the "ruined villages" along the Rhone (IV,1) that signify human oblivion still endure as signs of loss—recoverable, static points in Eliot's own structure of the human meaning of duration. The much-debated relation between determinism and freedom in Eliot's work,[27] too, suggests the presence of this monumentality of structure: the "doctrine of consequences"[28] in her novels that determines events as the intersection of multiple intentions, conscious and unconscious, is, on the one hand, an instance of Eliot's own appropriation of reality—her positivistic approach to psychology—and, on the other, of the transformation of human life into an archaeology of causes and circumstances, a constellation of signs. The metaphor of the human "web" in her novels is thus a part of this re-naturalizing of culture through a perception of the textural nature of meaning.

In *The Mill on the Floss*, this technique, in which human attempts to act on the world—to use it—acquire structural dimension, becoming spatialized and readable, had already been refined to great sophistication. We

need think only of the process by which Tom is handed over to Mr. Stelling—a pastiche of human intentions: Mr. Tulliver's complex desires for
independence, revenge, and provision for his son; Mr. Riley's desire to
have an opinion; his desire also to think well of his friend's friends both as
a reflection on himself and as a prospect of future back-scratching; his familiarity with Louisa Timpson's face; his general deference to classical
education. This human interchange acquires a life of its own as the idiosyncratic though overdetermined conjunction of all these human motives.
But the novel is prolific in examples of structural multiplicity in human
purposes: Wakem's motives for buying the mill, Mrs. Glegg's reasons for
relenting against Maggie at the end of the novel, the characteristic hereditary impulses of Tullivers and Dodsons. It is in this sense that Eliot's work
aspires to be "incarnate": that is, not by presenting human life as a series
of simple, single causes and effects, but by presenting it as a complex
structure of intentions so plural it acquires a massiveness of texture.
Human actions, rather than being consumed in time by the uses to which
they are put, are converted to palpability by their presentation as a deci-
pherable—but not a repeatable, instrumental—pattern.

The ultimate focal point for this structural principle in the novel is the
irresolution of Maggie's romantic life, and the defeat of morality as a tool
for human action. The last half of the novel is devoted to a stalemating of
Maggie's feelings, and, despite the tendency of critics to take sides here—
to defend or condemn Maggie's actions[29]—a large part of Eliot's intention is simply the dramatization of a moral conflict in which no single human interpretation, or theory of useful practice, predominates. Instead,
we are left with an "antagonism between valid claims,"[30] a nearly static
vision of human conflict that is impossibly urgent in its unsolvable multiplicity. For even if we can agree with Philip, for instance, that Maggie
"stupefies" (V,3) herself, we also know that his interpretation of her dilemma is tainted by his own self-interest, as well as by his lack of sympathy for her very real loyalty to her father: "Maggie . . . felt there was
some truth in what Philip said, yet there was a deeper consciousness that
for any immediate application it had to her conduct it was no better than
falsity." Similarly, while we cannot forgive Tom's lack of sympathy for
Maggie, we do feel, with Maggie, the occasional justice of Tom's
reproaches:

> she rebelled and was humiliated in the same moment: it seemed as if he held
> a glass before her to show her her own folly and weakness—as if he were a
> prophetic voice predicting her future failures—and yet, all the while, she
> judged him in return.   (VI,4)

This undecidability, which is underscored through the sympathetic, disinterested Dr. Kenn, who vacillates in his advice as he is caught up in the conflicting, equally compelling dimensions of the problem, is a primary experience for most readers. Dr. Kenn's confusion marks the limit of our attempts to prescribe a useful course for Maggie; the narrator seizes on his predicament to claim that "the great problem of the shifting relation between passion and duty is clear to no man who is capable of apprehending it: the question, whether the moment has come in which a man has fallen below the possibility of a renunciation that will carry any efficacy, and must accept the sway of a passion against which he had struggled as a trespass, is one for which we have no master key that will fit all cases" (VII,2). In this sense, Maggie's earlier moral standards, her attempt to apply the formulas of Thomas à Kempis to life, appear just as narrow a form of pragmatism as the material monomania of St. Ogg's. Morality, like economics, is deadening so long as its goal is functional efficiency.[31] For Eliot, both the moral world and the world of appropriated objects become emotionally expansive only when they are corporalized, when they are given a life greater than that of individual human intentions.

It should be pointed out here that such a static, corporal vision of the human world is not incompatible with a moral program, although it does work to make Eliot's moralism passive. For George Eliot, neutralizing self-interested appropriations through a perception of the corporality of human meaning is the first step toward selfless, disinterested—and in that sense "natural"—moral response. In her later novels, in which Eliot moves further away from a concern with the human use of objects and towards a more direct naturalizing of human psychology itself, the moral consequences of such perception are made clear. Thus, in *Daniel Deronda*, Daniel's central quest is for a discovery of his rootedness in a historical context, in a complex of overdetermined racial meanings. And his discovery of that context sparks his surrender to an impersonal and abstract cause that is larger than his own ability, as a character, to define it. Similarly, *Middlemarch* provides Dorothea with a detached complexity of perception that allows her to remove herself—specifically, with regard to Rosamond and Lydgate—from any sphere of recognizable personal appropriations. For Eliot, and for the Victorians generally, morality is identified with an absence of appropriative, interested motives, as if a complete denial of purpose (from the point of view of the self) might guarantee one's relation to eternity.[32] But the moral use of such perception in Eliot's work does not limit its implications. In *The Mill on the Floss*, Eliot refuses to speculate on the moral use of her vision of a naturalized human order: the suppression of any final moral action in the novel is one reason the ending seems rushed, bent as it is on fusing the human order with the natural through Maggie's death. Before adapting it to moral use, George Eliot was capable of seeing structural perception as an end in itself, the conversion of a debased human reality into the apparent permanence of nonhuman matter. And to understand the peculiar qualities of her moral judgements—not merely their passivity, but their strained mixture of passion with self-repression—we must first take this naturalizing impulse into account.

It goes without saying, too, that Eliot's strategy of exploring the human order to find in it the monumental status of matter has become a widespread modern one. The formal emphasis and self-consciousness of modern literature and art, not to mention the blatant attack on the nature of structuralism and its concurrent elevation of language as an institution more permanent than man, all indicate that our search for the eternal presence and authenticity of matter now proceeds largely, paradoxically, only within the field of the human itself. Eliot's moral purposes may ultimately have prevented her from recognizing the vast implications of this shift. But its presence in her work—and, perhaps, in the fundamental assumptions of the nineteenth-century social novel—suggests a profound link between modern humanism and more nonreferential literary preoccupations that usually remains obscured.

NOTES

1. *Experiments in Life: George Eliot's Quest for Values* (Detroit: Wayne State University Press, 1965), p. 3.

2. "*Middlemarch* and the Externality of Fact," in *This Particular Web: Essays on "Middlemarch,"* ed. Ian Adam (Toronto: Toronto University Press, 1975), p. 76.

3. "Incarnation: George Eliot's Conception of 'Undeviating Law,'" *Nineteenth-Century Fiction*, 29 (1974), 273–286.

4. Though such a reading is not the focal point of her argument, a good summary of this interpretation is Margaret Homans, "Eliot, Wordsworth, and the Scenes of the Sisters' Instruction," *Critical Inquiry*, 8 (1982), 223–242.

5. Hugh Witemeyer, *George Eliot and the Visual Arts* (New Haven: Yale University Press, 1979), p. 139, calls this scene "an anthology of motifs" from Dutch landscape painting. For a good discussion of the materialistic qualities of Dutch painting, see Roland Barthes, "The World as Object," *Critical Essays*, trans. Richard Howard (Evanston: Northwestern University Press, 1972), 3–12.

6. George Eliot, *The Mill on the Floss*, ed. A. S. Byatt (New York: Penguin, 1979), I, 1. Further references are given to book and chapter numbers in parentheses within the text.

7. Most critics accept Eliot's humanism as a close approximation of Feuerbach's *homo homini deus est*, often pointing to Eliot's own remark, very early in her career, that she agreed with Feuerbach entirely; see *The Letters of George Eliot*, ed. Gordon S. Haight, 7 vols. (New Haven: Yale University Press, 1954–55), II, 153 (hereafter referred to as *Letters*). For a good summary as well as an attack on Eliot's humanism as a disruption of her theories of realism, see U. C. Knoepflmacher, *George Eliot's Early Novels* (Berkeley: University of California Press, 1968). Interestingly, Knoepflmacher argues that in Eliot's novels the material world is always converted into a moral world.

8. Eliot's famous disclaimer of any intention to attack the Dodsons implies only that she did not consider them personally responsible for their values.

9. See Nina Auerbach's provocative article, "The Power of Hunger: Demonism and Maggie Tulliver," *Nineteenth-Century Fiction*, 30 (1975), 150–171.

10. This qualification includes discussions of Eliot's preoccupation with egotism: most critics have written on this subject, and there are good summaries in Paris, who sees the novels as a prescription for the transcendence of egotism, and in Reva Stump, *Movement and Vision in George Eliot's Novels* (Seattle: University of Washington Press, 1959). But it also includes recent "deconstructive" approaches to Eliot. These are more fundamental qualifications of Eliot's faith in human understanding, and in our abilities to control our own destinies through it. The most widely known of these are J. Hillis Miller's "Narrative and History," *ELH*, 41 (1974), 455–473, and "Optic and Semiotic in *Middlemarch,*" *Harvard English Studies*, 6: *The Worlds of Victorian Fiction*, ed. Jerome H. Buckley (Cambridge, Mass.: Harvard University Press, 1975), pp. 125–145. See also Jonathan Arac, "Rhetoric and Realism in *The Mill on the Floss,*" *ELH*, 46 (1979), 673–692. My chief quarrel with such approaches, persuasive as they are, is that they assume Eliot believed any human appropriations of reality must fail unequivocally—that is, they do not take into account what I will later describe as her attempt to naturalize such appropriations.

11. *Letters*, III, 279.

12. For a good statement of this impossibility, see Ermarth, p. 276.

13. But for a more positive reading of this and other scenes of immersion in the novel, see Auerbach, who places immersion within the novel's complex of Gothic motifs, although she tends to overlook the ways in which these romantic impulses are finally frustrated.

14. *Letters*, IV, 300. Further on in this same letter, Eliot reveals another paradox in the writing of *Romola*: "I felt that the necessary idealization could only be attained by adopting the clothing of the past."

15. *Letters*, VI, 216.

16. Other key remarks on this subject occur in "The Natural History of German Life," *Essays of George Eliot*, ed. Thomas Pinney (London: Routledge &

Kegan Paul, 1963), pp. 266–299 (hereafter referred to as *Essays*). But in this essay, too, Eliot does not so much reject theory as insist that it be as complex as human circumstances, that is, that science be specialized. On pp. 289–290, she writes:

> It has not been sufficiently insisted on that in the various branches of Social Science there is an advance from the general to the special, from the simple to the complex, analogous with that which is found in the series of the sciences, from Mathematics to Biology. . . . The more general science will not suffice to solve the problems of the more special.

Her anxiety, in such passages, seems only that reality be adequately described by theory, rather than that theory be used to predict reality. And, of course, the use of this kind of theory is well defined in the essay: the development of a social policy. More germane, perhaps, are her remarks in "Notes on Form in Art," *Essays*, pp. 433–434, in which she arrives at a conception of artistic form as "a set of relations selected & combined in accordance with the sequence of mental states in the constructor, or with the preconception of a whole which he has inwardly evolved."

17. George Eliot, *Middlemarch*, ed. Gordon Haight, Riverside Edition (Boston: Houghton Mifflin, 1956), Ch. 21.

18. See also "The Natural History of German Life," *Essays*, p. 287:

> One word stands for many things, and many words for one thing; the subtle shades of meaning, and still subtler echoes of association, make language an instrument which scarcely anything short of genius can wield with definiteness and certainty.

19. Sensitivity to the "plurality" of meaning, it should be noted, is often invoked by post-structuralists as a more authentic approach to experience than the economic conception of the sign/signified relationship found in traditional theories of reference. See esp. Jacques Derrida, "White Mythology," *New Literary History*, 6 (1974), 5–74. In particular, Derrida writes: "Language is only language to the extent that it can analyze and master polysemie."

20. Roland Barthes, "To Write: An Intransitive Verb?" in *The Structuralist Controversy*, ed. Richard Macksey and Eugenio Donato (Baltimore: Johns Hopkins University Press, 1970), p. 136, writes that the central discovery of modern "semio-criticism" is a "new type of objectivity" that establishes "the distinctive elements of [many] levels" within signs. He then argues that this linguistic plurality can lead us to find a "homology" within the structuration of discourse that reifies language in a liberating, expansive way, grounding man in its pre-human reality.

21. "The Eiffel Tower," in *The Eiffel Tower and Other Essays*, trans. Richard Howard (New York: Hill & Wang, 1979), pp. 3–17. Barthes is one of the few post-structuralist critics who extensively discusses the materiality of structure. However, as with most such concepts in his work, its treatment is fragmentary and unsystematic. His discussions of structure's materiality are most traceable, though, when they coincide with his theme of the text as "body"; see in particular *S/Z*, trans. Richard Howard (New York: Hill & Wang, 1974), pp.

111, 119–120, 190–192, for good discussions of the ways in which a text's structural plurality gives it the status of a "body."

22. "The Eiffel Tower, " p. 9.

23. John P. McGowan, "The Turn of George Eliot's Realism," *Nineteenth-Century Fiction*, 35 (1980), 171–192, brilliantly documents Eliot's conception of culture as a complex of fluid, structural codes, though he does not discuss how Eliot naturalizes these structures.

24. "To Write: An Intransitive Verb?" p. 144.

25. The structural dimension to these "networks" is suggested in several of the essays. In "Notes on Form in Art," for example, Eliot use metaphors of the human body to describe what she calls an "interrelatedness" in aesthetic form. But it is crucial to see that the concept of interrelation in this essay is precisely what allows Eliot to make an analogy between the organic and the inorganic: form is "the limit of difference by which we discriminate one difference from another . . . this is true whether the object is a rock or a man" (*Essays*, p. 433). Through the patterning of relations, man and nature merge. It is also crucial to see that interrelation is not described as a dynamic of resolution, but as the static juxtaposition of parts, as "difference," or as "unlikeness." For a fascinating rereading of Eliot's conception of the organic, see David Carroll, "'Janet's Repentance' and the Myth of the Organic," *Nineteenth-Century Fiction*, 35 (1980), 331–348. Carroll argues that Eliot's organic world is based in unresolvable oppositions, and he writes, p. 348, "George Eliot's view of the world is far more precarious than is usually acknowledged."

26. Witemeyer, p. 43, notes that Eliot was not a practitioner of spatial form, in the modern sense, since her works do not attempt to harness flux through repeated formal motifs. Even Witemeyer, however, does concede that Eliot attempts to slow the movement of time through her contemplation of objects.

27. There are many good discussions of this issue. See esp. George Levine, "Determinism and Responsibility in the Works of George Eliot," *PMLA*, 77 (1962), 268–279; and Felicia Bonaparte, *Will and Destiny: Morality and Tragedy in George Eliot's Novels* (New York: New York University Press, 1975).

28. For a good summary of Eliot's "doctrine of consequences," see Bonaparte, *Will and Destiny*, esp. pp. 13–25.

29. This aspect of the novel has, of course, drawn considerable attention. It seems appropriate here only to summarize a few of the main positions. Among those critics who defend Maggie, John Hagan, "A Re-Interpretation of *The Mill on the Floss*," *PMLA*, 87 (1972), 53–63, finds the love of Maggie and Tom genuine; Paris claims that renunciation enables Maggie to attain an objectivity like that desired by science; and Felicia Bonaparte, *Will and Destiny*, argues that Maggie attains wholeness by apprehending the greatest possible context for her crisis. Among those who condemn Maggie's behavior, U. C. Knoepflmacher attacks Eliot's attempt to find through Maggie an epic teleology; and Carol Christ, "Aggression and Providential Death in George Eliot's Fiction,"

Novel, 9 (1976), 130–140, finds Maggie's death a similar gesture toward the numinous. Critics who dismiss Maggie's course simply as an inadequate conception on Eliot's part include F. R. Leavis, *The Great Tradition* (New York: Anchor, 1954), who finds that Maggie represents Eliot's own ill-thought-out sexuality; and Barbara Hardy, *The Novels of George Eliot* (London: Athlone Press, 1959), who sees bad faith in Eliot's avoidance of the consequences of Maggie's renunciation. A more neutral reading is offered by George Levine, "Intelligence as Deception: *The Mill on the Floss,*" *PMLA*, 80 (1965), 402–409; Levine argues that Maggie's renunciation is the fatal consequence of defects in the world of St. Ogg's.

30. The phrase is from "The Antigone and Its Moral," *Essays*, 261–265. For a good reading of Eliot's attitude toward unresolvable conflict in tragedy, see Sara M. Putzell, "'An Antagonism of Valid Claims:' The Dynamics of *The Mill on the Floss,*" *Studies in the Novel*, 7 (1975), 227–244.

31. A similar argument is made by Mary Jacobus, "The Question of Language: Men of Maxims and *The Mill on the Floss,*" *Critical Inquiry*, 8 (1982), 207–222, although Jacobus defines Maggie's freedom from moral formulas more narrowly than I have, as a defiance of patriarchal hierarchies of meaning. Jacobus finds Maggie's "gift . . . for ambiguity" (p. 214) to be a characteristic of femininity in the novel—a persuasive reading, but one that ignores the tolerance for ambiguity accessible to characters like Dr. Kenn, or Philip Wakem at the end. In general, Jacobus's reading—as well as the direction set for her by Luce Irigaray's work—seeks to appropriate for feminist criticism a polemical opposition between determinate and indeterminate meaning that has its roots just as surely in the very dominant, patriarchal culture she intends to discredit, which has long been in rebellion against mimesis.

32. The genealogy of this idea is much more complex than I can suggest here. But see Gerald Graff, *Literature Against Itself* (Chicago: University of Chicago Press, 1979), p. 45, who traces the common ground linking aesthetic versions of "autonomy" from meaning with moral disinterest all the way back to Kant and to eighteenth-century aesthetic theory.

Thackeray Studies: 1979–1982

Robert A. Colby

In the mid-1970s Thackeray was characterized in a review essay as "a colossus in the shade."[1] Despite an upsurge of publication on him during the following years it was still possible for a reviewer in the *Times Literary Supplement* to observe that he is "one of the most unjustly neglected authors of the Victorian period."[2] He has not, of course, shared the academic limelight with Dickens for some time; neither is he nearly so conspicuous in the catalogs of university presses as George Eliot; even that "lesser Thackeray" Anthony Trollope has bounced out ahead of the greater one lately. It is true that a gathering of Thackerayans at a recent MLA meeting fit quite comfortably in a small hotel room without rubbing shoulders. Yet Thackeray has not really been ignored in recent years. During the period under review some ten doctoral dissertations were completed—perhaps a harbinger for the future. However, in current books it has generally been Thackeray's lot to share billing with others rather than starring, the tendency being to treat him in relation to various Victorian literary trends (satire, realism, author-reader relations, etc.). So he is an honored guest at the feast, if not a celebrity.

A notable exception is that without benefit of a centenary or other such occasion to commemorate, as enjoyed by George Eliot and Anthony Trollope, a special double number of the journal *Studies in the Novel* (Spring-Summer, 1981) published at North Texas State University, was devoted entirely to Thackeray.[3] The fifteen essays comprising this issue reflecting the latest trends in Thackeray study—textual, contextual, historical, iconographic, interpretative, by scholars from five countries—gave him a respectable showing in the 1981 Victorian Bibliography (*VS*, Summer, 1982). Comment on individual contributions is reserved for appropriate sections of the present review essay, but it can be observed at this point that the cosmopolitan nature of this homage to Thackeray is indicative of a widespread interest in him if not a large one by Dickensian standards.

341

Bibliography, Textual Scholarship, Publishing History

The semi-annual *Thackeray Newsletter*, inaugurated at Mississippi State University in 1974, continues to serve as an informative medium of communication among the fit though few devotees. Recent issues have brought to light obscure publishing history, such as the misleadingly dated editions of *Vanity Fair* brought out by Tauchnitz (May, 1980); out of-the-way publication like *The Heroic Adventures of Monsieur Boudin*, brought out in a limited edition by the Syracuse University Library Associates (more about this item later); biographical tidbits, like a hitherto unpublished account of Thackeray's death by his friend Theodore Martin (November, 1981); an offer of the Thackeray issue of *Costerus*, published in 1974 (its publisher has gone out of business) at a bargain price that is a "steal." (See May, 1982 issue). Scattered throughout are additions and corrections to the Colby-Sutherland census of manuscript locations in the *Costerus* issue. The checklists of "Thackeray Studies: Recent and Forthcoming" that conclude each issue are the fullest and most recent available, including even papers read at meetings.

The May, 1981 issue of the newsletter features a progress report on The Works of William Makepeace Thackeray edition underway, by Peter Shillingsburg, the editor of both. It appears that while the presses have not been rolling, there has been considerable activity in the editorial rooms. The text of *Pendennis* is actually completed and "ready to go," or would be except for the circumstance that the copy had to be prepared manually and is therefore not in computer readable form. The same holds true for *The Yellowplush Papers* (not at any rate the best choice to head off the edition). The collation of *Vanity Fair* has been held up by difficult decisions arising from the paucity of punctuation in the surviving manuscript. However, it and *Henry Esmond* are the first volumes in the edition to be "computerized," and are reported as "nearly completed." Meanwhile work has begun on some of the later volumes. "Once publication begins," concludes Shillingsburg on an assuring note, "the time between volumes should not be long." Thackeray has not been subject to such loving care since Anne Thackeray undertook the editing of the Centenary Biographical Edition in 1904, and she didn't have a computer or a collator.

Not much has surfaced lately about the still hazy history of Thackeray's relations with his publishers. John Sutherland, a close student of authors' contracts (or "agreements," as they were called in those days) reconstructs what he calls the "third phase" of Thackeray's career—the first being the pre-*Vanity Fair* period; the second the dealings with the firm of

Bradbury and Evans—in "The Thackeray-Smith Contracts" (*SNNTS* issue). On the basis of the unpublished correspondence between Thackeray and his last publisher, Sutherland conjectures that relations between the two cooled after *Henry Esmond*, judging mainly by the less generous terms offered for Thackeray's last books. However, after Thackeray's death, Smith was certainly generous to his daughter.

Biography

The Lamp of Memory has been turned on once more, without casting much illumination. If Margaret Forster's pseudo-autiobiography *Memoirs of a Victorian Gentleman* (1978; USA, 1979) has by now been shelved away as a useless book, Ann Monsarrat's *An Uneasy Victorian: Thackeray the Man* (London: Cassell, 1980) is most charitably labeled a superfluous one. Like other latecomers to Thackeray, Mrs. Monsarrat seems to regard him as her "discovery," asserting, in the face of the reams that have been published on him over the past fifty years, that while his books are accepted classics, "the life and character of their author is less well known than that of his rival contemporary Charles Dickens." Yet her own biography is little more than a condensation and conflation of that of Gordon Ray, eked out by details from Lionel Stevenson—not always with adequate acknowledgement. Her only contribution is some rummaging around in the papers of the Brookfield Family at Downside Abbey, not— to her credit—to dish up dirt, but to confirm that Thackeray acted with strictest propriety throughout what she coyly calls his "liaison danger-euse"—hardly qualifying this as a "new" biography.

Of far more value, if indirectly, is *Anne Thackeray Ritchie: a Biography* by the late Winifred Gérin (Oxford University Press, 1981), for continuity of the generations is a running thread through her book. In her words: "...to know Anne Thackeray is to rediscover Thackeray, to see him again in an entirely fresh light." Much is made, consequently, of Thackeray's precocious elder daughter's inheritance from him—artistic and psychological, as well as financial. As one would expect from so experienced a biographer as Mrs. Gérin, her last book is original and diligent in research (though she might have made use of Anne's correspondence with W. J. Williams of Smith & Elder housed at Princeton, which bears on the preparation of the Centenary Biographical Edition of her father's works). To be sure, gaps and enigmas remain, but Mrs. Gérin succeeds pre-eminently in conveying the passing of the Victorian era through a sensitive register who witnessed the Second Funeral of Napoleon as a girl (with her father) and lived long enough to help raise money for World War I. As a reviewer summed it up: "What English writer was teased by Thackeray and Virginia Woolf, knew them both intimately, and was afraid of neither?"[4]

Newly published correspondence provides some fresh detail on episodes in Thackeray's life. In "Thackeray and the Carlyles: Seven Further Letters" (*Studies in Scottish Literature*, 1979), Edgar Harden annotates these letters, housed in the National Library of Scotland, dated from 1840 to 1859, and addressed mainly to Jane. Among topics covered in this correspondence are: Thackeray's anxieties over his wife's madness; struggles to place his writing; the "Dignity of Literature" controversy; and an invitation to Thomas to contribute to *Cornhill*—which he refused. The long delayed publication of *The Letters of Edward FitzGerald*, edited by the late Alfred McKinley Terhune and Annabelle Burdick Terhune (Princeton University Press, 1980; 2 vols.) includes three letters from Thackeray to "his best and oldest friend," along with six from "old Fitz." It is true that most of these have previously been made available in Gordon Ray's edition of Thackeray's letters, or are quoted by Lady Ritchie in her introductions to the Biographical Edition of the works, but additional annotation has been provided here, and there are numerous references to Thackeray in other letters. The limited yield of this set, so far as Thackeray is concerned, is owing to FitzGerald's perverse decision to burn most of Thackeray's letters to him and to prune others. Something of a teaser is *A Divided Heart: Letters of Sally Baxter Hampton, 1853–1862*, edited by Ann Fripp Hampton (Spartanburg, S.C.: The Reprint Company, 1980), which brings into print for the first time two letters by the alleged original of Ethel Newcome to Thackeray, and one to her sister in which she refers to her acquaintance with him. This collection seems noteworthy mainly for what is omitted—nine letters that have been kept back for a supplementary volume of Gordon Ray's edition of the letters. Other letters by Sally are believed to have been burned.[5]

Criticism: General

Among recent macro-critical works, *Comedy and Society in Victorian England, 1820–1900* (Princeton University Press, 1980), Roger B. Henkle gives considerable attention to Thackeray, aligning him with lesser contemporaries like Peacock and Jerrold as exponents of what is called here "The Comedy of Radical Disaffection." Praising Thackeray for his "imaginative exuberance," Henkle, somewhat along the lines of John Carey, thinks it ironic that "a man who began his career so brilliantly exposing the humbug of the middle-class myths in the lesser literature should have spent his maturity solidifying variations of those myths." Thackeray figures prominently also in Robin Gilmour's *The Idea of the Gentleman in the Victorian Novel* (London: George Allen & Unwin, 1981). The chapter entitled "Thackeray and the Regency" relates *Vanity Fair* and *Pendennis* to the Silver Forks, as one would expect, but more importantly characterizes Thackeray as a redefiner of the gentlemanly ideal to fit a bourgeois society (a key concept of Gordon Ray's biography), though Gilmour emphasizes more his function as mediator between the "old" social values and the "new." In passing, Gilmour suggests that one reason for the "insecurity" of Thackeray's present-day reputation is the decline of the ideal of gentility—a part of the story quite possibly, but surely not the whole of it.

Thackeray looms large from a different angle in George Levine's *The Realistic Imagination* (University of Chicago Press, 1981), this time as parodist and deflator of pretension. In his chapter entitled "Thackeray: 'The Legitimate High Priest of Truth' and the Problematics of the Real," Levine contends that Thackeray helped both to shape and "subvert" the conventions of the realistic novel, prompted by an "aesthetic pluralism" reflecting his "profound uncertainty about the nature of reality." If one substitutes Eclecticism, the French philosophy that influenced Thackeray from his youth on, for "aesthetic pluralism" it is possible to interpret his "profound uncertainty" as open-mindedness.

The collection of essays assembled in honor of Edgar Johnson under the title *From Smollett to James* (University Press of Virginia, 1981) includes a charmingly written piece by Lionel Stevenson (posthumously published, sad to say) on "Thackeray's Dramatic Monologues." Surveying the various alter egos and *personae* created by Thackeray from Dorothy Ramsbottom to Arthur Pendennis, Stevenson concludes that Thackeray "played a role in developing the strategy of ambiguous self-revelation in prose fiction parallel to that which Browning played in verse."

Offhand one would expect Louis Auchincloss, also a lawyer-society novelist, to have something pertinent to say about Thackeray, but his essay on "Thackeray's Struggling Genius" in his book *Life, Law, and Letters* (Boston: Houghton Mifflin, 1979) is appallingly obtuse, worth preserving only for a resounding *non sequitur*: "Thackeray had only the dimmest conception of the potentialities of painting. Anyone who doubts this should read him on Turner after reading Meyer Schapiro on Cézanne."

Thackeray's Critical Journalism

One scholar who does not believe that Thackeray was blind to painting is Helene Roberts of the Fogg Museum Library. In "The Sentiment of Reality: Thackeray's Art Criticism" (*SNNTS* issue), she traces thirty-four of his identified "strictures on pictures" to then current aesthetic theories, and relates them to Thackeray's own pursuit of "truth to nature." She sees in his predilection for "simple, homely subjects" a sign of a shift in taste during this period from the elevated and ideal towards the real and affective. While Roberts does not deal directly with the fiction, it is possible to transfer to the novels Victorian ideas about pictorial association and emotional empathy that Thackeray clearly shared. Complementary in a way (though apparently unaware of Roberts's work) is Judith L. Fisher's "The Aesthetic of the Mediocre: Thackeray and the Visual Arts" (*VS*, Autumn, 1982), which contends that while as an art critic Thackeray does not belong on a level with Ruskin or Pater his "aesthetic choices are an invaluable guide to the growth of middle-class taste." Fisher makes an analogy—somewhat forced—between Thackeray's preference for genre (or "mediocre" art) and the characters of his novels who settle down to humdrum lives. Meanwhile three of Thackeray's hard-to-come-by pieces of art criticism from *Fraser's Magazine* ("A Pictorial Rhapsody," "May Gambols," "Picture Gossip") as well as one from *Ainsworth's Magazine* ("An Exhibition Gossip") have been reprinted in John Olmsted's anthology *Victorian Painting: Essays and Reviews, 1832–1848* (New York: Garland, 1980). So Thackeray can be read alongside his fellow gallery hoppers, as Helene Roberts recommends, though you had better bring along a magnifying glass, and one might wish that Olmsted had provided a more substantial introduction and some head notes.

Another area of Thackeray's critical journalism has been investigated by Donald Hawes in "Thackeray and French Literature in Perspective" (*SNNTS* issue). Contrary to some who have complained about the conventional prudery of Thackeray's judgments on Sue, Soulié, and other popular *feuilletonistes* of the day, Hawes finds that his "explicit delight in reading some French literature is unique among contemporary reviewers' attitudes," and that at times he sided with readers against some of the more solemn critics. The fact that Thackeray's reviews of French novelists were confined to the second rate (he never wrote about Balzac or Stendhal, for example) is not to be regretted, Hawes believes, for with his well-known ability to convert dross into gold, these Paris grub streeters undoubtedly helped him find his own way as a society novelist.

In "Thackeray's Journalism: Apprenticeship for Writer and Reader" (*VN*, Spring, 1980), Elizabeth Segel argues that Thackeray's use of a variety of *personae* in his "hack" work prepared readers for the disguise he assumed in *Vanity Fair* that seems to us so idiosyncratic, and that therefore he was not, contrary to received opinion, unknown to the public by the time when his masterpiece appeared.

Before *Vanity Fair*

Not much attention has been paid of late to the early fiction. The best of Thackeray's short narratives, *The Great Hoggarty Diamond*, a modern Arabian Nights tale as it might have been told by Theodore Hook, becomes for Peter Shillingsburg a test case in dating in "Publisher's Records and Analytical Bibliography: a Thackerayan Example" (*BC*, Autumn, 1980). Shillingsburg has turned up a previously unrecorded edition antedating what has been accepted heretofore as the first. Interest in *Barry Lyndon* seems to have subsided since the Kubrick film, the one article coming to light being Joseph F. Connelly's "Transparent Poses: *Castle Rackrent* and *The Memoirs of Barry Lyndon*" (*Eire-Ireland*, Summer, 1979), in which it is argued that while Thackeray undoubtedly drew on contemporaries such as Lever and Lover for his sources, this one comic novel by the "celebrated philosopher" of *Catherine* most influenced its technique.

Vanity Fair

Thackeray's most popular novel has as usual kept the word processors clicking. While explication and interpretation abound, the text has never really been fully glossed to everybody's satisfaction. The latest attempt is Oscar Mandel's paperback *Annotations to Vanity Fair* (Washington, D.C., University Press of America, 1981). This booklet can be commended for its amplitude of information on place names, people, and clothing (supplementing the Riverside and Penguin editions in these areas). On the other hand it ignores the speech "Before the Curtain"—including the Bunyan echoes that account for the title—as well as the wrapper design and historiated initials, so that the uninitiated for whom this aid is intended would have no idea that this novel was originally illustrated, or appeared in parts (in fact the compiler seems to be under the impression that it was first published in *Punch*). Quite possibly because Mandel is not himself a Thackeray specialist he has also missed a number of the contemporary literary allusions. This is adequate, in short, for a student who may not know what a benjamin is or the location of Vauxhall, but not for one curious about *Fatherless Fanny*, or the source of "the pursuit of fashion under difficulties."

Peter Shillingsburg has been making progress on the textual front. In "The Printing, Proof Reading, and Publishing of Thackeray's *Vanity Fair* . . ." (*SB*, 1981) he patiently isolates close to 250 variations within the six identified printings (who would have suspected there were so many!) of the first edition, 150 of which, he concludes are substantive. To further confound the confusion, he has discovered that parts continued to be issued even after the novel reached book form, so that format is no guide to printing sequence. In a sequel article "Final Touches and Patches in *Vanity Fair*: The First Edition" (*SNNTS* issue), Shillingsburg attempts to categorize these changes, and to assess Thackeray's possible part in them (i.e. "authorial" as against "editorial" changes). While he considers his evidence at present inconclusive, Shillingsburg thinks it sufficient to support defenses of Thackeray's authorial care and artistry (notably by Edgar Harden) against traditional disparagement. Meanwhile none of us can feel sure that we are reading the text of *Vanity Fair* precisely as Thackeray wrote it.

Such strictures are ignored in the latest Everyman reprint (London: Dent, 1979) which reproduces the same corrupt text from the first printing of 1908—a version that has previously been branded "unacceptable" in the consumer report that appeared in the Thackeray issue of *Costerus* (n.s., 2, 1974). All that is new really in Everyman redivivus is the introduction by A. O. J. Cockshut, which, however, dishes up some of the old bromides (Thackeray "was clever, but perhaps he was not deeply intelligent"). Hold on to your Penguin.

Whatever the state of the text, reading goes on. Some forty pages are devoted to *Vanity Fair* by Robert M. Polhemus in his *Comic Faith: The Great Tradition from Austen to Joyce* (University of Chicago Press, 1980) to demostrate, *pace* Cockshut, that Thackeray thought deeply about life and its mysteries. Subtitled "The Comedy of Shifting Perspectives," Polhemus's essay takes its point of view and imagery from the famous frontispiece of *Vanity Fair* depicting a melancholic clown looking into a cracked mirror. So this comic epic becomes "the Versailles of novels," scintillant with looking glasses, literal and figurative. Polhemus does not really sustain this metaphor throughout his study, but it is thoughtful and stimulating—if overlong. The darker side of Thackeray's satire engages Maria Di Battista in "The Triumph of Clytemnestra: The Charades in *Vanity Fair*" (*PMLA*, October, 1980), which elaborates in baroque mythological detail on the famous Gaunt House costume ball. Di Battista interprets the various tableaux that unfold in this episode as the "aestheticizing" of the "sadomasochistic yearnings" of the principal personages. Be that as it may, this is a learned and suggestive article, even if the extrapolations of myth do sometimes get out of hand—as when Becky is connected with both Procne and Semele.

Another kind of popular entertainment that Thackeray enjoyed and worked into his great "sentimental and comic history" is the centerpiece of Robert T. Bledsoe's "*Vanity Fair* and Singing" (*SNNTS* issue). We know that Becky enchants Jos and other men by her vocal accomplishments (among other things), but Bledsoe points out in precise detail how the songs Becky sings and, furthermore, the operas attended by characters in the novel serve as counterpoint to themes in the book. Much incidental music history of interest is packed into the footnotes of this essay. Two shorter pieces annotate historical details: In "George IV and Jos Sedley . . ." (*ELN*, December, 1981), John P. Frazee puts forward the Prince Regent himself as a prototype for some of the more fatuous traits displayed by Amelia's brother; Ira Bruce Nadel points out in "Becky Sharp and the Three Percent Solution" (*VN*, Fall, 1980) the generally unrecognized irony that by the time that *Vanity Fair* came out, the Consols that Becky sighs for as a firm rock upon which to found her respectability were actually unstable.

Pendennis

The fortunes of Thackeray's second major novel, a favorite with readers during his lifetime and throughout the nineteenth century, have been shaky since, but it seems now to be emerging out of neglect. Peter Shillingsburg once more shares with us some of his textual labors in "*Pendennis* Revised" (*EA*, October-December, 1981). There is even less to work with by way of manuscript evidence than with *Vanity Fair*, but on the basis of such fragments as are extant, as well as proof sheets, Shillingsburg assesses the significance of revisions, regarding them on the whole as improvements. "*The Weekly Chronicle's* Month-by-Month Reception of *Pendennis* and *David Copperfield*" (*VPR*, Fall, 1981) by Rebecca Rodolff affords us a unique contemporary slant through the only paper of the time to have reviewed Thackeray's novel alongside its great rival continuously as they came out. One discovery made here is that whereas previously *Dombey and Son* had been judged wanting by the *Chronicle* next to *Vanity Fair*, this time Dickens was thought to excel Thackeray. It is interesting to see the two writers pitted against each other literally.

In "Thackeray and Clough" (*SNNTS* issue), Ira Nadel points out parallels between *Pendennis* and Clough's *Bothie* on characterization, setting, and thought. The friendship between the two which Nadel believes amounted to a literary-symbiotic relationship is traced to Clough's death in 1861—two years after Thackeray died—reflected even in his last long poem *Mari Magno* for which Thackeray served as model for the Lawyer. Also stressing biographical background is the chapter of George Levine's aforementioned *The Realistic Imagination* entitled "*Pendennis*: The Virtue of the Dilettante's Dream'' which centers on the hero (really anti-hero to Levine) as surrogate for his creator, feeling himself out as man and writer, fusing the cynic and the sentimentalist in his makeup. Contrary to Thackeray's implication at the conclusion of the novel that Pen eventually succeeds in his calling, Levine sees him as reconciling himself to failure. (What Thackeray says is that George Warrington may be the superior talent, but that Pen's works ''have procured him more reputation.'') Patricia Meyer Spacks devotes a few pages of her *The Adolescent Idea: Myths of Youth and the Adult Imagination* (New York: Basic Books, 1981) to *Pendennis* as one of several examples of the Victorian propensity for glorifying childhood; she leaves out, however, the salient fact that Pen is a budding writer, which hardly makes him a typical child of the Victorian or any age.

Henry Esmond

Thackeray's great historical romance is evidently still much ''taught,'' though writing on it is less profuse than heretofore. The question raised by Wolfgang Schulze in '' 'François le Champi': Vorbild für 'Henry Esmond'?'' (*Archiv*, 1979) is not farfetched, little regard as Thackeray seems to have had for George Sand, inasmuch as the hero of this pastoral tale eventually marries the elder benefactor who raised him as a child. In ''The Writing and Publication of *Esmond*'' (*SNNTS* issue), Edgar Harden concludes, from the extant correspondence between Thackeray and George Smith, and other records, that this book which is generally regarded as Thackeray's greatest artistic achievement was, far from being long thought out and carefully planned as is commonly assumed, composed under as harried conditions as his other works. As for its popularity, Harden has found evidence that after some flurry created by the first edition, sales subsided, the second edition moving slowly. Interest in it was revived subsequently with the eulogies by Trollope and Pater. Deconstruction of the hero of this ''novel without a villain'' (as Thackeray referred to it) has abated, but still rears its head. In ''Henry Esmond's Love of Children'' (*NCF*, 1982), Marjorie Garson maintains that although Henry professes such an affection, his retrospective narratives of former playmates belie it, exposing him as self-serving and self-justifying, tending ''to perceive children of any age as his rivals. . . .'' Does that mean that Henry is disingenuous, or that Thackeray understood child psychology? J. Hillis Miller treats *Esmond* as a case study in ''Repetition and Irony'' in his book *Fiction and Repetition* (Harvard University Press, 1982). Because of his close identity with his creator, Henry, Miller proposes, should be added to the gallery of Thackeray's *personae* (Charles Yellowplush, Michaelangelo Titmarsh, etc.) as "a mask he wears, a name he goes by momentarily in the search by its detour to return to himself." In the course of tracking down the various echoes that resound through this novel—from events in Thackeray's own life, from history, from the Bible and classical mythology, Miller takes the reader on a dizzying detour of his own. "Clio and Three Historical Novels" by Dwight N. Lindley (*DSA* 10, 1982) treats *Esmond* in passing, contrasting its "private" view of history (pointed out by Lukács) with history unfolded as "grand event" in *A Tale of Two Cities* and the more philosophical conception of history in *Romola*.

Thackeray's lectures delivered during the early 1850s are of interest today primarily as the inception of *Esmond*, but they also reveal the interest in and care he took with historical research. In "The Writing and Publication of Thackeray's 'English Humourists,'" (*PBSA*, 1982) a kind of companion to his *Esmond* piece noticed above, Edgar Harden brings out how little control Thackeray had over their first publication, which took place during his absence in America, and consequently contained numerous errors not corrected until the second edition. Also bearing on the *The English Humourists* is Ian Ousby's "Carlyle, Thackeray, and Victorian Heroism" (*YES*, 1982). Questioning the assumption that Thackeray was trying to refute Carlyle's Hero theory of history in the lectures, Ousby believes that by mid-century the two men were finding a common meeting ground in seeking a compromise with the heroic ideal to conform to the needs of the modern world.

The Later Thackeray

The post-*Esmond* Thackeray continues to get short shrift. The late domestic tragedy that some diehards still regard as Thackeray's masterpiece is examined from the viewpoint of audience response by Michael Lund in "Reading Serially Published Novels: Old Stories in Thackeray's *The Newcomes*" (*PQ*, Spring, 1981). Lund argues that Thackeray brought something special to the serial format by building it on shifts of perspective and fresh variations on his themes ("old stories") rather than on mere "cliff-hanging." The monthly separation of reader from characters was also imitative of the cycle of leave taking and reunion in life. Though Lund scants some important aspects of serialization (author-reader rapport, topicality), he has opened up an avenue worth exploring. The extent of Thackeray's part in its illustration still is subject for conjecture. Some have argued that Thackeray should be regarded as a collaborator with

Doyle. John Olmsted in "Richard Doyle's Illustrations to *The New-comes*" (*SNNTS* issue) seems almost ready to argue the opposite—that much is owing to this "wayward artist," whom Thackeray at first took on reluctantly, and who proved a source of vexation to him—for bringing Thackeray's intentions to fruition. Examples are provided of various aspects of Doyle's genius, both in the realistic vein—fortunately inasmuch as there is no illustrated edition of *The Newcomes* in print. (Incidentally Olmsted goes along with those who have identified Doyle with Clive New-come's friend, the diffident genius J. J. Ridley.)

Few these days join the present writer as a torchbearer for *The Virginians*. One of them, Gerald Sorensen (who edited it for his doctoral dissertation) makes a strong case in "Beginning and Ending: *The Virginians* as a Sequel" (*SNNTS* issue) for Thackeray's American novel as a necessary complement to its predecessor rather than a mere appendage. In effect, Sorensen argues, *The Virginians* "completes the cycle that *Esmond* initiated," George's final thoughts in retirement "under vine and fig-tree" representing Henry's (and by indirection presumably Thackeray's) on the relationship of the individual to history.

Interest has been newly awakened in the much denigrated *The Adventures of Philip* for similar reasons, Thackeray's last completed novel bearing something of the relationship to *Pendennis* that *The Virginians* does to *Esmond*. In her aptly titled "Funeral Baked Meats . . ." (*SNNTS* issue), Juliet McMaster calls attention to its paradoxical nature "half the time celebrating energy and vitality, the other half giving way to the death wish." It is here in particular that we catch the mature Thackeray re-examining his youthful self, McMaster points out, making *Philip* of unusual biographical interest. The illustrations to this article, incidentally, treat us to some of the most grisly iconography in the Thackeray gallery. In "The Demystification of Laura Pendennis" (*SNNTS* issue), Ina Ferris discovers in the last incarnation of the "angel in the house" who had graced Pen's married life in *The Newcomes* evidence of disillusionment on the part of this model husband. Such second thoughts, Ferris suggests, may be Thackeray's tacit commentary on living by the letter rather than the spirit of the moral law. Thackeray's last novels are probably most fruitfully read as extended *Roundabout Papers*. These rarely studied meditative essays are sensitively examined by Richard Oram in "'Just a Little Turn on the Circle': Time, Memory, and Repetition in Thackeray's *Roundabout Papers*" (*SNNTS* issue). In these poignant and personal writings, in effect a farewell to his *Cornhill* readers, Thackeray, as Oram shows, both reviews his life and sets forth his ideas on time and immortality. These "essaykins" furthermore link up the Victorian and Romantic periods through intimations of Wordsworth.

Miscellaneous Writings

Thackeray is not much appreciated as the master he was of light verse, which in his hands was not light weight. Two obscure examples have surfaced lately. In "Thackeray's 'An Excellent New Ballad about a Law and a Lawyer,'" (*N&Q*, 1981), David O. Maury prints a previously unpublished ballad composed by Thackeray in 1832 while campaigning for his friend Charles Buller, then running for Parliament, in which he exposes the chicanery of Buller's opponent Lord Eliot and Eliot's election agent. In a different vein is "Early Verse by 'Unfortunate W. Thackeray,'" (*VN*, Fall, 1982), another youthful effort printed with commentary by Juliet McMaster, a mock romantic lyric composed by Thackeray while he was a law student, and possibly addressed to his cousin Charlotte Shakespear.

While the reprint presses have been virtually at a standstill so far as Thackeray is concerned, it is agreable to report two "firsts," which, though not exactly lost masterpieces restored, are of interest to students of Thackeray's satirical imagination. *The Heroic Adventures of Monsieur Boudin*, an illustrated comic book depicting the escapades and escapes of a heroic Boulogne fisherman captured by Nelson during the Napoleonic wars, hitherto accessible (much cramped and reduced) in the Centenary Biographical Edition of Thackeray's works, has finally been brought out in a handsome book by the Syracuse University Library Associates (1980). Gordon Ray has written an introduction to this sport, which diverted Thackeray shortly after *Vanity Fair* was published, placing it among his better known work, as well as translating the French captions, and providing useful historical notes. "Bluebeard at Breakfast," an unfinished blank verse playlet by Thackeray left in manuscript (now in the possession of Robert H. Taylor) has been printed, with introduction, notes, as well as title, supplied by Juliet McMaster (*DSA* 8, 1980). This was actually the last of several comic-grisly treatments in word and picture by Thackeray of this legendary uxoricide, who must have been an obsession with him, to judge by frequent reference, overt and subliminal, in the novels. In this incarnation Bluebeard takes on the unfamiliar guise of henpecked husband, relaxing over breakfast with a bachelor friend, and dispensing iconoclastic saws that sound suspiciously like his only begetter. The teasing question remains why Thackeray never finished this "wicked, witty, and diabolical'' (in his words) skit. McMaster thinks it is because Thackeray felt he could not sustain so lurid a story on this level of drollery.

Thackeray Abroad

Most of Thackeray's writings have been translated into many languages, both while he was alive and posthumously, with results ranging, a few happy exceptions set aside, from adequate, if uninspired, to ludicrous. In "Thackeray's French Dressers" (*SNNTS* issue), Sylvère Monod, well known to readers of this annual, points out, with examples, how "a small phalanx, which includes several nonentities and some scandalous bunglers," along with "people of real talent and expertise," variously handled and manhandled ten of Thackeray's works from *The Yellowplush Papers* to *The Rose and the Ring*. In this witty and erudite overview, Monod concludes that on the whole, while Thackeray attracted fewer "French dressers" (Dickens's phrase) than did his great rival, he was better served by them. Ironically *Vanity Fair*, which the French have taken to their bosoms since its first publication, has been generally botched in translation, while *Pendennis*, to which they have been indifferent, has fared well. Raymond Las Vergnas, one of France's leading Thackerayans, and himself a distinguished translator of *Henry Esmond* and *The Book of Snobs*, notes with regret in his introduction to Monod's essay that Thackeray's star is temporarily on the wane there, but looks to a turn in the circle.

In "Thackeray in Czechoslovakia (With a Glance at Other Slavonic Countries)" (*SNNTS* issue), Ludmila Pantůčková of the University of Brno reviews the dissemination of Thackeray's texts and reputation over Eastern Europe from the mid-nineteenth century into our times. We learn that while Dr. Pantůčková's country was behind the other Slavonic countries in recognition of Thackeray—Russian readers had access to all of Thackeray's major novels then in publication by the end of the 1850s; Poland by the 1870s; the first *Vanity Fair* in Czech (then Bohemian) was not published until 1880, and inadequately (sans illustrations and the "Before the Curtain Speech," omissions not to be rectified until 1930). Not only poor texts, but false images of Thackeray were perpetuated by earlier Czech scholars, owing to lack of access to authoritative sources, but the situation is now vastly improved, concludes Dr. Pantůčková, and thanks to the diligent labors of responsible scholars, "Thackeray is now an established name on the bookshelves of Czech and Slovak readers."

To judge by the *Index Translationum*, which lists recent translations of *Vanity Fair* stretching across Europe from Albania to Spain, Thackeray does not lack for foreign readers altogether. To discover that such minor works as *Catherine*, *The Great Hoggarty Diamond*, and *Lovel the Widower* have been published in Hungary, that *The Rose and the Ring* is a favorite book in Poland, and that the French cannot seem to get their fill of *The Book of Snobs* is to recognize that the Europeans have a wider appreciation of Thackeray than we do. It is dismaying to learn that Russia and Czechoslovakia are both ahead of us in producing scholarly editions (the latter "nearing completion" according to Dr. Pantůčková). Bibliographies furthermore indicate scholarly activity of various kinds on Thackeray in Italy, Germany, Yugoslavia, Japan, and India, but inaccessibility necessitates postponement of investigation of this area to a future review essay.

Adaptations

There has been no "Nicholas Nickleby" in the picture for Thackeray to bring him fresh recognition in the theatre or on television, but a few scholars have looked back on past performances. Postmortems continue over Stanley Kubrick's *Barry Lyndon*. In "Narrative and Discourse in Kubrick's Modern Tragedy"—a chapter in the collection entitled *The English Novel and the Movies* (New York: Ungar, 1981)—Michael Klein (one of the editors of this volume) anatomizes the various alterations that Kubrick made to Thackeray's rogue tale. Klein justifies them on thematic grounds—as making the film more of a "universal parable" than the story, evoking more sympathy for Barry than Thackeray does, and establishing him as "a figure of modern alienation." One wishes that Thackeray could have equal time. This book also contains an essay "Becky Sharp Takes Over" by Noel Carroll, a revisionist look at Rouben Mamoulian's 1935 film starring Miriam Hopkins, which made cinematic history as the first full-length Technicolor movie. Pointing out its reductiveness—though it owes more to Thackeray than to the Langdon Mitchell play on which it was nominally based—Carroll treats this adaptation not as a novel of the 1840s, but as a film of the 1930s, with its skirting of unpleasant moral issues, and its stress on Becky as "a role model for members of the aspiring classes."

Becky has been many things to many people, as is brought out by Robert A. Colby's historical retrospect "'Scenes of All Sorts. . . .': *Vanity Fair* on Stage and Screen" (*DSA* 9, 1981). This illustrated survey spans the various efforts, mainly misguided, to bring Thackeray's vast canvas to life on boards, on celluloid, and on tape, from John Brougham's *Becky Sharp* of 1849 (which ran for a week) to the rather tacky BBC TV "Masterpiece Theatre" presentation. The account comes to the unstartling conclusion: "Thackeray . . . remains unchallenged to date as his own best 'Manager of the Performance.'"

NOTES

1. Robert A. Colby, "William Makepeace Thackeray," in *Victorian Fiction: A Second Guide to Research*, ed. George H. Ford (New York: Modern Language Association of America, 1978), p. 114.

2. Peter Keating, "Victorian Lives" (review article), *TLS*, 7 December, 1979, p. 90.

3. The Guest Editor, Robert A. Colby, contributed a foreword and a review essay assessing the state of Thackeray scholarship over the years 1975–1979, which the present essay updates (along with the briefer "Recent Thackeray Studies" that appeared in *DSA* 8). The special number of *Studies in the Novel* will be cited throughout this essay: *SNNTS* issue.

4. *TLS*, 10 July, 1981, p. 776 (Review by Claire Tomalin).

5. Of additional biographical interest is *Thackeray: Interviews and Recollections*, ed. Philip Collins (New York: St. Martin's Press, 1982), 2 vols. This compilation, presumably following the lines of the one that Collins has assembled on Dickens, was announced but unavailable at time of writing.

ABBREVIATIONS

BC.	*Book Collector*
DSA.	*Dickens Studies Annual*
EA.	*Etudes Anglaises*
ELN.	*English Language Notes*
N&Q.	*Notes and Queries*
NCF.	*Nineteenth-Century Fiction*
PBSA.	*Papers of the Bibliographical Society of America*
PMLA.	*Publications of the Modern Language Association of America*
PQ.	*Philological Quarterly*
SB.	*Studies in Bibliography* (Annual)
SNNTS.	*Studies in the Novel (North Texas State University)*
TLS.	(London) *Times Literary Supplement*
VN.	*Victorian Newsletter*
VPR.	*Victorian Periodicals Review*
VS.	*Victorian Studies*
YES.	*Yearbook of English Studies*

Recent Dickens Studies: 1981

Sylvère Monod

The opening section of a survey article of the present kind cannot avoid damaging admissions, and it had been my intention to begin mine with excuses. A Shakespearian quotation suggested itself at once, because it had the merit of being alluded to in Chapter II of *Bleak House*, and I have a vivid sense of being sent, not to my account, but to the printer's, "with all my imperfections on my head," and they are many. It is, however, in part reassuring to find that such apologies are becoming a ritual gesture for the writers of annual surveys. There have been three pioneers so far; the most pioneering of all, Fred Kaplan, was the only one who did not express qualms about the possible incompleteness of his article, even though it covered two years rather than one; of the other two "surveyors," Robert Newsom, reviewing the publications of 1979, confessed: "I am undoubtedly ignorant of a number of important items published in 1979" (*Dickens Studies Annual 9*)[1]; and my immediate predecessor Sylvia Manning (*Annual 10*) went into more detail and explained that "many things are omitted" for one of three or four different reasons. By admitting that there are imperfections and gaps in the present survey, I am not therefore breaking new ground. It is sufficiently obvious that when the surveys are written by critics who have not been trained as professional bibliographers, imperfections are inevitable, even with the invaluable help of the excellent Checklists contributed by Alan M. Cohn and K. K. Collins to *Dickens Studies Newsletter*, and of the reviews printed both in the *Newsletter* and in the *Dickensian*. But it is not necessary to insist that such deficiencies are bound to be even more serious in the case of a surveyor who happens to live on the wrong side of the Atlantic and even of the English Channel. Let me, therefore, in my turn make a clean breast of my sins of involuntary omission: not all of the relevant publications, articles or even books, may have come to my knowledge, and of those that have, not all have proved obtainable, in spite of the valued support of the *Annual* editorial troika. Thus there is reason to fear that this essay, instead of having a few gaps in an otherwise fairly close-knit fabric, will appear to be mainly composed of gaps with a few pieces of fabric in between them. Again a quotation comes to mind, this time from Virgil's *Aeneid*: "*Apparent rari nantes in gurgite vasto*" (*anglice*: odd figures swimming are glimpsed in the waste of waters).

After such a chastening experience, never again shall I be tempted to make fun (as I fear I have done in the past) of bibliographers who invite authors to provide them with the information it is their responsibility to supply, or of the supposed British view that when there is fog over the Straits of Dover the European Continent is isolated. The European Continent *is* isolated from all but a small part of Anglo-American research, and there is nothing like playing at the bibliographical game to make one realize that information is hard to collect. Even so, however, there is plenty of material to describe and discuss; it will be done under the various headings which are more or less traditional or which suggested themselves as particularly convenient to deal with the kind of items that have accumulated in the course of 1981. Bibliography will be followed by Dickens' writings (editions and additions), then biography and history, then by studies of individual works, and finally (last but certainly not least, for that happens to be a particularly glamorous field in 1981) general studies of Dickens; a few sentences of overall impressions may try to squeeze themselves in at the end, and I know that I shall experience great difficulties if I attempt to keep them out altogether.

Bibliography

In that field the great year will probably be 1982 rather than 1981, with the publication of Cohn and Collins's *Cumulated Checklist*, covering the years 1970–1979, and also the bringing up-to-date of Brahma Chaudhuri's *Annual Bibliography of Victorian Studies*. Though not devoted to Dickens alone, this *Annual Bibliography* has already begun to be of service to Dickensian scholars everywhere. The speed with which its volumes have come out is breathtaking; the first installment was brought out in 1980 (covering the year 1977); 1981 saw publication of the volumes covering respectively 1979 and 1978; at least three more volumes were promised for 1982, those for 1980 and 1976, and a five-year cumulative volume; these were to be followed by a volume for 1981 before the end of 1982 and one for 1982 perhaps as early as August, 1983.

In addition the Edmonton Center (based at the University of Alberta) that is issuing these bibliographies proposes to provide on-line computer service for scholars. This center, which calls itself by the ugly name of Litir Database (almost seeming to negate in its very title the existence of the phenomenon of literature) enjoys all the benefits and suffers from all the drawbacks of computerized bibliographical work. It works fast and collects and sifts mountains of data; but it is not error-proof. Though it is too early to pass judgment on an achievement which is so evidently in progress, in every sense of the phrase, it can be said at this point that the policies outlined in the preface are sensible in most cases, though some decisions, in matters of both inclusion and exclusion, may appear controversial. *Nostromo* will not strike every reader as a Victorian novel; but it is surely safer to sin by excess than by default in such matters. A sad, perhaps crippling limitation is that only items written in English are included (Cohn and Collins do much better in that respect, but they deal with one author only). The general organization of the Chaudhuri (sorry, the Litir Database) volume appears satisfactory, and the four Indexes (by subject, author, title, and reviewer) are generous and convenient; but there are occasional errors and oddities. To give only one example: it seemed surprising to find only three entries for 1979 under the name of G. K. Chesterton; the *Chesterton Review* alone would account for far more items than that; but while the *Chesterton Review* is listed among the periodicals examined (many of which, incidentally, receive abbreviated titles different from the MLA format, and not always adhered to, which may create unnecessary difficulties for users), no article from it had been entered. In the volume for 1978, on the other hand, *Chesterton Review* articles are in fact listed, but with one omission and several inaccuracies. All the little errors that have been spotted in the course of a partial sampling are of course carried over into the Index or Indexes. In the Author Index, for instance, Adam Gillon having once been misprinted as Gillion, figures as two persons: Adam Gillion and Adam Gillon. Robert Newsom is slightly Thackerayized as Newsome (though that may be an unfair remark since there is a Lewsome in *Chuzzlewit*). Even so, one must compliment Brahma Chaudhuri and Litir Database on so much useful and disinterested work accomplished in the service of the community of scholars.

The other major contribution to Dickens bibliography in 1981 was of course Robert Newsom's inspiring essay on "Recent Dickens Studies 1979" published in *Annual 9*. It needs no description or discussion here.

Dickens' Writings: Editions and Additions

This is one of the sections which tend to make of 1981 a good, almost a brilliant year in Dickens studies.

Pride of place in that section must be given to the truly splendid edition of *David Copperfield* by Nina Burgis (Oxford University Press, Clarendon Dickens). It is admittedly an expensive volume (forty pounds sterling), but it is valuable, in spite of a definite lack of interest in the question of illustrations. With much recent scholarly work done by John Harvey, Michael Steig, and Jane R. Cohen, it is a pity that the Clarendon editors do not seem to devote much attention, either theoretically or practically, to that aspect of Dickens' novels, an aspect which he himself apparently never neglected. But with that single exception Nina Burgis has done superlatively efficient editorial work, worthy of her predecessors in that glamorous series and of its life and soul, general editor Kathleen Tillotson. The Clarendon *Copperfield* supplies abundant editorial material and applies intelligent editorial policies, in delicate questions like the retrieval of MS readings ignored by the compositors and unrestored by the author at proof stage, or in the treatment of accidentals; all of which is lucidly explained and justified in a substantial introduction. As to the textual notes, it is impossible in the format of a survey of the present kind to give any notion of their wealth, but their contribution to the reader's knowledge and understanding of Dickens' methods of work and their demonstration of his close attention to detail are of great interest. *Copperfield* is a magnificent novel in any form; it is understandable that Dickens loved it and worked at it lovingly. Rereading it in the new edition and with such additional helps to appreciation of the author's artistry is a highly pleasurable experience.

There have been in 1981 a new Bantam *Tale of Two Cities* and a reprint (Westminster Press, Philadelphia) with new illustrations of *The Life of Our Lord, Written Expressly for His Children* (a title in which the capital H of *His* is infelicitous).

If *Copperfield* is one of the greatest and most popular works written by Dickens, the Christmas story called "A Christmas Tree" is probably one of the least celebrated, so that a new and in some ways also glamorous edition of it comes as a surprise. It comes from Italy and presents itself as *Un Albero di Natale* by Charles Dickens and Mirando Haz (Milan: All'Insegna del Pesce d'Oro); the treatment given to Dickens' text in that edition is curious, but striking, and rather moving. The great feature is a sequence of twelve illustrations by Mirando Haz; there are in addition several essays, including one by Ada Nisbet, the others being contributed by Italian admirers of the illustrator and devoted to discussing the plates rather than the letterpress. The plates are beautifully printed (unlike the English texts) and offer a powerfully original reading of Dickens' Christmas story; some of the contributors are unscholarly, but the revelation of a true artist and of his dedication to Dickens is no doubt a significant event. "A Christmas Tree" had first been published in 1850 and was thus practically contemporary with *Copperfield*. It is a happy coincidence that the two works received royal treatment in the same year, though with enormous differences in scale and kind.

Through another felicitous coincidence, the fifth volume of *The Letters of Charles Dickens*, also published in 1981, again with Kathleen Tillotson as the moving spirit of the whole enterprise, covers the period just before and up to *Copperfield* (1847-1849). The editors of this particular volume are Graham Storey and K. J. Fielding. The book is as expensive and as rewarding as the Clarendon *Copperfield*; the Pilgrim Letters, like the Clarendon novels, are high-quality Oxford products. Even without the above-mentioned coincidence, the volume would be of considerable interest, for the three years it deals with were extraordinarily full and rich. It could be contended that between 1847 and 1849 Dickens reached the culminating point of his career. The editing is once more excellent; there are practically no detectable errors, and the annotation is admirable. The amount of research that goes into the footnotes alone is phenomenal. It must be a comfort to know that they have been read greedily by more than one reader, and found—what higher compliment could be paid them?—entirely worthy of the remarkably distinguished and lively company in which they appear, that of Dickens' own letters. Among the most striking features of the volume must be mentioned the sheer bulk of the correspondence: the superabundant energy of which they give evidence (in those days when there were no typewriters or any of the machines of various kinds that make things easier for us); the importance for the novelist of his "French connection" (visits to France, friendships with Frenchmen, flirtation with the French language); his authoritarian attitude to members of his family; the ebullient wealth of his ideas (including political ideas); and, of course, the image that one gradually forms of Dickens at work, whether in his collaboration with Angela Burdett-Coutts over the opening of Urania Cottage, or in relation to his strenuous (strenuous, and also, to be quite candid, slightly tiresome to the reader of the letters) private theatricals, or in literary pursuits, where it appears that he was ready to take on, in addition to his own writing, almost any number of other responsibilities, in order to help his friends, or mere strangers who applied to him for advice. The volume closes before Dickens has actually become editor of *Household Words*, but he has demonstrated to himself and to his correspondents that he is uniquely qualified for such a job.

Because one third of the 1248 letters in Volume 5 were hitherto unpublished, the book counts as an addition, and no slight one, to the corpus of Dickens' writings. A less bulky, but nonetheless welcome addition will be found in the thin volume ably edited by Fred Kaplan, *Charles Dickens' Book of Memoranda. A Photographic and Typographic Facsimile of the Notebook Begun in January 1855* (New York Public Library). I am delighted that this volume, which notoriously came out in 1982, was copyrighted in 1981, because it thus falls officially within my province and I enjoy the chance of saying how much I have found in it. Of course, fragments of the *Book of Memoranda* had been published before (by John Forster in the first place), but, astonishingly, no complete reproduction had yet been attempted. To the Dickens student such an instrument is valuable; one sees how Dickens' mind functioned in several directions, such as the creation of incidents, situations, themes, or in the quest for characters' names (the most eccentric creations being probably borrowed from real life). And the advantage of having Dickens' notes both in his own handwriting and in an almost impeccable transcription is considerable.

Another addition to the corpus of Dickens' writings is found in *Annual 9*, where Alec W. Brice (one of the world's two most dedicated Forsterians) and K. J. Fielding, now a senior statesman in the Republic of Dickens scholarship, published "A New Article by Dickens: 'Demoralisation and Total Abstinence.'" Their heading is amusing: no one (apart from spiritualists perhaps) expects Dickens to write new articles these days; admittedly it is difficult to describe such an item compendiously—uncollected? hitherto unidentified? hitherto unattributed? an article newly by Dickens? (*newly identified* is Brice's phrase in the title of his Edinburgh dissertation). This very good "new" article is against the National Temperance Association and against several individuals guilty of preaching fanatical teetotalism. Dickens advocates a distinction between use and abuse and is angered by what he regards as intemperate teetotalism; the writing is brilliant and his plea for moderation in preference to abstinence is eloquent. The ascription by the authors of this essay is based on circumstantial evidence and is convincing.

Biography and History

The tribute to Edgar Johnson by Alice Chandler, "Edgar Johnson / An Appreciation," in *From Smollett to James. Studies in the Novel and Other Essays Presented to Edgar Johnson* (Samuel I. Mintz, Alice Chandler, and Christopher Mulvey, eds., University Press of Virginia), and the checklist of Johnson's writings, call for mention in this place.

Johnson is seen as novelist and critic as well as biographer, but his books on Dickens and Scott are his most justly celebrated achievements. Chandler defines the virtues of the great Dickens biography, very properly mentioning the collaboration of Johnson's wife Eleanor; she also evaluates Johnson's attitudes and his stance as a critic free from modishness. The checklist reminds us that he had published two books on biography before writing his life of Dickens, and that, of his forty-three articles and introductions, twenty are on Dickens, which seems to me an admirable and indeed exemplary proportion: it makes him a specialist and an expert, but not a narrowly concentrated one.

Of the historical works on the Victorian period, one of the most profitable is Martin J. Wiener's *English Culture and the Decline of the Industrial Spirit* (Cambridge University Press), which deals with the history of ideas. It is very far from being a book on Dickens, but Dickens plays his part in it and is even integrated into a general trend which extends over more than a century. The central thesis of the book is that there has been a constant antagonism between the British *intelligentsia* and industrial development (if not material progress). Wiener analyzes the contradictions of Dickens' thinking in that respect, a deficiency which he had in common with Arnold and Ruskin among others. One emerges from reading this book with the conviction that Dickens, in numerous and distinguished company, unconsciously bore part of the responsibility for the eventual decline of Britain's industrial eminence.

Of considerable biographical value are the two volumes of *Dickens. Interviews and Recollections* edited by Philip Collins (London: Macmillan). They contain a very useful hoard of impressions. Dickens was not often subjected to formal interviews, but innumerable people reminisced about him, with frequent, if pardonable, amplification of their relationship with him (a phenomenon well known to students of French reactions to Dickens published soon after this death). Not all the items collected by Collins are of the first magnitude and many of them are untrustworthy about facts: some are disappointing, considering either the author's intrinsic merit (George Eliot) or Dickens' attachment to them (Marcus Stone); others cannot disappoint the reader grievously, because little enough was to be expected of them (some of the novelist's children, or of his schoolfellows, and several good ladies writing in what they imagine to be a literary style). Particular credit goes to Eliza Lynn Linton, and to J. and A. Fields. But nearly everything in this book, even, or especially, the contributions of the least famous and often most mediocre writers, deserves attention and adds something to our knowledge of Dickens and his circle of acquaintances. One of the highlights of *Interviews and Recollections* comes near the end of Dickens' life: it is the correspondence relative to the novelist's visit to Queen Victoria (it is, properly speaking, neither interview nor recollection of Dickens, but it is great fun, inserted by Collins with delightful and characteristic tongue-in-cheekism). Philip Collins has once more served the cause of Dickens studies in an able and decisive way.

Several items of biographical interest on a smaller scale were published in 1981. Michael Allen's "The Dickens Family at Portsmouth" (*Dickensian*, Autumn) is substantial, running to twelve pleasantly illustrated pages, and shows that the Portsmouth years (seven in all for Dickens' father) have been meagerly documented. The announcement of the future novelist's birth in a local newspaper reads amusingly: "On Friday, at Mile-end Terrace, the Lady of John Dickens, Esq. a son," which tends to show that John Dickens, Esq., resembled Mr Sapsea rather than a forerunner of modern feminism. The whole piece by Allen is interesting and useful.

Lawrence J. Clipper's "The Blacking Warehouse Experience Again: Another View" (*Newsletter*, September) does not contain much novelty, apart from one psychological suggestion and one or two odd statements: Dickens must have remembered, Clipper thinks, the less mournful aspects of the episode, and particularly the "happy circumstance" of his grandmother's death, which caused him to believe in miracles; among the miracles to be found in his novels there is the fact that "Florence Dombey falls into the clutches of Mrs. Brown."

Michael Hollington's "Dickens the Flâneur" (*Dickensian*, Summer) is a cultured and distinguished essay on Dickens' walks which have sociological and psychological implications, and were called by himself at first lounging, and later sauntering, though Hollington prefers the word *flânerie*. He refers interestingly to Balzac and Baudelaire, Lamb and De Quincey, and to Walter Benjamin. Hollington demonstrates that Dickens' narrative mode was to be influenced by his *flâneurship*.

"The Britannia Wine Set" (*Dickensian*, Summer) by Pieter Van Der Mewe (of the National Maritime Museum at Greenwich) is less ambitious; it describes the items of Dickensian interest at the Museum, items which were viewed by members of the Dickens Fellowship in October, 1982, when the Fellowship celebrated its own eightieth anniversary there. The story of the gift of plate presented to Captain Hewitt of the *Britannia* is interesting and elegantly told. It is sad to think that Hewitt had later to sell his wine set when he needed money. Van Der Mewe does not entirely dispel the little mystery that surrounds the episode: what was the real reason for this presentation, considering that Hewitt had done no more than his duty? Such presentations occurred now and again, but by no means always. Among the least unsatisfactory explanations I find two or three, connected with aspects of Dickens' personality (for there can be no doubt that he was the prime mover in the whole affair): there was his pleasure in acting with an aristocratic fellow-passenger; there was his need to believe that the crossing had been uniquely stormy and dangerous; and there was his urge to act, direct, and control, when he found himself among a group of other human beings.

"Dickens Incognito" (*Dickensian*, Summer) by Katherine M. Longley is a disparate, but erudite and witty article. Longley's claim that Dickensian scholars have neglected the revelations of Forster's *Life* about Dickens incognito is only in part substantiated, because the notion of "incognito" varies, being sometimes confused with Dickens' fondness for playing roles or with his delicate trickery (for instance, when he bought Maclise's painting under an assumed name). The section on the name of Tringham is especially amusing. An example of the unprofitable is on the contrary provided by Roy Nuhn's "Amateur Actor Dickens" (*Hobbies*, December). This little article deals without much novelty (apart from a few bizarre phrases) with the *Christmas Carol* and the public readings, of which a superficial account is given, though there are a few valuable illustrations, especially reproductions of picture postcards featuring the *Carol*. The conclusion of the essay is somewhat uncritical: "Overly sentimental it may well be, but the story is one of the most nearly perfect pieces of literature ever penned. Christmas would not be the same without it." The conclusion of the reader may well be that amateur scholarship is hardly fit to become a hobby.

James E. Marlow combines history and biography in "Sir John Franklin, Mr. Charles Dickens, and the Solitary Monster" (*Newsletter*, December); Marlow shows that Dickens' works provide many examples of anthropophagy (some of which are less convincing than others, like the case of John Jasper, who "(apparently) intends to consume the flesh of Edwin Drood (by means of quick-lime)"), but that the adventure of Franklin, lost on a Polar expedition and rumored to have resorted to cannibalism before he died, reinforced the novelist's obsession. Dickens tried to demonstrate that the accusation could not be true, mainly because it would have been too horrible, and in spite of some supposed evidence provided by natives and later travelers. Dickens' voice in this affair appears to have been singularly insistent and urgent and, as it happens, he was probably right.

A specific branch of biographical and historical studies that is attracting more and more attention is the history of the publication and reception of Dickens' works. Richard Maxwell's "Dickens, the two *Chroni-*

cles, and the Publication of *Sketches by Boz*" (*Annual*) is a valuable contribution in that field. It is interesting because it concerns itself with the change from journalist to author, and at the same time provides a chapter in the history of the British press: the fate of the *Morning Chronicle* under its successive editors, the creation of the *Evening Chronicle* as an offshoot, the way Dickens' *Sketches* were shifted from *Morning* to *Evening Chronicle* (though with republication in the morning newspaper) and later to *Bell's Life in London*, all these are clearly explained by Maxwell.

As for Ellen Casey's "'That Specially Trying Mode of Publication': Dickens as Editor of the Weekly Serial" (*Victorian Periodicals Review*, Fall), it is mainly a study of Dickens' editorship of *All the Year Round*, chosen because that journal regularly included fiction. Casey quotes a well-known and interesting letter to Mrs. Brookfield (written in 1866) and compares Dickens' editorship of twenty novels with his son and successor's editing of fifty-four. Dickens' principles are listed (there must be a sensational story, a prompt beginning, no excessive length of either novel or installments, incidents must be shown rather than told about). The article is not uninteresting but, insofar as its purpose is to show that Dickens was a better editor of fiction than his son, it can only demonstrate the obvious.

In "Fitzjames Stephen, Charles Dickens, and Double Reviewing," Christopher C. Dahl (*Victorian Periodicals Review*, Summer), concentrates on four articles in which Stephen discussed *Little Dorrit* and other popular novels. One article had appeared in the *Edinburgh Review*, whose editor Henry Reeve may have toned it down. That article was favorably reviewed in the *Saturday Review* by its author. Stephen, whose father was reputed to be one of the targets of Dickens' satire, disliked the Circumlocution Office section of *Dorrit*; Stephen's father, however, had cautioned him against fighting Dickens, and Dahl shows that the latter had in fact replied in *Household Words*, not without success, to the *Edinburgh Review* article.

Stephen, with Bagehot and Lewes, and some lesser lights like Stott and Whipple, are quoted in Philip Collins's essay "Special Correspondent to Posterity / How Dickens's Contemporaries Saw His Fictional World" (in the volume edited by Mintz, Chandler, and Mulvey). Collins shows that Dickens' contemporaries were divided between those who thought he would survive as chief witness of the age, and those who believed him to be merely ephemeral. In addition, he alludes to the fate of the epithet "Dickensian." It seems to Collins that many Englishmen of the time saw

England through Dickens' eyes (i.e., their vision was influenced by his), whereas Henry James and several other critics denounced exaggeration and caricature. Collins concludes with Dickens' own view of the question, which was fairly clear-sighted. It is a pity that this otherwise excellent essay carries a slight inaccuracy in its title (Bagehot's phrase, correctly quoted twice in the text, speaks of a special correspondent *for*, not *to*, posterity).

Studies of Individual Works

In spite of Dickens' dislike of "tabular statements" (expressed, of course, in *Hard Times*), it is in order to begin this long section with a few figures. The novel that received most attention in the 1981 publications discussed here was *David Copperfield* (examined in eight articles, editions, or chapters of books); *Bleak House* is a close second with seven; then come *Our Mutual Friend* and *Oliver Twist* with four each, followed by *The Old Curiosity Shop* and *Great Expectations* (three each); *Little Dorrit*, surprisingly, is the subject of only two essays, and thus ranks with *Pickwick*, *Barnaby Rudge*, *Hard Times*, and *A Tale of Two Cities*; each of the other novels, and four minor works (*Sketches*, *Christmas Books*, *Christmas Stories*, and *Life of Our Lord*) occasioned one publication in 1981, with the exception of *Dombey and Son*, which appeared nowhere in its own right, though one book about Dickens and others has a chapter on it and one on *Little Dorrit*. It may be significant—and such a shift seems to be one of the main trends of the year—that *Dorrit*, once, not so very long ago, a proud member of the somber trilogy, should have been left far behind by the other two, overtaken by Little Nell, and doomed to rub shoulders with Lucie Manette, Louisa Gradgrind, Emma Haredale, and Arabella Allen. "To have seen what I have seen, see what I see!" Amy may, Ophelia-like, exclaim.

The best contribution to *Pickwick* studies in 1981 is to be found in Alexander Welsh's *Reflections on the Hero as Quixote* (Princeton University Press). This stimulating book does not offer simply one separate chapter on Dickens' first novel—*Pickwick* is present everywhere (and there are also a few interesting lines on *Great Expectations*), mixed up, however, with much else. Welsh is a splendidly cultivated critic and treats German, Spanish, Russian and French, as well as English, novels. He studies two aspects of quixotic heroism, illustrated, among others, by the case of Mr Pickwick and Sam Weller: the two most relevant chapters are the first ("Foolishness, not Satire") and the fifth ("Victims of Circumstance")

where Welsh presents an entertaining, yet enlightening, comparison between Mr Pickwick and Abraham, suggested by Kierkegaard's reading of
the latter's story in Genesis. One may fleetingly regret that, while he was
at it, Welsh did not see fit to examine the quixoticism of Joseph Conrad's
Lingard, but there is every reason to be grateful for what he has achieved,
and especially for his circumstantial demonstration of *Pickwick*'s indebt-
edness to Goldsmith, and, via Fielding and Goldsmith, to Cervantes himself. The other *Pickwick* item is a short article by Glyn A. Strange called
"Paired Episodes in *Pickwick*" (*Newsletter*, March) with a rather arbitrary starting-point, to the effect that the Bath interlude "has escaped
close attention." This observation is followed by a jealous defense of the
newly discovered part of *Pickwick*. It then appears that paired episodes
are, in fact, something like internal echoes. Strange has a point, and it *is*
made, though it is somewhat slight and unduly magnified and exploited
for doubtful purposes: Strange believes that by using paired episodes the
"emergent novelist was deliberately attempting . . . to give shape to his
novels." It does not seem to have occurred to Strange that repetition may
be due to carelessness, and that "shape" ought to be something too visible to need this kind of ingenious ferreting.

Oliver Twist, together with *Our Mutual Friend*, is aimed at by Archie
Niman, in "A Case for Shakespeare and Dickens" (*Midstream*, October).
Its starting-point sets a new record for arbitrariness by asserting that most
people, on being asked who are the villains in English literature (but
where could someone be found to ask such an inane question?) would
name Shylock and Fagin and "would be hard pressed to name a third.
There can be little doubt, therefore, that for the vast majority these two
are the archetypes of villainy." Because these two are Jews, Niman believes he must go on to demonstrate that Shakespeare and Dickens were
not really anti-Semitic. The defense of Shylock is occasionally based on
odd arguments; for example, that not too much importance should be attached to his threats because "angry men in plays who intend to kill utter
much stronger threats than these." Concerning Dickens, the hesitant tone
betrays extraordinary ignorance of Harry Stone's essay "From Fagin to
Riah: Jews and the Victorian Novel" published in the very same journal
(Winter 1960) as Niman's, whose little piece is well-meaning, pure in
heart, but nothing could be more unscholarly and still gain publication.
Has *Midstream* lowered its standards? *Oliver Twist*, in addition to being
annotated by Suzanne Brown in *Oliver Twist: Notes* (London: Longmans), also has rather better luck at the hands of Iain Crawford than at
Niman's; Crawford's "Time and Structure in *Oliver Twist*" (*Dickensian*,

Spring) follows step by step the chronology of the story, in its connection with the seasons. This tracing is well done, though the reason for doing it is not entirely clear (that Dickens was occasionally a little hurried and careless had not been completely unrecognized). In "Poverty and Villainy in *Oliver Twist*: Unraveling the Paradox" (*Newsletter*, September), Katherine T. Brueck wishes to utter a protest against the twentieth-century view of Dickens' criminals as social victims. Brueck asserts that Dickens wanted to make them repugnant and gives a list of loathsome details. She is also addicted to edifying sentiments ("Oliver's worldly affliction indisputably softens the heart") but does not appear to recognize that the criminals in *Twist* are "indisputably" much more lively and attractive than Brownlow and the Maylies (Dickens may not have intended it that way, but there it is).

The single article on *Nicholas Nickleby* in my batch is Norman Russell's "*Nicholas Nickleby* and the Commercial Crisis of 1825" (*Dickensian*, Autumn). It is a useful historical note, showing that Dickens was using more specific material in *Nickleby* than in his earlier "Mudfog Papers." Russell recalls the mania for foreign investment (mainly in silver mines) that had led in 1824 to the "floating" of 624 schemes, most of which had been stillborn or not born at all; however, 127 had survived: hence a panic and the failure of thirty banks. And that is how Nicholas's father is ruined and dies, while uncle Ralph promotes a "bubble" company very similar to some historical examples. The article is interesting and accurate, but how Russell has avoided all mention of Tigg, Merdle, and Veneering, is almost incomprehensible. The Royal Shakespeare Company production of *Nickleby*, discussed by Sylvia Manning (*Annual 10*) was shown in New York in 1981 (before appearing on British television's brand-new Channel Four in November, 1982), lavishly reviewed, and turned into the subject of a whole book (Leon Rubin, *The Nicholas Nickleby Story: The Making of the Historic R.S.C. Production*, London: Heinemann).

The Old Curiosity Shop has been steadily gaining, or regaining, ground. Loralee McPike borrowed from *Finnegans Wake* the heading of her two-part essay "'The Old Cupiosity Shape': Changing Views of Little Nell" (*Newsletter*, Part I, June; Part II, September). McPike retraces the critical debate about *The Old Curiosity Shop* and particularly about Nell, quoting not only various contemporary reactions but also the author's own views, showing how hostile opinions came to predominate as early as the 1850s and 1860s, until Gissing and Chesterton came to Nell's rescue. She mentions the part played more recently by psychoanalytical criticism, and concludes on the situation now: "After 140 years of persistent exis-

tence, Nell seems to have achieved a modicum of critical acceptance.''
Notwithstanding that McPike has written a detailed, intelligent, and balanced account, but offers no individual judgment, her essay is devoted to
the history of criticism rather than to criticism proper. Joan (or John—
for she, or he, is called John in "Contents") D. Winslow, writes of "*The
Old Curiosity Shop*: The Meaning of Nell's Fate" (*Dickensian*, Autumn),
an article devoted to showing that Dickens established a system of images
to prepare for Nell's death—one might have thought the days of image-
hunting were over. Winslow's work is well done, but the essay lacks pun-
gency. Nell's fellow-guest at Master Humphrey's weekly banquet, *Barnaby Rudge*, has occasioned two very different pieces. Dvora Zelicovici's
"Grip the Raven: A Rehabilitation" (*Dickensian*, Autumn) protests
against the "vile slander" perpetrated by a distinguished *Annual* contributor, Leonard Manheim, who is guilty of not having seen any humor in
Grip. Zelicovici's essay is admittedly light and humorous, but it is very
slight; the present reviewer, for one, could hardly care less, one way or the
other. John P. McGowan's "Mystery and History in *Barnaby Rudge*"
(*Annual*) deals with a serious question: the nature of change, and he explores factors like the relationship between story and history (he sees a
link between the Riots and the Rudge plot), and also the relationship between authority, authorship, and fatherhood. McGowan is ingenious as
well as learned: his notes are impressive; there is practically nothing important on *Rudge* that he has not read; his tone is urbane; and he gives his
predecessors their exact due.

It is again by means of historical documents that one episode of *Martin
Chuzzlewit* is enlightened in Lowell L. Blaisdell's "The Origins of the Satire in the Watertoast Episode of *Martin Chuzzlewit*" (*Dickensian*, Summer). Blaisdell relates events of the summer of 1843 and describes an earlier satire published in the *Times* which influenced Dickens: O'Connell
had gained American sympathies by his vigorous campaign for an Irish
Home Rule, but lost them in May, 1843, by attacking slavery. According
to Blaisdell, Dickens did not content himself with "literal paraphrase,"
but entered into the spirit of the controversy so thoroughly that there was
even a historical figure unknown to the novelist but worthy of having
been the original of General Choke.

David Copperfield is discussed at greater length and in a variety of
tones and ways, though there is a certain concentration on Agnes and
Dora in the year's criticism. Arlene M. Jackson's "Agnes Wickfield and
the Church Leitmotiv in *David Copperfield*" (*Annual*) is a full-scale essay whose point of departure is the fact that Agnes's character and part

are seen as unconvincing and embarrassing by the modern reader. Although there have been religious interpretations of Agnes, she must also, Jackson thinks, be connected with the novel's image-patterns and with David's memory processes. Jackson is perhaps a shade too apologetic, in her readiness to accept criticism of Agnes but not of Dickens as her creator ("we know Dickens could have created a flesh-and-blood character if he had so chosen"); to her the problem seems to be illuminated by the consistency of the church-image. Jackson is clearly in love with Agnes, an emotion with which I can sympathize, and her conclusion is that Agnes's idealization by David, not Dickens, is understandable after what he has gone through. The article is not wildly exciting, nor even wholly convincing, yet it is in several ways (in its method, tone, writing, coherence) exemplary. Rebecca Rodolff's "What David Copperfield Remembers of Dora's Death" (*Dickensian*, Spring) is a neat *explication de texte* of an important passage. The commentary does not tell the reader much that is new, but that is in accordance with the rules of the game, since an *explication* should not tell anything that is not in the text. Susan Schoenbauer Thurin, in "The Relationship Between Dora and Agnes" (*Newsletter*, December) is unlike Jackson and Rodolff (though like them she discusses Agnes and Dora) in that she is clearly unsympathetic to Dickens' characters. Her phrasing can be overtly, and anachronistically, brutal: David "rather expects Em'ly to remain attached to him long after he decides she is too proletarian for him" and "there is a trace of sadism in his refusal to recognize the emotional needs of another. He glosses over this unsavory aspect of his character by depicting Agnes and Dora alternately bestowing one another on him." Another questionable aspect of Thurin's essay is that she seems to discuss David, Dora, and Agnes as persons rather than as artifacts. Her view is that Agnes and Dora are antithetical and complementary, that their relationship occurs only through David and has complicated sexual undertones.

Richard J. Dunn has located and published "Gissing's Introduction to the Rochester *David Copperfield*" (*Dickensian*, Spring). It is certainly worth having, though it is not very good Gissing. Apart from a few errors, such as finding only two instead of four "Retrospect" chapters, or regarding Ham as Mr Peggotty's son (since Mr Peggotty was a "bacheldore," this is a serious imputation), George Gissing does not seem to have put very much effort into his essay: listing characters and his reactions to them is a primitive mode of criticism. We thus learn that he took rather a rosy view of *Copperfield* as a happy novel, that he disliked the melodrama of Steerforth and Heep, did not care for Agnes, or for David as adult and as novelist, but worshipped Micawber (without really illuminating him). On the other hand, Gissing does write intelligently about Em'ly. The history of the novel's publication is examined in Rebecca Rodolff's other contribution of the year, "*The Weekly Chronicle*'s Month-by-Month Reception of *Pendennis* and *David Copperfield*" (*Victorian Periodicals Review*, Fall). Rodolff supplies much valuable information about the *Weekly Chronicle* and its exceptional coverage of the two novels number by number. Having already compared *Vanity Fair* with *Dombey*, to Dickens' detriment, it saw *Pendennis* as making a good start, but as tending to be eclipsed when *Copperfield* entered the field six months later. It is particularly interesting to find that the journal's criticism of each novel was influenced by knowledge of its competitor. Michael Lund's "Clocking the Reader in the Long Victorian Novel" (*Victorian Newsletter*, September) is a well-informed and relatively new study, in which the critic's return to the time-element in the novel is welcome and characteristic (time is so obviously relevant to fiction that it cannot attract the attention of the more refinedly subtle commentators). The notion of "clocking the reader" is not, however, made crystal-clear.

One *Bleak House* item connects Dickens and Trollope: that is Naomi Jacobs's "Of Grace and Grease: Two Oily Clergymen" (*Newsletter*, June). This truly appetizing title does not prepare one for the disappointments in store. The very first sentence of the essay and the paragraph that follows show the author going off on a learned track that has little to do with the novels evoked (*Bleak House* and *Barchester Towers*, with Chadband and Slope). It seems unjustified to treat the Chadband oil as identical with the oily remains of the late Krook; train oil has very little to do with machinery; and Slope, in any case, is clammny rather than oily, unctuous only in the moral sense; and not one of the few words quoted from *Barchester Towers* refers to oil or grease. In a different style, "Qualitative Progression and the Dual Narrative in Dickens' *Bleak House*" by Anthony Belmont, Jr. (*PAPA*, 1–8) will perhaps be found equally unprofitable. Much influenced by abstract theorists, especially Kenneth Burke, Belmont takes time to establish his basis, then deals slowly and deviously with the dual plot of *Bleak House* (with an interruption for more theorizing, on Empsonian grounds); eventually, the principle of comic relief (such a crude expression is, of course, never used by Belmont) is redefined in rather stilted fashion. Is that "qualitative progression?" The conclusion, in any case, is justified, though a little flat: "Charles Dickens was both an artist and a craftsman who was in complete control of his medium."

A much more elaborate and substantial contribution to *Bleak House* studies is found in the *Annual*: Sandra K. Young's "Uneasy Relations: Possibilities for Eloquence in *Bleak House*" is intelligent, earnest, and learned. Although she makes one mistake (confusing business and electioneering in a most unDickensian way), there is much food for thought in her essay. Eloquence, she shows, is practiced by both narrators, by other characters, and by Dickens; Young defends Esther with some eloquence of her own, though not always successfully, and insists on her serious use of language, even though Young is not blind to the disadvantages of rhetoric employed by the two voices in the novel. The truest eloquence eventually appears to be that of Mrs. Rouncewell's hands. *Bleak House*, then, results from Dickens' increasing disbelief in the effectiveness of speech. Nancy Aycock Metz contributes almost too much material in her "Narrative Gesturing in *Bleak House*" (*Dickensian*, Spring), which makes, but does not always unite, a number of valid points about several topical issues in the novel—its experimental character, its way of often telling the reader, in effect, "Look at this!", and the parody of that attitude in the Roman pointing from Tulkinghorn's ceiling, or about the importance of disease and contagion. George H. Ford's "Light in Darkness / Gas, Oil, and Tallow in Dickens's *Bleak House*" (in the volume presented to Edgar Johnson) is an offshoot of his work on the annotation of the Norton edition of that novel, providing a wealth of attractive and well organized information. Dickens' interest in light was constant (until he retired from "these garish lights"): dealing successfully with street gaslight, indoor gas, lanterns, oil lamps, rushlights and candles, and firelight, Ford does a great deal to resurrect our sense of the smells and other sensations involved in the old modes of lighting. Marianna Torgovnick's book *Closure in the Novel* (Princeton University Press) has a chapter on *Bleak House*. With a title and theme that are obviously Kermodish, Torgovnick nevertheless finds Kermode incomplete. She is aware of all the recent theories but has a cautious attitude to them and rejects the refusal of extratextual information and the condemnation of the intentional fallacy. She defines her idea of "closure," distinguishing between two main modes: epilogues and scenic endings. In her *Bleak House* chapter, there is in my view one serious flaw: she finds the introduction to Bleak House (Jarndyce's house) in Chapter III, whereas ordinary readers arrive there only in Chapter VI, and this has serious consequences for Torgovnick's appraisal of the imbalance between beginning and end (between aperture—?—and closure): she has obviously read *Bleak House* with great care, and in a good edition, yet her view that there are three introductory chapters and only two concluding ones is not borne out by the novel itself. Torgovnick also finds twenty-five years between 1836 and 1858. But her chapter nevertheless deserves great praise, for it compels rethinking about one aspect of the greatness of that very great novel. She does make her point that the absence of "an after-history chapter for Chancery," not only sins against the ideal of "circular closure" but also weakens the social impact of the book. She expresses herself wittily about Esther, whom she charges with a lack of honesty and depth in her final chapter (reflecting Dickens' own lack of an Eliot-like philosophy), and she dislikes Richard's death, and Jo's. Torgovnick makes no exaggerated claims for her system, and her other chapters deserve to be read, as several of them are relevant to her evaluation of *Bleak House*, if only because they make her standards clearer.

Hard Times is examined in "Mr Sleary's Lisp" by Sena Jeter Naslund (*Newsletter*, June): Naslund insists on the wholeness of Mr Sleary, in spite of his physical deficiencies, and on the effect produced by his lisp on the reader who has to make an effort to take in what he says; the presence of embedded puns in the lisping speech is not convincingly demonstrated. The character of Sleary is approached sympathetically, but the phonetic problems of the lisp are not discussed. The essay, however, derives from an excellent idea and is very readable, but the title is somewhat inaccurate and the idea incompletely exploited. *Hard Times* is also dealt with in one chapter ("How successful is *Hard Times*?") of David Lodge's distinguished book *Working with Structuralism* (Boston, London, and Henley: Routledge and Kegan Paul). The volume is a collection of previously published articles, the principle being that they show how one can be a contemporary of the structuralists and appreciative of their work without slavishly following them; thus one remains intelligible. The essay on *Hard Times* asserts that it is a difficult novel to evaluate as literature because of its historical context. The specific aspect of *Hard Times* Lodge calls "moralised theatricality." He then analyzes several forms of what other critics tend to term stylization in *Hard Times*. The ironic metaphor, substituted for realistic description, helps put across the ideological implications. Lodge's mild conclusion is that "we should perhaps be more impressed by the degree of [Dickens'] success than by the novel's imperfections."

Robert J. Heaman's "Love and Communication in *Little Dorrit*" (*Newsletter*, June) gives many good examples of the inability of the characters to communicate, but why demonstrate a proposition so self-evident as that "the power of communication is essential to love," and how can one seriously believe that Doyce's invention is no other than love, and that that is what he is attempting to patent? Besides, Heaman regrettably uses an Everyman's Library edition of *Dorrit* printed in 1908. No essay on *A Tale of Two Cities* has come to my knowledge, but there was a play based on that novel, by Chris Bond and Pip Broughton, performed at the Liverpool Playhouse in the Fall of 1981.

Great Expectations gets first-class treatment in two items. One is a reprint of Rowland McMaster's introduction to the Macmillan College Classics edition of 1965. Though collected in the conjugal volume *The Novel from Sterne to James: Essays on the Relation of Literature to Life* (London: Macmillan; by Juliet and Rowland McMaster), it belongs to 1965 rather than 1981; but it remains a worthwhile critical study of the least superficial aspects of *Great Expectations*, and contains some excellent things on a minor favorite like Trabb's boy and a major figure like Jaggers. Edgar Rosenberg's "Last Words on *Great Expectations*: A Textual Brief on the Six Endings" (*Annual*) shows that a Norton editor is in a privileged position to illuminate the textual side of a critical problem, though it does not perhaps give him the right, as he blandly suggests, to air his views as the "last words" and then call for a moratorium! His essay is full of meat, but there is one unfortunate misprint (the omission of *not* from a sentence is bound to alter its meaning); however, the eight close pages of notes give evidence of superb scholarliness. Rosenberg has no respect for Bulwer and hates *Copperfield*'s Agnes. His interpretation of the last interpolation (which accounts in part for his finding six endings instead of our usual two) will not convince everyone, but at nearly every point his survey of the pros and cons is masterly. Rosenberg is a lively, witty, sometimes slightly eccentric, always stimulating writer: when mentioning "the 100-odd commentators . . . who have specifically addressed themselves to the double ending," he inserts a parenthesis where I have left an ellipsis and the parenthesis reads "hyphen optional"; of Dickens he says that his "autocritical report cards hardly ever record anything less than an A + ." Only one thing could be better than such an essay, and that would be the long-awaited edition of which it is an expanded offshoot. But the Norton *Great Expectations* is far from being the only grand Dickens project that has been hanging fire rather too long.

Jerome Meckier discusses "Boffin and Podsnap in Utopia" (*Dickensian*, Autumn), that is, he uses one allusion to "Podsnap's technique" in *Brave New World* and one brief appearance of Boffin in *News from Nowhere*, to show that *Our Mutual Friend* is betrayed by Morris's partisanship whereas Huxley's tribute is relevant, and also, less surprisingly, that the three novels involved are different. "A Rhetorical Use of the 'Fancy' in *Our Mutual Friend*" (*Newsletter*, December) by Angus P. Collins is a slighter piece. Collins thinks he has found a neglected corner of *Our Mutual Friend* to explore and illuminate: Eugene's fertile imagination, he claims, is diversely used, and Pleasant and Bella are other imaginative characters; it is Bella's fancy which saves her final *embourgeoisement* from being morally inconsistent (which is interesting, but not unquestionable). On the other hand, the essay published in the *Annual*, "Charles Dickens' *Our Mutual Friend* and Frederick Somner Merryweather's *Lives and Anecdotes of Misers*," by Wilfred P. Dvorak, though falling into some excesses, tells a great deal that is valuable to know about the kind of book Merryweather had written, and the care and intelligence with which Dickens had read and borrowed from it, although there may be a confusion between avarice (the vice affected by Boffin) and covetousness (Wegg's attitude). Another part of the article, thinly connected with the first, tries to ascribe to Merryweather's influence on Dickens the general themes of *Our Mutual Friend* with regard to money; again it seems odd to describe Fledgeby (*Fascination* Fledgeby) as a miser. But the general conclusion is entirely acceptable.

Since the year 1981 was marked, among other more (or some will say less) positive characteristics, by a drying-up of the source of *Drood*-continuations, the most visible *Drood* item is Edgar Rosenberg's "Chronic Droodophoria: Mr F's Antiserums" (*Newsletter*, December), which is a reply to Mr F. (Robert Fleissner) who, in the *Newsletter* of March, 1980, had accused Rosenberg of joking too much about the deaths of Drood and Dickens and had opposed scholars to critics. Rosenberg's reply is predictably vigorous and witty, and boils down to asking questions like: can one study Dickens and not joke at least a little (many have done it, but with sinister rather than illuminating effect), and can any man joke too much? Not Rosenberg, certainly.

General Studies

This is the category which, together with that of editions and additions, makes 1981 an important year: with at least six considerable books, and a sprinkling of general articles and collections, even if not one of the six books arouses unmitigated enthusiasm, the whole is impressive.

One collective publication deserves mention here, though it is neither massive nor highly specialized. The special issue of the French journal *Romantisme* (No. 34) contained "Le Dossier Dickens," a section of twenty-five pages made up of three articles and a checklist of available French editions of the works. The articles are by Isabelle Jan (about the society described in the novels), and by the two scholars who are emerging as the best experts on Dickens in France these days, Jean Gattégno (writing here on "Dickens en son temps") and Anny Sadrin, who provides a study of the past, present, and future directions of Dickens criticism.

The ninth volume of *Dickens Studies Annual* includes eight articles on Dickens, and one each on Bulwer, Thackeray, Gaskell, Trollope, and Hardy. The separate Dickens items are described where each of them belongs; however, they were included in the present survey, not without hesitation because my predecessors had set me a different example, but I was influenced by a sense that the *Annual* has gained an important place in Dickens studies, and that, if mention of it in this place may seem complacent or even narcissistic, its omission would be needlessly crippling.

Two of the articles in the McMasters' collection (*The Novel from Sterne to James*) by Rowland McMasters are on general themes: "Dickens and the Horrific" had already appeared in *Dalhousie Review* in 1958 and "Dickens, the Dandy, and the Savage" in *Studies in the Novel* in 1969. Though these essays were thus respectively twenty-three and twelve-years old in 1981, they gain some additional weight by being brought together and made more easily accessible. The gist of their contents may be briefly recalled: the earlier piece deals with the influence on Dickens of the *Terrific Register*, which he had read as an adolescent; in the later one McMaster denounces the inconsistency of the novelist's attitude to Dandyism, i.e., the contrast between his theory and his practice.

Other short essays of general interest include Judith Knelman's "Trollope's Relationship to Dickens" (*Newsletter*, March), which draws attention to the partial contradiction between Trollope's dislike of Dickens as expressed in private and his public tribute to a brother-artist who may have also been a kind of unofficial brother-in-law of his own brother's. The conclusions are a little saddening, but the article is useful. Claude Fiérobe published in *Images de l'ailleurs dans la littérature anglo-américaine* (Reims, France) an essay called "Le train, image de l'ailleurs, dans quelques oeuvres de Dickens," a neat and accurate piece, illustrated by very well-chosen quotations. It offers nothing spectacularly new as to facts, but the integration of railroads into Dickens' imaginative vision is achieved with intelligence.

Of the books announced above, Harland S. Nelson's *Charles Dickens* (Boston, Twayne Publishers, TEAS 314) is the least specific, though perhaps, for that very reason, not the least ambitious, since it aims at being a general introduction to Dickens. It may be hailed as a good TEAS and a good first book. It has some disconcerting features, such as the opening quotation which is from Wordsworth because "it could be by Dickens himself." The assertion that the Smallweeds are Jewish seems doubtful; there is excessive addiction to interpreting the characters' names (with a likeable liking for puns but a clear disregard of likelihood and intentionality); and the organization of the final chapter, like that of the book as a whole, is surprising and unbalanced. But the method works after all and the book serves its purpose of introducing readers to Dickens (though it should not be accepted as a substitute for reading the novels themselves). The three semi-biographical and fairly general chapters on the urges behind Dickens' writing of fiction, on the relationship with his public, on his methods of composition, are followed by two much longer ones dealing with all the important aspects of the novelist's art and craft, examined first in his work seen as one whole, then in the specific case of *Bleak House*. In addition, Nelson provides valuable notes. His book also serves as an introduction to himself, and he appears to be a shrewd reader and critic and to have a pleasant personality, justifiably ambitious, without lacking modesty and simplicity; and in these respects his *Charles Dickens* contrasts instructively with the other, perhaps more important, books of the year.

Janice Carlisle's *The Sense of an Audience: Dickens, Thackeray, and George Eliot at Mid-Century* (University of Georgia Press) eccentrically sports a jacket illustration from *Cranford* and begins with comments on *Sartor Resartus*. The purpose of the book, clearly stated in the introduction, is "to answer a single question: how did the novelist's sense of moral responsibility to his audience affect the narrative form of his art?" Of the non-Dickensian chapters the most fruitful are those on *Esmond, The Virginians*, and on *Adam Bede*. The two Dickens novels studied are *Dombey and Son* and *Little Dorrit*. Carlisle finds complexities in the relationship between reality and imagination in *Dombey*, though she sees it as a novel about hope. She quotes Kathleen Tillotson's criticism with approval, and proposes her own intelligent reading of some aspects and episodes (such as Chapter 47 with its "infamous" sermon, and the treatment of time and tenses). The *Dorrit* chapter contains some questionable assertions (such as that there, "more directly than in any of his other novels, Dickens explores the moral status of fiction"), but also much interesting material about fictions and mysteries in that novel, and the narrator practicing the art of "How Not To Do It."

In Dennis Walder's *Dickens and Religion* (London: Allen and Unwin), the author's quiet humor will be appreciated (for instance, when he speaks of one W. J. Conybeare's "justly neglected classic"). Walder's point is that Dickens was probably a more religious author than has been said and than he himself believed. Walder sees him as in the main "a liberal Protestant with radical, Romantic leanings." Perhaps Walder has been a little too ready to spot religiosity or even religion where other readers fail—excusably—to perceive any, but he does show that Dickens' attitudes to churches and to Scripture reflect both the trends of his time and his strong individuality. Finding anything religious in Chapter I of *Martin Chuzzlewit* or in some passages connected with Mr. Merdle in *Dorrit* is probably going too far. But there are many excellent remarks and analyses in Walder's book: for instance, about Dickens' conception of goodness ("as an expression of willed rather than felt belief"), about Captain Cuttle's indiscriminate but eventually efficient religion, and about Dickens' profound hatred of the Old Testament.

It is particularly embarrassing for me to deal with the next item on my list, Mark Lambert's *Dickens and the Suspended Quotation* (Yale University Press), after Sylvia Manning stole my thunder a year ago and turned it into a stream of milk and honey, by proclaiming that Lambert's book was far and away the best Dickens book of the year 1980. It may have been (or, as Dickens said of the angelic music heard by dying Nell. "God knows. It may have been"). That is, it may have been better than the other books of 1980. But I cannot agree that it is a very good book. I seem to be in a minority, but a person who proclaims that the emperor, if he is not entirely without clothing, is at best thinly clad, is always isolated. Yet it is only fair to mention that, in addition to Manning's, Mark Lambert gained golden opinions from all sorts of people, such as Daniel Karlin (in the London *TLS*), though he had serious objections also, or Michael Mason in the *London Review of Books*; but *he* used Lambert mainly as a stick with which to thrash Colin MacCabe. In any case, the only opinion I can express with any force is my own, and that is not golden. Mark Lambert does not bear any responsibility for the unjustified lines in his book, a practice against which it will be necessary to protest until publishers give one good reason for using them. As far as Lambert himself is concerned, I am aware that I may be wrong, but do critics possess the right of wrenching words and phrases (such as *quotation* and *suspended*) from their obvious meaning? Lambert is really dealing with interrupted characters' speeches, or rather with the interruption of characters' speeches, in Dickens' novels; his title is, therefore, tendentious, for the novelist is not quoting the characters in any sense of the word, he is writing their speeches. I find it amazing that some of Lambert's reviewers accepted so uncritically the Lambert line. As to Lambert's main thesis, that Dickens interrupts his characters because he is jealous of them, it is good fun in a way, but it seems to me to hold exceedingly little water. Other deficiencies of his book may have contributed in antagonizing the present reviewer. There is his treatment of Norman Page's *Speech in the English Novel* (1973), for instance, of which Lambert coolly announces that one chapter "will prove a most valuable supplement to the present work." On the whole, this *Suspended Quotation* seems to be an extremely arbitrary, half-intellectual, half-verbal exercise. Misquoting *Bleak House* (by using an imperfect edition) is a venial sin. Cheating with the facts (or being unaware of them) is more serious, as when Lambert twice makes the public readings begin in 1853 instead of 1858.

Yet it would be most unfair not to state also and in the clearest possible terms that Mark Lambert is a perceptive, gifted, and amusing critic. If he were not so keen on showing that he is clever, his cleverness would be more magnificently apparent all the time. Such a book cannot be unprofitable because intelligence never is that; yet when I reopen the book I let myself be irritated again by things like the following (preceding a dialogue from *Pickwick* in which, to add insult to injury, Magnus is consistently called Magus): "Consider . . . the following exchange, which you, reader, are in a particularly good position to appreciate, since what you hold in your hand it not a low-priced reprint of all *The Posthumous Papers of the Pickwick Club* but that decidedly expensive commodity, a scholarly monograph." I hope my irritation is due to a sense that the book could have been so much more profitable if self-restraint had been exerted, and that in its present state it is decidedly too high-priced for complacent exhibitions of that kind.

John Kucich's *Excess and Restraint in the Works of Charles Dickens* (University of Georgia Press) is the only major 1981 product to derive wholly from a 1979 dissertation. It shares some of the virtues and some of the disadvantages of the Lambert volume, though both are in a rather subdued key here. The overexcitement and the quest for originality at any cost are there, but less vividly, and without the unnecessary archness. On the other hand, while the critical intelligence at work is possibly less original, it is applied with more perceptible profitability. The choice of four novels in which to study the theme is surprising: *The Old Curiosity Shop, Bleak House, A Tale of Two Cities*, and *Great Expectations*—four fascinating cases, but leaving out an abundance of potential material. The theme is really an interpretation or a reading of Dickens' work in the light of "erotic energy," especially in those four novels. Kucich begins with portentous but harmless generalizations; however, he is guilty of far too many errors; he interprets Hortense's use of "spiritual" as referring to "a kind of transcendency" whereas it is only a gallicism for *spirituel* in the sense of witty; he mistakes Mercy for Charity Pecksniff, misquotes the title of a book by Françoise Basch, and calls Estella Esther. And perhaps his analyses of characters read too much like case studies of real persons carried out in order to find out the laws of human behavior. The scholarly value of the book suffers from all this (though the notes are of high quality and show genuine erudition). There are several examples of critical *excess*, such as speaking of Tulkinghorn's "unstated lubricity" or of the "phallic rape hidden" in the name of Jaggers (very well hidden, if it is there at all). The eroticism of Amy Dorrit, like that of Nell, is more apparent to Kucich (who is looking for it) than to the average reader. *Expenditure*, a word wearisomely iterated and probably in the event more revealing than *excess*, may not be the key to everything in Dickens, but it seems to be *a* key to a reasonable number of things, and there are many interesting and suggestive paragraphs in Kucich's book. He is particularly good on Quilp, Headstone, Mr. George, Esther, on role-playing, and on *The Old Curiosity Shop* in general.

S. J. Newman, the author of *Dickens at Play* (London and Basingstoke: Macmillan), is also a little obsessed by the erotic, or at least the sexual. Newman writes about the early Dickens and privileges *Sketches by Boz* and *The Old Curiosity Shop* at the expense of *Pickwick* and *Oliver Twist*, for instance. The overexcitement found in the work of so many young scholars and critics is again present, and thus it is reassuringly demonstrated that it is not a purely American phenomenon, due to the presence of the "publish or perish" urge (for it is well known that in old Europe only a milder form prevails, something like "publish or vegetate, more or less"). In fact, Newman claims his right to excitement. Writing about Little Nell, he says that in her case "there is something there to get excited about." With him excitement takes two main forms: extravagant hyperbole and dazzling rapprochements. Among Newman's many encomiums of *Chuzzlewit* the following are worth quoting: "deepest, most sustained and ambitious attempt to come to terms with" the world, or "the culmination of Dickens's art . . . his greatest achievement . . . arguably his most far-reaching masterpiece . . . revolutionary in its mode and technique . . . the most blatantly brilliant expression of comic energy in Western fiction." Of course, when getting down to brass tacks, those superlatives will be forgotten and it will be discovered that "*Chuzzlewit* wears its art on its sleeve" or "is badly marred by the fact that its virtuous characters, unlike its vices, are uncreative, unintelligent and woefully undramatic." Newman does not appear to mind the contradiction. His reference to "Western fiction" is typical of his range: in a brief one-page conclusion he mentions twenty-three glamorous names. Some of his rapprochements are undoubtedly valid and illuminating, like his remarks on Miltonic echoes in *Oliver Twist*, but Marvell is rather far-fetched in connection with *Barnaby Rudge* even if "Both writers use fire alchemically"; and it may take more than a few words on a printed page to establish "Dickens along with Balzac and Berlioz, Wagner and Nietzsche as a central representative of the European will to power." Newman's book is not free from a few naïve expressions ("Boz nowhere writes himself plain Charles Dickens"). But, as in other cases, when Newman lets himself be a critic, and not a juggler, he is splendid, and writes very well, with intelligence, skill, lucidity, and wit. Each of the works examined in his book receives some illumination from his fresh approach and shrewd glance. Though it is becoming less and less infrequent, S. J. Newman's return to Dickens' early fiction is to be welcomed gratefully, like his sympathy with such hoary critics of Dickens as G. K. Chesterton, who still have so much to teach us. Newman's attitude to *The Old Curiosity Shop*, a novel which he takes with perfect seriousness and not unsympathetically, seems to be a sign of the times, or at least to be less isolated in 1981 than in any previous year—possibly since 1840.

If Mark Lambert was clearly fated to fall into my brutal and unworthy hands, Susan R. Horton's *The Reader in the Dickens World* (University of Pittsburgh Press) could well have been in my predecessor's basket together with her previous volume, for the Preface is dated June, 1979. Horton's work in fact began in 1971, but became two books, *Interpreting Interpreting* (1980) and the present one. There may be infinitesimal doses of the Lambertian attitude in Horton, as when she feels the need to assert "But I am not naïve"; her view of John and Bella's financial position at the end of *Our Mutual Friend* may however, sound a little simplistic, for she writes that they "in effect earn their right to wealth and comfort by proving they can endure life without it." Several Dickens quotations are badly mauled in her book (which prints "Don't" for "Dan'l" or "Whater" for "Whether") and it contains a few surprising or erroneous assertions: was Herbert Pocket (called by Pip the "pale young gentleman") a "bull-like-boy"? And how can a passage of Chapter XXI in *Copperfield* be a "*fore*shadowing of the death of David's baby half-brother" when another small coffin "will be built" (it *was* built, in fact, back in Chapter IX)? I have not found Horton's style very engaging, perhaps because the volume missed one final trimming that would have eliminated phrases like "as delightful . . . than." Yet Horton is genuinely fond of words, and of wordplay: the heading of one chapter can give some idea of her talent in that direction—"Sequence and Consequence: from Truckling Knave to Trickling Blood." She, too, pays a tribute to Chesterton's merits.

Her purpose in this book is to look for an explanation of the individual response to Dickens, and to reconcile ordinary appreciation and scholarly criticism. She examines contradictions within the Victorian frame of mind and within Dickens himself, asserting that the contradictions are expressed by the opposition between rhetoric and plots. After a good deal of theorizing in the best company (Jakobson and Culler), the reader exploring the Horton world finds himself or herself comfortably back in biography and ordinary psychology (for example, used to explain through Dickens' marriage why he passes from pathos or tragedy to farcical comedy). After dealing with various aspects of Dickens' rhetoric (insofar as it sets the reader to work), with "The World beyond the Dickens World," and "The Dynamics of Description," Horton concentrates in her final section on *The Old Curiosity Shop*. There are moments when her views are not wholly acceptable. When she writes that "the great amount of energy that radiates from Dickens's novels is actually in part our own. Reading Dickens, finally, is a participatory sport," this has a fine modern ring, but can it be true? If Dickens' energy is our own, why can't we give it equally to other writers? Yet there are several very good sections in that book: on Dickens as the reticent rhetorician, on his peripheral vision, on his various uses of the conditional, on his having forestalled through observation some of Henri Bergson's later findings, and on *The Old Curiosity Shop* generally, of which the reading suggested is valuable though a little strained, even if it does not depend too closely on the previous theorizing.

I hope it has by now become clear why I said that all these books are important (and I may add interesting) without being absolutely great. Among the general impressions derived from them there is also the weariness with which one comes across the note of diffidence about adding to the already enormous number of books on Dickens; diffidence is better than brashness, cocksureness, and arch wit, but since the books in which that note is sounded are published, it comes to the same thing in the end, and I suggest that it had better be omitted in the future. One of our 1981 authors' first sentence reads: "Anyone threatening to add to the daunting outflow of material continuing to gush, apparently inexhaustibly, from the well of Dickens studies, must have good reason for doing so." That goes without saying. Reason has been found, and thought good, or good enough.

Another general impression is that critics are again moved, and ready to admit that they are moved, by the death of Jo, Paul, and even, or especially, of Little Nell.

Reviews

Nothing, or almost nothing, has been said so far of reviews. Dealing with them at length would be a fascinating but exacting task. It would also be a case of "veels within veels," of reviewing reviewers reviewing the very books one has been surveying. I am therefore taking the liberty of merely comparing the achievement in this field of the two journals exclusively devoted to Dickens.

The reviewers for the *Dickensian* and for *Dickens Studies Newsletter* in 1981 have sometimes been the same individuals, but much more often not. There is obviously a large and growing body of experts to draw from, and it will soon be proper for some very old hands like myself to make our bow and leave the stage to younger and brighter lights.

But there are two points that can be made. The usefulness of reviewing in specialized periodicals depends on two factors: exhaustiveness and punctuality. In point of exhaustiveness, the *Newsletter*, with twenty-one items reviewed (in addition to its wonderful Checklists), wins by a short head since the *Dickensian* printed only seventeen reviews. But in point of punctuality the veteran journal wins hands down, since the *Newsletter* reviewed only one publication of 1981, three of 1980, thirteen of 1979, two of 1978, and one each of 1977 and 1976, while the *Dickensian's* reviews consisted of eleven 1980 books and six 1981 publications.

Conclusion

Last year, Sylvia Manning denounced ugly and inadequate ways of writing English. I dare not follow suit, though I suffer acutely from similar allergies; as a Frenchman, who am I to point out that students of such a master of English as Dickens should avoid pretentious neologisms, feel free to use *thief* rather than *larcener*, realize that *periphery*, not *peripheries*, is the singular, that there is a difference between *principle* and *principal*, or that *unexceptionally* does not mean without exception? Who am I to complain that the rules concerning the plural and possessive forms of proper names seem to have gone by the board? No one, obviously, and so I must refrain from making any such remarks and suggestions, though they turn out to be urgently called for, even in the most respectable cases, not excepting the two Dickens journals and this *Annual*. What I may do, in my own fit of austere magisteriality, is to insist on accuracy in such minor but not negligible matters as characters' names, titles, dates, and the like. Dickensian scholarship is as serious as any, but it will not earn and enjoy all the respect it deserves until Affery ceases to be printed as Affrey, Flintwinch as Flintwich, Dorrit as Dorritt, or Coavinses as Coavenes. Admittedly Dickens gave us a bad example, since he had the *Britannia*'s captain's name printed and engraved on expensive plate as Hewett instead of Hewitt. On the other hand, he was a remarkably conscientious and efficient proofreader, and that is an example that should be emulated by Dickens scholars. It is perhaps inevitable that French words and names should suffer at the hands of non-French-speaking compositors, but something will have to be done about it sooner or later, or we shall go on having as many as six bad misprints of French quotations in one shortish article. Nor is the writers' English spared: there are far too many misprints, of all sizes and kinds, everywhere.

On emerging from my fit I am pleased to repeat what I hope to have shown, that 1981 can be seen in retrospect to have been a lively, good, perhaps even great or vintage year in Dickens studies. And it is almost needless to wish us all many more like it, if not indeed "betterer and betterer."

NOTE

1. All references are given in the text of this essay. Since all the items listed and discussed belong to 1981, no date of publication is mentioned. For books, the name of the publisher and, if necessary, the place of publication, are given. *Dickensian* is printed in full, *Newsletter* refers to *DSN* and *Annual* to *DSA*.

Index

Contents of Previous Volumes

Volume 5 (1976)

Volume 6 (1977)

Volume 7 (1978)

Volume 9 (1981)